The
PRINCE
of
PARADISE

ALSO BY JOHN GLATT

Love Her to Death

Lost and Found

Playing with Fire

Secrets in the Cellar

To Have and to Kill

Forgive Me, Father

The Doctor's Wife

One Deadly Night

Depraved

Cries in the Desert

For I Have Sinned

Evil Twins

Cradle of Death

Blind Passion

Deadly American Beauty

Never Leave Me

Twisted

The
PRINCE
of
PARADISE

THE TRUE STORY OF
A HOTEL HEIR, HIS SEDUCTIVE WIFE,
AND A RUTHLESS MURDER

JOHN GLATT

ST. MARTIN'S PRESS

NEW YORK

www.stmartins.com

ISBN 978-1-250-03572-1 (hardcover)
ISBN 978-1-250-03573-8 (e-book)

St. Martin's Press books may be purchased for educational, business, or promotional use. For information on bulk purchases, please contact Macmillan Corporate and Premium Sales Department at 1-800-221-7945 extension 5442 or write specialmarkets@macmillan.com.

First Edition: April 2013

10 9 8 7 6 5 4 3 2 1

FOR KEN CRICHLOW

ACKNOWLEDGMENTS

I n its glittering heyday, the Fontainebleau was *the* gold standard in luxury hotel grace and sophistication. With its sweeping Art Deco design, antique French décor and furniture, the landmark hotel put Miami Beach on the map in the 1950s and '60s.

Built by the legendary hotelier Ben Novack Sr., the Fontainebleau laid the groundwork for today's Las Vegas. Indeed, casino mogul Steve Wynn often stayed there as a boy, learning valuable lessons for his future dream palaces.

For almost two decades Ben Novack Sr. and his ex-model wife, Bernice, reigned over Miami Beach. Always larger than life, they entertained presidents, heads of state, and movie stars at their dazzling Miami palace. World-class entertainers such as Frank Sinatra, Elvis Presley, and Jerry Lewis played the La Ronde Room, and iconic movies like *The Bellboy, Goldfinger, Scarface,* as well as an episode of *The Sopranos,* were filmed there.

In January 1956, Ben Novack Jr. was born and became the Prince of the Fontainebleau. Known to one and all as "Benji," he grew up in his father's seventeenth-floor luxury penthouse with room service at his beck and call. The little prince may have been spoiled and petted by the likes of Sinatra and the Rat Pack, but he received scant attention from his parents.

Naturally nervous, Benji grew up with a revolving door of nannies and housekeepers and developed a chronic stammer, which would plague him for life.

When Miami Beach fell out of fashion in the 1970s, Ben Novack Sr. went bankrupt, eventually losing his beloved Fontainebleau in 1977. A few years later, he died a broken man.

Ben Jr. then launched a convention-planning business and made millions, having absorbed considerable knowledge from his father. But in 1991, he fell in love with an Ecuadorian stripper named Narcisa Veliz, embarking on a roller-coaster marriage that would ultimately claim his life more than a quarter of a century later.

In April 2012, the final chapter in the long, strange story of the Fontainebleau Hotel was written in a federal courtroom in White Plains, New York. I attended every single day of the stunning nine-week trial, where Narcy Novack and her brother Cristobal stood accused of orchestrating the brutal murders of Ben Novack Jr. and his eighty-six-year-old mother, Bernice.

It played out like classic film noir, as the two siblings absolutely denied any involvement in the murders, claiming they were innocent pawns who had been framed by Narcy's daughter, May Abad.

In recounting the story for this book, I have used personal interviews, police records, and trial transcripts to report the events leading up to the murders of Ben and his mother. Regarding the alleged 2002 home invasion, I reviewed police records and interviewed participants, but no charges were ever brought, Narcy denied any wrongdoing, and evidence of the incident was excluded from the murder trial.

During my two years of exhaustive research for this book, I was helped by many people, some of whom wish to remain anonymous for obvious reasons.

I would especially like to thank Ben Novack Jr.'s aunt, Maxine Fiel, and his cousin Meredith for all their help. I especially enjoyed the afternoon I spent with them in upstate New York. I also owe a huge debt to Detective Sergeant Terence Wilson of the Rye Brook Police Department, for all his support and encouragement. I also received invaluable help from Ben Jr.'s close friend and mentor Charlie Seraydar, who was there for many of the key events in this book.

I would also like to thank Lenore Toby for sharing her memories of her time managing the Fontainebleau during its declining years, and her reminiscences of Ben Novack Sr. During our stay in Miami Beach, my wife Gail and I also shared a memorable brunch with Lenore and her charismatic late husband, Dr. Bernard Simmons.

Many thanks also to Ben Novack Jr.'s first wife, Jill Campion, who gave me a unique perspective on the Fontainebleau and Ben's early life, as he was getting his business started.

My gratitude also to: Eddie Argondizza, Chief Gregory Austin of the Rye Brook Police Department; Guy Castaldo, former mayor of Miami Beach; Alex Daoud, Dixie Evans, Scot Fleming, Pat Franklin, Mark Gatley, William and Rebecca Greene, the Reverend Temple Hayes, Douglas Hoffman, Cynthia Johns, Ed Kelly, Melanie Klein, Alan Lapidus, Rabbi Alan Litwak, Dr. Barbara Lunde, Richard Marx, Joe and Peter Matthews, Steve Palazzo, Sergeant Colin Pfrogner, Prince Mongo, Dr. Larry Robbins, James Scarberry, Donald Spadaro, Larry Sheehan, Howard Tanner, and Vincent Zurzolo.

I also owe gratitude to: Allen Alter, Jonathan Bandler, Tom Delehanty, Christine Fillmore, Bob Gilmartin, Susan Giordano, Dena Goldstein, Candace Eaton, Herb Hadad, Anthony Mercurio, Joe Occhicone, Special Agent John Sullivan, Chuck Stevenson, and Joe Viola.

As always, I would also like to thank my editors at St. Martin's Press, Charles Spicer, April Osborn, and Yaniv Soha for everything that they do, as well as Jane Dystel and Miriam Goderich of Dystel & Goderich Literary Management, for their invaluable help and advice.

I also want to thank David and Diana Hayes for all their hospitality during my Spring 2011 week in Fort Lauderdale, as well as Chris Bott in Miami.

Much thanks also to my wife Gail; Jerome, Emily, and Freddie Freund; Debbie, Douglas, and Taylor Baldwin; Trudy Gerstner, Gurch, Danny and Allie Tractenberg, Cari Pokrassa, Virginia Randall, Roger Hitts, Ena Bissell, and Annette Witheridge.

The
PRINCE
of
PARADISE

INTRODUCTION

When retired police chief James Scarberry heard in July 2009 that Ben Novack Jr. had been brutally murdered, with his eyes gouged out, he was not surprised. On the contrary, he had foreseen the event seven years earlier, when he told his old friend to leave his beautiful wife, Narcy, or he would die. Scarberry's warning came after the former Ecuadorian stripper hired thugs to beat up her wealthy forty-six-year-old husband, whose father had founded the legendary Fontainebleau hotel in Miami Beach. After mercilessly binding and gagging him with duct tape, the hired hands had held him at gunpoint for twenty-five hours while Narcy ransacked the family home.

On her way out, Novack's forty-five-year-old wife boasted that she could have him killed anytime she chose.

"If I can't have you, then no one will have you," she snapped at him. "You're not dead now because I stopped them."

Then she disappeared with more than $400,000 in cash and Novack's collection of Batman collectibles, worth millions.

After breaking free, Novack first called Chief Scarberry, who had once worked security for Ben Jr.'s father at the Fontainebleau. Scarberry then used his contacts in the Fort Lauderdale Police Department to launch a criminal investigation.

An active member of the Miami Beach Police Department Reserve and Auxiliary Officer Program for more than thirty years, Ben Jr. told detectives that Narcy had organized the home invasion and that he still feared for his life. Then he hired a lawyer and initiated divorce proceedings.

When brought in for questioning, Novack's statuesque wife told detectives another story. She claimed that they were both into hardcore sexual bondage and had been role-playing. The one-time exotic dancer then stunned detectives by emptying out onto a table a brown accordian file full of her husband's huge collection of amputee porn magazines, including his own photographs of naked disabled women.

Within hours of Narcy's police interview, Ben Novack Jr. had called off the divorce, refusing any further cooperation with detectives. Then he welcomed his wife back into their home, explaining to police that they had started marriage counseling to get their relationship back on track.

Baffled friends wondered if Narcy was blackmailing him by threatening to reveal his bizarre sexual secrets and ruin his thriving $50-million-a-year convention business.

"I told him," recalled Scarberry, "Benji, you're nuts. This girl could have had you killed, and you've got to get out of that relationship."

Ben Novack Jr. had refused to listen, so Chief Scarberry ended the friendship, and the two had not spoken since.

It was ironic that Ben Novack Jr. should die in a hotel room, for, a half century earlier, his father, Ben Sr., had built and run the legendary Fontainebleau hotel, transforming Miami Beach into *the* glamour capital of America and drafting the blueprint for today's Las Vegas.

Benji, as everyone knew him then, had grown up in the luxurious seventeenth-floor penthouse, pampered by nannies and fussed over by the likes of Frank Sinatra, President John F. Kennedy, Bob Hope, and Ann-Margret.

"He was the Prince of the Fontainebleau," explained his cousin Meredith Fiel. "Anything that Ben Jr. wanted, Ben Jr. got."

ONE

COMING TO
MIAMI BEACH

One hundred and ten years before the home invasion, Ben Novack Jr.'s paternal grandfather, Hyman Novick, first arrived in New York from Russia, seeking a new life. The poor Jewish teenager, who spoke only Russian and Yiddish, married a girl named Sadie, who was six years his junior. Sadie was first-generation American, born in New York from Russian parents.

The young couple settled down in Brooklyn, and Hyman, a cloth cutter by profession, opened a clothing store. In 1903, when Hyman was twenty-five and Sadie nineteen, they had their first child, Miriam. A year later they had a son they named Joseph, followed in 1905 by another daughter, Lillian. Two years later, Sarah gave birth to Benjamin Hadwin, who completed the family.

Between the 1910 and 1920 censuses, Hyman Novick lost his clothing shop and was reduced to driving a New York City taxi cab. Sadie was a homemaker, but their eldest daughter, Miriam, age seventeen in 1920, supplemented the family income by working as a stenographer. According to the 1920 Census, twelve-year-old Benjamin and his older siblings could all read and write.

A few years later, Hyman moved his family to the Catskill Mountains and went into the resort hotel business. He and Sadie founded and operated the Laurels Hotel and Country Club on Sackett Lake, five miles from Monticello, in the heart of what would soon become the "Borscht Belt."

All the Novick children helped out with the hotel, which was soon thriving. They worked in various capacities, with Ben at the front desk and his big sister Lillian in the kitchen.

As a young boy, Ben almost drowned in the Laurels outdoor pool, an incident that resulted in his having to wear a hearing aid for the rest of his life.

After their father died in the mid-1930s, Ben and his elder brother, Joseph, took over the hotel. But they argued and soon split up, with Ben moving to New York City and going into the retail haberdashery business with a man named Kemp.

The handsome Ben arrived in the city in the midst of the Great Depression. To get ahead, he Anglicized his name to "Novack."

He and Kemp opened a clothing store on Sixth Avenue called Kemp and Novack, but it was short-lived. Brusque and arrogant, Ben Novack soon fell out with his partner, and the two sold the store and went their separate ways.

It was during this time that Novack first met a young retail store designer named Morris Lapidus, who would later play a pivotal role in designing the Fountainbleau hotel.

"I believe [Ben] was also in the black market tire business," said Lapidus's son, Alan. "But my father never elaborated on that."

Two thousand years ago the Tequesta tribe first settled South Florida. They stayed until the sixteenth century, when explorer Juan Ponce de León arrived, claiming the land as a Spanish colony. In 1763, Spain handed Florida to Great Britain in exchange for Havana, Cuba. Twenty years later, Britain returned Florida to Spain in return for the Bahamas and Gibraltar. After the American War of Independence, Spain ceded Florida to America as part of the 1819 Adams-Onis Treaty, making it part of the United States.

Seventy years later, a rich Cleveland widow named Julia Tuttle bought 640 acres on the north side of the Miami River. In 1895, Tuttle persuaded Standard Oil tycoon Henry Flagler to bring his railroad to Miami and build a new town with a luxury hotel. On July 28, 1896, a few months after the railroad arrived, the City of Miami was officially incorporated.

If Julia Tuttle was Miami's mother, Carl Fisher was undoubtedly the father of Miami Beach.

Born in Indianapolis in 1874, Fisher made a fortune co-inventing Prest-O-Lite, the acetylene gas used in car headlights for night driving. After selling out to the Union Carbide Company for millions, Fisher devoted himself to the new sport of auto racing, buying the Indianapolis Speedway in 1909 and making a second fortune.

Three years later, Fisher moved to Miami, coming to the rescue of a New Jersey avocado grower, John Collins, who had begun constructing a two-and-a-half mile wooden bridge between mainland Miami across the causeway to Ocean Beach, to bring his avocados to market. Unfortunately, when the bridge was only half finished, Collins ran out of money. So Fisher struck a deal to lend him the $50,000 he needed to finish, in return for two hundred acres of uninhabited swampland Collins owned on the island.

Thus, on a handshake, was Miami Beach born.

Jane Fisher would later claim that the first time her husband set foot on the beach, he picked up a stick and drew a diagram in the sand, declaring that he would build the world's greatest resort on that very site.

Although the conditions were daunting (horseflies, snakes, and rats), Fisher's vision knew no bounds. He purchased another 210 acres and, over the next few years, set about taming the wild, primeval terrain. First he drained the swamps, pouring in acres of sand to form solid new ground on which to build. His motto: "I just like to see the dirt fly."

At first Fisher couldn't even give his Florida real estate away, as nobody wanted to live there. So he staged a whacky publicity stunt to turn Miami Beach's fortunes around.

In 1921, president-elect Warren Harding was vacationing in Miami Beach when Fisher arranged to have a baby elephant named Rosie be

Harding's golf caddy as a photo opportunity. The press loved it, and a picture of the smiling future president and his pachyderm caddy on Miami Beach made the front pages coast to coast. The shot caused an immediate sensation, transforming Miami Beach overnight into "a place you had to see to believe."

Fisher also persuaded his eclectic circle of friends—which included mobster Al Capone, newspaper publisher Moe Annenberg, and racehorse owner John Hertz—to build spectacular winter homes on the beach.

From 1920 to 1925 there was an unprecedented land boom in Florida, with Miami's population almost quadrupling. In 1925, Fisher's estate was valued at $100 million, and he celebrated by constructing Lincoln Road as the jewel of his Riviera resort.

The following year, Fisher turned his sights on replicating his success in Montauk, at the eastern tip of Long Island, New York. But this endeavor never took off and, along with the Great Depression, virtually wiped him out.

By the time Ben Novack arrived with his new wife, Bella, in February 1940, using the $1,800 he had received from liquidating his and Kemp's New York clothing store, Miami Beach was thriving. The rest of America might have been struggling in the Great Depression, but Miami Beach had become *the* winter retreat for the rich and famous. In 1941 the Duke and Duchess of Windsor vacationed there, attracting worldwide publicity in the wake of Edward's abdication from the British throne. Other famous regulars included Walter Winchell, Damon Runyon, and Eleanor Roosevelt.

Miami Beach had recently been dubbed "the ultimate Babylon" by influential *New York Tribune* columnist "Luscious" Lucius Beebe, and Ben Novack was determined to exploit it for all it was worth. But, initially, he was uncertain where to begin.

Legend has it that he started out selling expensive watches to the wealthy tourists and snowbirds now flocking to Miami Beach in the winter. He also dabbled in the import-export business, reportedly running a fleet of banana boats to and from Cuba. Before long, he gravitated back to the hotel business he had grown up in.

With his silver tongue, Novack easily persuaded some business partners to put up $20,000 for a one-year lease on the Monroe Towers on Collins Avenue at Thirtieth Street. He then spent a year fixing up the 111-room hotel, while Bella worked as a chambermaid.

Then everything changed.

World War II broke out, making Ben Novack rich beyond his wildest dreams.

In February 1942 the U.S. Army took over Miami Beach, using it as a basic training center for troops before they were shipped off to Europe. With its perfect weather conditions, Miami was the ideal place to train pilots and rehearse the Normandy invasion.

Almost overnight, an estimated hundred thousand men from the Army Air Corps and the U.S. Navy invaded Miami Beach, and nearly two hundred hotels were requisitioned to billet them. The U.S. government generously compensated hotel owners up to $10 a night ($141 today) for each room, not including food.

"Boy, did my dad clean up," Ben Novack Jr. told author Steven Gaines in 2006. "He raked in the profits, and he did so well that he got another hotel and did the same thing, and then another hotel with an army contract."

Ben Novack used his profits to buy a share in the Monroe Hotel before snapping up the Cornell Hotel and then the Atlantis, which became an army reception center. Over a five-year period, he bought up five hotels.

Of Ben's housing soldiers, Novack's future sister-in-law, Maxine Fiel, remembered, "He told me, 'I don't have to feed them. I don't have to give them anything. Just a bed.' And that's how he made his money."

As he prospered, Novack carefully cultivated his own unique sense of style, becoming rather a dandy. He began wearing elaborate bow ties and draping custom-made brightly colored suits over his lithe five-foot, six-inch frame. Every morning, his personal barber trimmed his thin mustache the French way.

Novack took great pride in his appearance. It would be the same approach he would later bring to his hotels.

At the end of the war, Novack went into partnership with Harry Mufson to build the Sans Souci, boasting that the new hotel would "wow" guests. Novack envisioned it as *the* last word in elegance on the ocean, with its own restaurants, shops, and a penthouse nightclub with fabulous views. Its French name, Sans Souci (meaning "without care"), he felt, would add a touch of class.

Ben Novack saw hotels as pleasure palaces straight out of a Busby Berkeley musical. He dreamed of transforming Miami Beach into an unparalleled paradise, like no other place in the world.

In the spring of 1945, his ambitions knew no bounds when he strolled into Manhattan's La Martinique nightclub and first set eyes on top photographic model Bernice Stempel.

Two

BERNICE

Bernice Mildred Stempel was born on December 2, 1922, on New York's Upper West Side. Her father, William Jack Stempel, had emigrated to America from London some years earlier.

The Stempels settled in New York and young William, whom everyone knew as Jack, grew up to become a successful furrier, dressing Manhattan's elite. Handsome and athletic, he was a welterweight boxing champion and a bon vivant, who liked the good life.

"He was a playboy," recalled his youngest daughter, Maxine Fiel. "He was a guy that knew all the politicians in New York and had his own card games."

One day, Stempel was in Gloversville, in upstate New York, during one of his frequent fur-buying trips to Canada. He stopped off at Worth's department store, where he saw a beautiful young Irish salesgirl named Rowena Sweeney Burton.

It was love at first sight.

"He thought she was just unbelievably gorgeous," said Maxine. "Red hair and blue eyes. And when my father wanted something, he was like a dog with a bone."

Over the next few months, the thirty-six-year-old Stempel, who was

Jewish, assiduously courted the twenty-one-year-old devout Irish Catholic. When he proposed marriage, she readily agreed.

After the wedding, he moved his new bride to Manhattan, installing her in his spacious West End Avenue brownstone. He then went into the insurance business and made a fortune.

In 1922 their first daughter, Bernice, was born, followed by Maxine, two years later. Rowena insisted on having the babies baptized Catholics.

Now a father, Jack Stempel did not allow his new family to cramp his playboy lifestyle in the slightest. He was already well known in New York society, cultivating influential friends and gambling away his nights in the speakeasies during Prohibition.

"He'd go out," said Maxine, "and do the same things as if he was unmarried. So he left [our mother] alone."

One day, Jack asked his best friend to keep his wife company nights, while he went out on the town.

"That was fatal," said Maxine. "He left her alone, and his friend, who was a salesman, was interested in her."

When Stempel discovered that his wife and best friend were having an affair, he threw Rowena out of the house and filed for divorce.

"It was all over the papers," said Maxine, "because my father was very prominent."

Jack Stempel won custody of his young daughters, but sent them to live with his two sisters. He refused to let their mother have any further contact with them. Rowena tried to fight for custody, but she had no money to challenge her ex-husband's expensive attorneys.

After a few months, Bernice and Maxine's aunts could no longer take care of them, so the sisters were sent to an orphanage. They were eventually fostered out to a German family named Reiser, who owned a restaurant in Far Rockaway, in Queens.

Bernice was a nervous child, and was so traumatized by her parents' bitter divorce that she withdrew into her own world.

"Bernice was older, but I always took care of her," said Maxine. "She wouldn't speak up, and I always had to."

. . .

In the early 1930s, divorce was rare. Most people stayed together, making the best of a miserable marriage. Bernice and Maxine Stempel, therefore, had a difficult childhood, growing up under the stigma of their parents' divorce. This tough childhood took a toll on Bernice, leaving scars for years afterward.

Their foster parents sent the girls to public school in Washington Heights, where their mother would try to visit them.

"She would come to the schoolyard to see us," recalled Maxine. "She was gorgeous. I adored her."

They missed their mother terribly, but spent the holidays with their father and his family. He would never let them see their mother, who eventually ended up in a mental health facility.

Both Stempel girls were unusually beautiful, turning heads wherever they went. They were skinny and pale, with striking red hair and freckles that they had inherited from their mother.

When Bernice was ten years old, an uncle recommended that she and her sister become millinary models for the big New York department stores.

"He was a buyer for a big firm," said Maxine, "and he suggested we go into [modeling], because he said you girls are so beautiful."

The uncle found them jobs modeling hats, jodhpurs, and other riding outfits for society outfitters in Manhattan, but they were paid a pittance.

At public school, Bernice was a good student with a talent for stenography. She was also a natural rebel, and often cut classes.

When she left school, Bernice was headed for a secretarial career, until she was spotted in the street by a talent scout for the famous Conover Model Agency, who immediately signed her to their books.

By 1940, Conover was *the* top fashion model agency in New York. It was founder Harry Conover who had invented and trademarked the term *cover girl*, and who headed a stable of *the* most beautiful models, specializing in the "well-scrubbed" natural American girl look.

The handsome and charismatic Conover turned his "girls" into the first supermodels, giving them suggestive professional names such as Choo Choo Johnson, Jinx Falkenburg, Dulcet Tone, and Frosty Webb.

After signing with the Conover agency, Bernice Stempel soon went to the top. Her natural red hair and cream skin made her one of his most sought-after girls. Overnight, the once-insecure girl was reborn as a poised, sophisticated young woman whose breathtaking beauty won her a string of lucrative modeling assignments.

"It helped her get self-esteem and to be validated," explained Temple Hayes, later to became a close friend. "She and her sister had started out in an orphanage, so it was wonderful for her to have those kind of doors open. And she was proud of surviving such a horrific [childhood]."

In the mid-1940s, Bernice moved into her own apartment with another model, and started going out on the town with her new, glamorous friends. At one party, she was introduced to Salvador Dalí, who immediately invited her to come to his studio and model for him.

When she arrived and the middle-aged surrealist ordered her to strip naked for a portrait, she fled.

"He wanted her to pose nude, and she refused and walked out," said Estelle Fernandez (not her real name), who would later become Bernice's best friend. "She told me he was absolutely crazy and he tried [to take advantage of her]. She would never use her body or do anything to [get ahead]."

Although many advertising directors employed the casting couch approach, Bernice Stempel never resorted to these measures to get modeling assignments.

Throughout the 1940s, she regularly modeled for Coca-Cola, as the clean-cut American girl in many of its ad campaigns. She also worked for Old Gold cigarettes, with her long shapely legs tap-dancing under a king-size pack in a popular commercial of the time.

Bernice was a regular at the ultra-exclusive Stork Club, becoming a favorite of its charismatic owner, Sherman Billingsley. She was also pursued by a string of admirers, some of whom proposed marriage.

"She went out with some very wealthy guys," recalled her sister, Maxine, "but she ended up marrying a nice middle-class good guy."

Arthur "Archie" Drazen was anything but a playboy, but Bernice fell for his charm. After they married, they settled down in a modest apartment at One University Place, Greenwich Village, overlooking Washington Square Park.

Then Drazen went off to Europe to fight in World War II, leaving his beautiful model bride alone in Manhattan, with all its temptations.

THREE

MR. ROMANTIC

Ben Novack first met Bernice Drazen at the fashionable La Martinique nightclub in early 1945, and was smitten. He was on a brief trip to New York, making arrangements for his new Sans Souci hotel and looking for a good time.

As he already knew one of the girls at Bernice's table, he casually came over to introduce himself, sitting down next to her.

Many years later, Bernice would explain that, for her, it was anything but love at first sight. In fact, she blew off the thirty-eight-year-old flashily dressed hotel proprietor, thinking him gauche.

After buying champagne for the table, Novack started boasting about his growing Miami Beach hotel empire. Bernice was not impressed. To the twenty-three-year-old model, Novack seemed overbearing and middle-aged. She also noticed the hearing aid in his right ear, with a large wire connecting it to a pocket microphone.

"But there was something about him," she recalled more than half a century later. "He was charming and vulnerable, and there was the way he walked and swayed his shoulders."

Ben Novack started bragging about the Sans Souci hotel, saying it would be the last word in grandeur and luxury. It was a one-way conversation, as Novack could not hear Bernice, and had to keep asking her to speak louder into the microphone of his hearing aid.

At the end of the night, he gave the model his business card and asked her to call him.

"And she glanced at it," said Maxine, "and dismissed him."

Refusing to take no for an answer, Novack then requested Bernice's telephone number. Once again she refused, saying she had to go.

"He flipped for her," Ben Novack Jr. would later tell *The Miami Herald*. "She didn't want to date a married man and made it very clear to him."

The next day, Novack returned to La Martinique, bribing the maître d' to give him Bernice Stempel's phone number. Instead, he was given the phone number for a young male friend of Bernice's, who had also been at the table.

Ever resourceful, Novack called the friend, saying he needed to get in touch with Bernice on a legal matter. He was then given a contact number for the Conover Model Agency.

"So he called up the agency and said he had a job for them," said Maxine. "He manufactured a shoot in Havana and said he wanted a very American girl type. Outdoorsy looking. Red hair. Freckles. He made the whole thing up."

A week later, Bernice and another model were sent to Havana for the modeling assignment, together with a makeup girl and a photographer.

When she came out on the beach in her swimming costume for the scheduled photo session, a smiling Ben Novack suddenly appeared out of nowhere.

"He had set the whole thing up to look like a job," Bernice later explained, "just so he could spend time with me."

His elaborate romantic ploy paid off. Bernice was so impressed that she started seeing him whenever he came to New York.

Her husband, Archie Drazen, was still fighting in Europe, and although they regularly corresponded, they had grown apart. There was also little passion between Novack and his wife, Bella, who was content to remain in Miami while he gallivanted around the world on business.

Before long, Ben and Bernice were lovers.

"He wined her and he dined her," said Maxine, "and she's still married."

All through their often rocky four-year courtship, Ben Novack wrote Bernice love poems, enlisting Maxine as an ally.

"He was in Florida sending her soft-shell crab and baskets of fruit," Maxine recalled. "He was a hotel man, so he would send beautiful things like wine, cases of liquor, and the top sirloin steaks. And he'd always say, 'Maxine, I want her to know how she can live if she marries me. This is how she'll live.'"

Maxine says her sister did not fall in love with her ardent suitor immediately. She was also romantically involved with a rich young man named Ivan Mogul, but his parents did not consider the beautiful young model marriage material, making him break off the relationship.

Soon after that, Bernice and Ben became serious, and when Archie returned from Europe, Bernice decided to end the marriage.

"She wrote him the 'Dear John' letter," said her sister. "She said, 'Arthur, I don't know if we're suited. You know I met somebody and I think you'd be happy with someone else.'"

Bernice even visited her mother-in-law to explain. She and Archie Drazen would remain friends for the rest of her life.

Maxine said their father had always encouraged his daughters to be socially ambitious.

"Bernice had ambitions," Maxine explained, "We inherited that from our father. He'd always say, 'Remember who you are.'"

Back in Miami Beach, Ben Novack spent 1948 trying to get his ambitious Sans Souci hotel off the ground. It was being built on 1.5 acres at the prime location of 3101 Collins Avenue.

He had hired architect Roy F. France to design his dream palace, but was unimpressed with France's plans, viewing them as run-of-the-mill and lacking that "wow" factor Novack so desired.

So he hired retail store designer Morris Lapidus, whom he had met years earlier in New York, to jazz things up. Lapidus had been designing retail stores for the A.S. Beck chain of shoe stores, but had absolutely no experience with hotels.

When Novack first asked him if he knew anything about hotels, Lapidus replied that he had "stayed at plenty," conceding that he had never actually designed one. Then, after seeing some preliminary sketches Lapidus did for him on the spot, Novack hired him to design the Sans Souci for a paltry $18,000.

"Local architects were not terribly imaginative," explained the designer's son, Alan Lapidus, "so they said, 'Let's bring down that guy that did our stores because he has a lot of flare.' So he would take their plans, which were pretty boxy and straightforward, and jazz them up."

Morris Lapidus, an early champion of Art Deco, brought stunning New York department store lobbies to hotels. Novack loved Lapidus's charming designs, which he called "intentional nonsense."

Novack and his partner, Harry Mufson, agreed that Lapidus should take over as San Souci's architect, and they had a celebratory dinner, which was attended by Ben's new girlfriend, Bernice Drazen.

Years later, Morris Lapidus would recall that terrible evening in his autobiography. Over dinner, Novack and Mufson got into a heated argument, hurling personal insults across the table.

"The air became blue with more four-letter words than I knew existed," Lapidus later wrote.

Eventually, Novack ushered Bernice out of the party, to save her embarrassment.

When the Sans Souci opened in 1949, it was an instant sensation. With its gleaming fin of blue glass tiles rising up the front of the building and its coral stone walls, it looked more like a pleasure palace than a humble hotel, even boasting a swanky nightclub.

Ben Novack's promotional brochure for his new hotel immodestly stated, "In Paris it's the Eiffel Tower . . . London, Buckingham Palace . . . and in Miami Beach, the Sans Souci."

. . .

Just weeks after the opening of the Sans Souci, Ben and Bella Novack adopted a two-year-old boy named Ronald. But it was Bella who bonded with the boy, as Ben was too busy with his latest hotel projects and his passionate affair with Bernice to care about much else.

Back in New York, Bernice's modeling career was on fire. She could now pick and choose her assignments, and had become *the* face of Coca-Cola, with a string of calendars, advertisements, and other promotions to her credit. She was the supermodel of her day, decades before the term would be invented.

In the summer of 1951 she took an extended European vacation with friends, traveling first class all the way. She sailed back to New York from Le Havre on the luxury French liner *Liberté*, arriving home on September 6.

Several months later, Ben Novack divorced Bella and had a nervous breakdown, going to Arizona to recover. As part of her divorce settlement, Bella received the valuable land tract on which the Sans Souci hotel stood. Some speculated that having to give Bella the land had driven Novack over the edge.

Years later, Bernice would blame Novack's breakdown on an elaborate practical joke perpetrated by his partner, Harry Mufson. One day he arranged to have all the furniture in Novack's office moved out, and he changed the door locks. After getting a locksmith to break in and finding an empty office, Novack suffered a panic attack, thinking he was losing his mind. Upon discovering that Mufson was behind the joke, he fled to Arizona.

Ironically, it was Mufson, concerned about his partner's mental health, who telephoned Bernice in New York, urging her to call Ben and raise his spirits. When she called, Ben turned things to his advantage, persuading her to marry him, saying it was the only thing that could cure him.

So seven years after first meeting him, Bernice agreed to give up her modeling career and move to Miami Beach and become Mrs. Ben No-vack.

In early 1952, Ben and Bernice were married by a judge in a simple civil ceremony at the Essex House, New York City. Jack Stempel gave his daughter away, refusing to let his ex-wife, Rowena, attend.

"My mother was alive," said Maxine, who came with her new hus-band, David Fiel. "But my father wouldn't let us know where she was. Bernice married a man just like our father: controlling, self-centered. Not particularly sensitive."

FOUR

BRICK BY BRICK

When Bernice moved into her new husband's luxurious Sans Souci suite, she fell into a deep depression. For the first months of her marriage she remained in her bedroom, wondering if she had done the right thing.

As Ben Novack had insisted she give up modeling, she felt she no longer had an identity, apart from being his wife. She rarely saw Ben anyway, as he was too busy running his hotel, now booked for months in advance. Her only social contacts were with the Sans Souci waiters and maids, who brought room service to the suite. It was a lonely existence she would soon learn to live with.

Most afternoons, Bernice would go to the hotel's private beach and sunbathe by the pool, finding little in common with the wives of her husband's business partners.

"The wives and I didn't get along," she later explained. "They were very cold to me, and so much older. Here I was, a model. They wanted to sit in a cabana and play cards all day, and I wasn't interested."

As soon as Ben Novack had the Sans Souci up and running, he was ready to move on to something bigger. A golden opportunity soon presented itself when the Harvey S. Firestone oceanfront estate went on the market. Well located on the bend of Collins Avenue at Forty-Fourth Street, the estate marked the boundary between Miami Beach's hotels and the "Millionaires' Row" mansions.

Built in 1918, at a cost of $350,000, by James Snowden of Standard Oil, the fifteen-room Italian Renaissance–style palace had long dominated Miami Beach. Harvey Firestone, the chairman of the Firestone Tire Company, bought it in 1924, renaming it Harbel Villa. He used it to entertain notables such as President Herbert Hoover, Henry Ford, and Thomas Edison.

When Firestone died in 1938, his heirs left Miami, and Harbel Villa fell into disrepair.

The Sans Souci lay thirteen blocks south of the abandoned estate. Every day, Ben Novack drove past it, lusting over its possibilities. With its commanding 950 feet of oceanfront, it would be far and away the biggest hotel in Miami Beach, if he could ever buy it and realize his vision.

Unfortunately, the Firestone estate lay right on the line dividing commercial buildings to the south and residential ones to the north. The rich and powerful Miami Beach citizens living nearby did not want any new hotels intruding on their exclusivity. They maintained that the four hundred hotels Miami Beach already had were quite sufficient, and any new ones would ruin the place.

In 1943 the late Harvey Firestone's heirs had first legally challenged the zoning laws, wanting to sell the land for the best possible price. For the next seven years, there had been a barrage of lawsuits, culminating in a state supreme court decision allowing the estate to be rezoned as commercial.

Novack had been following this case closely, and in late 1951 he and Harry Mufson began quietly negotiating with the owners to buy the Firestone estate. In July 1952 the two partners called a press conference to announce that their Sun N' Sea Corporation had agreed to purchase the old Firestone estate for $2.3 million ($19 million today). They told reporters they would tear down the Firestone mansion to build a "gigantic" 550-room hotel costing $10 million ($83 million today). It would be, Ben Novack boasted, the largest luxury hotel in Miami Beach.

On the eve of closing the deal, Harry Mufson discovered that Novack had double-crossed him by secretly syphoning off $15,000 in Sans Souci hotel money to get his Firestone estate deal under way. To make matters worse, he also discovered that only Ben Novack's name would go on the Firestone estate deed.

There was a heated confrontation between Novack and his partners at the Sans Souci, before Mufson stormed out and hired a lawyer to take legal action.

With just twenty-four hours to close the deal, Ben Novack started hitting the phones for financial backing.

Years later, Ben Novack Jr. claimed that his father had literally begged acquaintances he barely knew to trust him and wire the money, promising to send them contracts later.

"He put together the most unusual partnership," Ben Jr. told author Steven Gaines. "Some of the people he got weren't his choice, but they were willing to cough up the dough."

One of Ben Novack's new partners, one who put up big money, was Mafia boss Sam Giancana, who would soon play a major role in the new hotel.

In the wake of his battle with Harry Mufson, Ben Novack moved into the derelict Firestone mansion, using the dining room as his new office. Bernice took over one of the bedrooms and watched in admiration as her husband began working on the daunting logistics needed to start building the enormous seventeen-story pleasure palace he had in mind.

A few months later, in New York, Morris Lapidus picked up his morning newspaper to read that Ben Novack had selected him to be the architect of his new super-luxurious hotel, to be called "The Estate." It was the first he had heard of it.

Lapidus immediately called Novack, who explained that when he had been asked by a reporter who his new architect would be, Lapidus's was the first name that came into his head. Although Lapidus wanted the project, the hotelier now said he needed "a name" architect. Eventually, Lapidus persuaded Novack to allow him to design not only the hotel, but also the interior furnishings and everything down to the bellhops' uniforms. And he agreed to do it for just $80,000, a fraction of the going rate.

"My father made the devil's deal with Novack," explained Alan Lapidus. "It was an insane fee, but my father knew this was a chance to make his bones."

On December 17, 1953, Ben Novack met with his new architect and recently hired contractors in the Firestone mansion to discuss a time line for completion. He then shocked everyone by announcing that the opening ceremony would take place a year to the day from then.

"I protested this was impossible," Lapidus wrote in his autobiography, *Too Much Is Never Enough*. "The general contractor suggested that instead of preparing my plans in my New York office, I set up an office right here."

Lapidus agreed, and moved his wife and two sons to Miami Beach. He then started doing preliminary sketches for the new hotel, deciding to break way from straight lines and rectangles. Instead, he used curves and round buildings, as in his distinctive New York department stores. He later claimed the idea had come to him in the subway, on his way to work, as an epiphany.

"A sweeping curved building was what I wanted," he explained, "and what I hoped I could sell my client."

When Lapidus presented his client with twenty-six designs, Novack ripped them up and threw them in the trash can, saying he was going to "dream up his own shape."

A few days later, Novack called Lapidus in great excitement, saying he had "hit upon a marvelous idea," one that had struck him like a bolt of lightning while he was sitting on the toilet that very morning.

"Why not have a curved building?" he declared. "No one has ever designed a curved building."

Keeping "a straight face," Lapidus agreed, congratulating Novack for having such an inspiration.

Later, who had actually come up with the original idea for the hotel's iconic crescent shape would become a matter of contention. Half a century later, Bernice Novack would vehemently dispute Lapidus's claim that it was his idea.

"Ben designed [it] while sitting on the toilet of the Sans Souci hotel," she told *Ocean Drive* magazine in 2001. "He liked things that are round, like the feeling of embracing arms. He was in the bathroom for an hour and a half, and he came out with three pages of sketches."

In January 1954 the bulldozers moved in and razed the Firestone mansion to the ground. Then an army of 1,200 construction workers began work on Ben Novack's dream hotel. Once he was satisfied that construction was progressing well, he and Bernice sailed to Europe for an extended vacation.

During the trip—during which they took in England, France, and Spain—they drove past the stunning Fontainebleau Palace outside Paris, the summer residence of French kings dating from the twelfth century. But Ben refused to stop the car to look inside, saying he wasn't into historical places.

"I don't go for those foreign chateaux," he was later quoted as saying.

However, he did think the name "catchy," deciding on the spot that it would be perfect for his new hotel.

"Ben loved and was inspired by everything about French luxury," Bernice later explained.

On the way home, the Novacks stopped off in New York, where they visited Bernice's sister, Maxine Fiel, at her home in the Bronx.

"He liked my furniture very much," Maxine recalled. "He said, 'It's not fussy. It's French Provincial.' And he copied it for the bedroom sets at the Fontainebleau."

Morris Lapidus soon realized the enormity of his mistake in agreeing to design the Fontainebleau for a pittance. By June 1954 he had spent his entire fee, and he informed Ben Novack that he was quitting unless Novack came up with another $75,000.

Eager that his architect not abandon him and delay construction, Novack promised that if his partners liked the finished building, Lapidus would get the extra money upon its completion.

The architect reluctantly agreed to these terms, fearing his reputation would be ruined if he walked away from his first major project. So without consulting his wife, he spent their savings to keep them afloat, before taking out a series of personal loans when that money ran out.

Each morning, Ben Novack was the first on site in a hard hat and work clothes, like a general leading his troops into battle. Always hands-on in the hotel business, he now micromanaged everything.

That summer, Morris Lapidus got his teenage son, Alan, a job with the construction company, pouring concrete.

"I was fifteen," Alan remembered, "and we lied about my age."

Working there, the young boy witnessed Ben Novack's aggressive business style while attending some of the rancorous business meetings with his father.

"I remember [Ben] not being very pleasant," said Alan Lapidus. "Always imperious: 'I want this thing done and don't give me any goddamn excuses.' That's the kind of guy he was. Any problem could be solved if you swore enough."

Every afternoon, Bernice Novack came out onto the beach in her skimpy bathing suit to sunbathe. "She would just lie out there," recalled Lapidus, "and work would really come to a stop."

The Fontainebleau was the largest American hotel to be built since the war, and a New York–based building union soon arrived in Miami Beach to unionize the workforce. Fiercely antiunion, Ben Novack was livid when the union threatened to disrupt work and cause months of delays.

One day, at 4:00 A.M., Morris Lapidus got a call from the on-site night watchman, saying a bomb had just exploded. By the time the architect arrived, the police were already there. Lapidus could smell dynamite in the humid air.

Fortunately, the explosive charges had been set against a column supporting a two-story wing, so the damage was not serious, and was easily repaired. It was obvious, though, that the dynamiters knew what they were doing, and had not been trying to create permanent damage.

"Basically, the hotel workers' union was run out of town," said Alan Lapidus, "and it wasn't until much later that it was discovered that Ben Novack was behind the bomb. He had done it to break the union—which he did."

One week before the scheduled December 20, 1954, opening of the Fontainebleau, as the builders were making the finishing touches, Ben Novack took his partners on a tour of his new hotel. After a brief meeting in his office, Novack invited Morris Lapidus out to join them.

The tour finished up at noon by the new Olympic-size swimming pool. The partners stood there in awe, staring at the building's graceful curves, and at the fountains and statues on the immaculately laid-out seven acres of grounds surrounding it.

Then they congratulated Novack and his architect on their great achievement. It was at that point that Lapidus reminded Ben about the extra fee he was now owed, as Novack's partners obviously liked his work.

Novack threw Lapidus a blank stare, saying he had no idea what he was talking about. The architect was stunned, protesting that they had an agreement and that he had gone into personal debt to finance the work. Novack just shrugged, looked Lapidus dead in the eye, and said that this was the first he'd heard of it.

"Then [my father] snapped," said Alan Lapidus. "He had a total nervous breakdown and grabbed a two-by-four piece of lumber and started chasing him around the pool, screaming, 'I'm going to kill you, you son of a bitch!'"

It took four partners to subdue the architect before he blacked out.

He came around to find a group of Novack's concerned Fontainebleau associates pouring pool water over him.

Lapidus then told the partners about Novack's promise to pay him an extra $75,000 on top of the $80,000 they'd initially agreed to. It then emerged that Novack had told his partners, who'd financed the project, that he was paying his architect $250,000. It seemed he had pocketed the difference.

"They nearly killed Novack when they found out he had been stealing from them," said Alan Lapidus. "It was very unpleasant."

A few days later, the partners ordered Novack to pay Morris Lapidus the extra fee. The hotelier reluctantly agreed, but first insisted that Lapidus apologize for attacking him.

Lapidus swallowed his pride and agreed, in order to get his money.

"You *should* be sorry," Ben Novack barked at him. "Why didn't you talk louder? You were whispering, and you know that I don't hear well."

FIVE

"THE MOST PRETENTIOUS HOTEL IN THE WORLD"

On Monday, December 20, 1954, the Fontainebleau hotel officially opened with a grand ball for 1,600 specially invited guests. Two days earlier, Ben Novack had personally taken influential newspaper columnists such as Walter Winchell and Earl Wilson on a guided tour.

New York mayor Robert Wagner was among the celebrities who flew in for the grand opening. But the official guest of honor was the mayor of Fontainebleau, France, Homer Pajot, who would perform the opening ceremony, as well as provide a great photo opportunity.

Unsure what was expected of him, Mayor Pujot had brought along a tree from the Forest of Fontainebleau, which was promptly seized by Miami Airport customs agents. Novack's fast-thinking publicity man then purchased a replacement tree at a local nursery, which he had decked out in a French tricolor bow. Unfortunately, an eagle-eyed reporter spotted the florist's van arriving with it, and the next morning an embarrassing gossip piece ran in *The Miami Herald*.

Throughout the opening ceremony, Mayor Pujot, who didn't speak a word of English, looked lost and confused. No one had thought of hiring an interpreter for him.

The French mayor winced as Novack mispronounced the hotel

name—"FOUN-tan-BLOO"—and for years afterward, Bernice would complain that everyone pronounced it incorrectly, and that the correct French pronunciation should be used.

The tree-planting ceremony was held in the hotel's French gardens, copied from the ones outside the palace of Versailles. A smiling Ben and Bernice Novack stood inside the gigantic crescent-shaped aquamarine glass façade as Pajot kissed them on both cheeks. Then, to a round of applause, he presented them with a tablet inscribed in French, reading, "May the sun warm your day and the moon and stars bring happy evenings. And may you return again to taste the pleasures and elegant living at this most fabulous of all resorts."

Everyone then went inside to gasp at Morris Lapidus's amazing interiors, which Mayor Pujot later described as "a bouillabaisse."

That night, Ben and Bernice Novack hosted the opening ball in the La Ronde Room. Ben wore a black tuxedo, and at his side was Bernice, looking like a movie star in a white mink stole and glittering diamond earrings.

The guests danced past midnight, as Patti Page sang the "Fontainebleau Waltz" and Liberace played an 1882 German Steinway grand piano under a huge chandelier cheekily nicknamed "Sophie Tucker."

Even Eastern Airlines jets passing overhead tipped their wings in a salute that night.

The next morning, *The Miami Herald* carried a tongue-in-cheek report on the opening.

"Everything was French, including the confusion," the paper wryly observed. "Millionaires in their elegant glamorous attire lost their dignity as they scrambled for their tables. But the guests took it all in their stride. One gushed, 'You can't get in, you can't get a drink, you can't get anything, but isn't this the grandest hotel you ever saw.'"

Groucho Marx, soon to become a Fontainebleau regular, described the hotel as the Eighth Wonder of the World, but the architectural critics were not so kind.

"The nation's grossest national product," noted one. "A monstrosity," asserted another, forecasting that it would appeal to people who "don't know the difference between architecture and Coney Island."

Ben Novack couldn't have cared less, proudly proclaiming the Fontainebleau "the world's most pretentious hotel."

He now began referring to himself as "Mr. Fontainebleau," and wore a tiny golden replica of his hotel on a heavy gold chain around his neck.

But it would be hard even for the flamboyant hotelier to compete with his stunning creation.

According to the Fontainebleau press release, the hotel had cost $13 million ($106 million today) to build and employed nine hundred staff. The motif was French, and the main curved building had lovely, warm French white marble floors with black bow ties receding into the distance, elegantly winding stairways, and round columns. An estimated $1.5 million in French Provincial antiques and statues adorned the corridors and suites. Everything was decked out in over-the-top French period décor. The Presidential Suite even had a dummy fireplace, with a marble mantel from the old French embassy in Washington, D.C.

The focal point of the hotel's massive main interior was the two-story "Staircase to Nowhere," which Morris Lapidus had copied from the Paris opera house.

Guests would take an elevator to the mezzanine before slowly walking down the curved staircase, parading their jewels and furs to an appreciative audience below.

"When they walked down the staircase, they were stars," said Alan Lapidus. "They seemed to be saying, 'We're rich and we can afford it.'"

This nonstop display of affluence soon become one of the hotel's most popular attractions.

The future Las Vegas hotel magnate Steve Wynn vacationed at the Fontainebleau as a young boy, learning valuable lessons from Ben Novack that he would put to good use many years later. "The Fontainebleau invented the concept of the hotel as show," explained Wynn, who would later marry into the Novack family. "Not only was it grand, but it had the charisma of a place that was cool to be at. There was nothing but laughter in the lobby. Everybody was having the time of their lives, everybody was pretty, and everybody was rich."

Ben Novack never underestimated the importance of star power, carefully cultivating close friendships with the world's biggest entertainers. But it was through the influence of Mafia bosses and his Fontainebleau partners Sam Giancana and Joseph Fischetti that Frank Sinatra first started playing at Novack's beloved hotel.

In return for headlining midnight shows at the Fontainebleau's exclusive La Ronde Room nightclub, Novack presented the superstar with the key to his own permanent penthouse suite on the sevententh floor. Over the next twenty-five-years, Sinatra became synonymous with the Fontainebleau—and one of Ben Novack's closest friends.

Following Sinatra's example, other big stars started playing the Fontainebleau. The Rat Pack made the hotel its winter headquarters, performing many impromptu drunken sets at La Ronde.

"We had not just the Rat Pack," said the hotel's first head of publicity, Hal Gardner, "but also Judy Garland, Sophie Tucker, and Marlene Dietrich. Where else would you see Gary Cooper reading the paper or Groucho Marx having eggs Benedict? When Joan Crawford walked across the lobby, people would get up and applaud."

As a world-class entertainment center, the Fontainebleau transformed Miami Beach into *the* glamour capital of the world, drawing the rich and famous like a magnet. (Ben Novack enforced a strict evening dress code among guests all over the hotel, with suits and ties for men and cocktail dresses for women.) And the iconic crescent-shaped Fontainebleau became synonymous with Miami Beach on postcards and other memorabilia.

Incredibly, during the quarter of a century Ben Novack ran the hotel, there was never a single Fontainebleau sign inside or outside to identify it.

"If you didn't know what it was," explained future Fontainebleau manager Lenore Toby, "you didn't belong."

. . .

Soon after the Fontainebleau opened for business, Ben and Bernice Novack took up residence in a fabulous duplex suite on the seventeenth floor, nicknamed the Governor's Suite. Their majestic four-bedroom apartment looked out on the ocean and boasted a dining room, a billiard room, and a piano bar with a baby grand piano.

"They lived like royalty," said future Miami Beach mayor Alex Daoud, "and they acted like they were royalty. Ben could be very charming, and he could also be very cruel. He could be ruthless, but he was always very cunning."

Ben Novack now devoted himself to making the Fontainebleau a success, having little time or energy for anything else. He lived and breathed the Fontainebleau 24/7, and Bernice soon realized that she would always take second place.

"The Fontainebleau was his life," she later told author Steven Gaines. "It was his baby, his wife, his mistress, all his dreams and ideas together."

Resigning herself to the role of trophy wife, she spent her days shopping and fulfilling her duties as the Queen of the Fontainebleau. Her husband demanded she always dress in the latest fashions—it was as if she had a full-time modeling assignment for his hotel.

"You're always in a glass cage," she later explained. "People stared at me. They'd say, 'There's the owner's wife' or 'There's Mrs. Novack.' I didn't care for it. I didn't like the 'front' of the house."

Still, Bernice was constantly upstaged by her narcissistic husband and his ever more garish suits, bow ties, and jeweled bling (years before the word was coined). Plus, she soon discovered that although she might be living like a queen, wearing the most expensive furs and jewels, it all belonged to the hotel and she actually owned nothing.

On May 28, 1955, Ben and Bernice Novack flew to Paris for an extended European shopping vacation. On June 7 they checked into the luxurious Savoy hotel in London for a ten-day stay, before flying back to the States.

By the time Bernice arrived back at the Fontainebleau, she was pregnant.

. . .

While Ben Novack was in London, his estranged business partner Harry Mufson called a press conference. He announced that he had bought land directly north of the Fontainebleau, to build an even more elegant and luxurious hotel. It would be named the Eden Roc, after the gardens and swimming pool at the Hôtel du Cap-Eden-Roc, in Antibes.

His architect would be Morris Lapidus, who vowed to create an even more ambitious hotel than the Fontainebleau. Mufson's brief to Lapidus was to make the Eden Roc the ultimate in elegance and luxury, with "no French stuff like the Fontainebleau." When Lapidus proposed Italian Renaissance, Mufson replied that he did not care if it was "Brooklyn or baroque," as long as it had plenty of glamour and "screams" luxury.

"I want the Fontainebleau to fall flat on their ass," he told his architect.

When Ben Novack returned from Europe, Lapidus went to the Fontainebleau to inform him as a matter of courtesy that he had agreed to design the Eden Roc. Novack went ballistic, forbidding his former architect to design the rival hotel.

"I patiently explained to him that architecture was my profession," wrote Lapidus in his autobiography, "and my means of earning a livelihood. Ben claimed that I owed it to him to turn down my new commission."

When Lapidus said he would be designing the Eden Roc anyway, Novack banned him from ever setting foot in the Fontainebleau again.

"I left the hotel feeling like Adam being driven out of the Garden of Eden," Lapidus wrote.

Some years later, when Lapidus attempted to enter the Fontainebleau for a charity luncheon, Novack had security guards physically throw him out of the hotel he had designed.

At 9:00 P.M. on Thursday, January 19, 1956, Bernice Novack gave birth to a baby boy at a Manhattan hospital. When she went into labor, Ben

Novack jumped on a plane from Miami Beach. He arrived at the hospital two hours after his son, Ben Hadwin Jr., entered the world.

"Benji was already born when Ben came," recalled Benji's aunt Maxine. "He flew in from Florida and [Bernice] says, 'We have a son.'"

Maxine Fiel, who had been at the hospital with her sister since 2:00 that afternoon, said the new father displayed little reaction on learning that he now had a son and heir.

"Ben didn't ever show a great deal of emotion," explained Maxine. "He'd smile or something, but he never [seemed] very happy."

Novack first saw his baby son in the hospital nursery, and Maxine's husband, David, took photographs of him holding Benji for the first time.

The next day, Ben Novack flew back to Miami to take care of Fontainebleau business, and a week later Bernice brought their baby son home to the seventeenth-floor penthouse, where he would spend his childhood.

Six

BENJI

After Bernice's own difficult childhood, being a mother did not come naturally to her. A live-in wet nurse was hired to feed Benji, to be followed by a succession of nannies to look after him.

Although Ben and Bernice Novack would always be there for birthday parties and other family photo opportunities, Benji (as everyone called him) received little warmth or affection from his parents.

"I don't think [Bernice] even raised Benji," said Estelle Fernandez, later to become Bernice's confidante. "She had nannies that took care of him, and I think that's why their relationship was not a close one."

The year of Benji's birth, Ben Novack became obsessed with destroying the Eden Roc hotel, now rising fast across Collins Avenue. In the fall of 1956, several months before the Eden Roc's scheduled opening, he secretly purchased a ninety-nine-year lease on a parking lot dividing the two hotels. He was planning a massive new Fontainebleau extension, with a new wing and hundreds of extra guest rooms. There would be also a huge ballroom, to attract the lucrative convention business beginning to come to Miami Beach.

The Eden Roc officially opened just before Christmas 1956. It was clearly visible from the Fontainebleau, and to make matters worse, it was an immediate hit with the critics, who said it surpassed the Fontainebleau.

That holiday season, the two Morris Lapidus–designed hotels were the talk of Miami Beach—to Ben Novack's great annoyance. In revenge, he set to work planning his extension, which would include a seventeen-story blank concrete wall that would cut off the sunlight to the Eden Roc swimming pool and put the hotel out of business. The extension would be known as Fontainebleau Towers, and would double the size of his hotel.

The expansion was done under a veil of secrecy. The construction began on the rectangular gray slab of concrete towering over the boundary of the adjacent Eden Roc. Novack had deliberately positioned it to cast a shadow over his rival's pool between noon and 2:00 P.M., the most popular hours for sunbathing. Novack even gave his former partner Harry Mufson the proverbial finger by ensuring that the only break in the gray concrete wall facing the Eden Roc would be a large window in the upper-left-hand corner—the dining room of his and Bernice's new duplex.

Later, Ben Novack loved staring through his window as the noon shadow slowly crept over the Eden Roc pool, sending guests scurrying off in search of other places to sunbathe. It was said that he would sometimes open his penthouse window and spit at the rival hotel.

The media nicknamed his extension the "spite wall," as the bitter feud between the rival hoteliers made national headlines.

Forty-years-later, Ben Novack Jr. would dismiss any suggestion that his father had built the wall out of vindictiveness. "My father didn't give a shit what was going on next door," he maintained. "My father didn't even realize that the state of Florida is at a slight angle northeast and at 12:30 in the afternoon the wall would cast a shadow over the Eden Roc. Meanwhile, the result was the most god-awful ugly wall."

Mufson eventually sued Novack over the "spite wall"—unsuccessfully—and was forced to build a second swimming pool, giving Eden Roc's guests full access to sunlight.

. . .

From the very beginning, aside from models and movie stars, the Fontainebleau hotel also attracted a motley collection of thieves and con men, who preyed on the wealthy guests. Burglaries were common, and in the hotel's first two years an estimated quarter of a million dollars in jewelry and other valuables disappeared from guest rooms.

After Ben Novack's personal safe was robbed of $15,000 in cash, he hired retired New York City police lieutenant James Gillace to command a unit of twenty plainclothes security officers, who patrolled the hotel corridors around the clock.

Whenever Frank Sinatra or other A-list entertainers played the La Ronde Room, Novack hired additional off-duty Miami Beach police officers to work security in full uniform and ensure everything went smoothly. With free meals and other generous hotel perks supplied, the normally poorly paid police officers vied for a chance to moonlight at "the Blue," as they affectionately called it.

The FBI was also watching the hotel closely, as the Mafia were rumored to own a large stake in it, and had a strong presence there.

In March 1958, Frank Sinatra played a series of sold-out shows at La Ronde. A subsequent FBI report observed that the singer was staying at the Fontainebleau with movie star Lauren Bacall. It also noted that Sinatra had been seen with Joe Fischetti, a known Mafia boss and Al Capone's former lieutenant. Fischetti, it was said, had been ordered to look after Sinatra by mobsters "Lucky" Luciano and Frank Costello.

Ben Novack had known many of the Mafia families, going back to his time in New York in the 1930s. It was rumored the Mob had invested heavily in the Fontainebleau for "mineral rights," hoping to control Miami Beach gambling, if it were ever legalized.

"Basically, the [Fontainebleau] was mobbed up from top to bottom," said Alan Lapidus. "And that's when the Rat Pack came in and the whole thing started getting very weird."

Mafia chieftain Meyer Lansky used the Fontainebleau as his personal business headquarters. He lived in an apartment a few blocks north, but every morning, he'd arrive at the hotel with Bruiser, his beloved Shih Tzu, and spend the day there.

"He was a perfect gentleman to everyone in the hotel," recalled former desk attendant Robert Madiewski. "He would play cards either in the card room or out by the pool at his cabana, and use the pay phones in the lobby because the FBI had his phones at home wiretapped."

Chicago Mob boss Sam Giancana wintered at the Fontainebleau, and it was there that Sinatra introduced him to the beautiful actress Judith Campbell (later Exner), who became his mistress. A few months earlier, Sinatra had also set her up with then-senator John F. Kennedy, also reputed to have bedded Marilyn Monroe in a Fontainebleau guest room.

Giancana—who made millions of dollars a year from gambling in Cuba—is also reputed to have met CIA agents in his Fontainebleau cabana to discuss assassinating Fidel Castro.

On July 4, 1959, Sam Giancana threw a big wedding bash for his daughter Bonita at the Fontainebleau, which was duly noted by the FBI. Bernice Novack later described the $10,000 wedding ($75,000 in today's money) for two hundred guests, as one of the social highlights of her time there. She and Ben were photographed with the bride and groom at the lavish reception.

"While the wedding was very elegant and elaborate," Bernice told *Ocean Drive* magazine in 2001, "what I remember most was all the security . . . Sam and the hotel each had their own security, as the FBI and IRS agents and journalists were all swarming the lobby trying to get the names and photos of the guests going into the ballroom."

Although the Fontainebleau already had the reputation as a Mob hangout, Bernice said her husband never worried about the bad publicity.

"It was a public hotel," she explained, "and we couldn't keep anyone out."

For Christmas 1958, Ben Novack expanded his fabulously successful La Ronde Room supper club, where his headliners' minimum weekly salary was $35,000. Among the top stars already booked to perform for the holiday were Red Skelton, Jack Benny, Judy Garland, and Frank Sinatra.

In January 1959, Novack told *The New York Times* that La Ronde's larger capacity meant he could showcase the most expensive stars without putting up the minimum price of drinks.

Benji Novack grew up among all this glamour, wealth, and paranoia, and knew nothing else. As a baby, he was wheeled around the hotel in his stroller, to which was affixed a large sign reading, "Do Not Touch."

He was raised by a strict German nurse named Bella, who left a lasting impression on the little boy. When his aunt Maxine visited the Fontainebleau with his cousin Meredith, she was shocked at how the nurse treated him.

"Every time he would eat she'd wipe his mouth," recalled Maxine. "I said, 'Bella, will you leave him alone. He's going to drip. Wipe his mouth afterward.'" And I got so mad, I said, 'Benji, eat your hamburger. Do not wipe your mouth unless you feel something dripping.'"

The nurse also forced the naturally left-handed boy to become right-handed. His aunt believes this so traumatized him that he developed a terrible stutter, which remained with him for the rest of his life.

"I know why he stuttered," said Maxine. "He had that German nanny every minute. He had nobody else."

Meredith Fiel, a couple of years older than her cousin Benji, visited the Fontainebleau with her parents as a young child. She recalls her uncle Ben as being very cold and distant.

"He was this older, big man in charge of this big hotel," she recalled. "He used to pat me on the head, and that was it. I didn't have a 'sit on my lap' relationship with Ben Novack. We were never close."

Meredith also remembers her cousin Benji remaining with his nannies, with no interest in meeting other children.

"Benji didn't play with anybody," she said. "He didn't connect with me or really want to. When he had his tantrums, everybody would quake and shake at the thought of Ben Novack coming around."

SEVEN

"THE SUN AND FUN CAPITAL OF THE WORLD"

B en Novack Jr.'s pampered Fontainebleau childhood was like a Hollywood movie. When he was four, his nanny took him to see Frank Sinatra film scenes from *A Hole in the Head*, being shot at the hotel. Then, a few months later, Jerry Lewis took over the entire hotel for several months to direct and star in *The Bellboy* (which he'd also written). As a tip of the hat to the Fontainebleau's chairman of the board, the comedian had named the hotel manager character Mr. Novak.

"Benji was running around through it all," said Jill Campion, who was later to become Ben Jr.'s first wife. "All the stars came through there, and Benji knew them all."

Ben Novack Sr. was now the real-life star of the Fontainebleau. Always impeccably dressed in his own unique style, he ruled his kingdom from his executive office.

In March 1960, Elvis Presley checked into a penthouse suite at the Fontainebleau to shoot a Frank Sinatra television special. It was Presley's first public performance after being discharged from the U.S. Army, and would be filmed on the stage of the hotel's Grand Ballroom.

Ben and Bernice Novack were in the front row to see the two super-

stars perform duets of each other's songs: Sinatra's "Witchcraft" and Presley's "Love Me Tender."

After filming his special, Frank Sinatra and Elvis Presley led the Rat
Pack across the lobby in search of a drink. The first open bar they came
across was a bar mitzvah party. The stars walked in and were mobbed,
and had to leave after just ten minutes to get away from the fans.

The Sinatra TV special was broadcast on May 12, breaking viewing
records and exposing the glamorous Fontainebleau to millions all over
the world.

A few months later, Sinatra and the Rat Pack's Sammy Davis Jr.,
Dean Martin, Joey Bishop, and Peter Lawford played the Fontaine-
bleau. Davis had just married the Swedish-born actress May Britt, and
Ben Novack didn't want the black entertainer staying at his hotel.
Miami was still segregated, and Novack was afraid of upsetting the
other guests. Frank Sinatra thought otherwise.

"To Frank's credit," said future Miami Beach mayor Alex Daoud,
"he told Ben that if he had a problem with Sammy, he was going to
have a problem with him. And if Sammy couldn't stay there, he was
leaving. Ben Sr. said, 'Oh shit!' but there was nothing he could do."

That same day, Davis pulled up to the Fontainebleau front entrance in his red Cadillac, with his blond wife and several black friends
in tow.

"He waited until Ben Novack came out," said Daoud, "and honked.
I thought that was very funny."

From then on, Davis always sunbathed by the Fontainebleau pool
with all his friends, and Novack was powerless to stop him.

On July, 10, 1960, *The New York Times* ran an article on Miami Beach,
examining why some hotels flourished while others went bankrupt. As
the owner of the most successful hotel, Ben Novack was naturally interviewed.

"You can't buy your son-in-law a hotel and tell him to run it," Novack observed. "You've got to have know-how. And you can't switch

management every few months in a resort operation. A tourist likes to see the same faces. When he doesn't, he thinks you're in trouble."

The *New York Times* article noted that Miami Beach now welcomed more than two million visitors a year, coming for "the sun, sand and surf." With 378 hotels now vying for tourist business, many were going out of business. "The Fontainebleau is having its best year in its history," the article stated.

Novack credited his success to maintaining exclusivity, and keeping prices high. He criticized hotel owners who cut rates, and others who gave travel agents generous discounts to steer clients their way.

"That's inviting disaster," Novack explained. "A hotel has the same fixed charges. Fill it at reduced rates and you're still going to lose money."

Every day, Ben Novack worked long hours in his office, ensuring his hotel ran smoothly. He micromanaged everything, but still made a point to listen to everyone's advice, from his maître d' to a lowly bellboy.

"He was some hotel man," said his sister-in-law Maxine Fiel. "They had this big chandelier with about a thousand bulbs. One night he summoned his manager, Harold, and pointed up to it. 'Harold,' he said, 'there's a bulb up there that's blown out. I want it changed.'"

Novack was particularly obsessed with having clean ashtrays, constantly looking for used ones. "If he saw a dirty ashtray he would raise hell," said Richard Marx, who later did legal work for the hotel. "He was very fastidious and he wanted that hotel to be gleaming and clean and just perfect."

Even Morris Lapidus recognized his nemesis's genius for running the Fontainebleau. "Ben was a hotelier to his very fingertips," he wrote. "He knew hotel operations as few men do. But it went deeper than that. He knew what he liked [and] what his guests liked."

One afternoon, Bernice Novack and a couple of friends were walking through the hotel basement when Frank Sinatra's bodyguards ordered them to leave, as the great man was approaching.

"And naturally she didn't," said Guy Costaldo, who later became Bernice's close friend. "She said, 'Well, you tell Mr. Sinatra that Bernice Novack is walking through.' And then they both passed by each other."

When Sinatra heard what had happened, he sent her a pair of expensive diamond earrings as an apology. Attached was a note reading, "If you don't cotton to these mothers, you can always sell them to Swifty."

The singer was referring to the legendary Swifty Morgan, whom Damon Runyon immortalized as "the Lemon Drop Kid." Morgan hung around the pool at the Fontainebleau, acting as a pawnbroker for down-on-their-luck guests, who would sell him their wives' jewelry.

Over the years, Frank Sinatra gave Bernice many other presents, including a grand piano and his special recipe for spaghetti sauce.

"He liked her a lot," said Maxine Fiel, "because she stood up to him."

On January 9, 1961, Frank Sinatra checked into the Fontainebleau hotel to perform four nights at La Ronde. He was being tailed by an FBI agent, who later reported to J. Edgar Hoover that the singer had been seen at the hotel talking to Mafia boss Joseph Fischetti. The FBI would later claim Sinatra had "insisted" Ben Novack place Fischetti on the Fontainebleau payroll as "a talent agent," paying him thousands of dollars a year.

One night, Sinatra summoned Bernice Novack up to his penthouse to keep him company, as he couldn't sleep.

"He didn't like to sleep," said Maxine Fiel, "and just couldn't be alone. Bernice told me that they were all sitting there at five in the morning, and he says, 'Nobody leaves until I say so.' Bernice says, 'Oh, to hell with this, Frank, I'm leaving. I'm falling asleep.'"

On January 19, five-year-old Benji Novack flew to Washington, D.C., with his parents and Frank Sinatra to attend President John F. Kennedy's inauguration.

The next day, a heavy snowstorm blanketed the capital, almost necessitating cancelation of the inauguration parade. Nevertheless it went ahead, and the Novack family were in the Capitol Building to hear President Kennedy's historic inauguration speech. Later that night, they attended President Kennedy's Inaugural Ball, at which Frank Sinatra performed.

A year later, Benji and his parents were all photographed with the new president when he visited the Fontainebleau. A tuxedoed Ben Novack Sr. posed alongside President Kennedy with a wide smile and his hand on his young son's shoulder. Bernice looked radiant in a couture dress with matching top, wearing the diamond earrings Sinatra had given her. Little Benji wore a white tuxedo jacket and black bow tie. His wavy dark hair was combed forward and his eyes were full of pride.

Bernice Novack would treasure this stunning black-and-white photograph for the rest of her life. She carefully placed it in one of the many photo albums she compiled over the years showing her and her family with some of the most famous people of the twentieth century.

On February 12, 1961, the Fontainebleau made national headlines after a teenage guest went berserk in the hotel and gunned down a Miami Beach police detective and wounded another. Nineteen-year-old John Charles Cross from New Jersey reportedly started shooting when Miami Beach detective William Allsopp, sixty-two, summoned him to the executive offices and questioned him about his massive hotel bill and suspicious credentials.

Ben Novack and his head of publicity, Hal Gardner, were talking next door when shots ran out. They dove for cover.

After shooting the detective dead, Cross ran through the corridors of the Fontainebleau waving a .22-caliber pistol at scores of horrified hotel guests. He then dashed downstairs to the lower level of stores, as a bellboy lunged at him but missed.

The *Miami News* reported that the crazed gunman then grabbed Fontainebleau house detective Louis Behrens and forced him at gunpoint out of the back entrance.

"You're my way out of here!" he screamed, pushing the detective into his car before taking off toward Collins Avenue, a gun to Behrens's head.

A Miami Beach police squad car finally cut him off in front of the Montmartre hotel, and officers began shooting. When Behrens tried to grab Cross's gun it went off, shooting the detective in the knee. Then police rushed in and arrested Cross.

The next morning the *Miami News* devoted its entire front page to the murder, with the screaming headline "Murder at the Fontainebleau."

"[It was] the size of a war declaration," recalled Gardner of the headline. "Novack told me, 'Murder at the Fontainebleau! What are they trying to do to me?' I said, 'Don't worry. It'll be good.' And it was: The Poodle Lounge was jammed that night with people who wanted to see where the murder was."

Three days later, FBI agents arrived at the Fontainebleau and questioned Ben Novack about Sam Giancana's recent weeklong stay there. An FBI report released years later under the Freedom of Information Act stated that Novack was evasive, saying the Chicago Mafia boss had probably "just dropped by."

"[Ben Novack] volunteered no information," the report read, "and answered all questions tersely with no elaboration. He advised that it was not hotel policy to make records available to law enforcement agencies in the absence of a subpoena."

A few months later, the Florida attorney general labeled the Fontainebleau a "hangout for hoodlums."

Operating alongside Swifty Morgan's pawnbroker business was an ex-con named Max Raymond, also known as "Little Maxie," who had served a two-year sentence at Leavenworth for narcotics. Ben Novack gave Raymond the linen and lingerie store concession in the lower lobby. A subsequent investigation into the Mafia's ties with Ben Novack Sr. and the Fontainebleau would allege that Raymond was in fact the hotel's "resident muscle," and his real "concession" was running the Mob's invitation-only high-stakes card games there.

During Raymond's years at the Fontainebleau, he was arrested for gambling, burglary, and vehicular homicide, but never convicted.

"Maxie Raymond was always in the card room," Steve Wynn told

Ocean Drive magazine in 2001. "His leverage was that he was buddies with the union guys at the hotel."

Ben Novack's personal security force, composed of off-duty Miami Beach Vice Squad officers, turned a blind eye to the high-class prostitution conducted in the Poodle Lounge, where the maître d' took phone calls for the girls, even arranging assignations in return for a good tip.

"On a good night," said the Fontainebleau's former head of security Ronnie Mitervini, "you'd have six to ten different hookers working the Poodle Lounge. They were very classy, dressed conservatively, and came down for the winter not just from New York, but from little towns in the Midwest. They were the girls next door."

Whenever Frank Sinatra played the Fontainebleau's La Ronde Room, there was big money to be made. There would be long lines of fans in the lobby, desperate for tickets, and the only way to see the show was to discreetly tip the headwaiter $100.

"He'd make five thousand dollars a night when Sinatra was here," said hotel bellman Floyd "Mac" Swain, "and he had to split the cash with security and Novack."

Frank Sinatra was the engine driving the Fontainebleau, and whenever he was in residence, the money flowed. After the show, the action moved upstairs to the Sinatra penthouse suite, where anything could happen. The singer would party with his Mafia cronies Joe Fischetti and Sam Giancana, calling room service to send up the most beautiful girls from the Poodle Lounge, along with buckets of the best champagne.

"God, did they spend money," Ben Jr. later recalled admiringly.

The wild nights often finished with a drunken Frank Sinatra and his Mob pals in hysterics, throwing cherry bombs off the seventeenth-floor balcony.

Soon after JFK's inauguration, two writers who were working with Frank Sinatra on a film script arrived at his penthouse to discover him locked in the bedroom. Just before their arrival, the star had raised the silver salver that Room Service had delivered to his room to find a fully skinned lamb's head.

A shaken Sinatra viewed it as a warning from the Mob to use his influence to have President Kennedy tell his brother Robert, then attorney general, to stop waging war against organized crime.

The scene would later be immortalized by Francis Ford Coppola in *The Godfather*.

In the summer of 1961, Ben and Bernice Novack vacationed in France, dropping Benji off in New York to spend a couple of days with his aunt Maxine and cousins Meredith and Lisa, before going off to summer camp.

"Bernice asked me to take him," said Maxine. "Buy him some shoes and see him off to camp."

During the boy's brief stay, Maxine was shocked to see how socially inept and maladjusted the five-year-old appeared to be. Talking to her nephew, she was alarmed at how little he knew of the real world outside the Fontainebleau, and how lonely he was.

"He really was the little Prince of the Fontainebleau," said his aunt. "When he wanted his parents, he couldn't just go down and call for them. They were with presidents, diplomats, Sinatra, and the rest. This kid was stuck in a penthouse. He would make a few friends on the holidays, and then they would leave the hotel and he was alone again."

Despite his cousins' attempts to befriend him, Benji preferred to stay in his room and play alone.

On his first night there, the little boy ventured out to the kitchen, helping himself to ice cream and anything else in the freezer that took his fancy. He then left numerous open food containers littering the counter, as if expecting Room Service to clear up after him.

"He had everything open on the counter," Maxine remembered, "and my husband, David, and I had to tell him that we have to go to the store, pick out the food, buy the food, bring it home, and put it in the refrigerator. We don't just call down and say, 'Bring it up.' We told him that oranges don't come squeezed. I said, 'Benji, we're not a hotel. So if you want the ice cream, let me know, but don't open them all.'"

The next day, Maxine's husband David took Benji out on his boat, which was moored in a slip. He first warned him not to play on the slippery hull, in case he fell over the side.

"It was filthy water," Maxine recalled. "Everybody relieves themselves there before they go out sailing."

Benji would never take orders from anybody, and before long he was up on the hull. Then he slipped, falling headfirst into the polluted water.

"David had to jump in and pull him out," Maxine said. "Benji was a mess. He smelled to high heaven. We had to take him home, and David put him in the shower and shampooed his hair. David told him, 'When you're told no, it means no.' And something about that made them close. He bonded with my husband in a way he never did with his father."

Ben Jr. was shaken up. Later that night his aunt came into his bedroom to read him a story. "I put him on my lap," she said, "and he kept snuggling and went to sleep. He'd never had that kind of affection before, and he was a changed kid. We had that kid straightened out."

The next morning, they dropped him off at the summer camp, where Maxine introduced him to another boy. "I found a little friend for him," she said. "I said, 'You can be friends and if you get along, you can add people.'"

One week later, Benji called his parents saying he hated the camp and wanted to come home. "He couldn't get along with the other kids . . . he was arrogant," said his aunt. "So his father came up in a helicopter and picked him up. Oh, that'll win you friends. One week and you pick the kid up in a helicopter."

After the Fontainebleau put Miami Beach on the map, it spawned a string of new upscale, Art Deco–style hotels all over town. There was the Americana, Deauville, Doral, and Carillion, each trying to outdo the others in glamour and luxury.

In August 1961, Ben Novack upped the stakes by announcing that after Thanksgiving he was closing his hotel to the general public, to reopen it as a private club and health spa.

"I've always wanted to give a little more to my guests," he told the *Miami News*, "to improve facilities. Not only will this help the hotel but it will help the general Miami Beach area."

Bernice would later complain that the Fontainebleau had become part of the Miami Beach sightseeing tour, attracting busloads of gaping tourists who weren't even staying there.

"Guests from other hotels would bring their lunch in brown paper bags," she told *Ocean Drive* magazine, "and eat it in the lobby. They'd steal ashtrays, stationery, anything that wasn't nailed down."

Bernice hoped that making the Fountainbleau private would stem the flood of unpaying guests, but Ben Novack had an ulterior motive: Under new IRS rules, if a businessman was sent to a health spa by a physician for medical reasons, he could write it off as a business expense, and his wife could go along as a medical necessity. By privatizing, Novack hoped to lure business travelers to his resort, in a mutually beneficial arrangement.

But soon after Novack took the Fontainebleau private, there was such an outcry that he was forced to allow the public back inside again.

"It was a bad move," said *The Miami Herald* of the privatizing, "almost carny."

That fall, Benji Novack Jr. started classes at the Miami Country Day School. Every morning he would be chauffeured to the private preparatory school in North Miami, and then driven back at night. He was a very bright boy and a good student, but he would make few friends during his seven years there.

EIGHT

THE PRINCE OF
THE FONTAINEBLEAU

On January 19, 1963, Ben and Bernice Novack threw a lavish seventh birthday party for their son. As Benji had no friends his own age, a few children staying at the Fontainebleau were rounded up to join in the festivities. During the party, the hotel's publicity man organized a photograph of Benji on a horse, alongside his smiling parents. Ben Novack Sr. looked unusually casual and relaxed in a slightly unbuttoned shirt, his jacket bursting with his expanding waistline. Bernice looked radiant in a white scarf and a plain white dress, and the birthday boy wore a wide grin as he sat in the saddle, the center of attention.

To celebrate her son's birthday, Bernice Novack commissioned a portrait of him on the beach by the Fontainebleau. The oil painting would become one of her most treasured possessions, prominently displayed wherever she lived.

That summer, a movie crew took over the Fontainebleau swimming pool to film the waterskiing scene for the new James Bond film, *Goldfinger*. The hotel's distinctive exterior was also prominently featured in the tracking aerial shot over Miami Beach during the movie's opening credits.

Benji Novack eagerly watched the filming from the edge of the set, and was later introduced to Sean Connery.

"He knew all these stars," said his future wife Jill Campion, "from the time he was a little kid. He just ran around that hotel and was like the golden boy. Couldn't do anything wrong."

Beneath all the glamour and luxury, however, Ben Novack Jr. was a very lonely little boy, extremely self-conscious about his debilitating stutter. It was especially hard for him at school, where he was mocked by the other children.

"I know that the stuttering frustrated him," said now-retired Miami Beach police officer Joe Matthews, who moonlighted as a Fontaincbleau security guard and befriended young Benji. "He would body-talk."

Even at Halloween, Benji was on his own, being sent off trick-or-treating around Miami Beach in his father's chauffeured limousine.

"That was terrible," said his aunt Maxine. "He was a little king, but this poor kid didn't get any love."

Although the Novacks may have presented the image of the perfect American family in publicity photographs, they were anything but. Ben Novack Sr. was always on the lookout for beautiful young girls, and there was no shortage of available ones at the Poodle Lounge for his pleasure.

"Girls were there everywhere," said Dixie Evans, a retired burlesque dancer who worked the hotel switchboard. "For men with the money, there were plenty of girls around."

During his marriage to Bernice, Novack had numerous brief affairs. Over the years, he and his wife grew apart, eventually leading separate lives.

"Ben cheated on Bernice," said Estelle Fernandez. "I mean, she was aware of it, but she put up with it. He still showed her respect, let's put it that way."

Eventually, Ben Novack moved into his own bedroom in the penthouse, and Bernice asserted her sexual independence by seducing a string of handsome Latin bandleaders who played the hotel. Miami Beach was in the middle of a Latin boom during the 1960s, and the mistress of the Fontainebleau became a fixture at the weekly "Mambo Nights" at the Fontainebleau's popular Boom Boom Room.

In 1960, Cuban bandleader Paquito Hechavarria had joined the Boom Boom Room's seven-piece house band, and over the next few years he often accompanied Fontainebleau regulars Frank Sinatra and the Rat Pack.

Hechavarria recalled in 2001, "Can you believe that you had to wait in line to get into the [Boom Boom] room on a Tuesday. The Beach was full of dance teachers, teaching the Americanos how to dance cha-cha, mambo, tango, and the beginnings of bossa nova."

Hechavarria told the *Miami New Times* that he was just one of several Latin band leaders seduced by the beautiful Bernice Novack. "Let me tell you," he recalled, "she was a beautiful woman. She was hard to say no to."

Bernice also had a fling with the handsome Cuban bandleader Pupi Campo. When Ben Novack found out, he had the musician savagely beaten up and thrown out of the hotel.

"Pupi Campo," Fontainebleau manager Lenore Toby said, sighing. "That's the one that created the big scandal. That's when they split."

When Novack accused Bernice of cheating on him, a huge argument ensued. She then threw him out of their suite, saying she was getting an attorney and wanted a divorce. It was soon the talk of the hotel, as staff wondered what would happen next.

"I do remember the scandal," said Dixie Evans. "Obviously something happened, because why would the rumor go round that Mr. Novack had [Campo] beaten up? Why would he just go out and beat up the head musician? The show was great. Everybody liked him."

On Friday, August 14, 1964, *Miami News* columnist Herb Rau ran a cryptic blind item in his widely read "Miami Confidential" column: "Rumors are flying that a prominent Miami Beach hotelier and his wife are on the verge of extremism in the pursuit of individual liberty."

A month later, on September 7, Rau led off with another blind item: "It's a serious matter between a Miami Beach hotel owner and his wife," his column began. "She's been talking to her attorneys, and she's bantering around a figure in the millions as a divorce settlement."

On Tuesday, October 6, Bernice Novack sued Ben in circuit court, charging him with cruelty. She also asked for custody of their eight-year-old son, Ben Jr. The suit stated that besides being "a good wife," she had always offered her husband "industry and services" to help him run the Fontainebleau hotel. She also asked the judge to award her temporary alimony until the divorce could be heard in court, and that Ben Sr. pay all her court costs.

That morning, the *Miami News* carried the story with the headline "Novack Sued for Divorce." The following day, Herb Rau gloated in his column that Ben and Bernice Novack had "made the headlines" bearing out his previous two items.

After filing for divorce, Bernice moved out of the Fontainebleau, leaving Benji with his father. Then father and son moved out of the Governor's Suite and into a two-bedroom suite in another part of the hotel.

During the Novacks' acrimonious split, Dixie Evans, who by then was the chief night switchboard operator, fielded many dramatic telephone calls between them.

"We used to listen in and pull our key back," she recalled. "No, we didn't really eavesdrop . . . but as an employee you do kind of follow the trend. And when a phone call comes in, you know who to plug up and ring."

Maxine Fiel said that soon after they split Ben Novack desperately tried to win her sister back. "When she broke off with him, he would send cases of liquor . . . the best steaks."

Eventually, Bernice gave in, and in July 1965, just days before circuit judge E. Schultz was due to make his final ruling, she dropped the divorce suit and moved back into the Fontainebleau.

But the couple appeared less than optimistic that things would work out, stipulating that if the divorce suit were revived within two years, Bernice would receive alimony of $17,500 a year ($120,600 in today's money), and $7,500 ($51,600) in child support for Ben Jr.

Soon afterward, Bernice embarked on a passionate affair with Latin drummer George Rodriguez, whom she had met at the Boom Boom Room. "He played drums at the Fontainebleau," said Estelle Fernandez. "She went with him when she was having a hard time with Ben."

Once again Novack discovered Bernice's cheating, but this time he took the initiative and sued for divorce.

"George was her lover," said Guy Costaldo, whose partner was Bernice's hairdresser, Emmanuel Buccola. "And Ben had her followed, because he was terribly in love with her. They had helicopters following her. My lover Manny said, 'It was a very exciting time—running this way, that, and the other.'"

Bernice later claimed that even while her husband was having her followed, he was seeing another woman. "She was a bitch," Bernice said many years later, "She used to come to the hotel while the divorce was going on. She really pursued him, and I guess he fell in love with her."

On Saturday, January 15, 1966—four days before Ben Jr.'s tenth birthday—Ben Novack filed for divorce, accusing Bernice of infidelity and of being a bad mother. In the bitter suit, Novack charged Bernice with taking valuables and "letters of deep sentimental value" from his safety deposit box. He also accused her of being "cold and indifferent," and cheating on him with another man to cause him "mental anguish." He demanded the court give him custody of Ben Jr., claiming that Bernice had neglected the boy by failing to provide a religious education.

Three days later, the *Miami News* reported the story, with the headline, "Ben Novack, Wife Back in Court."

"Ben Novack, Fontainebleau Hotel operator, and his wife, Bernice, are back in divorce court," the article stated. "Mrs. Novack sought a divorce from him in 1964, but they kissed and made up."

In her countersuit, Bernice Novack claimed that Ben had told her that he was bored with their marriage, that he drank excessively and cursed at her.

Years later, Bernice would tell author Steven Gaines that she had been unhappy for many years, and no longer wanted to live at the Fontainebleau. "He would never buy me a house," she complained. "He was fooling around. He was attractive and rich, and women were after him. After all, he owned the world-famous Fontainebleau."

Soon after the suit was filed, Bernice Novack moved into a separate penthouse suite at the Fontainebleau, amid Ben's accusations that she had stolen valuable hotel furniture, art exhibits, liquor, and perfume.

The hotel corporation then sued Bernice in circuit court, demanding she return the hundreds of items that had disappeared from not only the luxury penthouse she'd shared with her husband, but also from the hotel.

NINE

"GAMBLERS AND HOODLUMS"

A s his parents battled in the divorce court, Ben Novack Jr. had the run of the Fontainebleau—to the annoyance of many. He got in the way of the staff, who were always too scared to complain about his boisterous behavior.

"He was in everybody's hair," recalled Lenore Toby. "He was a little tyrant. He had no discipline whatsoever. He was really Peck's Bad Boy," she said, referring to the 1934 film starring Jackie Cooper. Benji had been raised in the corridors and the lobbies of that hotel by the security officers, and had never had a real father and mother.

At that time, Ben Novack Sr. had given his adopted son from his first marriage, Ronald, a lowly job as a reception clerk, and kept his distance, never allowing Ronald to live at the hotel. Benji had little to do with his adopted half-brother, and avoided him, too.

"[Benji] didn't have siblings," said his cousin Meredith Fiel. "He had the Fontainebleau. The waiters. The waitresses. His nannies. That was his family."

In January 1966, ABC-TV broadcast the first episode of the *Batman* TV series, causing a sensation. Ten-year-old Ben Novack Jr. became a huge fan, and lived for the weekly shows. The small boy totally related to the caped crusader's fight for good against evil foes such as the Joker, Catwoman, and the Riddler.

He was now hanging around the Miami Beach police officers who worked security at the Fontainebleau, who took him under their wing. The precocious little boy latched on to the Fontainebleau head of security, Ronnie Mitervini, who became like a father to him. "Benji just hung on to him," said Toby. "He now wanted to be a detective, and his whole life was security."

"He was like a mascot to the police," recalled Officer Pat Franklin, "because his dad owned the Fontainebleau and would feed the cops for free."

Another Miami Beach police officer, James Scarberry, said that it was common knowledge that you had to take care of Benji if you wanted to keep getting the well-paying details at the Fontainebleau, along with the other perks. "We would be working at the hotel," said Scarberry, "and he would just tag along with us. Benji always wanted to be a policeman."

By the mid-1960s, the Mafia had quietly taken over the Fontainebleau hotel, reportedly paying Ben Novack $2 million a year as their frontman.

"Because it was run by the Mafia," Alan Lapidus explained, "there have probably been more movies and TV shows shot in the Fontainebleau than any building on earth. Jerry Lewis and all those guys made all their movies there to promote the building. Frank Sinatra had his own suite and there was definitely Mafia [involvement there]."

At 4:20 P.M. on March 1, 1966, the Miami Beach Police Department received a warning that an assassination attempt would be made on Frank Sinatra during his performance at La Ronde that night. The FBI was immediately alerted.

Sinatra "had received a telephone call from an anonymous male caller," the FBI's official report read, "who said, 'a hand grenade will be thrown at Frank Sinatra sometime tonight during the show.'"

That evening there was a heavy FBI and Miami Beach Police Department presence at the Fontainebleau, but nothing untoward happened.

A year later, Sinatra filmed *Tony Rome* at the hotel during the day while performing at La Ronde at night. He did the same thing in 1968, with *Lady in Cement*.

Whenever Sinatra and his entourage moved into the Fontainebleau, there was always an undercurrent of violence in the air. Sinatra was a heavy drinker, and unpredictable. He could explode at any time.

Once, at an after-party in the Poodle Lounge, Sinatra and Ben Novack Sr. were drinking champagne when the star reached over to an ice bucket to refill his glass. Discovering that the bottle was empty, he threw a tantrum.

"He was as drunk as a skunk," recalled Lenore Toby. "So he picked up the bucket with all the ice in it and turned it over Ben Novack's head, saying, 'You run a lousy hotel.'"

The Fontainebleau owner merely laughed it off, not wanting to upset the real chairman of the board.

On another occasion, Sinatra took umbrage at something and threw all the furniture in his room off the balcony and into the gardens below.

"Benji was later over there," said Toby, "collecting the furniture off the ground."

Sinatra always roamed around the hotel with a team of armed personal bodyguards to do his bidding. One night, the comedian Shecky Greene was opening for the singer, and cracked a joke about him.

"Sinatra got really pissed," said Pete Matthews, another Miami Beach police officer who worked security at the Fontainebleau. "Frank had some of his friends bounce him around to express his anger at comments that he made onstage. Benji told me he saw Greene, and he'd got the shit beaten out of him."

Years later, the comedian incorporated the beating into his act, joking that Frank Sinatra had literally saved his life. He'd tell the audience that five guys were beating him up when he heard Sinatra say, "Okay. He's had enough."

A couple of years before joining the Miami Beach Police Department, Pete Matthews had been driving along Indian Creek, by the Fontainebleau, when he spotted a young boy dressed in a full scuba diving outfit, complete with an oxygen tank, and wading around in the water next to the Fontainebleau's *Calypso* houseboat.

When Matthews asked what he was doing, Benji explained that he was retrieving the hotel's silverware, which Frank Sinatra had thrown off the side of the boat the night before.

"Frank was partying on the boat," said Matthews. "Sometimes he would go off on the deep end when he had too much to drink. He didn't like the utensils, so he'd dumped them over the side. Benji had such a terrible speech impediment that I spent ten minutes just trying to get it out of him."

By the late 1960s, Las Vegas was threatening to eclipse Miami Beach as America's leisure capital. For the Nevada desert town had one big advantage over the Florida beach resort: gambling. Despite Ben Novack and his Mafia partners' dream that Florida would one day legalize casinos, the religious vote up north always proved too powerful.

To add insult to injury, Vegas's thriving Caesars Palace Casino had stolen many of the Fontainebleau's designs and innovations, substituting a Roman theme for a French one.

But the confident Fontainebleau owner and president always talked a good game during press interviews. "Sometimes I am ready to give Miami Beach back to the Seminoles," he told *The New York Times* in February 1963, "but not today. Our volume now places us with the top five hotels in the world. We are enjoying 85 percent occupancy, and could do better if we had any way of bringing in guests on a stand-by basis."

Novack also dismissed any suggestion that the Caribbean islands were threatening Miami Beach. "Until last year we lost a great deal of business to Jamaica, Nassau and the Virgin Islands," he said. "Now these wanderers are coming back. They thought they wanted a complete rest, that peace and quiet were all they needed on a vacation."

Ironically, several months later, Novack decided to expand his empire and build a Fontainebleau Resort and Casino in the Bahamas, on one of the Cat Cay Islands. Unfortunately, his application for a license was ultimately turned down by a royal commission, on the grounds of "unfavorable police information on his character."

Talking to the Associated Press, Novack conceded that he knew a number of American underworld figures, but vehemently denied that they controlled either him or the Fontainebleau.

"Novack also said the Bahamian cabinet rejected his casino license application," read the AP article, "because it did not want a third casino in the colony, not because of police reports on his character."

In January 1967 *The Miami Herald* ran two investigative articles claiming that organized crime controlled the Fontainebleau. Two reporters had spent months examining thirteen years of the hotel's financial papers and had concluded that Ben Novack was a front for the Mob, which used his hotel to launder vast sums of money.

The first damning front-page exposé alleged that "gamblers and hoodlums" actually owned the hotel, which was run by Meyer Lansky, on behalf of a Mob syndicate called the Minneapolis Combination. The reporters branded the Fontainebleau as "a jungle of corporate and financial manipulation."

In the wake of the articles, eagerly picked up by other newspapers across America, Ben Novack's good name was put on the line. Powerful bankers and other financial institutions that provided him credit began turning their backs, and his complex web of financing soon dried up.

Novack sued *The Miami Herald* and the two reporters for libel, asking for $10 million in damages. The Knight-Ridder–owned newspaper refused to reveal its sources for the stories, claiming it was not in the public interest.

Miami Herald executive editor John McMullen explained this decision: "We don't believe that the authors of our laws," he said, "intended to permit assorted hoodlums, protecting organized crime interests, to refuse to testify and yet require a reporter, working in the public's interest, to divulge his confidential sources."

In April, the *Herald*'s lawyers made national headlines by subpoenaing Frank Sinatra to testify about the Mob's involvement in the Fontainebleau. Reluctantly, the singer gave his testimony in his suite at the Fontainebleau, with his attorney Milton Rudin present.

Under oath, Sinatra claimed he had no idea how much money he had made performing at the Fontainebleau over the years. He also denied there was any connection between Ben Novack and Meyer Lansky or Sam Giancana, although he admitted meeting the Chicago Mob boss. He testified that he might have played pinochle in the Fontainebleau card room "for a dollar or two," but was unaware of any other gambling there.

The following February, Sinatra canceled several performances at La Ronde after coming down with a mysterious case of viral pneumonia.

"I don't know when he'll open," a concerned Ben Novack told the *Miami News* on February 29.

A week later, Sinatra's distraught young wife, Mia Farrow, arrived at the Fontainebleau, her marriage on the rocks. Sinatra was furious that Mia was filming Roman Polanski's *Rosemary's Baby* instead of being with him while he filmed *Lady in Cement* at the hotel. Farrow had flown in from London in a final attempt to save her marriage.

"It was a hot and humid night as the taxi drew up to the Fontainebleau Hotel," she wrote in her 1997 autobiography, *What Falls Away*. "A giant sign said FRANK SINATRA in lights, and all the way out on the driveway, I could hear the band playing, 'It's my kind of town, Chicago is . . .' He was standing in that familiar smoky light with his tuxedo and microphone and hair and black tie."

Although Farrow's autobiography maintained she spent "a restless night" with Sinatra, Bernice Novack and Hal Gardner both claim that the singer refused even to see her.

"I found a young girl dressed in a T-shirt and jeans," the hotel publicity director later told *Ocean Drive* magazine. "It was Mia Farrow who had travelled from the filming of *Rosemary's Baby* to be with Frank. But he refused to let her come upstairs. Finally he sent down an envelope of money and told her to take the next plane home."

Bernice also recalled the incident, saying she felt terrible for the fragile young star. "She sat there like a little waif, a tiny little thing bent over with her arms over her knees. That was a horrible thing to do any way you look at it."

A few weeks later, with Ben Novack's imminent *Miami Herald* libel trial, the newspaper's lawyers again subpoenaed Sinatra. To avoid the process servers, he barricaded himself in his Fontainebleau suite. That night, when he went onstage at La Ronde, he recognized the process servers sitting in the audience.

"We're having a wonderful time in Miami Beach," he told the audience between songs. "Get a subpoena every day."

On April 10, circuit court judge Grady Crawford ordered the superstar to appear in Miami for a deposition, or be jailed for contempt of court. A few hours later, Sinatra abruptly left town to avoid testifying about Ben Novack, the Mob, and his real relationship with the Fontainebleau. Although he could not be extradited back to Florida, he faced arrest the next time he set foot in the state.

Then, on April 20, 1968, two days before the trial was scheduled to begin, Ben Novack suddenly dropped the libel action. In return, *The Miami Herald* agreed to publish a statement on its front page stating that he was the sole owner of the Fontainebleau's operating company. But the newspaper never had to apologize officially for the stories or retract any of its claims of Mafia involvement in the Fontainebleau.

There was much speculation that Frank Sinatra had pressured Novack into dropping the suit, refusing ever to perform at the Fontainebleau again as long as there was the threat of a jail sentence over his head.

TEN

"YOU'RE FIRED!"

In late May 1968, just days before the Novack divorce trial, Circuit Court of Dade County judge J. Gwynn Parker ordered Bernice to return everything she had removed from the Fontainebleau. The judge's order contained a five-page list of items.

Then on Monday, June 3, Ben and Bernice's attorneys reached an agreement for a "friendly" divorce, avoiding a scandalous trial. That morning, circuit court judge Hal P. Dekle was told that Bernice, who had been asking for custody of Ben Jr., now sought an uncontested divorce.

Although the terms of the property settlement were sealed, the *Miami News* reported that Bernice would receive more than $25,000 a year in alimony ($162,000 in today's money).

She was now a wealthy woman in her own right, although she would always complain about how little she had received from the settlement. "I didn't come out of it with too much," she explained. "Little more than my jewelry."

Bernice then moved out of the Fontainebleau, her home for nearly fourteen years. Defying a court order not to take anything from the hotel, she loaded up a truck with art, furniture, expensive china, and other items.

When Ben Novack discovered what she had done, he complained to Judge Dekle, who held Bernice in contempt until she returned the goods. Even after handing back some of the items, Bernice still kept assorted pieces of furniture and furnishings, including the piano Frank Sinatra had given her and her beloved oil portrait of Ben Jr. on the beach.

In September 1968, twelve-year-old Ben Novack Jr. moved to Fort Lauderdale to live with his mother, who enrolled him at the Pine Crest preparatory school. The exclusive private school had been founded in 1934 by a teacher named Mae McMillan, who tutored wealthy children whose parents spent the winter in South Florida.

Every morning, Ben Jr. would be chauffeured to the school in N.E. Sixty-Second Street, Fort Lauderdale, and then collected in the afternoon for the drive home. His chronic stuttering problem once again set him apart from the other pupils.

"He was different," remembered his schoolmate Cliff Dunaway. "A very nervous person. I don't know whether that was the problem with the stuttering, or whether it made him appear to be nervous. He seemed more standoffish [and] wasn't one of the crowd."

Still, Ben Jr. was immediately placed in the seventh-grade Honor's Class, and was an excellent student.

"He was very intelligent," said Dunaway. "Almost too smart for his own good."

Tall for his age, Ben Jr. nonetheless had little interest in sports. He joined the audiovisual department, helping out with the school's theater group.

It was while doing the sound and lighting for a production of *Julius Caesar* that he became friends with the young actor playing Brutus. Kelsey Grammer was a year older than Ben Jr. and also came from a broken home. Kelsey's parents had divorced when he was two, and a few months before they met, his father, Allen Grammer, had been brutally murdered in the U.S. Virgin Islands, where he had a controversial radio show. The killer, who had first set fire to his house before shooting him dead, was later found not guilty by reason of insanity.

The two troubled boys found much in common, remaining close for the next forty years.

"Benji's one friend was Kelsey Grammer," said his aunt Maxine. "They were just two lost souls when they met."

In January 1969, sixty-two-year-old Ben Novack Sr. married a beautiful young model named Janie Strong, almost forty years his junior. He had been seeing her all through the divorce, and after they married, he moved out of the Fontainebleau, setting up home in South Miami.

"She was a beautiful girl," said Lenore Toby. "She was elegant and very classy."

Novack had now visibly aged, and was no longer the dynamic entrepreneur he had once been. Although he still dressed in colorfully outrageous clothes—red pants with polka dots were a current favorite—his hearing had deteriorated further and his perfect white teeth looked artificial. But he still oozed charm and was as sharp as a tack.

"Ben Novack was a wonderful old codger," recalled Miami attorney Al Malnik. "If he liked you, he invited you to sit at his personal table at the Poodle Lounge for happy hour [where] there was always a surplus of girls."

As a young attorney, Malnik frequented the Poodle Lounge, but it was months before he would be invited to sit down at Ben Novack's table. When it finally happened, "I thought I had arrived," he said. "That was how the social hierarchy of the day worked: Who you were was where you sat at the Fontainebleau."

Although now almost deaf, "Mr. Fontainebleau" had by now stopped wearing a hearing aid out of vanity. "So you had to yell in his ear," said Malnik. "He wore outlandish clothes, bright green jackets and moccasins with no socks."

The Fontainebleau proprietor had recently had a major facelift, trying to recapture his youth. He was so delighted with the results that he threw a special party for his plastic surgeon, Dr. Larry Robbins, at his La Ronde Room.

"He had me invite twenty people," remembered Dr. Robbins, who is now retired, "and picked up the check for everybody. He would introduce me saying, 'This is Larry Robbins, who did my face but not my eyes.'"

Through his third wife, Janie, Novack became friends with a young Miami attorney named Richard Marx. "Janie had been a model with my wife, and they were good friends," Marx explained. "And based upon their relationship, we got together socially [and] all hit it off very well."

Soon after they met, Novack asked the young lawyer to do some legal work for him. "I was fascinated," said Marx. "I said sure."

Marx became the hotelier's go-to man, and as Novack was very litigious, there was plenty to do. "I basically gave a lot of advice to Ben," Marx explained. "I was his sounding board for a long time. He didn't always listen—or, let's put it this way—he always listened but didn't always follow through. He was a very independent thinker and never unsure of himself."

Novack also started taking Marx to football games, as well as going out socially with their two wives.

"Ben didn't suffer fools," said Marx. "He wanted perfection, and I always like a good challenge. I was [his] unofficial confidant."

Over their long friendship, Marx often visited the Fontainebleau, observing Ben Novack's unique business methods. "He was a hell of a hotel man," said Marx, "and he ran a tight ship. He lived and breathed it, and he was there twenty-four hours a day . . . that's all he cared about."

The attorney also got to know Ben Jr., who, when he wasn't in school, spent most of his time hanging around with the security officers. "Junior was just a little kid and he was always looking for a friend," said Marx. "He was kind of a loner, and I tried to befriend him because his father, unfortunately, did not spend enough time with him."

As he got to know Ben Jr., Marx realized how destructive his pampered upbringing had been. "Quite frankly . . . anybody growing up under those circumstances has a strange view of the world," he explained, "His privilege was infinite there for him, and yet when he walked out of that place . . . then what? So it was a two-edged sword."

Marx, too, noticed that the Fontainebleau staff catered to the young teenager's every whim, never daring to say no to him. "People would do whatever he said," said Marx. "If they crossed him, he would run to his father and there would be problems. So everybody acknowledged his importance there."

Miami Beach police officer Joe Matthews recalls one occasion when Benji felt that one of the head chefs had not shown him enough respect. "He wasn't a nice kid," said Matthews, "And he went into the kitchen and asked the executive chef, who was in charge of all the restaurants, for some kind of dessert." The chef replied that he was too busy, telling Benji to ask one of his staff to take care of it. Ben Jr. then ordered him to bring the dessert to him personally, and when the middle-aged chef refused, the teenager exploded.

"So Benji fired him on the spot," said Matthews. "Then the guy goes up to Ben Novack Sr. and says, 'What the hell's going on? Your son comes in and he wants the ice cream and he fires me?' And the old man said, 'Well, if he fired you, he fired you. Now get the hell out.' So the old man let everybody know that he was preparing his son to be the ruthless businessman that he was."

A few months later, Benji asked his father to book the eccentric falsetto ukulele singer Tiny Tim for ten shows at La Ronde, at a reported $60,000. "He told his father, 'Oh, you've got to book him,'" said Dixie Evans. "So his father bowed to the kid and said okay."

Tiny Tim, who had just married Miss Vicky in front of forty million viewers on Johnny Carson's *Tonight Show*, bombed at the Fontainebleau, playing to empty houses. And Big George, La Ronde's maître d', was furious there were no tips.

"He came down here with his hair all in his face and pulling out his pockets," Evans remembered of the maître d', "and he says, 'I didn't make any tips tonight. That kid got his way and nobody showed up.'"

In 1970, Ben Novack Sr. bought the Sorrento hotel, just south of the Fontainebleau, to expand his empire. He planned to build a spa and beef up the Fontainebleau's lucrative convention business.

Then disaster struck. His builders were in the midst of attaching a new wing onto the old Sorrento building when the entire building collapsed. Unfortunately, Novack's contractor did not have a proper insurance bond, leaving Novack financially liable for the repairs.

"So he was stuck for all that money," said Lenore Toby, "and he was unable to get financing, after *The Miami Herald* had said he was Mafia connected."

Novack was forced to take $3 million out of the Fontainebleau's cash flow to rebuild the wall and complete his ambitious new project.

A year later, he bought a large tract of land by Miami International Airport to build Fontainebleau Park, which he envisioned as becoming "the world's most majestic country club." He even had a special Fontainebleau Country Club crest designed, which he had sewn onto all his jackets.

"He was copying the Doral," explained Lenore Toby, "because they had a country club, and he didn't want to be left out."

Confident of success, Novack used millions of dollars of his own money for the project, which comprised a new hotel, two golf courses, and hundreds of condominiums and apartments.

"The land was laid out to create a beautiful little city," said Morris Lapidus, "with roads, parks, schools and everything."

Once again, the rumors of Novack's Mafia connections scared off the banks and other would-be investors, who refused to put up the rest of the $25 million required.

In 1972, he refinanced the Fontainebleau, taking out a $6 million mortgage, as well as buying a further 180 acres for his proposed Fontainebleau Park.

"He never got to build that, though," said Toby, "because he could not get the financing."

In June 1970, Ben Novack Jr. was officially put on the Fontainebleau payroll, working security for twenty-five dollars a day. He reported directly to the hotel's chief of security, Ronnie Mitervini. He would later describe his job as "Security—Property Protection and General Assignment."

Six months later, Ben Jr. turned fifteen, and as a birthday present, his father persuaded Miami Beach Police Department chief Rocky Pomerance to allow him to go out on regular patrols with detectives.

"That privilege wasn't granted to the average kid," said now-retired Miami Beach detective Joe Matthews, "but because of his father's influence, everybody allowed it to happen."

In return, Ben Novack Sr. showed his appreciation to the Miami Beach Police Department by lavishing hospitality on favored officers who moonlighted as security at the Fontainebleau.

"Well, there were two kinds of cops back then," explained Matthews. "Those that befriended Benji so they could get a free weekend at the 'Blue. And then there were those that felt sorry for him, because he never had any friends and stuttered to a point where you couldn't hardly communicate with him. You'd feel sorry for him because he would struggle so hard just to say a few words."

Joe Mathews's brother, Pete, now serving with the Miami Beach Police Department, became close with the teenager, taking him out on night patrols in his cruiser. "Benji was our biggest fan," said Pete Matthews. "Always taking an active part. I kind of befriended him, and we just hung out and walked around the hotel."

As he got to know Ben Jr. better, though, Pete Matthews observed how "arrogant and self-centered" he could be. He was also struck by how distant he was from his parents, especially his mother, whom the boy called "Bernice."

"When they were together," Matthews said, "there was no hugging, touching, kissing or anything. I didn't see any affection at all, but that was Benji's nature."

In December 1971, after just three years of marriage, Janie Strong Novack sued Ben Novack Sr. for divorce. She had fallen in love with a highly successful insurance magnate named Tom Cundy, whom she would later marry.

"Janie and Ben were just such a weird, weird relationship," said Richard Marx. "They were fraught."

Lenore Toby said Janie disliked Ben's cavalier behavior. "He was a womanizer," said Toby. "Frankly, I think she just had a little too much class for him. She was a nice lady, and she probably just could not tolerate all that was going on."

Years later, when asked why all three of his marriages had failed, Novack blamed the Fontainebleau. "My marriages didn't work because I gave the hotel too much time," he explained. "I worked seven days and seven nights a week. I was married to the Fontainebleau."

On January 19, 1972, Ben Novack Jr. celebrated his sixteenth birthday, receiving, among other gifts, a burgundy Lincoln Continental from his father's good friend Victor Posner. The reputed mobster, with close ties to Meyer Lansky, handed him the keys to the brand new town car at his birthday party. Other gifts included a gold dollar locket from movie star Ann-Margret and fat checks from Frank Sinatra and other members of the Rat Pack.

"They all bought Benji really nice birthday presents," said his future wife Jill Campion. "He was friends with Sinatra, Ann-Margret, and the Rat Pack. They were like family."

Since he was a small child, Ben Jr. had hung out backstage at La Ronde, forming close relationships with the stars who played there. He was never in the least intimidated by fame.

"He knew them all," said Pete Matthews. "He would be nonchalant, and wasn't in awe of them at all. He treated them like any other hotel guest. Apparently they knew his position and that his father owned the 'Blue.'"

Matthews remembers Ben Jr. hitting it off with up-and-coming comedian Woody Allen. "Nobody could be on the elevator with him," said Matthews of Allen. "He had very little communication, but I remember Benji clicking with him."

Ben Jr. now ran all the sound equipment at the hotel, capitalizing on his audiovisual experience at school. He also worked security for all the conventions held at the Fontainebleau, making contacts with the organizers, who returned year after year. Among the contacts that would prove especially invaluable in the years to come were leaders of the Amway family, who were impressed by the teenager's dedication and professionalism.

"He was everywhere," said Pete Matthews. "He knew everything that was going on and just had a handle on it."

Soon after his birthday, Ben Novack Jr. got his first driver's license and started driving around Miami. If ever he saw a road sign down or anything he considered amiss, he immediately called the Fontainebleau switchboard, asking them to report it to the police. "He would say, 'That sign is down,'" said Dixie Evans, "and [then he'd] give me the name of the street and the cross street, and I'd call it in."

Eleven

AHMED BOOB

S oon after his divorce was finalized, Ben Novack Sr. sailed off to Morocco in his luxury yacht, staying with the movie star Omar Sharif. Legend has it that one night on Sharif's yacht, Novack won the star's young valet, Ahmed Boob, in a game of cards. He then brought the handsome Moroccan, in his twenties, back to Miami to be his personal assistant.

"Ben won him in a card game," confirmed Robert Platshorn, who later became close friends with both of them. "He came to the States as Ben's valet."

Novack immediately put the rail-thin youth to work as his driver and right-hand man. "He was a gofer in reality," said Richard Marx, "and there at Ben's beck and call. He was extremely close to Ben and very loyal. He could be trusted with anything."

The hotelier, who had fought his way up to success, was "amazed" by Boob's streetwise intelligence, thinking him brilliant. Before long, Ahmed Boob had eclipsed his own son Ben Jr., whom Ben Sr. had never really considered as having the right stuff.

Lenore Toby, who later got to know Boob well during her time managing the Fontainebleau, believes he was the son Ben Sr. had always wanted. "Boob lived at the hotel and was a procurer of everything Ben wanted," said Toby. "Anything."

The young Moroccan soon became part of Ben Novack's inner circle, and the two were never apart. "When we would have social occasions," said Marx, "[Boob] would walk next to Ben and remind him of who the person was coming up next. The name of that individual."

Ben Jr. was visibly jealous of his father's new right-hand man, but there was little he could do. "I think Benji was annoyed that Boob took his place," said Toby. "Not that Boob would ever be the heir apparent of the Fontainebleau, but Benji thought he was going to be. It must have been hard for Benji when his father brings this kid from Morocco off the street, and makes him so important."

"Junior was just annoying people," Richard Marx said, "He was a pain in the rear most of the time, as far as the staff at the hotel were concerned. 'Just go away. Go away. Leave me alone.' Very few people paid attention to Junior."

On the other hand, Ahmed Boob, had a charismatic personality that endeared him to everyone. A few months after bringing Boob to the Fontainebleau, Ben Novack Sr. showed his appreciation by renaming the restaurant at the back of the Poodle Lounge Boob's Steak House.

"Boob was the host when he was around," said Platshorn. "The fixer, pimp, and procurer. A great personality. Everyone loved Boob."

In July 1972 a convicted Mafia hit man told a congressional committee in Washington, D.C., that Frank Sinatra was the Mob's front man at the Fontainebleau hotel. The New York *Daily News* carried the story with the headline "Sinatra Dodges House Crime Probe." When Ben Novack Sr. read it, he was furious.

"This is all crap," he screamed at *New York Times* reporter J. Anthony Lukas. "There are no Mafias in here. No Sinatras in here. My accountants can tell you that, my lawyers can tell you that. I built this whole thing with my blood and sweat."

The sixty-five-year-old Miami Beach icon was giving an interview in his office at the Fontainebleau. It was on the eve of the Democratic National Convention coming to town, which he had successfully lobbied for. But he was furious that hundreds of anti-Vietnam War protestors were also expected, and demanded they be run out of town or arrested.

"What right do these punks have to come down here and turn our beautiful city into a cesspool?" he asked. "Those Yippie faggots who believe in free love, free sex, love each other, all that. Let 'em go to work. I don't have time to take this summer off for a vacation."

At that point in the interview the phone rang, and his secretary informed him that the president of Venezuela was on the line.

"Ah, I'm too busy!" he snapped. "You handle it!"

"But Ben, the president of—"

"What does he want? Probably a hotel room for the Democratic convention. We'll do what we can. But tell him he can't have any of my women—not even for a president."

As for women, the aging owner of the Fontainebleau did not have to look any farther than the Poodle Lounge, where his protégé, Ahmed Boob, played host. The Poodle Lounge featured murals of erotic eighteenth-century paintings by the French artist Fragonard, with the faces of poodles superimposed on the women. Every evening the lounge was packed with ladies of the night.

"We would call them food-and-beverage hookers," recalled Lenore Toby. "They would just find someone and make a date with them, so they would take them out for dinner and drinks. And maybe a favor or two later."

The Miami Beach Vice Squad would also be in the Poodle Lounge, but officers always turned a blind eye to the goings-on there.

Ben Novack Jr. was well acquainted with the girls of the Poodle Lounge, having known many of them since he was a child. It is quite possible that he lost his virginity to one of them at a young age.

"I'm certain he had his first intro to the sordid type of life there," said Toby. "Right at the hotel."

. . .

In the summer of 1972, Ben Novack Jr. became close friends with a
Miami Beach police officer named Charlie Seraydar, who had worked
off-duty details at the Fontainebleau. The young cop was a favorite of the
hotel's security chief, Ronnie Mitervini, who regularly called him in.

"Benji was a young lad at the time," said Seraydar, "and we became
very friendly. He wanted to ride in the police car, so I allowed him to
ride with me. He loved the excitement of doing police things."

On late night patrols around Miami Beach, Officer Seraydar got to
know the teenager well, and the two bonded. "Benji was just an obnoxious, nice kid," Seraydar recalled. "Growing up in the environment he did,
he was very much self-centered and a loner. But he had a good heart
and would do anything for anybody."

After leaving the Fontainebleau, Bernice Novack was now living a qui-
eter life. She had settled down with her teenage son by the Coral Ridge
golf course, in an exclusive area of Fort Lauderdale. It was worlds away
from her days as mistress of the Fontainebleau.

"She wanted to live in a house with a picket fence like everybody
had," said Estelle Fernandez. "But Ben Sr. didn't like that lifestyle, and
he had been in charge. Now everything had changed."

Now fifty years old, Bernice was still stunningly beautiful. (She was
still dating musician George Rodriguez, who had his own room in
her new house.) Upon her ex-husband's recommendation, she had had
the first of three facelifts she would undergo over the next few years.
Her old Fontainebleau hairdresser, Emmanuel Buccola, still looked after her striking red hair, and was now a close friend and confidant. But
without the demands of the Fontainebleau's rigorous social life, Bernice
now dressed down, favoring smart shirts and slacks.

Also, she had found herself drawn to the spiritual life, joining the
Science of Mind Church in Fort Lauderdale, and volunteering for
church work. The Science of Mind Church dated back to the Institute

of Religious Science, which was founded by Dr. Ernest Holmes in 1927 in Southern California. Dr. Holmes had developed a philosophy for "positive thinking" using his own tools to find spiritual insight and peace of mind. In the 1960s his teachings were brought to Florida by Ministers Drs. Norman and Dorothy Lunde.

"This church has been established to provide a place where questing people may gather," the church's mission statement read, "to pursue freely the search for Spiritual Truth. It is our conviction that man's capacity to grow and unfold in spiritual consciousness is unlimited."

"Bernice was still living at the Fontainebleau and married when she first met my parents," recalled Dr. Barbara Lunde, who now runs the church. "My parents were invited to go over there all the time. It was *the* big place."

After moving to Fort Lauderdale, Bernice became an active member of the Science of Mind church on N.E. Twenty-Sixth Street, regularly attending weekly services. She also arranged social fund-raisers, such as fashion shows and lunches.

On Saturday, February 24, 1973, she organized the church's annual fashion show luncheon. "Bernice Novack, chairman of this event," read the February edition of the church magazine, "tells us that featured this year will be the beautiful clothes from Frances Brewster Resort Fashions on North Ocean Boulevard."

One of her assistants for the event was Jeanne Cummings, a Fort Lauderdale real estate agent who had found Bernice her new house. Cummings still fondly remembers Ben Jr., who was with his mother when Cummings drove her around. He'd show off by running to the garage of every prospective home they looked at and tripping the lock.

TWELVE

OFFICER BENJI NOVACK

I n January 1973, Ben Novack Jr. turned seventeen and officially joined the Fort Lauderdale Police Department Youth Auxiliary. Six months later, he graduated from Pine Crest School with school service awards in audio/visual, technical, and journalism. He then enrolled at the University of Miami, for a major in mass communications and a minor in marketing. But his main interest in life was law enforcement.

On February 8, 1974, a few weeks after his eighteenth birthday, he applied to join the Miami Beach Police Department as an auxiliary police officer. He listed his special qualifications as having a good knowledge of radio and television equipment and being a member of his college Honor Society.

He had now moved out of his mother's house and was living in an apartment in the Fontainebleau.

In September 1974 he was accepted to the Southeast Florida Institute of Criminal Justice, to train to be an auxiliary officer. Over the next three months, he underwent the exact same 160 hours of intensive training as the regular cadets, and studied various aspects of law enforcement, including the legal system, prosecution, defense, and sentencing.

On December 17, Ben Novack Jr. officially graduated from the academy, becoming a bona fide member of the Miami Beach Police Department. At a special ceremony he received a certificate showing that he had successfully completed the necessary training to join the department.

"So Benji went to the police academy and got certified," said Officer Pete Matthews. "He was an auxiliary or reserve officer. They had uniforms. They had guns. They had everything, including arrest powers."

As an auxiliary officer, Ben Novack Jr. was expected to serve two ten-hour shifts a month, riding details with fully qualified Miami Beach police officers. Pete Matthews now became his regular patrol partner.

"Very few people wanted to team up with Benji," Matthews explained, "because he was just high maintenance. But I liked the kid and he was always obliging."

Officer Matthews often took the new reserve out on his midnight shifts, but soon realized that the hyperactive teenager's unbridled enthusiasm could present problems. "He would get pumped up and excited," said Matthews, "and kind of shoot from the hip. I remember one time I said, 'Benji, you're going to have to tame it down.'"

The enthusiastic young reserve now proudly wore a Miami Beach Police Department uniform and carried a concealed gun in a shoulder holster. He wasn't above breaking the law himself, though. He loved driving fast, and a year earlier his new red Thunderbird had hit an ambulance in Miami. He was later charged with careless driving, but ultimately found not guilty.

"Ambulance ran red light w/out using caution," he wrote in a report. "I was charged but found not guilty."

Pete Matthews was now anxious whenever the young reserve got behind the wheel of his black-and-white squad car. "Now I'm not over-reactionary," Matthews explained. "I don't get excited. I just kind of slow the pace down, but Benji was the opposite. He would drive too fast on these calls and I would say, 'Oh my God! Put the safety belt on.'"

Early one morning, the two officers were heading out of Miami Beach, responding to a fatal accident on the MacArthur Causeway, when the reserve hit the accelerator hard.

"I said, 'Benji, slow down for God's sake, we're doing one hundred miles an hour,'" recalled Matthews. "And then he put the siren and blue lights on. I mean it was four A.M. and there was nobody there and Benji's driving like an idiot."

Suddenly, as they approached the accident site, Novack slammed on the brakes, sending his partner, who wasn't wearing a seat belt, straight into the dashboard. Then he accidentally put the squad car into reverse instead of park, and after they both jumped out, "the patrol car started going backward," said Matthews. "And I said, 'Benji, look at the car!' I wouldn't run after it. I didn't give a shit, but Benji chased after the car and jumped in, slamming it into park. But that was Benji."

In September 1974, Lenore Toby was hired to manage the Fontaine-bleau. Born in Boston, the ambitious career woman had been running the rival Eden Roc (for the last six years) when it had temporarily closed. A vice president at the Fontainebleau had then hired her.

When Ben Novack Sr. found out, he was livid. "What are you crazy, bringing a woman in?" he screamed. Nevertheless, Novack finally re-lented, appointing Toby manager of his 1,250-room, five-star hotel.

"He was a genius," Toby recalled, "but he would call everyone a rep-robate. His favorite expression was 'He's nothing but a reprobate.'"

Toby says her new boss was the most amazing person she had ever met, with a unique style of his own. "Ben Novack was interested in fash-ion," she said. "He used to wear these pink cashmere jackets with plaid pants. He always had his hair puffed up and combed."

Each morning, his beloved elder sister Lillian Brezner arrived at the hotel to spend the day, although no one was quite sure exactly what she did. "She was dowdy, horrible," said Toby. "I never knew where she lived or where she came from."

One morning soon after Toby arrived, Ben Novack Jr. stormed into her office ordering her never to call him Benji again, as he hated it. So she asked what he wanted to be called.

"Ben," he told her emphatically. "Not Ben Junior. Just Ben."

Although he was still studying at the University of Miami, his fa-ther had promoted him to a Fontainebleau vice president, with a

$15,000-a-year salary, a company car, and an apartment. He even had his own personal assistant, who worked in sales.

Now six foot, three inches tall, Ben Jr. had grown a full beard, to appear older and be taken more seriously.

"He was very immature for his years," said Toby. "He was all over the place, but he really envisioned himself as the chief of security."

Benji now patrolled the hotel corridors with a huge chain of keys and a chattering police radio hanging around his neck. "It was a joke," Toby said. "He was still playing policeman. You'd think at his age he would have moved on to something else. Everybody laughed at him, they really did. He was an annoyance to people who would just tolerate him, because you never knew how daddy was going to react."

Toby also sensed that the teenager craved his father's approval, but never got it. "Benji was belligerent, because he was trying to make his place in the world," she said. "I don't think his father respected him or thought he'd be anything but a playboy. I don't know what went on behind their closed doors, but he was not a happy kid."

In December 1974 the Fontainebleau celebrated its twentieth anniversary. Miami Beach had undergone a seismic change since the hotel opened, with tourism plunging by half over the last ten years, as Las Vegas surpassed it.

Three years earlier, Ben Novack had welcomed the opening of Disney World in Orlando, forecasting that it would draw millions of new visitors to Florida, ultimately benefitting Miami Beach. But he had been proved wrong, when it in fact began syphoning business *away* from the Fontainebleau and the other hotels.

Other negative factors were cheap air travel, and package vacations to the Caribbean islands. The growing cruise industry had also cut into profits, as the luxury floating palaces offered gambling.

By the mid-1970s the Fontainebleau was surviving on convention business alone. It had been an uphill struggle for Ben Novack Sr. since the Sorrento wall had collapsed.

"Social business had declined terribly," explained Toby. "The main account in those years was IBM. They had several meetings back to back during the height of the season, and that kept the hotel afloat for the rest of the year."

Ben Novack was now mortgaged up to the hilt, owing millions to the banks and other lenders. After he paid his huge monthly bills, there was not enough cash to maintain the Fontainebleau, and it was becoming badly run-down. Its French Provincial furniture now looked outdated, and there was no money to replace it with something more contemporary.

Years later, Ben Jr. described the condition of the Fontainebleau hotel rooms as deplorable. "TV sets needed to be replaced," he said. "Wallpaper, furniture, fixtures and equipment needed to be modernized."

In February 1975, the *Miami News* reported that Ben Novack Sr. was being investigated by the Internal Revenue Service for possible tax evasion. The story, later picked up on the wire services, claimed that the IRS had compiled a detailed dossier of Novack's sex habits, drinking, spending, and other social activities.

THIRTEEN

THE BLACK TUNA

GANG

In late 1976, Ben Novack Sr.'s protégé, Ahmed Boob, threw a party on the *Calypso* houseboat, moored across from the Fontaine-bleau. Among the guests were two New Yorkers, Robert Plats-horn and Robert Meinster, who had just started smuggling millions of dollars worth of marijuana from Colombia to Miami.

"That's where we originally hooked up with Boob," Platshorn recalled. "And that party cemented our relationship. Right about that time we brought in our first load, maybe fourteen hundred pounds or something."

Over the next few months, the two smugglers became close friends with Boob. He began catering their parties for prospective buyers through Boob's Steak House, as well as providing girls from the Poodle Lounge as the entertainment.

Boob arranged for Platshorn and Meinster to move into the Fontaine-bleau's $1,000-a-night Governor's Suite, where Ben Novack Sr. and his family had once lived. He even pulled strings for Platshorn to take over the barbershop concession in the basement lobby, and the hotel's yacht charter business.

"Thanks to the owner's valet, Ahmed Boob, we based our smuggling and distribution operations [at the Fontainebleau]," Platshorn wrote in his 2010 autobiography, *The Black Tuna Diaries*. "With its miles of underground parking and service corridors, we could move around and reappear in any part of the hotel, without using public elevators or hallways. Because we owned and operated the barbershop and yacht club at the hotel, our presence there was unremarkable."

In his book, Platshorn vividly described checking into the Fontainebleau's Governor's Suite. "Ahmed Boob was waiting in the lobby," he wrote. "A short bone thin, hawk nosed, dark complected Moroccan. Boob was a combination, meeter, greeter, host, dealer, concierge and pimp. Most times Boob was either coked up or luded out.

"Only occasionally, he could be found at his restaurant, 'Boob's Steak House,' located in the hotel lobby. After his usual greeting of a big hug and a couple of very sloppy wet Moroccan man-kisses, he informed me that Robbie and Gene [Myers] were up in Penthouse A, and that he was sending me up a steak and a Caesar's Salad from Boob's."

Boob then led Platshorn through the kitchen, and into the service elevator up to the seventeenth floor, so Platshorn couldn't be followed.

Platshorn maintains that neither Ahmed Boob nor Ben Novack Sr. knew of his massive smuggling operation, and played no part in it. But hotel manager Lenore Toby says that nothing happened at the Fontainebleau without Ben Novack's knowing about it, so he must have received a cut.

"Absolutely," she said. "He was part of that. He had to have been. He was so close to Boob, I don't know how he wouldn't have known his actions. I knew that Boob was involved in drugs. He was high all the time. He was living on that boat more than in the hotel, and had parties all the time."

Over the next few months, Platshorn and Meinster ran their massive drug-smuggling operation from the luxurious seventeenth-floor oceanfront penthouse. They would later become infamous as the leaders of the "Black Tuna Gang."

Fifteen years later, a U.S. Tax Court report listed the gang's involvement with the Fontainebleau hotel during 1977 and 1978:

"The purposes of the Hotel suites," the official report read, "were to provide a place for payments of money, to host elaborate parties for petitioners and their friends at which drugs were freely available. And to create the aura of wealth and importance. Further, the Hotel was the most prestigious in Miami Beach, and [they] hoped that this factor would help to establish their credibility in the drug trade."

The U.S. Tax Court report mentioned Ahmed Boob by name, claiming he personally arranged for discounts on the expensive penthouse suite, which was always paid for in cash.

"Platshorn and Meinster," the report stated, "received a special discount rate on accommodations as a result of the influence of Ahmed Boob, owner of Boob's Steak House and a close associate of the owner of the hotel, Ben Novak [sic]."

Over that period, Lenore Toby noticed how Boob was taking keys and using them to let friends into rooms while the guests were not there. On numerous occasions she would check a guest into the hotel only to have him come back to Reception complaining the room had been used.

"And I had said, 'Boob, listen,'" she recalled. "'You have to stop doing this. You can have all the rooms you want, but please let me know in advance so I can put them out of order.'"

Now in his early thirties, the Moroccan liked using a bedroom right next to the suite Ben Novack Sr. was presently living in. One night, Toby gave the suite to an important lady travel agent and sent up a basket of fruit.

"There was a small gun lying next to the basket of fruit," Lenore said, "so she thought it was a gift, as those toy cigarette lighters were popular then. Then she pulled the trigger, shooting a bullet through the wall of the room."

After their first huge Colombian drug run, the Black Tuna Gang celebrated with a wild party on one of the Fontainebleau houseboats. The party, fully catered by Ahmed Boob, included the gang's rich drug buyers from New York and Philadelphia and other associates.

Platshorn later described the highlight of the party as "some ladies Boob had dragged out of his bar at the hotel."

. . .

It is impossible to know if the Fontainebleau hotel's vice president of security, Ben Novack Jr., was aware that multimillion-dollar drug deals were going down in the same penthouse suite he had grown up in. He was always extremely loyal to his father, and would never have wanted to cause a scandal to blacken the Fontainebleau's name.

Although Ben Novack Jr. never had a steady girlfriend, he regularly visited the strip clubs around the Miami Beach area, for rowdy nights out with his cop buddies.

"This was my zone," said Officer Pete Matthews, who worked Vice. "So I knew all the clubs and club owners. And I would prearrange everything."

There were always available women for the handsome bearded heir to the Fontainebleau fortune, and like his father, Ben Jr. was attracted to tall, beautiful, busty women.

A natural flirt, he dated a string of showgirls whom he met at the Fontainebleau and local strip clubs. And he always sent his favorites to cosmetic surgeon Dr. Larry Robbins. "He had a lot of girlfriends," said Dr. Robbins, "and yes, he brought them all to me."

Ben Jr. particularly enjoyed watching the world-famous plastic surgeon perform breast augmentation operations on his dates. And Dr. Robbins was only too happy to oblige him. "I used to let Ben come in and watch the surgery," he remembered. "I would always give my advice, and he always said, 'I want to pick the size.' So I said, 'Okay, Ben, whatever makes you happy.'"

On June 7, 1976, it was revealed that the Fontainebleau hotel owed $1.3 million in back taxes, and faced being sold at a public auction. A few days earlier, Ben Novack Sr. had told the Miami Beach City Council that despite a "fairly good" tourist season, "We don't have the money to pay the taxes." He said he was now making arrangements "so we can pay our taxes very soon, I hope."

The iconic hotel was said to be two years in tax arrears, and had until November 1 to settle its debt, or county officials would seize the hotel and sell it to the highest bidder.

In early 1976, twenty-year-old Ben Novack Jr. had fallen in love with an attractive air stewardess, after meeting her on a flight. Within a couple of weeks they were engaged.

"They were pretty serious," recalled Pete Matthews. "I met her a couple of times, and she was a very stunning woman."

Nevertheless, in the fall of 1976, Matthews played Cupid, setting Ben Jr. up on a blind date with the daughter of a neighbor.

Jill Campion was a shapely six-foot-tall, twenty-nine-year-old Las Vegas showgirl taking a break from dancing to decide on her next move. Matthews told Benji he had to meet her, so they concocted a ruse for her to come to the Fontainebleau.

"He set us up on a date," said Jill, "and I thought it was a job interview."

After the interview, Jill nervously asked Ben Jr. if she'd gotten the job. "Ben says to me," she remembered, "'Well, I'm sorry that I can't hire you for anything at this hotel.' And I said, 'Why?' And he goes, 'because we have a policy that you can't date anyone that works in the hotel, and I intend on dating you.'"

Then, after admitting that the interview had been a setup, Ben Jr. took her to Boob's Steak House for a champagne dinner.

"And that was the beginning," she said. "He swept me off my feet."

A few days later, Ben Jr. took Jill for dinner at the exclusive Celebrity Club at the Diplomat Hotel. As they walked into the restaurant, Jill was shocked by his rudeness to the maître d'. "I said, 'Who the hell do you think you are?' And he looked at me like nobody had ever talked to him like that before. And that began our little challenge."

Ben Jr. loved the way Jill stood up to him, always calling him out for his rudeness.

"He ordered people around," she explained, "and talked to them as if they were servants. Like he owned them and they didn't matter. It was degrading."

During their first few dates, Ben Jr. was charming and flirtatious, rarely opening up about himself. He stuttered badly when he started speaking, but once he got into the flow of a conversation, he improved.

He claimed to run the Fontainebleau, adding ten years to his age to make himself seem more worldly. He also showed her the gun he always carried, explaining that he had done so ever since a threat to kidnap him as a child.

One night over dinner, Ben Novack Jr. suddenly announced that all his girlfriends must have boob jobs, which he would be happy to pay for. Without missing a beat, Jill replied that, being a dancer, she had already had hers done.

Soon after they met, Ben Jr. broke off his engagement to the steward- ess, amid bitter allegations from both sides. "It was ugly," said attorney Richard Marx. "There were overtones of maybe blackmail involved."

On Friday, November 5, the Connecticut General Life Insurance Company, one of Ben Novack Sr.'s biggest creditors, filed to place the Fontainebleau in foreclosure on the hotel's first mortgage. Novack frantically hit the phones, managing to come up with $250,000 to save his hotel.

That month, as Novack battled for survival, he stopped paying his employees' health insurance, and was often late with paychecks. To save costs, he ordered his bar staff to pour cheap champagne into Dom Perignon bottles, and then charge customers for the good stuff.

With the Fontainebleau in serious financial trouble, Ben Novack Sr. started receiving numerous offers of backing to keep him afloat. "It was as if he had two great eagles on his shoulders," said Toby, "saying, 'All the con men of the world, here I am.'"

He began courting possible backers, taking them for expensive din- ners and giving them free rooms at the hotel. But each month, as the mortgage checks went out, the noose on the Fontainebleau tightened.

At one point Frank Sinatra stepped in, offering to buy the Fontaine-bleau. And when Ben Novack refused to sell, the two had a knockdown fistfight.

"They beat the living hell out of each other," recalled Robert Plats-horn. "It resulted in black eyes, bruises and cuts. Ben was a bear in those days and Sinatra would fight at the drop of a hat."

The fight became common knowledge around the hotel, and Ben Jr. was upset that his father had turned down Sinatra's generous offer.

"I remember the fistfight," said Jill Campion. "Benji told me that Sinatra wanted to buy the hotel and his father had refused. This was when they were starting to have problems. [Others] also offered to buy it, but he wouldn't let it go. He just couldn't sell it."

After the fight, Ben Novack Sr. threw Frank Sinatra out of his suite, and the superstar never again played the Fontainebleau.

That Christmas, ten thousand members of the Hotel Employees Union Local 355 went on strike, demanding higher wages and better working conditions. The Fontainebleau and six other Miami Beach hotels were picketed by maids, waiters, bellhops, and bartenders.

At around 7:00 A.M. on December 27, with temperatures in the for-ties, a combative Ben Novack Sr. stormed out of his hotel to confront the one hundred striking picketers lined up outside the front entrance.

"That's the thanks I get for giving them jobs," Novack raged to *Miami News* reporter Bill Gjebre.

Novack vowed that he would never allow the strikers, mostly Cuban immigrants, to disrupt his hotel service, threatening to sack them and hire new ones. He told the reporter he was already using his executive staff to make beds and wait tables.

"There are a lot of jobs here for people," he said. "We'll function."

FOURTEEN

DECLINE AND FALL

Ben Novack Jr. fell hard for his new girlfriend, Jill Campion. Most evenings he took her out on the town, to expensive restaurants and nightclubs.

"The thing Ben and I had in common was a love of the night life," said Campion. "Me being a showgirl dancer was fitting for his lifestyle. We were always getting dressed up and going someplace to be seen and have fun and, on his part, do some business. It was all about packing in as much as we could."

Ben Novack Jr. was also very generous.

"He bought me jewelry and clothes," said Jill, "but he was very exacting on how he wanted me to dress and wear my hair."

Although Ben Jr. always looked slightly unkempt, with his full beard and thick bushy hair, open-neck shirts, and leather jackets, he insisted Jill dress like a sexy fashion model. "He wanted me to be as skinny as possible," she recalled. "So I used to take diet pills and exercise."

In one photograph of the couple, taken backstage with Frank Sinatra after a show, Jill towers over the singer, wearing a sexy top and wraparound shawl.

"I look at the picture today, with me and Sinatra, and I'm embarrassed," she said. "I'm half-dressed. That's how [Benji] wanted me to be."

Before long, he introduced Jill to his parents.

"[They] called him Benji," she remembered. "He always tried to get away from it as an adult."

Jill immediately noticed that he was far closer to his mother than his father. Most weekends, he would drive Jill to Fort Lauderdale for dinner with Bernice and George Rodriguez.

Although Ben Jr.'s mother was always friendly to her face, Jill always felt she strongly disapproved of the relationship. "His mother ran that show," she explained. "She was very charming and lovely, but I know she wasn't happy with him being with me."

Jill felt far more comfortable with Ben Sr., who at seventy years old still exuded charm and flirtatiousness. "There was just something about him," Jill said. "He was very charismatic and so charming he could make you melt. His eyes were just dreamy."

She sensed that Ben Sr. was not particularly close to his son. "He would send messages to Benji through me," she said, "If he wanted him [to do something], tell Benji this and tell Benji that. So I don't think they talked a lot."

She also met Ben Sr.'s right-hand man, Ahmed Boob, one night at his steak house. "He was quiet," she remembered. "He was just there, and you almost wouldn't notice him. So he didn't draw any attention to himself, and I think probably with good reason."

A few weeks after they met, Jill Campion moved into Ben Jr.'s modest two-bedroom apartment at Fontainebleau Park, in southwest Miami. Soon afterward, he took her to Victor Posner's house for dinner.

"You walk in and there was this palatial pool," she said, and "we were served by a bodyguard with a gun on his shoulder."

Campion introduced her new boyfriend to her circle of friends, who found him rude and socially inept. He would criticize the way they dressed or wore their hair, suggesting how they could improve themselves. In spite of this, Jill's best friend Dovie Ann Hart became close with him. "Ben could be critical of me," Dovie said, "but he was constructively critical. I think he treated me somewhat like a sister. Ben could be very direct with his poignant remarks . . . and not everyone would have been comfortable."

One night Jill brought Dovie along to a cocktail party at a mansion in Bal Harbour. Ben Novack Sr. was also there, and immediately invited Dovie to have dinner with him. During the meal, the elderly roué told the attractive young woman that if she became his girlfriend, she would be well taken care of.

"He said he wanted to date her," said Jill, "and told her he would treat her very well. Dovie refused ever so respectfully. She said he had become a bit crusty by then, so [they stayed] friends."

After a night out on the town, Ben Jr. and Jill often checked into a room at the Fontainebleau. Over the first few months of their relationship, they spent much time at the hotel, and she observed him working hotel security.

"He was in and out with his beeper," she said, "because he ran the hotel and was always getting beeped."

One night while they were staying there, Campion discovered that Ben Jr. was cheating on her with the stewardess he'd been engaged to when they met. "He probably hadn't even broken up with her," said Campion. "One weekend, he had her and me in different rooms at the Fontainebleau. He kept running out, saying he was 'working the hotel.'"

In January 1977 the Fontainebleau went into state court receivership, owing a staggering $27 million ($101 million in today's money) in back taxes. On January 31 the hotel took center stage again when millions of TV viewers watched aerialist Karl Wallenda walk a tightrope between it and the Eden Roc hotel, as part of an Evel Knievel stunt special. But despite the hotel's grand reputation and continued exposure, Ben Novack Sr. was forced to file for voluntary Chapter 11 bankruptcy little more than two months later, on April 6. The *Miami News* reported the story the following day, saying that it would be business as usual at the Fontainebleau, which Ben Novack Sr. would still run.

"We were at death's door," explained Lenore Toby. "The hotel went about its business every day, but there was no pay."

Although creditors were now circling like vultures, Fontainebleau manager Toby ran it on a shoestring. "I could be an expert in running a hotel without any money," she said. "We couldn't afford to do the laundry, so we would change the bottom sheets into top sheets."

That summer, Ben Novack Sr. desperately tried to raise funds to satisfy his hungry creditors. He also quietly began moving his money and assets to hidden offshore accounts, funneling large sums into his sister Lillian Brezner's name.

"When he was losing the hotel," said Jill Campion, "I'd go to dinner with [Ben Sr.] and he'd say, 'Listen, tell Benji to be nice to his aunt Lillian. Because that's where my money is.'"

Ben Novack Jr. was obsessed with the then-top-rated TV cop show *Hawaii Five-0*. He modeled himself after the show's star, Jack Lord, complete with his bouffant hairstyle, and used Lord's character's catchphrase, "Book 'em, Danno," at every opportunity.

Every morning, he would struggle in front of the mirror, trying to straighten his curly brown hair with a blow dryer to look like his hero. Jill, who was working as a stylist in a top Miami Beach salon, now cut his unruly hair.

One afternoon in the summer of 1977, she returned to their apartment to find an engagement ring in a box on her dressing table. It was the exact same $2,000 gold ring with a single diamond that he had given his stewardess fiancée and then taken back after they split.

"That's how he proposed," Jill said. "That was it. He didn't say a word. I'm like, 'Okay.'"

By the late seventies, the Fontainebleau could no longer afford the A-list stars who once headlined there. Frank Sinatra now played other venues in Miami Beach, and Las Vegas had long taken over as America's leading entertainment resort.

Soon after they met, Ben Jr. took Jill Campion to see the C-list singer Pia Zadora, whose career was being bankrolled by her rich husband,

Meshulam Riklis, who was more than twice her age. It was a vanity gig: the Israeli millionaire had rented La Ronde so Pia could have her own show.

"We just couldn't afford to compete with Las Vegas," Lenore Toby explained. "We couldn't even afford to buy new linens for the hotel."

FIFTEEN

PARADISE LOST

A t the end of September 1977, circuit court judge Dan Satin ordered Ben Novack Sr. to pay $3.2 million to creditors or have the Fontainebleau Hotel sold at auction. The judge ruled that Novack owed the money to the land-developing firm of Roland Security and must forfeit the hotel to satisfy the loan if he could not come up with the money.

At a hearing, Judge Satin explained that he could not allow the Fontainebleau's iconic importance to Miami Beach to influence his decision. "It just has to be considered," he said, "as another piece of property. The court will offer it to the highest bidder."

Ben Novack Sr. immediately announced that he would be appealing the decision at the state level.

The Roland International Corporation and especially real estate tycoon Stephen Muss, who had a big stake in it, were determined to get the Fontainebleau at all costs. Under foreclosure rules, anyone could bid for the hotel, but Roland had a huge advantage, as Novack owed it so much money.

Over the next few months, Novack did everything possible to raise the necessary cash to postpone the bankruptcy court order until his appeal to the state supreme court could be heard.

Attorney Richard Marx watched his friend and client desperately fight to save his beloved hotel. "Eventually the cash ran out," said Marx, "and [Ben] fought like a tiger to maintain it. He tried everything possible. Went to as many people as he knew to raise funds and kept running into a brick wall."

One evening, Novack, who was now officially bankrupt, summoned Lenore Toby to his private office on the mezzanine, atop his Stairway to Nowhere. When she got upstairs, she was surprised to find his door closed, as it was usually open. His private secretary told her to go right in, as she was expected.

Lenore slowly opened the door and cautiously entered, discovering her boss sitting at his huge antique conference table, which was covered with stacks of hundred-dollar bills from money that he had secretly squirreled away over the years

"Sit down," he ordered, "and start counting piles of nine thousand, nine hundred dollars each."

The hotel manager started counting, while Novack made various phone calls to raise more money.

"After I did about six piles," said Toby, "I said, 'Mr. Novack, I just want to know why you are having me do this?'"

Novack explained that he did not have to legally report sums under $10,000 to the IRS. He told her that he was using only his most trusted employees to help him out. Then he asked her to take a pile of $9,900 to the bank and bring him back a cashier's check.

"That was the only way he could get cash," Lenore said. "He had no money and was stealing from himself now. He did that with other people that he trusted around him. Can you believe that. He was amazing. He also had some private deals none of us knew about."

During those desperate times, Ben Novack Sr. became close to Robert Platshorn, who was still using the Fontainebleau's Governor's Suite to run his multimillion-dollar marijuana smuggling operation. According to Platshorn, Novack now enlisted his help to raise money to save the hotel.

"At one time," said Platshorn, "we had scraped up a suitcase full of cash from various sources. That was only supposed to be for emergency backup, in case he came short when it came time to pay off the bankruptcy."

It was supposed to be a secret, so as not to attract undue attention. Unfortunately, the ever-vigilant Ben Novack Jr. asked some Miami Beach Police Department officers to protect the suitcase.

"Benji drafted a whole squad of cops to guard it," said Platshorn, "and that was the last thing on earth that one wanted. It just killed the whole deal. I mean nobody knows what's in the suitcase, until you make a big deal of it."

Finally, Ben Novack Sr. was outmaneuvered by Stephen Muss and his Roland International partners, who bought the Fontainebleau Hotel for $27 million.

Right up to the eleventh hour, Novack believed he had saved the hotel after a Canadian investor came forward with the money needed to bail him out. The day of the hearing, the investor suddenly changed his mind, and the judge ordered the sale to go ahead if Novack couldn't come up with the money by the beginning of January.

"The Fontainebleau was literally sold on the courtroom steps," said Toby. "It was so sad."

That Christmas, as Ben Novack Sr.'s January deadline loomed, Robert Platshorn hosted a lavish Christmas at his new home a few blocks away from the Fontainebleau.

"Available for consumption at this party," noted the U.S. tax inspectors in an official report, "were Thai sticks, a very potent type of marijuana cigarette, along with cocaine, which was freely available to the guests."

On New Year's Eve, the Black Tuna Gang leader and his partner, Robert Meinster, threw another wild party.

"Large quantities of liquor and expensive food such as stone crab were provided," noted the U.S. tax inspector. "Cocaine was freely available in open saucers throughout the house."

. . .

On January 4, 1978, Ben Novack Sr. failed to post a $10 million cash bond, missing yet another deadline. Now, unless his attorneys could come up with a new legal loophole by January 9, the sale to Stephen Muss and his partners would become final.

Ben Novack Sr. had reached the end of the line. He was a beaten man, and he knew it.

"Those final days were all heartbreaking and sad," said Lenore Toby, "so we said, 'Well, what can we do?'"

All the top hotel executives then pitched in, buying Novack a platinum pocket watch and having it engraved, "Ben Novack. Mr. Fontainebleau Always."

"And then nobody wanted to give it to him," Lenore recalled. "They were so horrified. It was the night before they were throwing him out of that hotel. So I was designated to be the one to bring the watch to him."

When Toby went up to Novack's suite, her boss came to the door in a bathrobe, a large Scotch in his hand. He had obviously been drinking heavily.

"He was a mess," she recalled. "His hair was flying all over the place and he was wheezing. It was *the* most pathetic sight I have ever seen."

When she told him she had a gift from the staff, he told her to sit down, saying he had to make an important phone call.

"He was trying make a deal to save the Fontainebleau," she said, "It was so sad. It was really terrible."

She winced, hearing him say that if the money could be there by seven the next morning, they would have a meeting to save the Fontainebleau.

"He had to leave the next morning, mind you," she said, "and still trying to the last minute to make a deal, hoping against hope that he could save his hotel."

Early the next morning, all the staff of the Fontainebleau assembled in the lobby to say their good-byes to Ben Novack Sr. Without saying a word, he slowly filed past them in the lobby, shaking hands and visibly close to tears.

Then he walked out the Fontainebleau's front door for the last time and was driven away. He would never return.

Some months later, *The Miami Herald* dubbed Stephen Muss, the new owner of the Fontainebleau, "The Most Powerful Man in Miami Beach."

The land developer told a reporter that he had bought the hotel "out of civic duty," calling it a barometer of Miami Beach's success.

"He didn't know enough about the hotel business," said Lenore Toby. "And he didn't trust anyone that was running the hotel, so he decided to bring in a national chain to operate it for him."

So, after announcing a $40 million renovation, Muss hired the Hilton Hotel Corporation to operate the Fontainebleau. And finally, after nearly a quarter of a century of the hotel's never having any sign outside, the new owner erected a huge forty-four-foot sign reading, "FONTAINEBLEAU HILTON."

"When Hilton put their name up, it should have been in the bathroom," Ben Novack Sr. fumed. "That's how much work they did there."

Sixteen

STRIKING OUT

B en Novack Jr. could only watch helplessly as the Fontainebleau slipped through his father's fingers. Growing up as the
Prince of the Fontainebleau, he had always expected to inherit the kingdom one day.

"This was his whole identity," said Richard Marx. "He was devastated."

So the young man decided to strike out on his own. He asked the
high-level contacts he knew at Amway International for a job, utilizing
what he had learned at the Fontainebleau to organize the organization's
conventions. Amway agreed, putting him on a $45,000-a-year salary.

"He was Ben Novack's son," said Lenore Toby. "They were thrilled
to have him. He had actually made a friendship with the owners of
Amway, and they were impressed with him. So they took him under
their wing and he became their Johnny-on-the-spot."

The hugely successful Michigan-based direct-selling company specialized in health, beauty, and home care products. Its morale-boosting
conventions for the worldwide sales force were crucial to its success.

"They were paying him to run their conventions," said Ben Jr.'s fiancée,
Jill Campion. "He was just employed by Amway."

Ben Jr.'s conventions were highly successful, and he was well respected. He now regularly entertained the Amway board of directors, taking them out on the town.

"There were twelve board members," said Campion, "and we always went out to dinner with them and their wives after the shows."

After leaving the Fontainebleau, Ben Novack Sr. moved in with his sister Lillian Brezner in Bal Harbour, Florida, until he could find a place of his own. He fell into a deep depression and seemed rudderless, trying to come to terms with his great loss.

"He was vegetating," said Robert Platshorn. "My wife and I would have him over to the house for dinner, maybe every week or two, just so he'd have some company." At their meals, Novack would drink heavily, and the old spark would return. "And he'd regale us with stories of the good old days of the Fontainebleau," said Platshorn.

During their protracted engagement, Jill Campion discovered that her fiancée was a compulsive liar and lived in a fantasy world. He was also constantly unfaithful to her. "Benji was definitely a liar," she said. "He would just lie to everybody to get what he was after."

He would often call Amway's head office in Ada, Michigan, pretending to be traveling all over America on convention business when he was actually home in Miami Beach. He'd also go to the airport with an empty suitcase to meet Amway clients for business meetings, claiming to be in transit between flights.

"He thought he was James Bond," said Jill. "He'd say, 'Patch me into so-and-so.' He was always trying to appear more successful than he was."

Meanwhile, in Fort Lauderdale, Bernice Novack was getting on with her life. She, too, had been saddened when Ben Sr. lost the Fontainebleau, but what hurt even more was when he had then sued to have his alimony terminated, claiming he could no longer afford it.

"She kept taking him to court for her money," said Jill Campion.

Ben Jr. appeared to rely on his mother to bankroll his extravagant lifestyle, as his fledgling convention business was still not earning him enough to cover his expensive tastes. "His mother held the purse strings," said Campion, "because he was still on salary from Amway and did not make that much money."

Bernice was now on the board of the Science of Mind Church as treasurer, and becoming more active. A photograph in the church's *Creative Life* magazine showed Bernice, now fifty-six, posing with the seven other board members. The former model was still very glamorous, with her signature bright red hair and fashionable attire.

"She was so gorgeous," recalled Dr. Barbara Lunde, whose parents ran the church. "She was our treasurer for a long time."

The former First Lady of the Fontainebleau now devoted herself to organizing the church bazaars, with the same enthusiasm she had once brought to the hotel. "She loved going through the old clothes, furniture, and stuff coming in," said Dr. Lunde, "and setting it all up and pricing it."

Bernice and George Rodriguez were now a devoted couple, but Bernice told friends they had no plans to marry, as she didn't want to lose her alimony.

Although Ben Novack Jr. was still a dedicated Miami Beach Police Department Reserve officer, he also indulged in cocaine. On one occasion he flew to New York City for the opening of his cousin's new fashionable roller rink and bar. The following day, Jill Campion flew in to join him, and he collected her from the airport in a limousine.

"It was really late at night," she remembered, "and the streets were dark."

Under Novack's instructions, the limo drove deep into Spanish Harlem, pulling up outside a dilapidated old house.

"We got out of the limousine and knocked on the door," Jill

remembered, "and they opened a little peephole and let us in. There was this huge party. [Then] there were a couple of very young girls all over him."

Ben Jr. later admitted taking the girls out the previous night, and giving them cocaine. He had come back tonight because he had run out and wanted more.

"I was shocked to see him with cocaine," said Campion. "I think he did that so he could be the big man, because that's what people wanted. But I'd never seen him do that before."

On May 1, 1979, Robert Platshorn and Robert Meinster were indicted, along with the other members of the Black Tuna Gang. They were charged with smuggling five hundred tons of marijuana into the United States over a sixteen-month period. It marked the first ever joint operation by the Drug Enforcement Agency (DEA) and the FBI. Ahmed Boob was never charged with being any part of the illegal operation.

After handing down the indictments, federal law enforcement then targeted Ben Novack Sr., suspecting him of having used the Fontainebleau to launder some of the gang's millions.

"He certainly didn't, and took great exception to it," said Platshorn in 2011. "There was an incident where he was about to punch out an agent in the DEA office . . . for impugning his integrity."

Platshorn was eventually sentenced to sixty-four years' imprisonment for smuggling marijuana. He was finally freed from federal prison in 2008, after serving almost thirty years. He still remains evasive about whether Ben Novack Sr. was aware of the smuggling operation.

"They tried to force him to testify against us," said Platshorn. "He never saw what we were doing. Whether he knew or not is a different story."

In early June, Ben Novack Jr.'s best man, Pete Matthews, threw him a bachelor party, and several of their friends from the Miami Beach Police

Department came. Matthews had organized a dinner, followed by a tour of strip clubs around Miami Beach.

"It was fun," he said. "We went to three or four of the strip places that were active on the beach . . . the Gaiety, the Place Pigalle—we hit them all."

At one of the clubs, a stripper was doing an exotic pole dance to everyone's delight. "Benji slipped a dollar in her garter," recalled Matthews. "She was up and down the pole, and had all kinds of bills sticking everywhere from every crevice in her body."

Then one of the bills got dislodged and fell to the floor.

"Benji palmed it," Matthews said, laughing, "and I said, 'Ben, I don't believe it.' He said, 'I'll give it back to her the next round.' That was always Benji, God love him."

On Tuesday, June 19, 1979, Ben Novack Jr. married Jill Campion in an Orthodox Jewish wedding conducted by Rabbi Irving Lehrman at the Temple Emanu-El in Miami Beach. Several months earlier Campion had converted to Judaism, to please her new husband and his family.

"Yes, they did want that," said Jill. "I went to the Oceanside with Rabbi Lehrman and got in the water. I went through the whole thing."

The bride and groom were married under a traditional chuppah. Jill wore a long flowing white gown and a matching white hat, and carried a bouquet of flowers. The bearded groom wore a loose-fitting white suit and pink shirt with a wide striped tie. During the service, Ben Jr.'s large pyramid-shaped yarmulke fell off, though the guests were too polite to notice.

A proud Ben Novack Sr. attended the wedding, appearing on good terms with his ex-wife Bernice, who brought along George.

After the service, Ben Jr.'s parents posed together with the happy couple under the chuppah. Ben Sr. looked debonair in a white open-neck shirt and a large gold chain, his chevron mustache combed immaculately. Everyone in the picture is smiling, except Bernice, who was against the wedding, as Jill was eight years older than her son.

The maid of honor, Dovie Ann Hart, remembered Bernice being

unusually subdued on her son's wedding day. "Bernice did not appear to be happy about the wedding," said Hart, "but she was very gracious."

Then, after a small family reception, Ben Jr. kissed his new bride good-bye and drove to Miami International Airport for a business trip.

"He got on a plane by himself," said Jill. "That was our honeymoon. He said we'll have a big party later."

On July 4 of that same year, Bernice Novack threw a lavish wedding party in her garden for her son and his new wife. The bride had made her own low-cut white gown and a lace shawl. Looking very relaxed, Ben Jr. wore a white waistcoat and an open-neck shirt.

"It was very nice and fully catered," Jill remembered. "And they had tables all over the yard, with umbrellas."

Ben Sr. arrived alone, wearing a bright pink silk shirt, with various gold chains dangling from his neck. His sister Lillian and her husband, Harry Brezner, also attended, and Maxine Fiel flew in from New York with her daughters, Meredith and Lisa.

Ahmed Boob came with a beautiful redhead, and happily sipped champagne and posed with Ben Jr. and Bernice for photographs.

None of Ben Jr.'s celebrity friends showed up, although many sent gifts. Frank Sinatra and his wife Barbara gave the newlyweds a beautiful crystal platter with a card attached reading, "Dear Jill and Ben— Wishing you a long, happy and wonderful life together—Love & Kisses, Barbara and Francis."

Among the guests were several important Amway executives and their wives, and several of Ben Jr.'s friends from the Miami Beach Police Department.

At one point, to everyone's delight, a man burst into the garden, complete with a monkey on his back and clashing cymbals, to deliver a singing telegram: a humorous song to the bride and groom.

Later, everybody posed for photographs around a huge wedding cake with a miniature bride and groom on top.

"It was very modest," best man Pete Matthews said of the event. "The reception was in the backyard, and it was really nice."

A few weeks later, when the caterer's bill came in, Matthews received a phone call from an angry Ben Jr., who had his mother on the other line. They informed him that they intended to challenge the bill and demand a discount, as processed turkey had been served instead of real meat.

Seventeen

MARRIAGE

Soon after they married, Ben Novack Jr. admitted to being almost five years younger than he had claimed. He was taking a shower and suddenly called his new wife into the bathroom, saying he had something he had to tell her.

"Listen, I'm not really twenty-seven. I'm twenty-five," he told her.

Jill Novack, who was now in her early thirties, told him that it was no big deal. Then, a few weeks later, he confessed that he was actually only twenty-three years old, and had been only twenty when they first met.

"I felt such a fool," said Jill. "That's why his mother wasn't happy with me, and was so upset about the wedding."

After their wedding, Ben Jr. concentrated on organizing Amway conventions all over the country. By 1980 he had built up so many contacts in the convention business that he quit his Amway job and set up his own company, Novack Enterprises, Inc., appointing himself president. He would still do Amway conventions, but now he would be able to take on new clients.

"He started his business from people he knew," said Richard Marx, whom he had recently hired as a legal adviser. "And I admired Benji to be able to do what he did. He accomplished something. He truly did. And he did it basically away from his father."

Ben Jr. was now on the road most of the time, organizing Amway conventions and courting new corporate clients. He would often take his beautiful new wife along, viewing her as a great business asset. "We went out to dinner with his business associates a lot," recalled Jill. "I attended parties and traveled with him."

One time, he brought Jill along to an Amway convention he was running at the Playboy Club Retreat in Lake Geneva, Wisconsin. "We ran into Rip Taylor and hung out with him," Jill remembered of the flamboyant comedian. "I colored his hair and mustache and we had a great time."

On another trip to Las Vegas, Ben Jr. brought her backstage to meet Neil Sedaka, whom he had known since he was a child.

"We'd get all dressed up and have carte blanche to backstage," Jill said. "And you'd meet everybody. He was close to all those heavy-hitters: Sinatra, the Rat Pack, Ann-Margret. We were rubbing shoulders with them and were treated like royalty. It was very, very nice."

In retrospect, Jill believes Ben Jr. viewed her as a "trophy wife," a way to replicate his father's relationship with his mother at the Fontainebleau. "I was that trinket," Jill said. "I was a showgirl dancer, but I could hang out with the respectable people."

In 1980, Ben Novack Sr. moved into a new condo development on the Seventy-Ninth Street (now John F. Kennedy) Causeway, eight miles west of Miami Beach. He bought a small stake in the Racquet Club in North Bay Village, and started managing it. It was a steep fall for the man who had once commanded one of the world's most glamorous hotels.

Since the breakup of his third marriage, the septuagenarian had dated a string of beautiful young women, some young enough to be his granddaughters. Bernice was furious when he fell for an eighteen-year-old schoolgirl, and even went along to her high school prom as her date.

"That's ridiculous," said Maxine Fiel, "Give me a break."

After that short-lived relationship, Novack started dating a former Miss Uruguay in her late twenties named Juana M. Rodríguez Muñoz.

As a token of his love, he presented her with the same heart-shaped hammered gold ring Bernice had worn during their marriage.

When Ben Novack Jr. learned that his father's new girlfriend was wearing the ring, he was furious, and cornered the girl in the street, demanding it back.

"The same bad choices," Richard Marx explained. "Both Junior and Senior . . . seemed to have problems with women. And they paid a price for it. They paid a big price for it."

Before long, Jill Novack discovered that her new husband had been cheating on her during his frequent out-of-town business trips. "He had met this woman," said Jill, "who was running his convention for [a] hotel, and they liked each other."

One evening, he took Jill along for dinner with another couple at their favorite hangout, the Celebrity Room at the Diplomat Hotel. "And all he could do was talk about this woman," Jill said. "I stormed out crying."

Ben Jr. followed her out of the restaurant and into the parking lot, where they started arguing. Soon afterward, Jill found the woman's phone number. "So I called her," Jill said. "She admitted to it and said it was nothing. You know how things get really intense when you're doing a convention. Yeah I know."

Another major problem in the marriage was Jill's mother-in-law, Bernice, who used her money to control her son. "His mother ran the show," Jill explained. "In person, I got on with her great. She was very charming and lovely . . . but she wasn't going to be happy with any woman."

"At eleven o'clock every night," Jill remembered, "his mother would call him on the phone because the rates went down then. And finally I said, 'You know eleven o'clock is not a good time for your mom to be calling us,' because sometimes we'd both be in bed and didn't want to be disturbed. I told him to tell his mother to stop calling, and that was an issue."

According to Jill, she and Ben Jr. enjoyed a normal sex life during their marriage. "He never asked me to do anything kinky or weird," she said. "The only thing is he had one or two soft-porn films, a pretty story and a filter with lenses. A couple of times he turned those on."

To make extra money, as well as fulfill a long-cherished dream of being a private eye, Novack set up his own security company, called Eagle. In addition to supplying security guards for special events, he also conducted discreet surveillance for divorce attorneys.

"Once, he was hired to follow someone's wife," said Jill, "to prove if she was having an affair."

One night, Ben Jr. had parked his burgundy Lincoln Continental outside a condominium, hoping to use his high-powered camera to photograph the wife and her lover in a compromising position.

"It turned out to be uneventful," Jill said. "At around two A.M. he had me bring him food and drink and sit with him to keep him company. He was lonesome and bored."

During his rare downtime, Ben Jr. loved to mix his own rock-and-roll tapes, using his expensive customized sound system.

"I remember him with a headset mixing music tapes and stuff," Jill said. "But he never really shared that with me. I sewed a lot."

However, Ben did share his passion for jazz with Jill's best friend, Dovie Ann Hart. "Ben loved jazz," Hart said, "and he had an entire music room devoted to his 'state-of-the-art' electronic sound system. I loved jazz, too, so we listened together and discussed the artists."

Pete Matthews was in awe of the expensive high-tech equipment in Ben Jr.'s Fontainebleau Park apartment. "He went first class with all the high-end technology," said Matthews. "With the TVs and the stereos."

Although he never skimped on anything for himself, Ben Jr. was parsimonious when it came to anybody else.

"We were celebrating a birthday party for Jill's mom," Matthews said, "and Jill and Benji came and he bought a bottle of wine. It was a fun night. And I remember Benji leaving with Jill, and he turns around and looks at the wine. Then, in front of everyone, he says, 'Oh, I see they didn't open it, so I'll take it home.' I couldn't believe it. He took the wine and left. That was Benji. I don't think he really cared what people thought. He just spoke his mind and did what he wanted to do."

· · ·

To save money, the newlyweds opened a joint savings account, both putting away a few dollars a week. One day, Jill checked on the account, which should have had $2,000 in it, and discovered it empty.

"He was traveling, and I called him out on it," she said. "He could make you mad."

After Ben explained that he had transferred the money into a new account in his mother's name, as it was a good investment, his wife decided to teach him a lesson.

"He had over $20,000 worth of electronics," said Jill. "We had televisions. We had music equipment. So I packed up the whole apartment. Everything." Then a girlfriend helped her move everything out to her mother's house. "I went over to my Mom's and stayed there," Jill said. "And when he got back in town, he walked into an empty house. First off he called his mother, who told him, "You see, I told you. She wanted your money."

When a furious Ben Jr. arrived at her mother's house to confront her, Jill immediately gave him back everything, saying she just wanted to teach him a lesson.

"Here's your stuff," she told him, "I don't want it."

She then agreed to come home, but things between them would never be the same again.

In early 1981 they decided to buy a house together, hoping to get their marriage back on track. Jill was overjoyed, as this had always been their long-term plan.

"We're buying this house," she recalled, "and everything is going well. [Then,] on a Sunday morning, he came in with a document in his hand and says, 'I can't do it.' I said, 'You can't do what?' And he says, 'I can't buy this house and put your name on it. My mother won't let me.' She held the purse strings."

Jill then became suspicious that he was cheating again, and looked at his planner. There, to her horror, she found divorce papers Ben Jr. had had an attorney draw up saying that the two of them were no longer married.

"Well, I called my attorney," she said. "He checked the court, and there was no record that we had been divorced. When Benji came back, I held [the document] up to him and said, 'What's this for?' And he looks at me with those big eyes."

He then confessed that he had invented the divorce for his mother, so she would stop nagging him about not putting Jill's name on the deed for the new house.

"And we're still going to her house at weekends as usual for dinner," Jill said, "and she's thinking we're divorced, and never even said a word to me. That's just weird."

Recently, Bernice had even taken Jill to one side and confided that she had a twenty-four-carat gold purse in her safety deposit box that would one day be Jill's.

"Why tell me that if you don't want me there?" she asked. "But she was very nice to me in person."

A few weeks after the divorce document incident, Ben Jr. coldly handed her a separation agreement offering a $2,000 settlement. When Jill complained that it was not enough even to get an apartment, he reluctantly agreed to double the figure.

"Two months later he called me back," she said. "We weren't divorced yet. And he says, 'I learned my lesson. Please come back. I'll rip up the separation agreement and put your name on the house.' And I said no, because I knew if I went back it would be twice as hard to get out the next time."

On March 18, 1981, they were officially divorced after less than two years of marriage. Jill accepted a $4,000 payoff and gave him back her engagement ring.

"It was all congenial," she explained. "It was like his mother was in control. She broke us up and she did it with a smile on her face."

In April 1981, two weeks after his divorce was finalized, Ben Novack Jr. bought a house on the water off Atlantic Boulevard in Pompano Beach, a short drive from his mother. He now spent most of his time on the road, organizing conventions for Amway and his other clients.

When he was at home, he still went out in his uniform on patrol for the Miami Beach Police Department. After seven years as a volunteer, he had an excellent attendance record, somehow managing to log the required shifts each month.

"He was very proficient," said Officer Pete Matthews, who still partnered with Ben Jr. on midnight patrols. "He wrote an excellent arrest record, and the citations were flawless. He knew what he was doing, and I never had to second-guess him."

On May 8, 1983, Ben Novack Jr. was promoted to fully sworn reserve status. To qualify, he had to pass a thorough background investigation, a psychological examination, and a polygraph test. He also had to explain in writing why he was applying for the promotion.

"For the past nine-years [I] have enjoyed being able to devote time each month," he wrote, "to help serving community, help people and do my share in upholding the laws of our government, for which I have a very high regard."

However, Officer Novack's dream of ever making the detective bureau was handicapped by his uncontrollable stutter. "Ben desperately wanted to [make detective]," said former Miami Beach Police field training officer Pat Franklin. "He had a very bad stuttering problem and this precluded him, because he couldn't use the radio. He couldn't speak under stress, so he was frustrated."

To make matters even worse, some of his fellow police cruelly ridiculed his stuttering behind his back. "They would make offhanded remarks over the radio," said Matthews, "which I found very disturbing. They never did it in front of him . . . just behind his back."

Ben Novack Jr. often went out partying with his friends from the Miami Beach Police Department. He particularly loved the local strip clubs, where he had a reputation as a big spender who was more than generous to any stripper who took his fancy.

One night in August 1983 he was at the Follies International Club in Hialeah, Florida, when a beautiful, young, blond Ecuadorian stripper named Sylvia caught his eye. He stayed all night, slipping dollar bills into her garter whenever she danced.

On his way out, he gave her his business card, asking her to call him.

Later, in the girls' dressing room, Sylvia, whose real name was Narcisa Cira Veliz Pacheco, asked the other girls who the tall, generous bearded man was. When she was told that Ben Novack Jr. was the wealthy heir to the Fontainebleau hotel fortune, she tucked his card safely away in her pocketbook for safekeeping.

EIGHTEEN

NARCY

B en Hadwin Novack Jr. and Narcisa Cira Veliz Pacheco's child-
hoods could not have been more different. Whereas Ben had
been raised like royalty in the Fontainebleau's seventeenth-floor
penthouse, Narcisa, or Narcy, as everyone knew her, came
from humble peasant stock.

She claimed to have been born on November 28, 1956, in Guayaquil,
Ecuador, although she would later be accused of being older. Known as
the Pearl of the Pacific, Guayaquil is the biggest city in Ecuador, rest-
ing on the banks of the Guayas River, which flows into the Pacific
Ocean.

Founded by the Spanish in 1538, Guayaquil has a violent and troubled
history. In 1687 it was ransacked by pirates, who massacred the male
population before kidnapping the women for their pleasure.

Over the next several hundred years, Guayaquil was continually oc-
cupied by several countries, including Spain and Peru.

On May 24, 1822, the Republic of Ecuador was established after
gaining independence from Spain.

With a population today of more than thirteen million, Ecuador is
one of the poorest places on earth. The average annual wage in 2011

was just $4,500, and 65 percent of the population was officially below the poverty line.

While Narcy was growing up, her parents owned a grocery story and a large dairy farm and grew cocoa beans. They had six children: Estilita, Leticia, Blanca, Carlos, Cristobal, and Narcy, who was the baby of the family.

In Guayaquil, the practice of voodoo, brought over by African slaves in the seventeenth and eighteenth centuries, is commonplace. As a young girl, Narcy learned voodoo spells and the various herbal mixtures for hexes and other dark arts. Later, she would claim to be a voodoo queen of the dark underground religion.

Cristobal and his sister Estilita first came to America in July 1974 on tourist visas, remaining in Brooklyn after those visas ran out. Two days after arriving, twenty-one-year-old Cristobal found a job in a bakery.

"In Ecuador they grew up together," said Cristobal's Chinese born fiancée Laura Law. "They all came over at different times."

The next sibling to come to America was Carlos, who lived in Queens. Then, in 1978, their little sister Narcisa, then twenty-three and affectionately known in the family as Mi Niña (meaning "Little One"), moved over with her husband, Angel Abad, and two-year-old daughter, May Azalea, settling in Hialeah, in southern Florida.

Hialeah had a strong Latin American population, and the religion of Santeria, as well as voodoo, flourished there. When the marriage broke up several years later, Narcy sent May to live with her elder brother Cristobal, who was now living in Richmond, Queens.

"I was like her father," said Cristobal. "I taught May how to read and write."

Back in Hialeah, to make ends meet, Narcy found a job as an exotic dancer in a seedy strip joint called Follies International Club, by the Hialeah Speedway.

"Sylvia was the name she used," recalled Big Fannie Annie, the club's featured entertainer. "A lot of girls come like she did, very quiet and innocent at the beginning. But once they start dealing with men they get a little more hardcore. There are a lot of gold diggers."

At first the heavily accented Sylvia worked days, when there were far fewer customers than at night. Annie befriended the unsophisticated Ecuadorian girl, taking her under her wing and showing her the ropes.

"I tried to help her," Annie explained. "I sold her a few costumes, to get her going. At the beginning she was a little shy, but it doesn't take a girl long to see that money out there and how to get it. She soon got more confident and more cocky."

Follies International was an all-nude club, and Sylvia could earn anywhere between $500 to $1,500 when she worked nights.

"The girls would get totally nude," said Annie, "and get up on the tables to dance. Then [the customers] chose the girls they liked."

In the beginning, the diminutive Sylvia often stood alone on the table naked, as the predominantly Latin clientele preferred American girls. "They wanted a blonde with big boobs—something they weren't getting at home," Annie explained. "So Sylvia went blond, and it did help, although she had small breasts."

The seasoned strip club veteran also had Sylvia shave off her pubic hair, as it was losing her tips. "Those girls loved to bend [over] when they're dancing on the tables and give the men a little show," said Annie. "So Sylvia shaved her bush down."

As she got to know Sylvia, Big Fanny Annie was struck at how she never talked about her past. "Most of the girls will tell you everything," she said, "but Sylvia was kind of private about that. I knew that she had been married and then separated, and sometimes she'd bring her little girl into the club around Christmas. She was cute."

Sylvia was not popular with the other girls, as she was often irritable and had a bad temper, which could explode without warning.

"I'll never forget one Christmas," Annie said. "She was sitting with some guy, and his wife came in and started yelling, 'Come home! You have children!' And Sylvia screamed at her, 'Bitch. Can't you leave him alone!' She told her to leave him alone because she was making money off him. But that really pissed off the wife, and in the end the owner told [Sylvia] to go into the back room or she'd be fired."

Another Follies stripper, Cynthia Johns, who danced under the name Stormy Shea, remembers Sylvia having an affair with one of her wealthy customers. "He was a guy we called the Silver Fox," Johns said. "He was a lot older, with silver hair, but he had money."

Cocaine was rampant at the club, according to Big Fanny Annie. "Cocaine was why those girls changed," she explained. "And they changed hard. I know the people she went with, and they were heavy into it."

Sylvia also became close with an older stripper named Brenda Ryan (not her real name), who used her as an interpreter for her Latin customers.

"Brenda was smart and a hustler," said Annie. "She broke Sylvia in. Real hardcore. She kind of trained her."

Brenda taught Sylvia the art of giving customers hard-luck stories, to get bigger tips.

"I've sat and listened to her stories," said Annie. "You tell them your mother's dying and you need money, or my baby's sick and I need to buy medicine, or I don't have the money to pay my rent. She would just pour it on for maximum sympathy and of course money."

There was also big money to be made from meeting customers for sex, after the club closed.

"After work," said Annie, "the girls all met up with whoever was paying the most. Or they'd get the money and then go out the back door to meet the guys in the parking lot. I mean these girls were as tough as they come, and Sylvia learned to be real tough to survive. She soon changed and adapted."

All the strippers at Follies International knew Ben Novack Jr., who often came in with his policeman friends. The tall, bearded businessman never had any shortage of nude table dancers, as it was common knowledge that he bought his favorite girls new boob jobs.

"Ben was a party guy and had a little entourage," Annie said. "All the girls liked him because he threw money around. Somebody said that his father owned *that* hotel, and I said, 'Oh, that's good. This is the wrong place for him to be.' Somebody was going to latch on to him. Obviously it was Sylvia."

. . .

In the summer of 1984, within a couple of months of meeting Ben No-vack Jr., Narcy Veliz quit Follies International and moved into his Pom-pano Beach house. But he refused to allow her daughter, May, to live with them, so the eight-year-old girl moved to Naples, Florida, to live with Narcy's sister Leticia.

Soon after Narcy moved in, Ben Jr. brought her to one of his cos-metic surgeons, to watch her get a new pair of breasts, designed to his exact specifications. It would be the first of several breast augmentations he would have her undergo over the next few years.

Officer Charlie Seraydar first met Narcy at a Miami Beach Police Department social function. "He told me that he had a girlfriend that was a bombshell," Seraydar recalled. "And of course I know Ben's taste and that she was going to be a blond bimbo." However, Seraydar was impressed with Narcy, soon giving her his stamp of approval. "She was a really nice lady," he remembered, "and took care of him hand and foot. Ben was demanding, not just in business but in his personal life. And this lady Narcy knew exactly what to do to take care of him."

On July 21, 1984, Miami Beach Reserve Officer Ben Novack Jr. won a commendation after rounding up a major auto-theft ring. Now finally assigned to the detectives' division, Officer Novack had been on patrol in Miami Beach in an unmarked police car when he noticed a black Datsun driving erratically, with two white males inside.

"At that point," wrote his superior officer Sergeant Tom Hunker in his official letter of commendation, "Novack attempted to stop the vehicle by using the revolving blue light in their police vehicle. However, the Datsun increased speed and began to flee."

Officer Novack pursued the Datsun at high speed through the streets of South Beach. The two suspects eventually bailed out of their vehicle and made a run for it. Novack apprehended one, while the other was stopped by another officer.

"Due to [Officer Novack's] actions," wrote Sergeant Hunker, "a

potentially dangerous situation was kept in hand. Reserve Officer Novack interviewed both subjects, who admitted to having stolen at least
five cars in the last thirty days. Due to Novack's interrogation and follow-up investigation, numerous auto thefts are to be cleared by auto
theft detectives."

A few weeks later, Ben Novack Jr. was with Charlie Seraydar, testing
out his new forty-two-foot Hatteras yacht, when his mobile phone rang.
It was Narcy, who had just discovered that Ben was seeing another woman
on the side.

"Narcy was threatening to burn the house down on Atlantic Boulevard," Seraydar said. "And he's pleading with her not to burn it down
and to calm down. 'No, don't do anything. I don't have anybody else.'
Apparently she was very jealous.

"I thought, 'Boy, are you in for a long, fucking hard ride.'"

NINETEEN

"I AM
MR. FONTAINEBLEAU"

On Saturday, November 19, 1983—after being forced out of the North Bay Village Racquet Club in a lengthy legal battle—Ben Novack Sr. auctioned off his personal collection of Fontainebleau furniture, furnishings, and memorabilia to raise money. Nearly six years after losing his beloved hotel, the seventy-six-year-old iconic hotelier was a shadow of his former self. And he had little sentiment for all the French Provincial furniture and furnishings that had once adorned the Fontainebleau.

All his debts had now been paid, so the profits from the auction block would be his.

The preview for the auction was held on a chilly Thursday morning in a shabby warehouse on the outskirts of Miami. Bernice Novack attended, along with Ben Sr.'s other two ex-wives, Bella and Janie.

"After losing the hotel," Bernice said later, "the fire wasn't in him. He was older and wasn't well."

At the warehouse, a visibly ailing Ben Novack Sr. slowly escorted reporters on a tour of several hundred of his Fontainebleau treasures. His once-fashionable clothes had been replaced by plain peach-colored slacks, a short beige jacket, and a matching hat.

"You're looking at the end of an empire," he announced. "These are the shreds of an empire. 'The courts took all the sentiment out of me. These, these are things. Just things. Why should I be sad?"

But it was sad to witness the now-frail senior citizen, cane in hand, trying to recall some of his treasures, helped by auctioneer Jim Gall.

"God bless the people who acquire some of these things," Novack reflected. "Let them enjoy them. I never really enjoyed them."

Miami Herald reporter Mary Voboril accompanied Novack on his unsentimental journey.

He passed by a smallish Russian clock flanked by little onion domes [Voboril later wrote], marble desks fitted with gilt ink-wells and bronze lions but no pens, lampstands fashioned out of gamboling bronze nymphs, rows of delicate crystal.

"I had more glasses," Novack said. "Lots and lots of glasses; boxes of glasses."

"I think they were Lalique," said auctioneer Jim Gall.

"A lot of what?" said Novack, bending closer.

"His hearing is not as good as it once was. Neither is his memory."

During the tour, he suddenly lashed out at Miami Beach for not doing more to help him save his Fontainebleau.

"I did enough for Miami Beach," he snapped, "but I did not get them to reciprocate. They got what they deserved. Decline."

His mood only brightened when he proudly told the *Herald* reporter and photographer how he had won a retraction from their newspaper after it dared accuse him of Mafia involvement.

"*The Miami Herald* tried to bury me as Mafia," he declared, "until they apologized to me in the front section of the paper. The Knight Boys apologized. Hah. They said, 'Ben, don't go to court against us.'"

When asked how much money he expected to make from the week-end auction, Novack replied he hoped to get just enough to buy Bernice a lavalier that she particularly wanted.

"I hold my weight down," he suddenly said out of nowhere, "because I have no money to buy food."

Then, a few minutes later, he announced that he had enough money to last him for the rest of his life.

At the end of the tour, Novack was asked if he would like to be remembered as the man who built the Fontainebleau.

"I *am* Mr. Fontainebleau," he replied, after a brief pause. "Look, I have it right here."

Then, reaching into his shirt pocket, he pulled out a miniature replica of the crescent-shaped Fontainebleau on the end of a heavy gold chain. Somebody then asked how he had got it, but he could only scratch his head, unable to remember.

The following day, Ben Novack Sr. was admitted to the hospital with dangerously high blood pressure, and was too ill to attend the auction.

On Saturday morning, almost five hundred people turned up to bid on the Fontainebleau treasures. Bernice Novack came with some friends, immaculately dressed in white hose and tan heels, her trademark red hair perfectly styled for the occasion. She appeared indifferent, down-playing any feelings she might have had about witnessing the final nail in the Fontainebleau's coffin.

"You lose the sentiment for it," she told a reporter. "They just become objects. I hope the people who buy them find great happiness with them."

There was no shortage of buyers, as item after item was eagerly snapped up, raising a total of $200,000. A Chinese palace vase on a rosewood pedestal went for $6,750, while a cigar box given to Ben Novack Sr. by former Cuban president Fulgencio Batista fetched $125.

Among the other items for sale was a montage of photos of Ben Novack Sr. with movie star Ann-Margret, going for $25, and a chamber pot for $75.

However, some of the most valuable Fontainebleau items had long since found their way to Bernice Novack's Fort Lauderdale home, where they were now housed in a special museum.

Three weeks after the auction, Ben Novack Sr. bounced back, sinking more than $1 million into a brand-new nightclub in Boynton Beach. He had now relocated to the scenic oceanfront community sixty miles south of Miami Beach, vowing to transform his club into a world-class resort.

"It looks like a lovely area for good clean exploitation of nice people," Novack explained to *The Miami Herald*. "We're here. We're full of ego and ready to go."

His latest idea was Alcatraz, a prison-themed entertainment park. He had transformed an old A&P supermarket on South Federal Highway into an entertainment prison, complete with a restaurant, bar, and disco.

After entering through a velvet rope, guests were first "booked" by staff dressed as prison guards, before having their mug shots taken. Then they were escorted to individual cells, either to be seated on toilet seats behind bars, or to be placed in a mesh-screened booth to prevent "contact visits."

Dinner was served by waiters in full warden outfits. Afterward, "inmates" were directed outside into "the Yard," to play on a huge pool table dug into the ground, using croquet mallets instead of cues.

At the December grand opening, a wheelchair-bound Ben Novack Sr. was so confident of success that he was already planning franchises in three other Florida locations.

"People don't want to spend the big prices anymore," he explained, as his former Miss Uruguay girlfriend looked on admiringly. "We built something we think will be for the everyday public."

Bernice Novack also attended the Alcatraz opening, with her personal hairdresser, Emmanuel Buccola, and his partner, Guy Costaldo.

"It was very exciting," Costaldo recalled. "Ben was ill and in a wheelchair at the time, but all these people from the Fontainebleau were

there. It was a very unique place. There would be alarms constantly going off, like someone was escaping. It was different."

While his father was devoting himself to Alcatraz, Ben Novack Jr.'s
convention business was going from strength to strength. He had now
renamed his company Convention Concepts Unlimited, and was starting
to make big money. His training at the Fontainebleau hotel had proved
invaluable, and he was now using every trick in the book he had learned
from his father.

In late 1984, Mark Gatley, who ran the Niagara Falls Convention and
Visitor's Bureau, received a phone call from Ben Novack Jr. out of the blue.
"He said he had an Amway program for us," Gatley recalled. "Do we have
dates and space to do a meeting in the Niagara Falls Convention Center?"

The meeting was a success, and over the next few years Gatley would
host many Amway conventions for Ben Novack Jr., getting to know him
well.

"Well, Ben was a very difficult, tough businessman," Gatley said.
"He argued about the price . . . and got what he wanted. But he was a
gentleman who paid his bill on time."

The president of Convention Concepts Unlimited often demanded
that a preconvention meeting be held on Thanksgiving or other major
holidays, with little thought for anyone's family obligations.

"That was unusual," Gatley explained, "and I think he did it because
he wanted to make a deliberate entrance into a community. It was very
unorthodox from an industry standpoint, and would unfortunately set a
tone in many cases."

Ben Novack Jr. soon gained a bad reputation in the tightly knit convention industry as being difficult to please.

"[Everyone] found his character interesting," said Gatley, "because
he would be complimentary, and then he would add that 'but' in the
second sentence, and there would be something wrong."

Ben Jr. also played up his Fontainebleau heritage, using it to repri-
mand any convention center that failed to measure up to his demanding
standards.

"He was extremely hands-on," said Gatley. "And you look at his history. We knew he grew up in the hotel business."

One particular trick Ben Jr. had learned from his father was especially exasperating to the industry. He always refused to sign any contracts requiring payments up front, which gave him an escape clause to back out at any time without having to pay a cent.

TWENTY

"A DREAMER
AND A CREATOR"

fter Club Alcatraz predictably bombed, Ben Novack Sr.
scaled things down. He took over the concessions for the
City of Hollywood public golf course, paying the city
$84,000 to run the clubhouse restaurant and bar. Within
a few months this, too, tanked, with Novack's company going out of
business.

"Terrible," said his former Fontainebleau manager Lenore Toby. "It
was mortifying. Horrible."

On the thirtieth anniversary of the opening of the Fontainebleau, Ben
Novack Sr. was now living in exile in the Boynton Beach neighborhood
of Ocean Ridge. Although the former Miss Uruguay Juana Rodríguez
Muñoz, now thirty, was his constant companion, his ex-wife Bernice
visited daily, ensuring that he took his medication and ate properly.

"They couldn't live with each other," explained Maxine Fiel, "and
they couldn't live without each other. Bernice would go and see Ben with
Miss Uruguay there, to see that he was okay and that he had his soup.
It was the strangest thing."

Maxine believes her sister still carried a torch for her ex-husband,
and wished they had stayed together. "Toward the end," said Maxine,
"Bernice said, 'I never should have divorced him.'"

To mark the hotel's thirtieth anniversary, Ben Sr. granted an interview to *Miami Herald* writer Mike Capuzzo, revealing that he had never returned to the hotel since losing it six years earlier.

Published on Sunday, February 19, 1984, the story, carrying the headline "The Sand Castle," painted a sad portrait of a beaten old man still fighting for his just credit for designing the Fontainebleau.

"I entertained kings and queens and presidents all over the world," Novack told Capuzzo. "The glory I got being Mr. Fontainebleau will go on forever . . . but there was no glory in building a failure. Miami Beach went from being one of the most gorgeous places in America to the dumps . . . including the Fontainebleau."

The article wryly noted that "old friends" were becoming concerned about Novack's often erratic thinking. "[He] says he's a millionaire in one breath," read the article, "a pauper in the next. On its 30th anniversary, Novack sometimes wishes he had never built the hotel."

In the article, Novack again bitterly attacked Morris Lapidus for daring to take any credit for the Fontainebleau's iconic design. "It was my idea to have the curved building," he declared. "It was my idea to decorate it. It was my idea to build it. It was my idea to pay for it. He helped. He was part-and-parcel of me. We worked together. He did a lot of the décor. He's a very clever man. But Ben Novack designed that building."

For balance, Morris Lapidus was also interviewed for the article:

"This is an illiterate man who thinks he designed the Fontainebleau," said the now-world-famous architect. "He has grand delusions. He had no more to do with it than a man sweeping a street. He's the greatest egotist in the world. He's a man I once tried to kill and almost succeeded."

Ben Novack Sr. lashed out: "He's full of crap. The idea came to me in a bathroom. When I thought of the Fontainebleau I was in the john and sitting on it. My wife was witness to it."

At the end of the article, Novack attempted to articulate his life achievements:

"They say Ben Novack built Miami Beach," he said. "I don't know. I gave it all I had. Everything I've ever done was on a grand scale, and it was all successful. My heroes are the famous people of the world. I always loved winners. Those are the heroes—winners. When you lose, you're not a winner. I did my duty. They can never destroy the Fontaine-bleau."

In October 1984, Ben Novack Sr. signed over his power of attorney to his twenty-nine-year-old son before being admitted to a nursing home after leg surgery. Two months later, Ben Jr. filed a suit seeking the return of money and jewelry from his father's young girlfriend, Juana Rodríguez Muñoz, including a $100,000 loan, a $15,000 ring, a gold bracelet, and a money clip. He also sought an injunction barring her from communicating with his father.

In the suit, Ben Jr. claimed that his father had paid her for "companionship."

Three months later, Ben Jr. asked a Dade County Circuit Court judge to declare his father mentally incompetent, and appoint him and Bernice Novack as Ben Sr.'s legal guardians.

Ben Jr. would later reveal that his elderly father spent the final eighteen months of his life hovering in and out of sanity.

"He would never want the world to know how he spent his last days," said Ben Jr.

On Saturday, March 30, 1985, Ben Novack Sr. suffered a major stroke and was admitted to Mount Sinai Medical Center in Miami Beach. Five days later, as her seventy-eight-year-old boyfriend fought for his life in intensive care, Juana Rodríguez Muñoz's attorney filed papers to stop Ben Jr. and his mother from being appointed Ben Sr.'s guardians. Her motion pointed out that as Ben Jr. "may stand to inherit substantially all" of his father's estate, appointing him guardian would be a "conflict of interest."

She called for "a totally disinterested third party" to be made guardian, and a full investigation into how the elderly Novack had been kept "over-sedated," and "held virtually incommunicado from his friends."

Rodríguez Muñoz's motion blamed Ben Sr.'s treatment for causing the stroke, alleging that his son had improperly obtained power of attorney and was now using it to "harass" her.

She claimed to have lived with Ben Novack Sr. on and off for the last five years, calling their relationship "a labor of love" motivated by "genuine care and concern."

On Thursday, April 4, Ben Novack Sr. rallied and was taken out of intensive care, and listed as in good condition.

"Novack Improving, But Fight for Fortune Takes Turn for Worse," read the headline in that morning's *Miami Herald*.

Then, on Friday morning, he suffered a relapse, and at 10:38 P.M., Ben Novack Sr. died, after his heart and lungs finally gave out.

Ben Jr. handled the funeral, arranging to have his father's body brought back to Miami Beach for a Saturday night viewing.

The next day, *The Miami Herald* carried a front-page obituary for the man who had changed the face of Miami Beach forever.

"I'll only be stopped by God," it quoted the hotelier as saying at his darkest moment, nearly eight years earlier, after losing his dream.

Further inside the paper was a death notice, paid for by Ben Novack Jr.

"Ben, 78," it read, "debonair Hotelier and Entrepreneur, came to Miami Beach in 1940. A Dreamer and Creator, he owned and built six hotels, including the San Souci and Miami Beach Flagship Resort, the Fontainebleau, which he owned and ran for twenty-four years.

"His greatest love was Miami Beach. He is survived by his loving son Ben Jr. and sisters Miriam Spier and Lillian Brezner."

That Monday, a service was held at the Riverside Chapel.

"It was a whole big thing," said Guy Costaldo, who went with Bernice. "A lot of people from the hotel were there. It was a mob scene."

Later, Ben Novack Sr. made his final journey back to New York, to be buried in the Novack-Spier family mausoleum at the Mount Lebanon Cemetery in Queens.

A month later, Juana Rodríguez Muñoz filed a $500,000 slander suit against Ben Jr. for claiming she had provided paid companionship for his father.

"It could turn into a contest for the will," speculated attorney Richard Marx, who now represented Ben Jr. "It's a very sad situation."

In April 1987, Rodríguez Muñoz abruptly dropped the suit, after both sides came to an undisclosed agreement.

Exactly how much money Ben Sr. squirreled away in offshore accounts or other hideaways may never be known. His will left Bernice $2,500 a month for the rest of her life, and set up a $60,000-a-year trust fund for Ben Jr. Maxine Fiel estimates that Ben Sr. left his son around $1 million and all his possessions. His sister Lillian was also well taken care of.

Ronald Novack, Ben Sr.'s long-forgotten adoptive son with his first wife, Bella, who was now suffering from mental illness and virtually homeless, received just one dollar under a codicil. This ensured that Ronald could never contest his will.

Twenty-One

"THE MEETING PLANNER FROM HELL"

In the wake of his father's death, Ben Novack Jr. was now a wealthy man in his own right, no longer having to rely on his mother for money. As the personal representative of his father's estate, Ben Jr. had agreed to pay Bernice the $2,500 a month for the rest of her life. But now he was no longer reliant on her; he could do whatever he wanted.

Charlie Seraydar says Ben Sr.'s death had a profound effect on his son, who had always struggled to be recognized in his own right. He now also started adopting some of his father's character traits.

"It was a very tumultuous time in Benji's life," his good friend explained. "He had stepped into taking over his father's character and he was obnoxious."

He also decided to finally do something about his debilitating stutter, enrolling at a special speech therapy school in New York.

"He pretty much overcame it and found a way to control it," said Seraydar. "He used to tell me it had to do with thinking about what to say first and putting the sentences in your head, so you know what words to say."

In the summer of 1987 Ben Novack Jr. bought a luxurious fifty-foot Cary boat, using $524,000 from his inheritance. He christened her

White Lightning, and moored her right outside his Pompano Beach home. The powerful boat had four 625-horsepower engines and could reach sixty knots.

"He loved it," said Seraydar, "and that was an extension of him. He used to come up to my house in it, and we would always go out on the boat. He would never venture out more than ten miles."

The new boat owner especially delighted in having his well-endowed new girlfriend Narcy pose on deck as his human figurehead.

"After Narcy's boob job," said Seraydar, "he used to put her on the bow of his boat and ride up-and-down the Inter-Coastal . . . so people would see her."

He also held top-level Amway business seminars on board *White Lightning*, writing them off as business expenses. Often he would be joined by Miami Dolphins star football player Tim Foley, who also worked for Amway and was a close friend.

That summer, Ben Novack Jr. was so busy running Amway conventions that he missed some shifts at the Miami Beach Police Department. On September 26 he wrote a memo to his department superior, Sergeant John Tighe, explaining the situation and making sure he received the proper credit.

> *I have had an emergency business situation in Columbus, Ohio, for the months of August and September, and therefore have been unable to fulfill the normal hour input requirement. I did return to Miami last week for the main purpose of not missing the range qualification with my service revolver and in fact should be credited with ten hours for September 21, 1985. (Left home at 7:15 A.M. and returned at 5 P.M.) I qualified with a 271 on the PPC and 1098 overall ("Expert").*
>
> *I believe that my business situation will resolve itself to where I will be back on schedule and fully able to comply with my monthly hour input during the month of October and from that point forward.*
>
> *Once again, many thanks for your understanding and the Department's working with me during this time.*
>
> *Respectfully submitted, Ofc. Ben Novack Jr.*

. . .

After her ex-husband's death, Bernice Novack, now sixty-five, decided to sell off some of her jewelry, including the diamond earrings she had been given by Frank Sinatra. She took them to a small jewelry store in Fort Lauderdale, but the owner suggested she go to a bigger one, in Bal Harbour, as the earrings were out of his class.

While there, she struck up a conversation with the saleslady, Estelle Fernandez, finding immediate rapport. "We became friends instantly," recalled Estelle. "I mean we were like sisters."

A few days later, Bernice returned to the store, telling Fernandez that she'd sold the jewelry for a good price. "One of the jewelry stores bought it from her," said Fernandez. "I guess she needed money at the time, as I don't think Ben left her anything."

Over the next few months, the two women began meeting regularly for Chinese dinners, soon becoming confidantes.

"Bernice was very private," said Estelle, "but she told me stuff she wouldn't tell anybody else. She did not want anybody to know she was a foster child [or] know her age."

In late 1987, Bernice was devastated when her close friend and hairstylist Manny Buccola was diagnosed with AIDS. They had remained close since the Fontainebleau days, and each week he visited her home to do her hair.

Bernice began taking care of him, and started working with various AIDS charities, raising money and awareness for the disease.

"I got her involved," explained Guy Costaldo. "When my lover was ill, a priest here was opening a second-hand store called the Poverello Center, selling used furniture for money to buy food for people with AIDS." Bernice started donating furniture and clothes to the center, joining the committee so she could be more actively involved.

"She supported them in every way she could," said Barbara Lunde. "This was early on, when no one was mentioning [AIDS]. She gave a lot of stuff to that store and she used to go there all the time."

The Reverend Temple Hayes, who had first met Bernice at the Science of Mind Center in Boca Raton, said Bernice made AIDS her personal cause long before it was fashionable to do so. "Bernice was an old soul," said Temple. "She volunteered at an AIDS place and was very open-minded. She had some friends that were gay back then when unfortunately AIDS hit. She really helped support that organization and took it to heart."

As Buccola's conditioned worsened, Bernice visited him daily to nurse him and keep his spirits up.

"When Manny was ill," said Costaldo, "I went to work, and she'd stop by every day to see him. We became friends through his illness."

During their evenings together, Bernice regaled the couple with stories of her glamorous time at the Fontainebleau, and all the stars she had known. She loved to show them her personal scrapbooks with candid photographs of her posing with presidents and movie stars.

"She was a very exciting woman," said Costaldo," and owning the Fontainebleau hotel, she would tell stories. Manny knew a lot of them, because he worked there. All about the heyday of the Mafia and very interesting stories if she got talking. We always bugged her to write a book."

During Manny's final days, Bernice encouraged the couple to be blessed by a priest.

"It wasn't a marriage," explained Costaldo. "Manny wanted to do it, and he was ill. It made him happy. Bernice was there. We had Mass said in the living room, and she was here for the party."

A few weeks later, in July 1988, Manny Buccola died. Bernice attended the funeral with Estelle Fernandez.

"She loved him dearly," said Fernandez. "I don't usually like that kind of thing, but I went because of her."

From the very first time Bernice Novack set eyes on Narcy Veliz, she detested her. Although she may have disapproved of Ben Jr.'s ex-wife, Jill, the former Ecuadorian stripper posed a far greater threat. But Bernice was powerless to do anything, as she no longer exerted any financial control over her son. So she kept quiet and bided her time.

Her sister, Maxine, met Narcy soon after she moved in with Ben Jr.

"This one was no beauty, and Bernice hated her," said Maxine. "She was so uneducated and spoke with a thick Hispanic accent. [Bernice] said, 'Maxine, if I want to see my son, I have to be nice to her.'"

Charlie Seraydar believes Bernice suffered from so-called Jewish mother syndrome. "She didn't like her from day one," said Seraydar. "You know the Jewish mothers never think their sons' girlfriends are good enough for them."

To many, Ben Jr. and Narcy seemed a good match, and Pete Matthews had never seen his friend so smitten.

"He was devoted to her," said Matthews. "I've known many women that Benji socialized with . . . and I've never seen any warmth or compassion or sincerity in any of his relationships that I was aware of, except Narcy."

Matthews observed that Narcy did not fit Ben's usual taste in girls, making him wonder what special qualities she possessed. "It was surprising," he said. "Narcy was not tall and kind of on the zaftig side. The girls that had appealed to him over the years were very tall, very sleek, and not overly bosomed, with an hourglass figure. Everyone has a stereotype, and she was not that. But apparently she did something to attract him.

"I never talked to Benji about that but there were always rumors that she was kind of a free-spirited young lady, if you know what I mean. And Benji never really confided in me any of his fetishes or anything. It was just one of those things that he didn't discuss."

Narcy now worked alongside Ben Novack Jr. in his Convention Concepts Unlimited business. She joined a small staff that included William Roszell, who set up the company's computer programs. It was a cash-only operation, and Novack picked up thousands of dollars in bills at each convention. He was now earning millions of dollars a year from his business, much of which went unreported. According to Roszell, Novack was hiding large sums of cash in offshore accounts, to evade the IRS as his father had done. "He would basically get kickbacks from conventions," said Roszell," who left the company in 1991.

Bernice did the books for her son's company, now listed as a religious organization. Narcy, too, soon proved a great asset when Ben started bringing her along to Amway conventions. Her Spanish would be invaluable in building up the growing Hispanic Amway convention business.

"In the years that he started his business," said Charlie Seraydar, "she was right there with him."

The last weekend of July 1990 they did a major Amway convention, at the David L. Lawrence Convention Center in Pittsburgh. After it was over, Ben Novack Jr. complained he had been overcharged, and threatened to pull out of two future conventions at the center.

The *Pittsburgh Post-Gazette* covered the story, reporting how every other organization had always given the convention center high marks in the past.

"Novack said convention center officials tried to wrongfully extract a fee for a percentage of the merchandise his company sold at an Amway sales and marketing seminar," the story read. "He also complained about the quality of food and food service at the hall and a lack of cooperation with the hotels."

The center explained that Novack's complaints were the result of "an honest staff error and a misunderstanding caused by his verbally abusive overreaction."

Mark Gatley said this behavior was quite normal for Ben Novack Jr., now known in the industry as "the meeting planner from hell."

"It goes back a long way," Gatley explained. "He would ask for certain things free or with a huge discount. If we wouldn't bend, he'd call the chairman of my board or the mayor. He'd threaten to first, and we'd go, 'He's not going to do that.' But he would, and you'd end up having to cave in."

On the other hand, Novack always paid his bills, however reluctantly, and brought lucrative Amway business to convention centers all over America and beyond.

"Everybody knew who he was," said Gatley. "And when he came into your community, everybody said, 'Brace yourself, here comes Ben.'

At the end of the day, you'd say, 'Well, did he complain?' Yeah, it's Ben. We expect it."

In the summer of 1990, Ben Novack Jr. hired a building contactor named Joe Gandy to build an extension on his Pompano Beach house. Soon Gandy would become his trusted right-hand man, just as Ahmed Boob had been for Ben's father at the Fontainebleau.

"When I met Ben," Gandy remembered in 2011, "he was living out of a Pompano house . . . a little house on the water. Every neighbor hated him. They hated him across the canal. They hated him everywhere. He just made enemies. As soon as you looked at the man, you could tell he was an asshole."

Gandy already knew about Novack from a friend who had once worked at the Fontainebleau. "He told me stories about Ben before I ever met him," said Gandy. "I know about him having his ass beat at the Fontainebleau when he was fourteen, and when he was seventeen he was peed over, because he didn't like marijuana."

The first time Gandy met Ben Jr., he could hardly understand a word he said. "He stuttered so bad," said Gandy. "His head would go back and forth like a bubba doll, and the eyes and stuff. It was terrible."

After finishing the extension, Ben Novack Jr. hired Gandy to be his go-to man, to run various errands. Gandy was one of the few people Ben Jr. trusted, and he soon became privy to some of Ben's darkest secrets.

"Anything he wanted me to do I would do," Gandy said. "Ben would take me wherever he needed to go. He'd give me big wads of money that you couldn't imagine, to buy all the toys he wanted."

TWENTY-TWO

MRS. NARCY NOVACK

In December 1990, Ben Novack Jr. asked Narcy to marry him, and she readily agreed. The day after Christmas, they took out a Broward County marriage license, but it would be another nine months before they went through with the ceremony.

That spring, Ben Jr. informed his fiancée that he wanted her to convert to Judaism to please his mother.

"She converted for Ben," said Charlie Seraydar, "and that blew Bernice away, for Narcy still practiced voodoo at the house. She was very open about it."

Then, on August 15, 1991, the day before they were due to get married, Ben insisted Narcy sign a prenuptial agreement drawn up by an attorney. The agreement listed Ben Novack Jr.'s assets at $3.2 million, with $1.57 million in liabilities. It stated that if they divorced within ten years, she would receive nothing. After that, she would get a single payout of $65,000, plus her expenses. Narcy was also excluded from ever benefiting from Ben's life insurance, trusts, gifts, or any business interests.

"Upon the death of either Narcy or Ben," read the agreement, "the estate . . . of the deceased shall descend to or vest in their respective heirs-in-law . . . as if no marriage had ever taken place between Narcy and Ben . . ."

However, the agreement could be superseded by a valid will.

The following morning, Ben Novack Jr. and Narcy were married in an Orthodox Jewish ceremony, with just a few close friends and family present.

After the ceremony Ben Jr. and his new bride left for a honeymoon tour of Hong Kong, Fiji, and Australia.

"It was a nice wedding," Charlie Seraydar recalled. "But you could tell that Mama Bernice was not a happy camper. She asked me to talk to Benji to see if I could dissuade him, but Benji was his own guy and did what he wanted."

Soon after they were married, the couple took out a $150,000 mortgage on a home in the prestigious Miami neighborhood of Snug Harbor. But most of the time the newlyweds were out of town, running conventions all over the world.

Three months before their wedding, Narcy, who was now applying for U.S. citizenship, had become a grandmother when her sixteen-year-old daughter, May Abad, gave birth to a son she named Patrick. The unmarried teenager, who was still living with her aunt Leticia in Naples, Florida, soon became pregnant again, giving birth in June 1993 to another son, named Marcello.

"May would come visit [Narcy and Ben] for a week or two," said Charlie Seraydar, "but she was always sent back. She had always been shunted from pillar to post, and it wasn't until her teenage years that Narcy had any interest in May. And I guess the solidifying factor was actually the grandkids. That's what really put them all together."

Although Narcy doted over her two grandsons, she wanted little to do with her own daughter.

"There were always hard feelings and animosities between May and her mother," Seraydar explained.

In 2009, May would tell a reporter for *The Miami Herald* that her mother physically abused her as a young child. According to May, Narcy would punish her by making her kneel on sharp beer caps until her knees bled, or whipping her with an electrical extension cord.

"If I told you half the stuff she did," she said, "you would wonder why I was still standing."

According to Joe Gandy, Ben Novack Jr. disliked his stepdaughter, whom he occasionally employed as a gopher. "He hated May," said Gandy. "May and her mother would go sometimes three or four years [without] talking at all. No kids came by. No nothing. Then they would make up, and Ben would let her back in the office to work."

Although Bernice Novack had initially shunned May when she started working in the office, she gradually warmed to her, finding common ground in their mutual dislike of Narcy.

"Bernice put up with May," said Estelle Fernandez, "because May kind of wore her down with how miserable Narcy was to her. She took a liking to her because of it."

On December 2, 1992, Bernice Novack celebrated her seventieth birthday with a small party for her close friends. A few weeks earlier, a middle-aged couple named Bill and Rebecca Green had moved into the house next door, but she had still not met them. On the morning of her birthday, Bernice looked through her window to see a large sign near her new neighbors' front door reading, "Lordy, Lordy, Rebecca is 40."

"It was my wife's fortieth birthday," said Bill Green. "So I made this sign and hung it out on our trellis. When Bernice saw that, she came over and knocked on the door, and we became good friends after that."

Rebecca Green said that although they shared the same birthday, Bernice never revealed her age. "She didn't want anybody to know," said Rebecca. "So for years we celebrated our birthdays together . . . but nobody knew how old she was."

Bernice was now living alone with her pet terrier, Mitzy. George Rodriguez had moved out after she caught him cheating on her. But they remained close friends.

"There was a period of time when they weren't connecting," Bernice's friend Temple Hayes explained. "There was a sabbatical or a dry spell."

Once a week, thirty-four-year-old Temple and Bernice had a girls' night out in Fort Lauderdale. First they would dine at Bernice's favorite

Chinese restaurant, then go back to Bernice's home. Over cocktails, Bernice would bring out her treasured photo albums from her days at the Fontainebleau and start leafing through them.

"I had goose bumps," Hayes recalled. "She knew Frank Sinatra and the Rat Pack, and had dinner with the Kennedys. I mean she had all these photographs of Sammy Davis Jr. I mean to be around all these stars all the time, and it was just a typical day in her life."

Sometimes Bernice took her young friend into the parlor, instructing her on makeup secrets she had learned as a model.

"We had a rare intimate [relationship]," Temple explained. "There were times that she told me that I was the daughter she never had. She taught me a lot about grace . . . about being elegant and class."

One night, Bernice became emotional as she spoke about her tragic childhood, and being raised in an orphanage with her sister.

"She was proud that she had survived such a horrific [past]," said Hayes, "and that was part of her story. She would say, 'Temple, anyone can amount to anything . . . look at me.'"

Bernice also voiced her strong disapproval of her son's marriage.

"She didn't like Narcy from the beginning," said Temple. "It haunted her . . . and she wondered what her son had gotten involved in. I think she felt that Ben had married down on the ladder. She didn't feel she was authentic."

There were times when Bernice became so upset that she refused even to speak Narcy's name.

"I remember her saying several times," said Hayes, "'The woman that my son knows whose name I will not speak out loud.' I'd go, 'Bernice. Goodness.' And we'd kind of laugh and she'd give me a little smirky smile."

In May 1993, Ben Novack Jr. became front-page news in Pittsburgh, Pennsylvania, after pulling out of three major conventions when he couldn't get his own way. Several months earlier, Novack had insisted that Amway be allowed to sell clothing and grooming products to its own operatives at the upcoming meetings. But as the convention center was publicly funded, city law dictated that anything available at retail stores could not be sold there.

In the past the rule had been waived for Amway, but now the Downtown Merchants' Association had taken on Ben Novack Jr., and were refusing to make an exception.

The *Pittsburgh Post-Gazette* weighed in with an editorial, labeling the president of Convention Concepts Unlimited as "difficult," but warning that upsetting him could damage the city financially.

"Ben Novack Jr., of Miami," read the April 28 editorial, "has done a lot of complaining about food quality and service at the center, as well as treatment from Pittsburgh Hotels. As difficult a customer as Mr. Novack has been to satisfy, Pittsburgh doesn't want to risk . . . developing a reputation for being uncooperative in the sales area."

A month later, when the Public Auditorium Authority banned Amway sales in the convention center, Novack pulled the plug on three major meetings.

"The way the deal has gone down," said the *Post-Gazette*, "the Pittsburgh area is the big loser."

Although Ben Novack Jr. loved making money, he enjoyed wielding power even more, just as his father had done.

"Ben Novack wanted to live life like his father," said David Mann, a former Sheraton Birmingham, Alabama, conventions manager, who often worked with Novack in the 1990s.

According to Mann, Ben Novack Jr. would constantly be popping pills during conventions to stay awake. Before he even checked into his hotel, he would send over a four-page list of demands that had to be complied with. "When he arrived in your hotel on Thursday," said Mann, "till the time he departed on Monday, he literally took over your hotel."

One time, Novack had ordered Mann to call his general manager at home at 2:00 A.M., complaining that he couldn't get a tunafish sandwich. But few dared ever challenge him, as his Amway conventions generated so much business.

At the end of every convention, Ben Jr. and Narcy held court in their hotel suite, paying off the hotel management.

"He always settled with his black American Express card," said Mack Gatley. "His bill paying was well known in the industry. He would argue about little things, but he paid his bills."

Then he and Narcy would leave town with thousands of dollars in cash stuffed into a suitcase, moving on to the next convention.

Eventually, Ben Novack Jr.'s rude and aggressive behavior caught up with him. He was blackballed by at least one hotel chain, because he was so rude to the staff. He also fell out with the American-based Amway families because of his bad attitude.

Some believe that Narcy saved his business, by helping him forge a closer relationship with the Latin American and Hispanic Amway families, who picked up the slack.

"Allegedly, he had a break with some of those U.S. families," said Gatley. "Maybe they didn't like [his] demeanor. But at the end of the day he apparently did get a hook into the Hispanic Amway business, and that's what he was doing from a certain point forward."

From then on, Ben Jr. and Narcy, who had been promoted to registration manager, would work closely on Amway's international conventions.

"Narcy was important because of the language barrier," said Gatley, "because [Ben] couldn't speak Spanish. We would assume that her involvement was to bridge that language barrier . . . help him chase this business and bring it into the fold."

In May 1993 the Miami Beach Police Department asked Officer Ben Novack Jr. to fill in a new personal history questionnaire, as it had lost his original one. The long-serving volunteer replied with a sarcastic memo to his female superior, Detective Lee Ann Gutierrez.

Lee Ann, in accordance with your memo . . . requesting that I fill out a new Personal History Questionnaire to replace the two previous editions that I filled out and which now for some reason can not be located, I am pleased to do one better.

I am happy to report that my filing system seems to be a little bit more intact. I did keep photostatic copies of both the original "Applicant Questionnaire" that I filled out when applying for the Auxiliary Police Position back on February 8, 1974 (19 years ago) and the second Personal History Questionnaire that I filled out when converting to fully sworn (Reserve) Status on May 8, 1983 (10 year [sic] ago).

Since I am not applying for a new position at this time I am sure that these will serve a more appropriate role in returning my file to its original complete status.

Please let me know if you need anything else. Ofc. Ben Novack Jr.

Twenty-Three

2501 DEL MAR PLACE

I n early 1994, Ben and Narcy Novack moved to Fort Lauderdale to be closer to Ben's aging mother. Narcy arrived first, on a reconnaissance mission to scout out suitable properties on the water, ones with mooring facilities for Ben's yachts.

She found a spacious two-story, six-bedroom house on sale for $825,000 in the exclusive Seven Islands development and immediately put in a bid. Several days later, her husband arrived to vet 2501 Del Mar Place, before arranging a $625,000 mortgage.

Soon after moving in, they discovered that the six-thousand-square-foot house was infested with termites, and would require expensive treatment to be rendered habitable.

"Bernice had a fit," recalled Estelle Fernandez. "She said they paid over a million dollars, so you'd think they would have known about [termites] before. She said Narcy had wasted the money."

Then Ben Jr. brought in Joe Gandy to organize a construction crew to renovate the new house from top to bottom.

"When he moved to Lauderdale and bought the big house," said Gandy, "we had four or five guys working sixteen to eighteen hours a day, seven days a week on it."

Novack also had Charlie Seraydar plan the secret locations for his various safes, along with full outside video surveillance.

"Security was a big factor in his mind," said Seraydar. "All of that stuff was installed at my direction."

Two years later the Novacks bought two adjoining lots in Del Mar Place, taking out a second $400,000 mortgage. They converted a large house on one of the lots into business offices for Ben Jr.'s flourishing Convention Concepts Unlimited business.

Money was no object as Joe Gandy and his team transformed 2501 Del Mar Place into Ben Novack Jr.'s exclusive compound, complete with its own street sign reading, "Novack Drive." They built a state-of-the-art gym and weight room for Narcy, and an enormous fish pool in the backyard behind the new office. By the side of it was a large mermaid statue that had once adorned the pool at the Fontainebleau.

"They put pink quartz stones around the edge of the pool, so it looked very glamorous," remembered Estelle Fernandez. "There was a little bridge to walk over."

Ben Jr.'s fifty-foot Cary boat, *White Lightning*, was now moored behind the house, near a newly constructed seawall. He started taking her on short trips up and down the Intracoastal Waterway.

"It was a classy neighborhood," said Charlie Seraydar, "so he could put his shiny boat out there."

Gandy also constructed a large storage area behind one of the houses, to store Ben's growing collection of antique cars. Ben had also begun amassing old Coca-Cola collectibles, in honor of his mother, who had once modeled for the company.

"He was a Coca-Cola freak," said Gandy, "Anything Coca-Cola. He had a collection that you could not imagine. It was just unbelievable."

Narcy now started going on spending sprees, buying hundreds of pairs of designer shoes, many of which she never even wore. Always frugal, Bernice strongly disapproved of her daughter-in-law's excesses, but didn't dare complain to Ben.

"The woman was a tremendous spendthrift," said Maxine Fiel. "Her house looked like a shoe store. Coming from a dirt-poor country in Central America, and to suddenly have all this money. She just bought everything. It bothered my sister a lot, but she didn't want to interfere as she wanted to see her son."

Approaching forty, Ben Novack Jr. was a multimillionaire, boasting on his new company Web site that his business generated $50 million a year. Yet he still counted every cent.

"He had more money than God," said Joe Gandy, "but he was stingy. He would pay me, but we'd argue a little bit about the bill first."

Novack now started giving his trusted right-hand man other tasks besides supervising construction and helping with his conventions. Ben had always led a secret life, having several mistresses around town to be available at his beck and call. Now he had Gandy set them up in apartments, and take care of all their bills.

"He always had two or three women," Gandy explained. "I knew everything. I had to pay every bill, because he wouldn't give them cash. I would go pay the condo bills and the furniture bills, or whatever they would need. The groceries and everything, I took care of. That became my main job."

Soon after moving into 2501 Del Mar Place, Ben Jr. and Narcy Novack met their neighbor Robert Hodges, also known as Prince Mongo. The colorful eccentric had known the Brazilian family who had previously owned the Novacks' house, and he now started socializing with Ben and Narcy.

"Ben didn't have many friends," recalled Mongo. "He was kind of sarcastic in his own way. He was deliberately insulting . . . an arrogant person."

As Mongo got to know his new neighbor over cookouts and sailing trips, he realized that there was a good side to Ben that Novack rarely let people see.

"I understood him," said Mongo. "Under that skin he was a nice person, and I didn't really care what he was. He'd fly off sometimes and say, 'Hell . . . you're an idiot.' Whatever. That's okay. Everybody's an idiot once in a while."

Narcy often invited Mongo over to their house for a cookout, where they would be joined by Ben.

"Narcy and I became very close," said Mongo, "I would go to the house all the time to visit, and Narcy would cook me a bag of popcorn and some dried fruit."

Narcy had now reinvented her past, as befitting her new social position. She now claimed to have been the pampered daughter of a rich Ecuadorian family before moving to New York and becoming a successful fashion designer.

"She said she was wealthy when she met Ben," said Mongo. "She claimed that her father was a shrimp farmer and [her family] were very wealthy people. That she had a big business in New York and was a designer at a clothes manufacturer in the garment section."

After Ben Novack Jr. opened up his new offices next to the house, his mother came to work for him as office manager. (Ben had also hired a young man named Matt Briggs, along with several freelancers, to help him run conventions.) He gave her the title of vice president of Novack Enterprises. Every morning, Bernice Novack drove seven miles to the office, putting in a full day's work before going home.

Now in her mid-seventies, Bernice Novack looked far younger. She had had three facelifts and her teeth capped, and her striking red hair was always perfectly styled.

Many of her friends could not believe that she had gone back to work, her first job since being a Conover Girl more than half a century earlier.

When Estelle Fernandez questioned her about it, Bernice said it gave her access to her son.

"She wanted to be able to see Ben," said Fernandez. "Ben was very rude to his mother. He never called her 'mother'; he called her 'Bernice.' But Bernice loved him and that was her son. So by working, she got to see him."

One Passover Bernice invited Estelle Fernandez and her husband to a friend's Seder. Bernice was there with George Rodriguez, with whom she'd remained close friends. Ben Jr. and Narcy also attended.

"It was the first time I met Benji," said Fernandez. "I had never seen eyes like that. They were so dark. He had a lot of black hair and a black beard. He looked like a terrorist. He really did, and just looking at you, you'd be frightened."

On the rare occasions Estelle saw Ben Jr., she found him cold and unfeeling.

"He was extremely emotionless," she said. "[Bernice] would say it's very hard. She's all by herself and her son is not a touchy-type person. He has no emotions toward her. She said, 'I know he loves me, but he doesn't tell me.'"

In the late 1990s, Ben Novack Jr. started living big. He now ran approximately sixty conventions a year all over the world, and the money was pouring in.

He bought an island in the Bahamas, as well as a half-share in a Citation II private jet, with his friend Jerry Calhoun, who had made millions renting his customized coaches out to touring rock bands.

"They shared the expenses," said Mongo, who was part of their circle, "like a lot of people do that own jets. And their friendship developed from there into the partnership."

But Novack was so rude to his pilots that they refused to fly him anywhere.

"Pilots wouldn't fly the man, because his attitude got so bad," said Joe Gandy. "He had to fly commercial, although he owned his own jet."

Gandy, who now spent most of his time with Ben Jr. and Narcy, either at conventions or at their house, was in a perfect position to observe their increasingly hostile relationship.

"I was there everyday with them," he said. "In the beginning [Narcy] was decent. She was normal. But she then turned into [being] just like him. An asshole."

Later, Narcy would claim that she and Ben liked kinky sex, enjoying

S&M and heavy bondage. Most of their sexual relations involved Ben being tied up or restrained in handcuffs. He was also obsessed with amputee pornography, a taste he'd developed during his childhood at the Fontainebleau, after photographing some visiting handicapped children.

Narcy always suspected that Ben was cheating on her, and was constantly trying to catch him out.

"She was on his ass twenty-four hours a day," said Gandy. "He couldn't take a shit without her following him. He'd try and go outside and talk on the phone, but he couldn't because of her. He had phones hidden everywhere. It was crazy."

Whenever she confronted him with her suspicions, it led to violent arguments.

"They would have these horrific fights," recalled Prince Mongo, "and they were famous for tearing up the bathroom. I would see Gandy in the hardware store buying fifteen-hundred-dollar gold-plated fixtures. I'd say, 'Gee what are you building over there?' He'd say, 'Well, they got into a fight yesterday and they tore the bathroom to smithereens.' It was a wild thing, but that's what they'd do."

After one particularly bad fight, Mongo saw Narcy with a black eye, and heavy bruises to her face. "Ben would sometimes hit her," he said. "And she was ashamed. I've never heard her say anything bad about Ben, other than he hit on her. She was unhappy a lot of the time, and she hated it."

Joe Gandy witnessed numerous arguments over the years. "They battled every which way there is," he said. "They chased each other with cars down the street. You wouldn't believe it."

Twenty-Four

PARANOIA

In 1999, Ben Novack Jr. launched an ambitious new Convention Concepts Unlimited Web site touting his experience at his father's Fontainebleau hotel. He had developed a new company logo showing a little figure standing beside a check-in desk with the motto "CONTACT THE EXPERTS—That's Us!"

"Your convention," the site's homepage stated, "whether a once-a-year meeting for a few or multiple events for a few thousand, is very important to you, so why take chances?"

The company president claimed that his team of "hotel-trained negotiators and coordinators" had more than seventy-five years combined experience and a proven track record. The company also claimed to organize sixty events a year, generating $50 million.

"For over twenty years we have utilized this expertise," the site continued, "combining our talents to conduct events of all sizes, from California to Maine, Washington to Florida, as well as Hawaii, Canada, Mexico, the Caribbean and Central and South America."

"[Ben Novack Jr.] did meetings in so many different places," said Mark Gatley, who was now in charge of the Broward Convention Center in Fort Lauderdale. "He was extremely busy and knew all the ins and outs. You would marvel at his business acumen . . . and then hold your breath and wonder where he was going to find fault with what you were doing."

In July 1999, Ben Novack Jr.'s longtime friend Jim Scarberry was appointed the police chief of Hollywood, Florida. And Ben viewed this as an opportunity to set up his own reserve program.

"It was closer to his Fort Lauderdale home than Miami Beach," said Scarberry, who is now retired and runs his own private investigation agency. "But he also wanted to be in charge of the reserve program and have the take-home Hollywood [police] car."

To pitch the idea, Novack invited Scarberry and his wife to his home for dinner. It was the first time they had met Narcy Novack.

"She was dressed to the nines," recalled Scarberry, "with the extreme tightest clothing you could get. Eventually we heard she was a former stripper, which fit . . . the way she dressed."

Over the next few months, Ben Jr. lobbied hard for his own reserve program and police car. "But it wasn't a priority on my list to get Benji in the reserve program in Hollywood," said Scarberry. "I had so many other things going on at the time."

That same summer, seventy-eight-year-old Bernice Novack became convinced that Narcy was trying to poison her. She told her best friend, Estelle Fernandez, that her daughter-in-law practiced voodoo and that her own life was in danger.

"They all worked in this little area," Estelle explained, "but not Narcy, who seldom worked there. One day Bernice put her bottle of water in her little refrigerator, and when she went to drink it she [thought] it tasted funny. She drank it anyway."

A few hours later, when she got home, Bernice's throat swelled up and she could hardly swallow. A lifelong asthma sufferer, she thought she was going to die.

Bernice also told her friend how Narcy had often boasted of using voodoo spells against people she didn't like, and now felt that she was the target.

"Narcy did practice voodoo," said Fernandez. "She made dolls and she'd stick pins in them. She also grew a lot of herbs in her front yard . . . some of them boiled down could be a little bit poisonous. So Bernice knew she couldn't eat anything from her. You couldn't trust her."

Bernice confided her fears about Narcy to others.

"She called me up," recalled her sister, "and said, 'Maxine, I'm so deathly sick,' I said, 'What happened?' She said, 'Well, I got up and wasn't feeling well, so Narcy brought me a glass of water. After that my jaw closed and I couldn't speak.' She said it was the most awful feeling. She couldn't swallow."

Joe Gandy never ate anything cooked by Narcy, as he suspected she had tried to poison Ben, too. "A couple of times Ben went to the hospital from eating her food," he said. "It was a dangerous fucking situation."

On Labor Day, Ben Novack Jr. invited Prince Mongo to the annual Kruse International Classic Car Auction held in Auburn, Indiana, as he wanted to buy a rare 1970 Jaguar XKE Convertible and a 1957 Thunderbird. Mongo, who was staying at his second home near Memphis, Tennessee, declined, not wanting to leave his pet Rottweiler alone.

Ben insisted he come, offering to remove the backseat in his private plane to accommodate the large dog.

"I said if you do that, you have a passenger," said Mongo. "So Ben says, 'Okay.'"

The Thursday before Labor Day, Ben and Narcy flew in their private plane to Millington, Tennessee, to collect Mongo and his pet. They then flew on to the Indiana auction. After they landed, as arranged by their friend Jerry Mohoney, a coach picked them up and took them to their hotel.

At the auction, Mohoney let them use Willie Nelson's original fitted coach, which he was selling, as their "relief zone." "We could go there and use the restroom on the bus," said Mongo. "There were Cokes, drinks, and food [and] we could eat on the bus."

On Saturday, Ben Jr. bought the E-Type Jaguar he wanted, ordering his pilot Doug to fly back to Fort Lauderdale to collect the money for it.

"So Bernice had to go to Ben's lock-up box to get the money for Doug," said Mongo. "[Ben] actually sent Doug home two times, because he bought two cars and he didn't get [enough] money."

In the late 1990s, Ben Novack Jr. got serious about his Batman memorabilia, setting his sights on building up a world-class collection. Up to now he had quietly bought up the pieces on eBay, occasionally visiting comic book conventions. He now knew all the major dealers in Batman comics, toys, and other related items, but had been careful not to let them know his identity or long-term intentions, until he was ready.

"Guys that move in the circles that Ben moved in are usually covert," explained Chicago-based Batman dealer Scot Fleming, "until they get a trust built up with a dealer. So I was probably selling things to Ben for years and not knowing it."

Around the millennium, Novack finally revealed himself, and began cultivating relationships with all the major dealers of Batman memorabilia worldwide.

"Ben was not around in any shape or form before the millennium," said England's top Batman dealer, Ed Kelly. "Ben collected all sorts of things. He was a collectorholic."

Once he had unmasked, Novack started buying anything and everything relating to the world of Batman. He was especially interested in items from the 1960s *Batman* TV series, which he had loved as a young boy.

"Ben collected all over the mark," said Fleming, "but he really, really liked the vintage stuff. So anything that was tied into the older-looking style—the sixties—that's mostly what he bought from me."

Every morning, boxes and boxes of Batman stuff started arriving at 2501 Del Mar Place, and it was Joe Gandy's job to store them.

"The Batman stuff overruled the house," he recalled. "Every morning there were boxes of Batman toys on the front porch ten foot tall. They were from all the different places that had Batman stores. It didn't matter what it was—Batman pogo sticks or Batman basketball. Everything you could think of for Batman."

Soon the house became so crowded with boxes of Batman stuff that Gandy rented out a large warehouse to store everything. Over the next few years, there would be another four such warehouses needed.

"Every month we had to get a Ryder truck," he said, "and take it all to the warehouse."

Scot Fleming estimates that Ben Novack Jr. was now spending up to $100,000 a year building his collection. He concentrated on the rarest, most-sought-after Batman comics and other memorabilia. He even had Joe Gandy build a Batman museum in his house, to exhibit his finest pieces.

Just as he had done in the convention business, Ben Novack Jr. now applied his aggressive business methods to collecting—and soon gained a bad reputation.

"Ben considered himself part of a tiny group of guys [who] outbid each other," said Fleming. "And there was a friendly competition that was probably not so friendly at times. A lot of guys had issues with Ben."

Ben Novack Jr.'s Batman collection was as important to him as the Fontainebleau Hotel had been to his father. And he approached it with the same obsessive determination and single-mindedness. Within a couple of years he was on his way to achieving his dream.

"Ben was one of the top five Batman collectors of the world," said Fleming. "It's a very small group of people. They all know each other. They're all extremely upscale people with a lot of disposable income. As far as dealers go, we always refer to them as "shoppers" and not "collectors.""

Novack frequently called his favorite dealers from airports, while in transit to or from a convention. He often seemed lonely, wanting to chat about important new Batman items coming up for sale.

"I spoke to him tons on the phone," said Kelly, who, in England, was five hours ahead of Ben. "He used to phone me when he was on a flight going to conventions, mainly because he was flying at odd times and I used to keep very odd hours. It was mainly related to Batman collecting, because fanatics will only talk about the sort of things that interest them."

On one occasion, Scot Fleming asked Ben why he had started his Batman collection, but Novack was strangely evasive. "It's very nostalgic for a lot of these guys," said Fleming, "'When I was four my Dad and I watched the show,' or 'I had comic books.' I have to assume it was nostalgic for Ben, because of the theme of most of the stuff he bought. But he never shared any of that."

In May 2001, after twenty-six years as a Miami Beach Police reservist, Ben Novack Jr. underwent a forty-hour recertification course at the Miami Dade Community College. He was teamed up with his good friend Officer Pete Matthews, who was in the same class.

Now nearing retirement, Matthews, who had known Ben Jr. since he was a child, immediately noticed how "despondent" he appeared to be. One day over lunch, he asked him what was wrong.

"He said [Narcy] had been unfaithful," recalled Matthews. "She had [had] a relationship and he had found out about it. It was devastating, but he was working through it."

Matthews asked if he and Narcy were seeing a marriage counselor, but Novack said no.

After observing his male chauvinism over the years, Matthews had never seen Ben Jr. show the slightest emotion over any woman before.

"I don't know the sequence of events," Matthews said. "Thinking back, it's unusual, because the kid that I knew would have just said, 'Forget about it.' So I knew he was troubled by her [infidelity]."

Over the next few months, Ben and Narcy Novack's relationship spiraled downward. Although they put on a good face at conventions, they were constantly bickering. And their arguments behind closed doors were getting increasingly more violent.

August 16, 2001, was their tenth wedding anniversary, but there was little to celebrate. Ben Jr. now wanted out of the marriage, as he felt it was threatening his business. He was also still reeling from the shock of discovering that Narcy had been unfaithful, even though he himself kept several mistresses.

"He had all the women you could imagine," said Joe Gandy. "With that kind of money, you can imagine the women he had, and every one of them was there for money. There was no love. Narcy, too, you know. She was a titty dancer when he met her over in the strip club."

Narcy had long grown accustomed to her husband's extravagantly wealthy lifestyle, and to having everything she desired. She loved the good life and had no intention of ever losing it.

"Narcy wanted the red carpet in front of her feet," said Joe Gandy. "She thought she was a Novack, just like Ben, who was a big name with a lot of power."

Narcy was well aware that under the 1991 prenuptial agreement she had signed, even though the marriage had now survived a decade, she would still receive only $65,000 plus expenses were she and Ben to divorce. It appeared she was determined to leave with far more than that.

In January 2002, Miami Beach's prestigious *Ocean Drive* magazine carried a lavish fifteen-page salute to the glory days of the Fontainebleau hotel. Entitled "Swinging at the Fontainebleau—The Rat Pack, the Mob, and Dazzling Dames," the article had the full cooperation of Bernice Novack, who had even made available select photographs from her private collection.

Among the colorful photos was one of Ben Novack Sr. with Jerry Lewis, one of him with Irving Berlin, and one of a glamorous Bernice at a Fontainebleau grand ball with Joan Crawford. In another treasured shot, the Novacks share a joke with Frank Sinatra and Walter Winchell. On a more sinister note, one photo shows Ben Sr. and Bernice posing with powerful Chicago Mob boss Sam Giancana at his daughter Antoinette's wedding.

The seventy-nine-year-old former First Lady of the Fontainebleau was interviewed for the article, still insisting that Morris Lapidus, who had died a year earlier, had had nothing to do with designing the Fontainebleau.

"Ben designed the Fontainebleau while sitting on the toilet," she said defiantly.

When the article was published, Bernice was so delighted that she handed out signed copies to her closest friends. She also visited the Fontainebleau for the first time in many years.

"She went in, and everybody remembered her," said Estelle Fernandez, who accompanied her that day. "And she said hello to everyone. 'Oh, you're still working. I'm glad.' They all still loved her."

TWENTY-FIVE

"I CAN HAVE YOU KILLED ANYTIME I WANT"

On Saturday, June 8, 2002, Ben and Narcy Novack went out to dinner at a Mexican restaurant and then went home and retired to bed. At 1:00 A.M. on Sunday, three armed men suddenly burst into their bedroom. As Ben went for the Smith & Wesson handgun he always kept by the bed, he heard Narcy shout out, "Look out! He has a gun on his nightstand."

He was then pinned to the bed by one of the men, while another put a pillow over his face, trying to asphyxiate him. The third snatched his gun, hitting him hard across his head with it. His arms were then shackled in front of him with his own police handcuffs and he was blindfolded with a surgical eye patch.

As Narcy left to disable their elaborate house alarm system, Ben was tied to the heavy metal frame of a leather chair with thick ropes. Narcy then threatened to cut off Ben's penis and throw it in the canal behind their home. She was referring to what Lorena Bobbitt (who had also been born in Equador) had done to her husband John.

The men then threatened to kill him if he spoke or even moved. He was hit over the head again with his own gun, to make the point.

Over the next twenty-five hours, while Ben was held in the bedroom at gunpoint, Narcy Novack ransacked the house. She seized

$370,000 in cash kept in a safe under the stairs, as well as taking Novack family heirlooms, jewelry, antiques, firearms, important business documents, items of Batman memorabilia, and various firearms. She also cleared her closets, packing up all her clothes and her hundreds of pairs of designer shoes, and gathered together her toiletries and perfumes.

Helplessly bound to a chair hour after hour, Ben Novack Jr. was able to peer under his blindfold and see his attackers, who took turns guarding him. During the attack, he heard Narcy make several phone calls to an ex-boyfriend from the Follies strip club named Leo, who had just gotten out of jail. He also overheard one of the attackers mention the name of a well-known organized crime boss whom they appeared to be working for.

Periodically, he was allowed to relieve himself in a disposable urinal to the side of the chair.

At 7:00 P.M. on Sunday evening—eighteen hours into his ordeal—he heard Narcy call her yoga teacher, Rada Sevakananda, who also looked after their neighbors' pet dogs. She asked her to come straight over to help pack up some boxes, which she was taking to a warehouse.

Soon afterward, Novack heard the woman arrive and the sound of boxes being packed and sealed with a tape gun. Sometime later he heard the men loading boxes into a diesel truck parked outside.

Finally, as Narcy removed Ben's blindfold, he pleaded with her to release him. She said she would call a neighbor in a few minutes to do so.

Then she looked her husband straight in the face and told him, "If I can't have you, then no one will have you. The men that helped me . . . will come back and finish the job. I can have you killed anytime I want . . . you're not dead now because I stopped them."

At around 2:30 A.M. Monday morning, Prince Mongo, who was in Memphis, Tennessee, received a frantic call from Rada. After calming down, she said Narcy had called an hour earlier asking her to return to the Novack house to move some furniture out of the second-floor hallway, so the maid wouldn't throw it away.

When Rada pointed out that it was the middle of the night, Narcy insisted it must be done immediately.

"So Rada went over," said Mongo, "and when she went upstairs, the bedroom door was open. Ben was tied up by the door with duct tape, looking at Rada. She went ballistic. She didn't know what to do. And Ben was shaking his head and his eyes were bulging."

After Rada pulled the tape off his mouth, Novack told her to cut the rope tying him to the chair. Once he was free, he telephoned his mother, asking her to drive over immediately. He then begged Rada not to call the police, saying the men would come back and kill him if she did.

Rada waited until Bernice Novack arrived before fleeing the house and calling Mongo.

The first person Ben Novack Jr. called after being set free was his eighty-year-old mother. Then he called Charlie Seraydar.

"He tells me that he's just been robbed in a home invasion robbery," remembered Seraydar. "And he is scared out of his fucking mind. He's screaming, 'They stole my money! They stole $440,000!'"

Seraydar told him to calm down and call the police. When Novack said he could not, the former Miami Beach cop asked why. "He said, 'I think my wife was involved,'" said Seraydar. "I said, 'Get the fuck out of here. What makes you think that?'"

"He goes, 'Well, when the guys busted through the bedroom door, she said, 'Look out, he has a gun on his nightstand.' I go, 'You've got to be kidding me.'"

Seraydar called a retired cop friend of his called Fred Walder, asking him to go straight over to 2501 Del Mar Place and give Ben a gun to protect himself.

At 1:59 A.M. on Monday, while waiting for his mother to arrive, Ben Novack Jr. called the Fort Lauderdale Police dispatcher, to report the incident. He informed her that he was an officer with the Miami Beach Police Department. The dispatcher said someone would get back to him.

"He stated his wife came into the residence with 3 armed men," read the official report, "robbed him and left him tied for approximately 25 hours."

Then Novack called Hollywood police chief Jim Scarberry, asking what to do next, without mentioning Narcy's involvement.

"He was very scared," said Scarberry. "He said he had been a victim of a home invasion robbery. That the people had told him not to call the cops or they'd come back and kill him. He didn't want a bunch of Fort Lauderdale cops in uniforms and cars rushing to his house."

Novack asked Scarberry to use his contacts with Fort Lauderdale Police to explain the situation called with the utmost discretion.

"He assured me the bad guys had left," said Scarberry, "and that there was no safety issue for the cops. So I kind of coordinated that through our detective bureau."

Soon afterward, Sergeant Salters of the Fort Lauderdale Police Department called Ben Novack Jr. to follow up on his complaint. In the meantime, Bernice Novack had arrived, and the officer could hear her talking in the background.

"[He] refused to allow a marked unit to respond to his residence," said Salters. "While I was speaking with him I could hear him [discuss] the return of his money."

Novack told him that the men responsible for the home invasion were still watching his house, and would know if police responded.

Salter said, "I explained to him that we did not have any detectives in unmarked cars working at this hour that could respond to his location. I asked if I could call him back, and he agreed."

A few minutes later, Sergeant Salters received a call from Police Chief Scarberry, who had been referred by Dispatch. Scarberry informed Salters that Novack's father had once owned the famous Fontainebleau hotel, adding that he had known Ben Jr. for years.

"I explained to Chief Scarberry the dilemma Mr. Novak [sic] has placed us in," Salters later wrote in his report, "when he is making these allegations and does not want a marked unit to respond. I informed him I would offer Mr. Novak [sic] the option of making his report via landline."

After the call, Sergeant Salters called the Miami Beach Police Department, verifying that Novack was a reserve officer and known to them. Then he instructed an Officer Johnson to call Ben Novack Jr. and take his statement.

"Ben advised [that] his wife Narcy [had] orchestrated the robbery, with the unknown males," Officer Johnson later wrote in his official report on what the police referred to as a "suspicious incident."

Novack then gave the officer a detailed account of his twenty-five-hour ordeal, calling it "well organized."

"The suspects . . . took turns guarding him," he wrote, "while removing jewelry, documents and money and various other items. He claims total loss is approximately a million dollars."

Officer Johnson reported Ben's claim that the home invaders had threatened to kill him if he even spoke or made a move, and that periodically he was hit on the head with a gun.

"When the suspects were leaving," Johnson wrote, "Ben plead for his life and requested to his wife to be released. Ben claims Narcy called a neighbor to come over in 10 minutes to help her move some items. When she came over she found Ben tied up."

The officer also reported that Novack had refused any medical treatment for cuts on his mouth and badly bruised arms, saying there would not be much forensic evidence to be found. He also insisted that no mention be made of the incident over the police radio, in case his assailants were listening.

"[He] urged that forensics cannot respond," Johnson reported, "because no marked vehicles can be observed for fear that his life could still be in danger. He claims someone is still watching his property."

Powerless to do anything while Novack was refusing to allow officers to come to the house, Officer Johnson could only give him a case number for any subsequent investigation.

"Due to Ben's request for police not to respond at his home," Johnson wrote, "I have no physical observation to substantiate his claim as to the events that occurred other than the information taken by phone."

TWENTY-SIX

FALLOUT

At 8:00 A.M. on Monday, Detective Steve Palazzo of Fort Lauderdale Police Department's Violent Crimes and Robbery Division began his shift. As soon as he walked into police headquarters, his superior, Sergeant Patrick French, assigned him to the Ben Novack Jr. home invasion, handing him a copy of Salters's report.

"Ben had refused to allow any officers or marked patrol cars to come to his house," said now-retired detective Palazzo. "So I guess it was his choice to wait until a detective was available."

Detective Palazzo called Novack, who immediately informed him that he was a Miami Beach Reserve Police officer with almost thirty years' experience. He also stated that he was "close personal friends" with several police chiefs and "very well connected" in the local business community.

"He insisted that something should be done immediately to locate and arrest his wife," Detective Palazzo later wrote in his report. "He insisted that police in plainclothes and unmarked vehicles should respond to his residence but that we must not make our presence known to anyone in the area as the culprits may still be watching his house."

At 10:00 A.M., Detective Palazzo and Sergeant French drove up outside 2501 Del Mar Place in an unmarked police car. A disheveled Ben Novack Jr. came to the front door and let then in. He then brought them into a small room, where his elderly mother was waiting.

Palazzo immediately noticed that Novack had cut lips and bruising to his face. There were also red marks on his wrists.

"He had been bound," said Palazzo, "there was no question about it. And he had been struck in the face. That was obvious."

Novack pointed to a floor safe, which was open and empty. Then he led the detectives upstairs to the master bedroom, as his mother followed.

"We noted a reclining chair," Palazzo wrote later, "surrounded by ropes and binding items . . . a pair of handcuffs hanging from the left side of the chair."

Although it was daylight, the curtains were closed, bathing the bedroom in darkness. There was a small table with food on it next to the reclining chair, and a stool behind that.

Novack said the pillows and top bed sheet had been taken, and he showed them Narcy's large bedroom closet, which was bare except for some shoeboxes and hangers.

"She obviously took a lot of her belongings," Palazzo noted. "All her clothes were gone, but his stuff was all still there."

Novack then brought them into the en suite bathroom, pointing out that Narcy's marble countertop to the left of the faucet was bare, while Ben's side was full of his toiletries.

They then went into a room next door, which was being used as an office. Inside were several metal file cabinets, with drawers missing.

"He told us that these cabinets contained all of the files and documents for his business," Palazzo wrote. "He [had] had $440,000.00 in cash in the safe which was company funds [and] she had no rights to the money."

When the detective asked if Novack had documents to prove the money had existed, Novack said no, as it was his company's petty cash.

"Novack explained that his father was a former owner of the Fountain Blue [sic] Hotel in Miami," Palazzo wrote. "His father is deceased."

Novack then explained the setup of his company, saying he was the

CEO and his mother the vice president. "His wife is not a corporate partner," Palazzo wrote, "and has no official standing in the company, but does work with him for the business. He stated that she has no legal rights to take the documents. That she had no rights to the money."

Then, for the first time since they arrived, Bernice Novack spoke, confirming that everything her son had said was true.

"Bernice Novack stated that her son and Narcy have had ongoing problems for years," Palazzo wrote, "[and] Narcy has a strong dislike for her."

Then Bernice suddenly claimed that her daughter-in-law had tried to poison her the previous Saturday afternoon, just hours before the home invasion. She said she and Narcy had both been working in the company offices in the building next door, and she had been drinking out of a plastic water bottle. After Narcy had left, Bernice said she drank some water and had "a burning feeling in her mouth."

"Within hours," the detective wrote, "her entire mouth was numb. She produced that water bottle which had a small amount of liquid in it. She stated that she is certain that she was poisoned and her mouth is still numb."

Detective Palazzo advised Bernice to go straight to the hospital for treatment, and get her blood tested. He then took the bottle into evidence, in case anything was later discovered in a blood analysis.

Ben Novack Jr. then told detectives that early Sunday evening, while being held hostage, he heard his wife call their friend Rada. Although his bedroom door had been closed, he later heard the Indian lady downstairs for a long time. As the men had left the house several hours earlier, only he, Narcy, and Rada remained.

"I asked why he chose not to call out to [her]," Palazzo wrote, "and he stated that he was fearful that Narcy would harm him [and] that he was still bound to the chair."

Then Detective Palazzo called headquarters, requesting that Narcy's name and birth date be run through the police computer, for her vehicle license plate number. Once that was obtained, he issued a county-wide all-points bulletin for her car to be stopped immediately so she could be brought in for questioning.

"During this time," Palazzo wrote, "Ben Novack was very busy on the telephones conducting his business. The phone seemed to ring constantly."

The detective asked if Novack had a recording device, in case Narcy telephoned, and Novack showed him a special phone with a microcassette built into it.

Then, despite Novack's protests, Palazzo summoned Detective Carol Coval, a forensic technician, to the house to process the crime scene.

While they were waiting for her to arrive, Narcy Novack called. Ben turned on the cassette recorder before answering.

"After the call," the detective wrote, "Ben Novack played the tape recording for me. The entire recorded conversation seemed to deal with Ben trying to get Narcy to return his property. He repeatedly talked about the company records and files as well as the missing money from the safe. Narcy disputed the amount."

The detective heard the tape only once, as Ben refused to let him take it, saying it was the only blank tape he had. But he did agree to keep recording Narcy's calls, and gather evidence against her.

Then Palazzo asked why Novack hadn't asked his wife about the savage attack or about being held hostage for a day. He explained that this evidence would be vital in proving Novack's serious allegations against Narcy.

"He told me that he was unaware of that," said the detective, "and would try to get more on the next call."

At 11:45 A.M., Detective Carol Coval arrived and started photographing and processing the alleged crime scene. Detective Palazzo brought her upstairs to the master bedroom, where she saw the tan leather chair in the middle of the room, which Novack claimed to have been bound to during his ordeal.

"Connected to the bottom of the metal frame," Detective Coval later reported, "was a pair of handcuffs hanging down. Draped over, through and around the arms and back of the chair were numerous Terrence cloth strips of material and cloth type white ropes. Lying on the floor next to the chair was a box with a disposable urinal."

After photographing the bedroom and bathroom with 35 mm color film, the forensic technician processed the upstairs rooms for fingerprints, finding just one partial latent print on a small refrigerator in the bedroom. They then went downstairs and into Ben Novack Jr.'s Batman museum.

"That was an office with Batman collectables [*sic*] covering every square inch, both on the floors and walls," Detective Coval observed. "A floor safe had been uncovered and the carpeting was pulled away."

Then Novack handed Coval a plastic green tape dispenser that he told her "they" had used to seal the packing boxes, and a pair of latex gloves he said he had found in the house.

Finally, Coval photographed the injuries to Novack's lips, face, and wrists, before returning to police headquarters with Detective Palazzo.

While Fort Lauderdale detectives were processing her house, Narcy Novack was across town at Broward County Family Court swearing out a domestic violence injunction against her husband. She was now staying in a motel just outside Fort Lauderdale, and wanted to have Ben thrown out of the house so she could move back in.

In her petition, Narcy wrote that she was the victim of domestic violence, and in imminent danger from her husband. She claimed that the previous Thursday, he had savagely beaten her up in their home.

She wrote out her petition in capital letters and poor, ungrammatical English.

BEN—NOVACK MY HUSBAND—SLAPPED ME & PUNCHED MY STOMACH, SPIT ON MY FACE AND THREATENED. HE IS A BAD PERSON & USES A BAGED OF POLICE OFICE OF MIAMI BEACH TO POWER FOR PERPOUS—EN CASE Y WILL CALL DE POLICE MY SELF—HE SAID HE WANTS MI TO ROT IN JAIL & HE WILL DO ANITING TO ASURE THAT TO HAPPEN & HE WILL USE HES CONNECTION EN CASE Y LEAVE HIM.

She also stated that Ben had guns and police hunting rifles at the house, and he must leave 2501 Del Mar Place so she could move back.

Asked why she could not get another, safer place to live in, Narcy wrote, "WI HAVA A BISNES TUGUETER. WORK—SAME PLACE." She also asked the court to order Ben to provide her financial support and temporary alimony.

That afternoon, Detective Steve Palazzo returned to his office to check out Ben Novack Jr. and his allegations against his wife.

"Obviously, we're dealing with a very bizarre situation," said Palazzo in 2011. "There's a guy who's claiming to be a police officer making these wild allegations."

The detective first called Narcy's Indian friend Rada, who confirmed she knew the Novacks and was aware of their ongoing marital problems. Rada confirmed that she had been in the Novack home at around 7:00 P.M. on Sunday, but had not seen Ben Novack Jr. She also agreed that Narcy had called her at around 2:00 A.M. asking her to return to the house to help move some furniture out of their bedroom. Rada had gone over and then found Novack bound to a chair. She had cut him free and waited with him until his mother arrived.

"She stated that in the light of this event," said Palazzo, "she does not want to speak with me. She is moving out of the area as fast as possible."

TWENTY-SEVEN

"UNUSUAL
SEXUAL GAMES"

On Tuesday morning, Ben Novack Jr. arrived at Fort Lauderdale Police headquarters to make a taped statement under oath. Since Detective Steve Palazzo's visit the day before, Ben had called and texted him dozens of times, for updates on the investigation.

He was taken to an interview room, where he repeated that Narcy had orchestrated the home invasion. He even brought along a surgical eye patch that he said had been used to blindfold him. There had been further calls from Narcy, he told Palazzo, and he was now negotiating with her to return his money and business documents.

After Novack made his statement and left, Detective Palazzo and Sergeant French discussed how to proceed with the investigation. They decided to call Narcy's cell phone there and then and record the call. She answered, agreeing to come to the police station for an interview.

"She told me that she was anxious to tell her side of the story," said Palazzo, "[and] agreed to be at the police station the following morning."

At 7:30 A.M. on Wednesday, Ben Novack Jr. called in Pat Franklin for help. The retired Miami Beach detective, who now ran his own private investigation company, had once worked security details at the Fontainebleau, where he had first met Novack as a teenager.

"So I said to Ben," Franklin recalled, "'to what do I owe the pleasure of this call?' And he began to tell me a very bizarre tale."

Initially, Franklin thought it was a joke, as Ben spoke in whispers, as if scared someone might be listening. But Franklin soon realized Novack was deadly serious.

"He told me that the police in Fort Lauderdale were not doing their job," said Franklin in 2011. "That he didn't think that they believed him and were not acting quickly enough for his liking."

During their conversation, Narcy Novack called her husband's cell phone, and he held it up to his landline so the private investigator could listen in. Franklin then overheard Narcy admitting to being involved in the home invasion.

After hanging up with Franklin, Ben Novack Jr. called Detective Palazzo, informing him that he had now hired a private investigator. He said Pat Franklin intended to follow Narcy after she left the police station later that morning, and get his property back. He also invited the detective to call Franklin, saying he had proof Narcy was involved in the attack.

"I called Franklin," Palazzo later noted. "He advised me that he had in fact heard Narcy Novack talking about details of the incident."

The private investigator said that he had met Narcy several times in the past, and recognized her distinctive accent. He then asked Palazzo if he had any problems with his taking the case and putting Narcy under surveillance.

"[Palazzo] inferred that he had problems with [Ben's] story," said Franklin, "but if I found out anything I should give him a call."

After hanging up, Pat Franklin called his new client and negotiated a $3,000 retainer to take the case. Novack told him to come straight over to his house.

When he arrived, the front door was ajar, so he let himself in, calling out that he was there.

"Ben came walking downstairs," the private investigator recalled, "and he definitely was shook up. He looked as if he was beaten about the face. He had abrasions and a swollen eye and had clearly been beaten or manhandled. He had ligature marks on his wrists."

Novack brought him into the living room, which was full of Coca-Cola memorabilia, including a large old Coke machine. They sat on the couch and Franklin asked Novack to tell him what had happened from the beginning.

"He told me two stories about Narcy," Franklin said. "I don't know which one's the truth to this day."

In his first version of the incident, Novack said he and Narcy were with another woman for a bondage threesome. "They were going to have sex together," said Franklin. "They were going to tie him up in a chair at the foot of the bed, and Narcy and the woman were going to have sex."

He said they had tied him to the chair and blindfolded him when some men suddenly burst into the bedroom, hitting him in the face.

"He wasn't sure where Narcy was in all this," Franklin said. "And I said, 'Well, did you hear her voice?' and he goes, 'Yeah, I'm not sure what she was saying. It was very confusing. There was a guy and different voices.'"

Novack said he thought there were six men there, and had no idea what had happened to the other woman.

Pat Franklin then asked Ben to take him upstairs and walk him through the chain of events. Once inside the bedroom, Franklin observed foursquare impressions in the shag carpet at the foot of the unmade bed, impressions that matched the feet of an orange reclining chair.

At the foot of the bed were identical nightstands, with the door of the right one open. Franklin asked where his gun was, and Novack replied that his attackers had taken it. Franklin's follow-up question was from where, and Novack pointed to the nightstand with the open door.

"I said, 'Ben, you've got two identical nightstands on either side of the bed,'" said Franklin, "'How do they know to go to that one?'"

When he said Narcy had told them, the private investigator became suspicious.

"I said, 'Why don't we start over and why don't you really tell me what happened."

In his second story, Ben Novack Jr. recounted the original version he had told police.

"He was asleep," Franklin said, "and that two men jumped on the bed, covered him with the sheet and pillows and began pounding the shit out of him. He screamed and reached for the gun, at which point Narcy said, 'He's got a gun!'"

The assailants then threw him in the chair and tied him up.

"He said that Narcy was on the phone during this with someone named Lou," Franklin said. "And he knows of a Lou that just got out of prison, who Narcy had dated when she was dancing as a stripper in Hialeah."

Novack told the investigator he thought Lou was still watching the house, and was in touch with Narcy.

Franklin asked Novack what he wanted him to do. Novack replied that he wanted Narcy and his money back, and was prepared to drop the criminal prosecution in return.

"I said, 'Ben, you know this is pretty dangerous shit,'" Franklin said. "'She just sent you a home invasion robbery with a [guy] she used to date that just got out of prison.' He goes, 'I want her back.'"

Novack then gave the investigator Narcy's cell phone number, and Franklin called and left a message.

"I said, 'Narcy, this is Pat Franklin. I understand that you've had some trouble with Ben, and I want to talk to you before we move forward. I think that there may be a way to resolve this matter without pursuing formal charges.'"

That afternoon, at 1:35 as arranged, Narcy Novack arrived at police headquarters in her Mercedes, carrying several large bags and boxes. As Detective Palazzo brought her into an interview room, she explained that these were items she had taken from the house.

Then, before the detective could say anything, she opened up a large brown accordion file and emptied the contents out onto the table in front of him.

"She began by showing me a large number of photographs of naked and partially clothed women," Palazzo later reported. "She showed me several magazine pages of women with artificial limbs . . . and photos of women with artificial limbs posing nude or partially nude."

Narcy then started telling Palazzo, in explicit detail, about her husband's strange sexual desires. "She insisted that he was into many different and unusual sexual games," wrote Palazzo. "They are both into bondage and most of their sexual relations involve handcuffing each other to the reclining chair in the master bedroom."

Narcy Novack said their relationship had always been violent.

"She said that he has often battered her," Palazzo noted. "On one occasion several years ago, she received a broken nose after Ben hit her. He later took her to a plastic surgeon. She was put to sleep by the doctor and insisted that when she woke up, she not only had a nose repair, but also breast implant surgery. While she contends that this was done against her will, she never made a complaint to anyone."

It was some time before Narcy allowed the detective to speak. He then told her that their interview would be taped, and he began reading her Miranda rights.

When he turned on the tape recorder, Narcy announced she needed medical attention, explaining she had come straight from a doctor, who was treating her for allergies.

"She said she was not feeling well," Palazzo wrote. "That she was supposed to wait for one hour before leaving, to allow the medicine to take effect."

Detective Palazzo offered to put the interview on hold until she was feeling better, but Narcy wanted to continue.

"She denied ever tying Ben to the chair," reported Palazzo, "and said he was only handcuffed on one hand. She denied that he was ever attacked in the bed and said that he got into the chair willingly to have a sexual encounter."

Narcy then claimed that on Sunday morning Ben had been working in his office next door when a moving van arrived at their residence. He had later come home to discover she was moving out. She refused to identify who was helping her move, saying she had sent them away when Ben came back, to avoid an argument.

"She told me that she and Ben talked for several hours," Palazzo reported, "eventually decided to have sex. She got in the chair and Ben handcuffed her and performed sexual acts on her.

"She said that Ben then got in the chair and once she handcuffed him, she decided that she would leave him there while she continued to remove her belongings."

Narcy told the detective that her husband had been unable to get out of the chair to summon help, as it was too heavy for him to move. She denied that he had been blindfolded or bound to the chair at any time. When Palazzo asked about the portable urinal found in the master bedroom, Narcy explained that they both used it while watching television, or in the middle of the night. She explained that Ben likes the portable urinal, so he doesn't have to get out of bed and wake his cat.

The detective then asked her about removing all her husband's business files. Unfazed, Narcy replied that she had taken them only to find certain photographs and documents she could later use as ammunition in a divorce. She said that she had already agreed to return them.

"When asked about taking the money . . . from the safe," Palazzo wrote, "she told me that it was equally her money."

Narcy also insisted that she had taken only $5,000, and not the $440,000 her husband was claiming.

"Throughout the statement," Palazzo wrote later, "I did not confront her with any inconsistencies or untruths. I allowed her to provide whatever explanation she chose."

Narcy told the detective that there had been ongoing problems in the marriage for the last seventeen years.

"It is a sick vicious circle," she declared. "I have left him twenty times, or forty times, or fifty times. He has . . . gotten me back. He goes to my sister . . . he goes to my brother . . . we kiss and make up. It's a vicious circle that I need to break it."

After turning off the tape recorder, Detective Palazzo left the interview room to brief his superior, Detective Jack DiCristofalo on Narcy's version, telling him it was riddled with inconsistencies.

"[Narcy] was unbelievable," Detective Palazzo said. "I'd never met anybody like her. She was obviously lying, but her arrogance was what struck me the most. Just very, very bizarre."

The two detectives then agreed to go back and confront her with the discrepancies between hers and her husband's versions of what had happened. When they did so, Narcy changed her story, saying that she had planned it all several days earlier. In preparation, she told the detectives, she had rented a U-Haul truck and a car, in case she could not use her own.

"She admitted that several things she told me were untrue," Palazzo noted in his report. "That she lied because she was afraid that Ben Novack would hurt her."

Although Narcy now admitted to tying Ben up with a rope, she insisted that the incident had begun on Sunday morning while her husband was working in his office. She told the detectives that she had also threatened to cut off her husband's penis and throw it in the canal, but would never have done this, as she was "not that nasty."

She now admitted hiring someone, whom she refused to identify, to help her move and return to the house later while Ben was tied up.

"She asked that he help her scare Ben," Palazzo wrote, "into believing that several men were in the house armed with guns. He did this and was paid $200."

She said she was now staying with a friend, whom she refused to identify, in Kendall, forty-two miles south of Fort Lauderdale. She also spoke of plans to stay with her sister Leticia in Naples, joining her daughter, May Abad, and two grandsons.

She told the detective she had filed for a restraining order against Ben, but would return everything she had taken if he accepted responsibility for his actions that led up to this. She viewed the incident as the only way she could escape Ben without being hurt.

"From the onset of this investigation," the detective observed, "it was apparent that the entire incident is related to a domestic disturbance.

After hearing Narcy Novack's version, it became clear that there was even more history between the two than either chose to share with us."

Detective Palazzo then left her in the interview room, going back to his office to call Ben Novack Jr. He explained that Narcy was now threatening to expose Novack's most intimate sexual secrets if he went ahead and prosecuted her.

"For several minutes," Palazzo wrote, "he pondered dropping the charges. I explained the problems with the case and the low likelihood of obtaining a conviction. I felt certain that Ben Novack would not continue to desire prosecution once his property was returned. I also believed that, as confusing to me as it is, the two would get back together in the near future."

After Ben Novack Jr. agreed not to prosecute if his business documents were returned, Detective Palazzo went back to the interview room and told Narcy this. She then agreed to give back all the items immediately, but when Palazzo called Novack to tell him this, Ben Jr. suddenly changed his demands, insisting that she return the $440,000 in cash she had taken. When Palazzo told Narcy this, she maintained that the sum had been only $5,000. Palazzo called Ben again to confer.

"He said he would forget the money," Palazzo noted, "if I would draft a letter indicating that she waive all rights to any future claims against Ben, his estate or his business. I informed him that his request was out of line . . . that he should contact a civil attorney and not rely on the police department to settle his legal issues."

Twenty-Eight

"I CAN'T BELIEVE
WHAT I'M HEARING"

O n Thursday morning, Narcy Novack called Pat Franklin, who had been leaving messages on her cell phone for two days. He explained that Ben now wanted to drop the formal charges and urged her to meet with her husband to work out an agreement. Narcy said she would think about it.

"About an hour later," Franklin remembered, "she called me from a coffee shop and gave me the directions there."

When the investigator arrived, he saw Narcy seated in a booth and looking out of the window.

He came in a side door and slid next to her on the banquette in the booth, he recalled. "And she jumped. I said, 'If you don't trust me, I hope that shows you can, because I could have had you arrested right now.'"

He then sat across from her in the booth and waited for her to speak.

"She started venting anger," Franklin said. "I mean she really harbored a great hatred for Ben and couldn't stand him, calling him a bastard. And she alluded to his various perversions. 'You don't know what he makes me do. He makes me go with other men and blah, blah, blah. He spits. He stutters.' All in her broken English. She's very emotional."

Franklin suggested they call Ben from the coffee shop, so he would know she was all right. The private investigator had an ulterior motive in this, wanting to prove to his client that he had done the first part of his job and found Narcy.

"So I put her on the phone," Franklin said, "and she begins to sob like a baby. Giving him baby talk. And I'm scratching my head, because I can't believe what I'm hearing."

Narcy told Ben she was sorry for what had happened, promising to make it up to him. She then broke down in tears, begging him not to prosecute and get her sent her to jail.

"So finally she hands me the phone," Franklin said. "I said, 'Ben, I'm with her now. She's going to help us. She's agreed to take me where she has your property.

"And I'm nodding at her, like I'm putting words in her mouth. We never had that discussion yet, but I'm using this moment, and Ben is sort of a prop for me at this time."

Franklin told his client that he felt Narcy was genuinely sorry and would take him immediately to collect his property. He promised to call Novack back when he and Narcy got there.

"And when I hang up," Franklin said, "her tears dry up and she winks at me. And I'm like, 'What the fuck is this?' She winks [again]. She's a bullshitter and she's letting me in on her secret.

"I just smiled and said, 'Narcy, you work with me on this thing and you'll be fine.'"

After leaving the coffee shop, Narcy directed Pat Franklin to a public storage facility eleven miles away, off Interstate 595, in Davie, Florida. Once there, she led the way to a twelve-by-twelve storage unit, produced a key, and opened the padlock.

"It's filled from floor to ceiling with boxes, furniture, and clothing," Franklin recalled. "And I looked at her and said, 'You didn't do this alone.' She goes, 'No.'"

Narcy said it had taken six guys to bring everything over in a truck. Then she walked over to a desk, pulling out the brown accordion file she had shown detectives the day before.

"You want to know what kind of sick bastard your client is?" she asked Franklin. "Well, open it up."

The private investigator said he would rather talk first about what she had done with the contents of the safe, but Narcy insisted he open the file.

"So I look at it," Franklin said, "and there's a folder in there of pictures. Some are dated from the sixties and seventies. Some are Polaroids. And there're a variety of pictures and photographs of amputees—male, female, and children. Peculiar. Some of them were being fitted for prostheses.

"I'm certainly no prude, but I've never been aware of any kind of fetish involving amputees. But I guess there are all kinds."

As he quickly thumbed through the hundreds of photographs, he noticed one from the 1960s showing a young bikini-clad female amputee on crutches outside the Fontainebleau hotel.

After Franklin inspected the locker, he called Ben Novack Jr. to tell him he was with Narcy and had recovered Novack's property.

Novack immediately asked if Narcy had shown him any photographs.

"I said, 'Yes, she did,'" Franklin said. "He goes, 'Well, I'm not interested in that anymore. She's blackmailing me over this.'" Then he explained that he had first become interested in amputees as a young boy, at the Fontainebleau. "Ben told me," Franklin said, "'Well, you know my dad used to do charity work, and that's how I got interested in that.'"

Franklin then handed the phone to Narcy. They had a brief conversation, with Ben agreeing to drop all criminal proceedings against her and not file for divorce.

"He's scared of those pictures," Franklin said. "It's as simple as that."

A few hours later, Detective Steve Palazzo met with Ben Novack Jr. at his home. Novack informed the detective that Narcy had agreed to return everything she had taken. He then signed a "lack of prosecution" form, indicating that he was not going forward with the case.

He told Palazzo, however, that he would "immediately file for divorce, and never wanted to deal with Narcy Novack again."

On Friday morning, Ben Novack Jr. called Narcy; he recorded the telephone call on his microcassette recorder. Novack's first priority was persuading Narcy to return all his company files, as his business was now at a standstill and his reputation on the line. With three upcoming conventions and next month's mortgage due, Narcy's actions were now threatening to ruin Convention Concepts Unlimited.

"Don't worry about it," Narcy told him. "Tell me which is the first file that you need."

When he told her he desperately needed all the paperwork for three upcoming conventions, Narcy coldly replied she would try to get to it when she had time. She said it would have to be tomorrow, as she didn't have the files in one place.

Then Novack cautiously broached the subject of the $440,000 in cash she had taken, offering to negotiate. Narcy immediately disputed the figure, refusing even to discuss it with him now.

Then he implored her to return a drawerful of personal bills she'd taken, as their credit rating could suffer if payments were late. "Narcy," he pleaded. "I've got to make the mortgage payment."

"One day less is not going to make any difference," she told him.

After Narcy agreed to return the rack of files to him the next morning, Novack had one further question.

"Could you put the Batman picture in, please?" he asked.

"No," she snapped. "You and I have to talk about that. Listen I don't want to deal with you too long. If you give me the room to move around, it will make it a lot easier for you to get that stuff. If you start claustrophobing me, you're not going to get a thing."

When he told her that he urgently needed to make a 2:00 P.M. post office deadline, to send off files and papers for the conventions, Narcy flew into a rage.

"Don't give me no time, okay," she shouted.

"I need to get the work out," Ben reasoned.

"I understand. But you need to understand that what you did last night was not right, because we agreed on something."

Then Narcy accused him of hiring a divorce attorney.

"I haven't done anything," Novack said defensively. "We agreed."

Then she hung up.

A few minutes later, Ben called her back, trying to get evidence on tape that she had masterminded the attack.

"Narcy," he said. "Can I ask you a question?"

"Yeah, but quickly," she said, "because I cannot talk more than two minutes."

"Okay. Could you tell me why you felt it was necessary to have these guys come in and almost kill me, while they try and get this stuff."

"I don't know what you're talking about," she answered.

"Narcy," he continued, "why didn't you just ask me for what you wanted?"

"I cannot talk," she replied. "You're making no sense, okay. I don't know where you're coming from with that."

"Narcy. Narcy. Why was it necessary to do that?"

There was a long silence before she hung up on him again.

Ben immediately called back, pleading for his business papers before he left for Texas, and asking her to return two guns she'd taken.

"That's a lie," she told him.

"Okay, Narcy, the two guns that are missing are the ones that you took out. One that was in my black bag and the one in the night table, that I tried to get when they assaulted me."

"I don't understand what you're talking about," she said.

"Okay, Narcy, could you just tell me where the guns are?"

"I told you . . . what you're talking about, I don't know."

"Narcy," he pleaded, "please tell me where they are because that's—"

Then the line went dead.

He called back, asking if the "guys" who had attacked him had taken the guns.

"Listen," she told him, "I don't know what you're talking about.

What guys you're talking about or what?" Then she said her cell phone battery had run out, and asked where she could get more batteries. "Listen, let me tell you one thing," she said. "If it is not [working], you are not going to be able to reach me."

When Ben patiently told her the name of an AT&T store where she could get more, she said it was too far away.

"Narcy, please tell me," he pleaded. "Will you bring my files back?"

She said she had "a lot of sewing" to do before she could return anything.

"I need my receipts, Narcy," he implored. "I need my paid bills."

"Bye," she said, hanging up again.

When he called back, Narcy accused him of taping their phone calls.

"I just don't want you to be talking nonsense on the phone," she shouted. "You're taping everything."

"I'm not taping anything," he said. "I'm just talking about files—"

"You have a detective and you're taping everything and you're trying to get—"

"Narcy," he reasoned, "I'm not doing anything except asking you about my files. I'm not getting into any nasty—"

"You need to call me back," she told him, hanging up.

He called back, and Narcy accused him of trying to trap her, saying she could hear voices in the background.

"I'm not trying to trap you at all, Narcy," he told her. "I just would like to know when I can get those files. I'm desperate for them."

"Don't trap me," she warned. "You are not giving me enough room to move, okay."

"Narcy, could you just tell me what time they'll be here?"

"You have no time with me," she said angrily. "You're not timing me."

"Narcy, can you have somebody drop them off before—"

She hung up again, and for the rest of the day refused to answer her phone.

. . .

On Saturday, June 15, one week after the home invasion incident, Narcy Novack called Detective Steve Palazzo with some news.

"She advised that she had been in constant contact with Ben Novack," he reported. "They are negotiating the return of the property and possibility of getting back together."

Twenty-Nine

"THE WOMAN IS ABSOLUTELY WHACKO"

On June 17, Detective Steve Palazzo received an angry call from Ben Novack Jr., demanding that he arrest Narcy immediately for threatening his life. The detective refused, advising Novack to hire an attorney instead and get her threats on tape.

"Throughout the whole thing," Palazzo said, "I kept telling Ben, 'You need to get as far away from her as you can. You need to get restraining orders [and] see a divorce attorney. The woman is absolutely whacko.'"

The next morning, as a precaution, Palazzo arranged to have a patrol car drive past 2501 Del Mar Place, to see if Narcy's car was there. After learning that it was not, Palazzo called Ben Novack Jr. and asked if he had seen his wife recently.

"He said that he was busy," Palazzo wrote, "and would call me later."

Suddenly the detective heard Narcy's distinctive voice in the background, and asked Ben if she was with him.

"He told me it was none of my business," Palazzo wrote, "and he would call later. Then . . . Narcy picked up another phone in the house.

Both began speaking. Narcy stated that they were getting back together. They had arranged to get counseling. Suddenly both began to argue."

The detective turned on his tape recorder and recorded the conversation. Now they both admitted that Narcy had been back home for days, and that Ben had gotten her a room in a hotel after she took his amputee photographs to the police.

"The two continued to argue," Palazzo wrote, "and eventually blamed me and the police department for interfering in their lives."

Then Novak said he had only let her back to the house to record her threats against him on tape. On hearing this, Narcy announced that she was leaving and never coming back.

"The conversation is preserved on tape," Palazzo wrote, "and will be placed in evidence along with the other tapes."

The next day, Narcy went to Broward County Family Court and swore out another complaint against her husband. A judge then evicted Ben from his own house, allowing Narcy to move back in.

The following morning, Ben Novack Jr. hired Fort Lauderdale attorney Don Spadaro to help him get back in his house.

"He was just very upset," Spadaro recalled in 2011. "He had been physically removed from the house when they served him with the restraining order."

Then Novack recounted to Spadaro how he had been held at gunpoint in his bedroom while some men took $440,000 from his safe, and that Narcy had been involved.

"So he told me this wild story," Spadaro said, "and his focus at that point was that he wanted to get in the house, because all his business paperwork and whatever was in [there]. He felt that his business was going to go down the tubes if he couldn't get in there."

After their meeting, Spadaro filed for an emergency hearing at Broward County Family Court, which was held the next day in front of circuit court judge Geoffrey Cohen.

"We were able to convince Narcy to modify the restraining order," said Spadaro, "so that he could get back into the house."

Under the order, Ben Novack Jr. would be allowed to reside at the residence "to conduct his business," while Nancy stayed in the guest-house and could enter the main residence only to do her laundry.

"No other harmful conduct shall occur between the parties," ordered Judge Cohen, who called another hearing for June 25, to rule on Narcy's restraining order.

After the hearing, Novack told his new lawyer that if Narcy refused to drop the restraining order and didn't return his money, he was filing for divorce. He then had Spadaro draw up a divorce petition on the grounds that the marriage was irretrievably broken down.

As they drafted the divorce petition together, Novack insisted that the attorney incorporate Narcy's alleged threats against his life during the home invasion.

"I would never have put them in but for Ben's insistence," Spadaro explained. "I said, 'Ben, if you want me to put this in there, you've got to tell me straight from your mouth.' And of course I had him sign this."

Section 10 of the divorce petition read, "That the petitioner is fearful that when the Respondent received notice of the filing of this Dissolution of Marriage that violence will come to him as the Respondent previously has falsely imprisoned Petitioner in order to remove assets, including but not limited to cash, furnishings, antiques, family heirloom jewelry, firearms, and business files necessary for Petitioner/Husband's business."

Section 13 was even more damning:

"That the Petitioner/Husband is fearful that unless this honorable court enters a restraining order against the Respondent/Wife, that his life is in danger. The Respondent/Wife has threatened: a) 'That if I can't have you, then no one will have you.'; and b) that 'the men that helped me remove the property from the house will come back and finish the job . . . I can have you killed anytime I want . . . you're not dead now because I stopped them the other night.'"

. . .

On Wednesday, June 19, Don Spadaro filed the divorce petition, along with the couple's original August 1991 prenuptial agreement, in circuit court. Two days later, Ben Novack Jr. posted a $50,000 bond and was granted a temporary injunction against Narcy, freezing all the cash and the rest of his belongings that had been removed from the house. These included all the pornographic photo albums, magazines, and negatives Narcy had taken.

In her order, circuit court judge Patricia Coralis granted Ben Novack Jr. exclusive use of the marital home. "Narcy Novack is hereby restrained from coming in the marital property," read the order, "and/or entering the marital home . . . pending further order of the court. Narcy Novack is also further restrained from molesting, harassing, physically hurting or abusing the husband . . . at any time or any place."

On Tuesday, June 25, Narcy Novack told Judge Cohen at an evidentiary hearing that Ben was violently abusive and a pervert, lusting after amputee porn.

"She goes forward and testifies 'he's hit me in the stomach,'" said Spadaro, who cross-examined her. "And she's Hispanic, so her language is whatever, but she certainly described that he slapped [her] and spit on [her]."

After Narcy's testimony, Ben Novack Jr. told the judge that he had been held hostage under Narcy's direction for more than a day, with a gun to his head. Then Detective Steve Palazzo took the stand to testify about the ongoing investigation.

"And I think Judge Cohen was kind of shocked," Spadaro recalled.

Bernice Novack attended the closed hearing, sitting next to her son. Estelle Fernandez had offered to go with her for moral support, but Bernice had refused.

"She was so mortified," Estelle recalled. "She said, 'No, I don't want anybody to know how my daughter-in-law is.' And then in court Narcy was telling all these stories about Ben having this fetish with amputee models and pictures. And Bernice would say, 'Oh my God. She's crazy. She's crazy.'"

By the beginning of July, Ben and Nancy Novack had reconciled again, after she agreed to repay $175,000. Then, on July 10, after she paid a first installment of $75,000, they both signed a "Confirmation of Understanding" and had it notarized.

This six-point document, which Novack's divorce attorney, Don Spadaro, had not been consulted on, stipulated that "certain private items" must be kept private or the agreement was void. It also stated that Ben would agree to drop the divorce action and allow Narcy to come back home.

It read:

1. That Ben and Narcy wish to do everything possible to reconcile their relationship and move forward with their lives, together.
2. That Ben and Narcy have agreed to seek marital counseling from a professional in this field. Narcy will locate some qualified individuals for this and together Ben and Narcy will mutually agree on which one or ones to utilize. This action will be done immediately.
3. That Ben and Narcy have agreed to other certain private items that will be honored mutually by both parties to keep this document and agreement valid. Should any of those items not be honored by one or both parties this agreement ceases.
4. That Ben and Narcy will place a privately agreed sum of money into a joint investment, chosen by mutual agreement, and which can subsequently be touched only by both parties together and neither one individually.
5. That upon full completion of #4 above, Narcy will return to the house and Ben will drop the Marriage Dissolution action and all related actions in that filing.
6. If at any point during the 8 month period following the

completion of the above actions it becomes apparent that the relationship is not going to work out, that Ben will provide for a reasonable and mutually agreeable house or apartment for Narcy to reside in, at Ben's expense, for a period of one year following.

A few days later, Ben Novack Jr. brought Narcy to Don Spadaro's office and instructed Spadaro to drop the divorce action. As Narcy waited in the foyer, Novack went into Spadaro's office and handed him a copy of the "Confirmation of Understanding" and a receipt for $75,000.

"He came in and said [they'd] reconciled," recalled Spadaro. "And I brought him in here, because she was in my waiting room. Then I closed the door and said, 'Are you crazy? [How can anybody] that went through what you went through, go back and reconcile?'"

The attorney asked how Ben knew Narcy wouldn't have somebody break into the house again to rob him, perhaps killing him the next time. Novack replied that he still loved Narcy, and they were back together.

"I still tried to convince him that he was nuts," said Spadaro. "After what he went through, having a gun put to his head. But I have since learned that they had some sort of kinky sexual thing going on . . . that he enjoyed, and he wanted to keep that relationship together.

"That was pretty much the end of my involvement. When he walked out of that door that day I never saw him again."

Seven years later, May Abad would allege that her mother had blackmailed Ben Novack Jr. into paying her $6,500 a month, threatening to go public with his fetish for "photographs . . . involving nude bodies with amputated arms and limbs."

When Hollywood police chief Jim Scarberry learned of the reconciliation, he was appalled. Although they had spoken almost daily since the home invasion, it was weeks before Ben told him that Narcy was behind the attack.

"I had asked him how the investigation was going," Scarberry said. "He told me that Narcy had apologized, and they were going to get back together."

Chief Scarberry said he was "nuts," and warned him that Narcy might kill him the next time. Ben replied that he still loved Narcy and they were going into marriage counseling to work things out. Then Scarberry told him never to call him again.

"I was hoping that would entice him to make a decision to get away from her," he explained. "But that didn't happen, and that was the last time I spoke to him."

Charlie Seraydar found out that the divorce had been called off only when he called the Novack house and Narcy answered the phone.

"That surprised the hell out of me," Seraydar said, "because Ben was calling me every single day. Then I happen to call him back one day and she answers the phone. And she was as nice as shit to me, and I was nice to her."

When they next met, Seraydar told his old friend that he was a "fucking idiot" for taking Narcy back, after what she had done. "I just said, 'Ben, I'm not going to pass judgment on you, but look what you were put through.' And he says, 'I know, but we're going to marriage counseling, and I'm seeing a psychologist.'"

Seraydar then asked why he was going back to Narcy. Ben replied that he still loved her and did not want to lose everything that he had built up over the years.

"Then I said to him, 'Is it worth your life?'"

Ben's old school friend Kelsey Grammer was also concerned Ben had gone back to Narcy. "It seemed like classic abused-victim behavior," the actor later told *People* magazine. "He was terrified of her."

By the fall of 2002, Ben and Narcy Novack were back living and working together, as if nothing had happened. But Bernice Novack could not forget her son's frantic call for help, or rushing over to his house to find him bruised and battered.

"Bernice was so upset that she went into counseling for the longest time," said her neighbor Rebecca Green. "She was just so disturbed by it."

To make things even worse, she saw her daughter-in-law every day, at the Conventions Unlimited office. Always extremely private, Bernice would discuss what she was going through only with her closest confidants.

"Well, she called me and told me the entire story," said Barbara Lunde. "She said, 'Please do a prayer for me, so I will know what to do.'"

Bernice also confided in Temple Hayes, saying she had hoped it would be the end of the marriage. "She was appalled and flabbergasted," said Hayes, "that someone could have done that to her son . . . she feared for his life. She knew Narcy was into Santería and even wondered if she had put some kind of spell on her son.

"She felt Narcy was involved in some kind of Spanish Mafia, and said, 'There you go. I knew what was going to happen. She only married my son for what he has, and because she wants to control him. She brought in these hit people to show him what she would do if he ever tried to leave her.'"

Bernice was especially hurt by Narcy's allegations that her son was into bondage sex, telling her sister she refused to believe it. "Bernice said, 'It's a lie,'" said Maxine. "She tied him up, and they kept him there with a gun to his head until he opened that safe."

When Estelle Fernandez asked how Ben could possibly stay with Narcy, Bernice said it was because he had always hated to be alone at night.

"But I think Narcy must have had loads of stuff on him," Estelle said, "like offshore money, bank accounts, and stuff like that. He knew he couldn't trust her to keep her mouth shut, and that's the real reason why he stayed with her."

For Ben's sake, Bernice now did her best to get on with Narcy, but it was always an ordeal. When friends asked why she was still working six days a week, Bernice explained that she was only doing it to protect Ben.

"His mother was extremely worried about him," Fernandez said. "She stayed mainly because she wanted to see Ben."

A few months after the home invasion, Prince Mongo told Bernice how sorry he was about what had happened. "I said, 'How does he stay in the house with Narcy under those conditions?'" said Mongo. "She said, 'I told him he has to sleep with one eye open.' I said, 'I would tell him to sleep with both eyes open.'"

Thirty

"TIME MUST MOVE FORWARD!"

O ver the next several years, Ben and Narcy Novack did appear to get their relationship back on track. Convention Concepts Unlimited was thriving, and money was rolling in. None of Ben Novack Jr.'s clients or business contacts had any idea of what had happened, or how perilously close the company had come to imploding.

In the wake of the home invasion, the Miami Beach Police Department questioned Reserve Officer Novack about the incident, having him write out his version of events in an official report. Soon afterward, he was told that his services were no longer needed.

"There was a little bit of an embarrassment in the department," explained Charlie Seraydar, who had retained close ties to the Miami Beach Police Department after retiring. "And that would have been the last time he donned the uniform."

On May 5, 2005, Ben Novack Jr. wrote a letter on Convention Concepts Unlimited notepaper to Miami Beach police chief Donald De-Lucca, with the heading "Resignation/Retirement."

"It was good sitting down with you a few weeks ago . . . to discuss the past, present and future," it began. "Having been a sworn and certified police officer for more than 30 years . . . I have certainly seen a lot of changes."

The letter went on to explain that because of the "tremendous growth" of his business, he could no longer devote sufficient time to serving in the Reserve Unit.

"I feel that the best course for me may well be to 'retire,'" he explained, "and go out on a very high note with many fond memories of the past 30+ years."

He promised to let the chief know if the situation were to change, thanking him for allowing him to attend several upcoming police courses in order to maintain his state certificate for the next four years.

"It saddens me to leave something that has been part of my life for 30 years," he wrote, "but time must move forward!"

After leaving the Miami Beach Police Department, Ben Novack Jr. devoted all his spare time to building up his collection of Batman comic books and memorabilia. As he could no longer live out his Caped Crusader fantasy on the streets of Miami in a black and white, he now lived it vicariously through his Batman toys and comics.

"I must have sent him five hundred boxes over that period," said British dealer Ed Kelly. "He would pay for all the shipping, and I would just fill boxes for him and send it."

Novack now went to all the Comic Cons around America, getting to know the dealers and making useful contacts.

"He would have a whole army of people searching for stuff for him," said Kelly, "and he'd buy it through auction houses and dealers. He was very good at negotiating and I'm sure he got things at great prices. But of course because he was buying so much of it, people would give him good prices."

Although Ben and Narcy's close friends were aware of their marital problems, these were never discussed when they met socially. The Novacks were now regulars at Robert Woltin's Italian restaurant Louie Louie, on Las Olas Boulevard, a few blocks from their home.

"I met him at my Miami nightclub Façade in 1987," said Woltin. "He was a customer at my restaurant and he would eat there with Narcy on the weekend."

They were often joined for extended dinners by Prince Mongo and Jerry Calhoun.

"Ben would order a five-hundred-dollar bottle of wine," said Mongo, "and drink the whole bottle. Narcy may have one glass."

Although Mongo was close to the couple, he was aware of Ben's stable of kept women around Miami. "Joe Gandy would take those whores money all the time," said Mongo, "to pay their rent secretly. I didn't like Gandy and what he was doing undercover. And that's why Ben never got rid of him. Ben was using him, because you won't cut off your left hand, will you."

Ben Novack Jr. now had several mistresses whom Gandy catered for, who had all received new breast enhancements from their rich benefactor. "There [were] three he had," said Gandy, "that I used to drop money with. And every one of them goes with him [for] money. None of them were with him for love, including Narcy."

Gandy could earn up to $5,000 a week from his boss, running his secret errands and helping with conventions. "I was making a lot of money every week," Gandy said, "but I put up with a lot of shit. I wanted to kill him a thousand times."

Periodically, Narcy's daughter, May Abad, would arrive with her two teenage sons to stay for a few weeks. But Ben never allowed the boys in the house, in case they messed with his Batman collection.

"He would send them to my house for the night," said Mongo, "because Ben didn't want them sitting on his sofa. He didn't want them touching Batman. He wanted them regimented. When they came in the house he said, 'Don't move!'"

Mongo recalls May, who worked as a barmaid, as being in her own world and never close to her mother or her stepfather. "She didn't really care about Ben," he said. "But she cared about her kids."

Several years running, Mongo was invited to Passover Seder at the

Novack home, where Narcy prepared a traditional kosher meal. "Ben would be at the head of the table," he said, "and we'd have the kosher wine and all the rituals. We'd have to put on our yarmulkes, and May and the kids would be bored to death."

According to many, Ben Novack Jr. disliked his stepdaughter intensely. Although she occasionally worked on conventions for him, he tried to avoid her as much as possible.

"He hated May to death," Joe Gandy confirmed. "Sometimes May and her mother would go three to four years without talking. No kids came by. No nothing. Then they would end up making up, and Ben would let her back in the office to work. But Bernice couldn't take her at all."

Charlie Seraydar, who has known May since she was a little girl, says she had a very difficult upbringing. "May was always a problem child," he said. "She has her issues with her kids, very similar to the issues she experienced with her mother. I thought she was a nice kid. The problem is her mother."

On January 19, 2006, Ben Novack Jr. turned fifty, and made a will, leaving virtually everything to Narcy. He even wanted their caskets to be buried next to each other at his family's mausoleum in Queens, New York.

Narcy would inherit all his property, but if his eighty-three-year-old mother survived him, Narcy would receive only $200,000 and half the 2501 Del Mar Place. In the event that Narcy died before him, he bequeathed $250,000 each to her grandsons Patrick and Marchelo Gaffney, and $100,000 to their mother, May Abad.

At the end of his will, Novack stipulated that his death would automatically void his and Narcy's contentious 1991 prenuptial agreement, and be superseded by his will.

Ben Novack Jr. was now running up hundreds of thousands of dollars a month on his coveted black American Express card, for his business and personal expenses. But while he was living big, Bernice Novack shopped in thrift stores and watched every cent.

"She loved these huge flea markets in Pompano Beach," said Temple Hayes. "Once, we went and spent the whole day there, looking for bargains."

On one trip to New York, Hayes brought Bernice back a ten-dollar imitation Rolex watch she had bought on the street. "Bernice loved that thing so much," remembered Hayes. "She was so tickled. She wore it faithfully all the time."

The former mistress of the Fontainebleau was now known in several Fort Lauderdale stores as a demanding customer and extremely hard to please.

"Bernice loved to shop," explained Guy Costaldo, "and she liked to return. She'd take it home, try it on, and then didn't like it and return it. And I used to tease her, saying, 'The girls in Saks must shake when they see you, because they don't know if they're getting a commission this week or not.'"

Eventually, Bloomingdales banned her from the store, because she had taken back so many clothes.

"We'd go shopping," said Estelle Fernandez, "and we'd all buy stuff. And the next thing you know Bernice is returning everything. She really didn't need it. She just did it for the thrill."

Where once the former model had dressed like a queen in the most expensive haut couture—and still had those clothes, now carefully stored away and labeled in boxes—she'd now throw on an old shirt and jeans to go to work.

"She had no use for those clothes," said Fernandez, referring to Bernice's former classy wardrobe. "That was a different life and a different lifestyle. She was now down to wearing nothing, because she worked in this office with these lowlifes. She didn't even want to put makeup on. She said she had no reason to get dressed."

Although Ben Jr. was often rude to her, his devoted mother refused to hear a bad word about him. While her son and Narcy were traveling around the world running conventions, Bernice looked after Ben's two cats and tidied up their cluttered home as best she could. Ben had always had a pet cat since childhood, and often seemed more attached to his cats than any human being.

"Ben doted over those cats," Temple Hayes recalled. "When [he and Narcy] would travel, he wanted [Bernice] to go over two or three times a day, especially if one of the cats was not feeling well. He stressed a lot about his cats. Sometimes he would even talk to them on the phone. Ben even had a small cat cemetery in his backyard, where his pet cats over the years were buried. There were these beautiful little tombstones of his kitties," said Hayes.

Ben was still highly dependent on his aging mother, regularly calling her late at night to talk. He made no allowances for her being in her mid-eighties and in declining health, and thought nothing of calling her in the midst of a heated argument with Narcy and asking her to drive over and provide moral support.

"This is when he used his mother," explained Estelle Fernandez. "'I can't handle Narcy. You have to come over.'"

Narcy would then come on the line, complaining that Ben was watching pornography on his computer. He would deny it.

Then the old lady would drive over to Del Mar Place at midnight to make peace between them.

"It was horrible," said Estelle. "She'd say every day, 'I never thought my life would be like this.'"

All the stress in her life was starting to take its toll. Bernice became depressed, and her doctor put her on the antidepressant Xanax and its generic, alprazolam. Also, her asthma, which she had always suffered from, was getting worse. She started suffering chronic asthma attacks in the middle of the night, and had to keep an oxygen machine by her bed. She even began sleeping with her clothes on, in case she had an attack and had to go to the emergency room in the middle of the night.

"She was afraid," said Fernandez. "She didn't want to go to the hospital in her nightgown, and would be prepared."

Whenever she had an attack, she would immediately phone Ben for help. On the many occasions she was unable to reach him, or he was out of town, she drove herself to the emergency room.

That Christmas, a man followed Bernice Novack home from a mall where she had been buying presents. He waited until she had driven her car into her two-car garage, and then attacked her.

"As she stepped out of the car, he grabbed her heels," said Estelle Fernandez, "and dragged her out of the car. Then he grabbed her purse and ran to a car parked nearby and drove off."

The old woman was so shaken up by the attack that Ben Jr. had Joe Gandy fit dead bolts on every door of her house, for extra protection.

THIRTY-ONE

LIFE WITH THE NOVACKS

In early 2007, Prince Mongo moved to Daytona, and Ben and Narcy Novack sailed there to visit him. On the way, their fifty-foot yacht *White Lightning* broke down at Vero Beach, so they rented a car to complete the journey. Ben then ordered Joe Gandy to bring the yacht back to Fort Lauderdale to be completely refitted, at a cost of more than $2 million.

While in Daytona, Ben and Narcy viewed available houses, as they were thinking about relocating. Ben wanted to be near the water for his boats, with Bernice remaining in Fort Lauderdale to run the Conventions Concept Unlimited office.

Over the next few months, Ben and Narcy also looked at properties in South Carolina, Key West, and Tampa. They especially liked a house by the water in St. Augustine, which Ben thought would make an excellent museum for his Batman collection, and sent Mongo an air ticket to come see it.

"They flew me in to Jacksonville," Mongo said. "Ben picked me up and we looked at the house, and I flatly couldn't stand it. They did not buy that house, although they looked at many others around my area."

During the trip, Mongo viewed houses with them during the day and socialized with them at night. "After that home invasion thing," he said, "they were getting along better than they ever did. We'd go out and eat every night and they were chummy chummy. They smile, they laugh and talk and seemed normal. And I said, 'Jeez, it's good that you're all getting along so good.' Narcy said, 'Well, he's been better lately.'"

One night, Mongo took Narcy to one side and asked her why they wanted to move out of Fort Lauderdale.

"That was an awful mystery to me," Mongo said. "Narcy told me, 'Ben is acting so strange, he wants to get out of town now. He wants to buy a house and leave Fort Lauderdale.'

"I said, 'How can he possibly, with his lifestyle, want to leave Fort Lauderdale?' And Narcy said, 'It seems like somebody's shaking him.'"

A month later, an excited Ben Novack Jr. announced that they were buying a house in Seattle, Washington.

"I said, 'You've got to be kidding,'" Mongo recalled, "'It's raining all the time in Seattle. What are you going to do about the boats?' Well, Ben always had an answer. 'You can boat in California day to day.'" I mean they were jitterbugging around . . . jumping like hot popcorn."

In late 2007, Ben and Narcy Novack visited New Jersey for a convention and, while there, bought some furniture. Narcy's elder brother Cristobal Veliz, who divided his time between Brooklyn and Philadelphia, had just been laid off from his bus driving job, so Ben hired him to drive the furniture back to Fort Lauderdale.

"Narcy called," said Cristobal's Chinese-born fiancée, Laura Law, "and they have a meeting to arrange to move the furniture, as Ben wants to move it to Florida."

Recently, Narcy Novack had become closer to her two older brothers, Cristobal and Carlos. Every February, Cristobal, Laura, and his two young children from a previous marriage vacationed in Florida. They spent a couple of days with Ben and Narcy before visiting his other two sisters and a niece, who were scattered around Florida.

During their brief visit in February 2008, Ben Novack Jr. was his usual brusque self, trying to avoid Narcy's family as much as possible.

"Ben Novack is very picky," said Law. "Nobody can go inside their house, and guests can only stay in the guesthouse."

During their stay, Laura Law observed her in-laws and felt that something was wrong. "They are like a husband and wife," she said. "But sometimes they argue. They are not happy."

Every night while they were there, Ben worked late on his computer in his second-floor office, drinking one coffee after another. "And when there was no coffee on the table," said Law, "Ben was not happy. He would be on his computer and shout, 'Narcy, coffee! Narcy, coffee!' And Narcy makes a cup of coffee and brings it up to him."

On one occasion, after an argument, Narcy refused to make him coffee. Ben then complained to Cristobal that his sister wasn't talking to him, asking if he could mediate and tell Narcy to stop being so angry.

"My husband was in the middle," said Law.

The next day, Ben bought Narcy some jewelry to make up with her. Narcy refused to accept it, telling Ben that she didn't want his gifts anymore.

"And then Ben was so mad," said Law.

Several weeks later, Ben Novack Jr. answered a sex advertisement on a Fort Lauderdale–based escort service Web site called Cityvibe.com. The advertisement had been placed by an attractive $300-an-hour prostitute named Rebecca Bliss, who had fallen on hard times after a former boyfriend shot her a year earlier.

Born Rebecca Dabakey in Grand Rapids, Michigan, the heavily tattooed and pierced forty-year-old brunette had a troubled history. After dropping out of the Kendall College of Art and Design, she had married and had a daughter. In 2002 her marriage broke up and she lost custody of the now-seven-year-old girl and moved south to Fort Myers, Florida, to work as a tattoo artist.

"I got my first tattoo when I was sixteen," says her Web site, "and have had a passionate love for body art ever since."

Three years later, she moved to California to start a new career as a porn star, as she owed her ex-husband thousands of dollars in child support. Over the next several years, under the name Mona Love, she starred in hardcore movies such as *Mona Love: Housewife Willing to Do Anything*, *Mona the Love Warrior*, and *Mommy Blows Best*.

In 2007 she retired from porn and moved back east to work as a tattoo artist. A few months later, her boyfriend shot her three times in her right hand and leg, effectively ending her tattooing career.

Then she moved to Miami and became a prostitute to survive.

Apart from advertising on Miami Internet sex sites, Bliss also had her own raunchy Web site, in which she boasted, "Have skills will travel . . . MI, NYC, CA, FL."

In February 2008, Ben Novack Jr. answered one of her online ads, and they began e-mailing each other.

"I included my phone number," said Bliss, "and he was able to call me, and we started speaking."

Soon afterward, they met for a coffee at a Starbucks in Fort Lauderdale so Ben could look her over, and he liked what he saw.

"The first date was just sexual relations," Bliss would later testify. "He paid me six hundred dollars, but we also talked."

Over the next few months, Ben began seeing Bliss regularly and they'd speak almost every day on the phone.

"We got a lot closer," she said. "And we talked a lot more every day on the phone."

That April, Vincent Zarzuela, who owns Metropolis Collectibles, the largest vintage comic dealership in the world, first heard about Ben Novack Jr. He was tipped off by a friend that Novack was spending big on vintage Batman comics, and would be at the upcoming Supercon in Florida.

"I figured, 'Hey, a new serious customer,'" said Zarzuela. "'I'd like to get away to Florida for a few days.'"

Several weeks before the show, the New York–based dealer received a call from Novack, who was interested in some of Zarzuela's rare Batman comics. Zarzuela arranged to meet Novack at the convention, to which he would bring the rare Batman books Ben was interested in.

On May 23, the first day of the Florida Supercon, Zarzula was at his stall when Ben and Narcy Novack came over and introduced themselves. "He reminded me of an old-school kind of hippy," Zarzuela said. "He had a lot of very big rings on him, the turquoise New Mexican cowboy type. He even had one of those Western-style bolo ties. A denim shirt. Curly blackish hair. His wife, Narcy, was also there. You meet so many collectors' wives, but she seemed okay."

As Narcy looked on, Ben Novack began thumbing through the stacks of Batman comics Zarzuela had brought, soon zeroing in on the ones he wanted. "He was rather stern in his negotiations," said the dealer. "Like I gave him a price, and he was, 'No, you'll have to do better than that.' It was kind of funny, because most customers don't talk like that. But we worked it out. Once we struck the price, he'd run it on his black Amex card. When you see a black Amex card you know the guy's got deep pockets, because there are not a lot of those around."

After striking a deal, Novack relaxed, and began discussing his passion for Batman comics and collectibles. "He loved Batman," said Zarzuela, "and I found him to be a passionate collector. He told me he was having a Batmobile made, and had all the working doodads and gadgets, down to the parachute shot out of the back."

Novack proudly announced that he was close to building complete sets of *Batman* and *World's Finest* comic titles, which would be worth millions.

"He's what we call in this business 'a completest,'" said Zarzuela. "He was working on his want list and he had very specific things."

At this first meeting, Novack and the dealer found a rapport, and when Zarzuela returned to New York, he shipped Novack the comic books he had wanted, whose cost totaled more than $100,000.

Over the next year, they remained in close touch over the phone and by e-mail.

"Ben had the potential to grow into a very big customer," said

Zarzuela. "What I would consider a good customer. A guy you want to keep doing business with, because he had the passion and the means to pay for his passion."

In early June of 2008, Ben Novack Jr. invited Rebecca Bliss to move to Fort Lauderdale so she could be closer to him. He offered to find her an apartment and pay all her expenses, on condition she gave up escorting.

While she looked for a suitable new home in Fort Lauderdale, he installed her in the luxurious Elizabeth Arden Red Door Spa in Weston, Florida. Over a period of two weeks, she ran up thousands of dollars in expensive spa treatments and other luxuries, paid for by Ben's company Black Amex card.

"[Ben] even bought me a toy poodle," Bliss said.

She eventually settled on a $1,220-a-month luxury apartment in an exclusive Fort Lauderdale gated community called Falls at Marina Bay, which boasted a "country club lifestyle" by the water. It had a club-house, a health and fitness club, and a movie theater.

"I called [Ben] to let him know that I had found something," Bliss said, "and he came over and looked at it. He agreed it was nice and said he was going to pay for it."

On the June 22, 2008, Marina Bay residency application, Ben Novack Jr. listed himself as Bliss's spouse. He cosigned the fourteen-month lease on apartment 204 in the name of Novack Enterprises, Inc., listing his assets as $10 million. He also put down a $250 security deposit as well as a small one for Bliss's four-year-old toy poodle.

As it was unfurnished, Ben told Bliss to go shop for furniture and then bill him.

"I went to Rooms to Go in Fort Lauderdale," Bliss recalled, "and I got a living room set, a kitchen set, and a bedroom set, costing some-where between nine thousand and and ten thousand."

After she moved in, Ben bought her a new cell phone, taking away the old one with her old clients' numbers on it.

He then assigned his right-hand man, Joe Gandy, to look after her.

"[Joe Gandy] came over to take me to do some errands," Bliss explained. "He would take me to pay my utility bills."

That summer, Ben Novack Jr. invited May Abad and her sons to move back to Fort Lauderdale and live in his guesthouse. It was agreed that May would work in his office doing customer service and helping out at conventions, while her sons Patrick, sixteen, and Marchelo, fifteen, went to a local school.

The plan was for Narcy to spend less time in the office, and eventually May would take over.

"According to Narcy," said Ben's cousin Meredith Fiel, "they were giving May a second chance, and grooming her to be part of the business."

This despite the fact that Narcy and her daughter had always had a very strained and combative relationship, often placing Ben in a difficult position.

"So May was fishing from both wells," said Charlie Seraydar. "Whoever would take care of her. It was a convoluted relationship between them all."

In July, Bernice Novack made out a new will, leaving most of her estate to the Jewish Federation. Her previous will, signed on November 12, 2004, had directed that she be cremated and that her ashes be mingled with those of her beloved pet schnauzer Micah and scattered at the Fontainebleau.

That earlier will left everything to Ben Jr., except $50,000, which would go to her sister Maxine, and $15,000 to each of her nieces, Meredith and Lisa. If Ben failed to survive her, everything would go to his nearest relation, Narcy.

Bernice told Estelle Fernandez that she now wanted to update her will, making sure Narcy never received a cent of her money or any jewelry.

"Her biggest desire," said Fernandez, "was never to let Narcy get anything of hers. Not one thing."

Fernandez then suggested Bernice set up a trust fund for her son, so he'd receive the money over a period of time. When Bernice told Ben about her plan, he was furious, ordering her not to, saying he and Narcy had two big mortgages to pay off.

"Well, Bernice never ever could make up her own mind," said Fernandez. "She had this quirk and just couldn't make a decision. So she drew up the will, leaving the money to the Jewish Federation. She was going to have an attorney do it, but never got around to it. And it just lay there on her desk."

Over that summer, Ben Novack Jr. fell in love with his new mistress, Rebecca Bliss. Although he rarely visited her apartment for sex, they would speak every day on the phone, developing a serious relationship.

"[I was] his girlfriend," said Bliss. "I loved him. We talked every day about everything going on in our lives. He was giving me everything." In one example of his largesse, he bought her $10,000 in digital musical equipment, which he installed in the apartment so she could start a new career as a DJ.

"He wanted me to do that instead of escorting," Bliss explained. "I did it for friends."

Later, Bliss would testify that Ben had asked her to be patient, saying he intended to divorce Narcy so they could be together.

In late August, Narcy Novack began to suspect that her husband was having an affair. Looking for evidence, she searched through his personal papers and found several credit card receipts slips for furniture.

"She got suspicious and called Bernice over," said Estelle Fernandez. "So they both went through his stuff and found out he was buying furniture for an apartment."

When Narcy confronted Ben with the evidence, he admitted to having a girlfriend but refused to give her up.

"Narcy was catching on that he was a whore hoffer," said Joe Gandy, "There were more whores than she could have guessed, and she was driving him crazy. So he filed for divorce."

Said Gandy, "I told him, 'Well, you sleep with a bunch of fucking rattlesnakes in a tank, you're going to get bit.'"

May Abad later claimed to have first discovered the incriminating receipts, asking her stepfather about them. Ben told her that he wanted a divorce, but promised to take care of her and her two teenage sons.

"My mother was very jealous," Abad told *Miami Herald* reporter Julie Brown. "He had a girlfriend on the side close to 40. It's part of my dad's life."

Charlie Seraydar believes there were other reasons Ben wanted to leave Narcy, and it wasn't to do with other women. "No, those were just extra-curriculum," said Seraydar. "But he was preparing to file for divorce, because things were getting ugly at home."

Ben and Narcy were now constantly arguing in the office, where it was an open secret that she had caught him cheating. May Abad later recalled how her mother would often light candles, as part of a voodoo ritual, after their fights.

"Somebody was going to kill somebody," said Joe Gandy. "We all knew it."

After discovering that Ben was planning to divorce her for Rebecca Bliss, Narcy Novack decided to have them both arrested. In early September she secretly contacted the Miami/Palm Beach office of the FBI saying she had information about her husband's illegal activities regarding an immigration fraud scheme.

On September 8 she met with FBI Special Agent John Wiley at a Fort Lauderdale coffee shop. She informed him that Ben was using his convention company as a front for arranging sham marriages. The following weekend, a Vancouver-based Iranian businessman was bringing in a number of energy soft drink distributors to a convention her husband was organizing at the Flamingo hotel in Las Vegas.

"The attendees from Canada would disappear in sham marriages," said Agent Wiley. "She stated that her husband Ben had set up two women in South Florida to be part of the sham marriages [and] was providing the services. He was also involved with prostitutes in the USA."

Narcy also gave the agent Rebecca Bliss's name and address, saying her husband had set up the former exotic dancer in an apartment with the sole purpose of Bliss's marrying a foreign convention attendee. She named a second woman, Shandra Lopez of West Palm Beach, claiming that Ben had also arranged a sham marriage for her.

At the end of the meeting, Narcy offered to discreetly provide more incriminating information against her husband, but insisted she remain anonymous.

"She said that if I call I should pretend to be from a mortgage company about financing," said Special Agent Wiley. "She feared retaliation if anyone found out she was talking to law enforcement."

A few days later, at a second meeting with the FBI, Narcy Novack made further claims about her husband's purported criminal activities. She told an agent that Joe Gandy was supplying Ben with "baseball-sized" supplies of cocaine. She also claimed that Ben and his friend and business partner Jerry Calhoun used a private airplane to make questionable trips back and forth to Mexico.

FBI agents duly filed reports about Narcy's claims, but they were not deemed credible, and no action was taken.

A month later, prior to boarding a Continental Airlines flight home after a convention in Puerto Vallarta, Narcy informed Mexican customs officials that Ben was traveling with $10,000 in illegal American cash. She told the Federales how her husband often masqueraded as a retired Miami Beach police officer, when he had never worked in law enforcement. She questioned how he could afford their extravagant jet-setting lifestyle, inferring he was involved in illegal activities.

As a result, when Ben and Narcy landed at Houston Airport, Ben was stopped by customs officials. Eventually, after hours of questioning, he was allowed to leave after U.S. Customs and Border Protection officers verified that he truly was a retired police officer with a permit to carry a concealed weapon.

A couple of weeks later, Narcy Novack was interviewed by FBI agents regarding her claims to Mexican customs agents, which she vehemently denied ever making.

In January 2009 a furious Narcy Novack made a call to the cell phone Ben had given Rebecca Bliss. Narcy demanded Bliss stop seeing her husband and offered her $10,000 never to speak to him again.

"She said she was Ben Novack's wife," Bliss recalled, "and did I know he was married. Just a lot of yelling. . . . She told me there were a lot of girls and I wasn't the only one.

"She mentioned that she knew I had a daughter in Michigan and she would help me fund her and give me money if I leave Ben. I said no."

When Bliss hung up, Narcy called back immediately.

"She was just yelling, 'We're not going to get a divorce.' There were more girls and he doesn't love me. She said that if she couldn't have him, no one could."

After Bliss stopped answering her calls, Narcy began investigating the former porn star, tracking down telephone numbers and e-mail addresses for Bliss's mother and an old boyfriend. She also obtained details about the Marina Bay apartment Ben had set Bliss up in, even contact numbers for the Marina Bay staff.

Then in mid-January, the complex's assistant property director, Joyce Errica, received a call from a Mrs. Novack informing her that her husband, Ben, had died and would no longer be paying Rebecca Bliss's rent.

Errica told her she did not know what she was talking about, and suggested she send her a copy of Ben Novack's death certificate.

"She said she would bring in the death certificate, and she hung up," said Errica. "She never called again."

THIRTY-TWO

A FAMILY PLOT

Investigators believe Narcy Novack now decided to make good on her 2002 threat to murder her husband, fearing she would lose everything in a divorce. Under Ben's 1991 prenuptial agreement, Narcy would receive only $65,000, but she wanted the whole of Ben Jr.'s $7.2 million fortune. So she recruited her elder brother Cristobal Veliz to help her.

First, however, they cold-bloodedly decided to kill Bernice Novack, who was executor of Ben's estate, ensuring that everything would go to Narcy after Ben was disposed of.

To help plan the attacks with Cristobal, Narcy bought an old flip phone from a neighbor's brother for $200, which had an unlimited Boost Mobile monthly plan. She explained to the seller that she wanted a phone that Ben couldn't access or track.

Over the next few months she would use her secret cell phone number 954-816-2089 to brief Cristobal on Bernice's and Ben's habits and movements. Cristobal would talk to Mi Niña (My Little One), the family's pet name for his sister, for hours at a time.

In December 2008, Narcy's brother drove to Miami with a teenage family friend called Francisco Picado, to make contacts and recruit some hired hands for the killings. Fifty-five-year-old Veliz had first met Picado in 2003, when the boy was twelve, after renting a room in his mother's house at 1499 Jefferson Avenue, Brooklyn. As Picado grew up, Veliz, who worked in a bakery, had become a father figure to him.

Now eighteen, Picado had recently started dating a Miami high school student named Keyling Sanchez, and invited Veliz to drive down with him to visit her, and thus save on expenses. Veliz, who lived in Philadelphia, was only too happy to go.

"We would go to be with women," Veliz explained. "I would have fun with women down there."

In Miami, Veliz and Picado both stayed at the home of Keyling's mother, Tomassa Ortez, at North West Fourth Terrace, which was also used as a day care center. During their stay, seventeen-year-old Keyling introduced Veliz to several women.

Veliz started making contacts by befriending several of Keyling's family friends. These included twenty-seven-year-old Melvin Medrano, who owned a local car wash; his lover José Carlos Castillia, and a Nicaraguan friend of Keyling's brother Luis named Cesar Mairena.

While in Florida, Cristobal also spent time with Narcy in Fort Lauderdale, and investigators believe that this is when they took their plot to the next stage.

On Monday, February 2, Cristobal Veliz made a second trip to Miami, driving Francisco Picado's Nissan Murano. Over the last few days, he had been in close contact with Narcy on her secret cell phone, and prosecutors believe that she had now given him the go-ahead to make preparations for the murder of her mother-in-law, Bernice Novack.

As soon as they arrived in Miami, Veliz withdrew $750 from his account at the Bank of America to cover expenses. He then contacted Melvin Medrano, offering him $2,500 to participate in the attack on Bernice Novack.

On Wednesday, Veliz asked Francisco Picado to drive him to Fort Lauderdale, directing him to a gas station near Las Olas Boulevard, just a couple of blocks away from Ben and Narcy Novack's compound. They parked across the street, and Veliz explained that they were waiting for Bernice Novack's Infiniti to pass by.

"He wanted to check the route that her car would take on her way home," said Picado.

Suddenly they saw Bernice's tan Infiniti emerge into Las Olas Boulevard; they followed it. But a few minutes later they lost it in traffic, and Veliz instructed his young friend to turn back to Miami. On the drive back, Picado asked Veliz why he needed to know the old lady's route home.

"He said that somewhere along it they were going to [hit] the car," Picado later testified. "They would go out and help her and then assault her."

Picado then asked why Veliz would want to beat up the old lady, and Veliz replied that his sister was paying for it and wanted Bernice "hospitalized." He explained how Narcy hated how Bernice treated her, and how she told her son, Ben, to force Narcy into sex. Veliz also claimed that Ben had fitted his sister with breast implants while a doctor had been treating her for a broken nose.

Two days later, Veliz telephoned Cesar Mairena, whom he had met in December, offering him fifty dollars to drive him to Fort Lauderdale. They met up at Keyling Sanchez's house, where Veliz was staying, and on their way north they stopped at a gas station to fill up Mairena's white Impala.

On arrival in Fort Lauderdale, Veliz directed Mairena to Bernice Novack's house at North East Thirty-Seventh Drive, but they got lost and stopped at a gas station to buy a map. While there, Veliz called Narcy on his cell phone for instructions on how to proceed.

"He said 'Mi Niña' a couple of times," said Mairena, "so I knew it was a lady."

After getting clarification from Narcy, Veliz directed Mairena to the Coral Ridge County Club, where they drove past Bernice's house several times, looking for her car.

"He wanted to see what it was like," Mairena explained. "It was a nice middle-class neighborhood."

Mairena drove up and down NE Thirty-Seventh Drive for a few minutes, before Veliz told him to drive back to Miami.

The next day, a Saturday, Cristobal paid Mairena another fifty dollars to drive him back to Fort Lauderdale.

"I drove by the house, like the first time," Mairena said. "Then we turned around again."

During the drive back to Miami, Veliz asked Mairena if he would be willing to hit an old lady in the face for money. "I told him no," Mairena later testified. "He told me he was trying to [hurt] the lady, because she supposedly did some harm to his sister. He wanted to pay her back."

Later that day, Veliz and Picado drove back to Brooklyn, arriving on Sunday morning. After spending a few hours at his fiancée Laura Law's Brooklyn apartment, Veliz drove with her to Florida for their annual family vacation.

The following Wednesday, February 11, Cesar Mairena got a call from Cristobal Veliz asking him to make a third trip to Fort Lauderdale. Once again they met at Keyling's house, but this time Veliz directed Mairena to a car wash at a nearby Chevron gas station.

"Mr. Veliz said he was going to meet somebody who was going to go along with us," Mairena said. "He told me that he had got somebody to do the [old lady] harm."

After collecting the man from the car wash, Mairena drove them to Fort Lauderdale, and Veliz told him stop at a mall, as he had to buy something. While Mairena waited in the car, Veliz and the man went into a sports store, emerging a few minutes later with a bag of power-walking weights for the attack.

They then proceeded to NE Thirty-Seventh Drive, where Veliz pointed out Bernice's house to the attacker, whom he never referred to by name. Veliz ordered him to wait in the bushes by the old lady's house and "hit her in the face and hurt her" when she came home.

After dropping the man off by the house, Mairena waited with Veliz at a nearby strip mall, where he called his sister to see if Bernice had left the office yet.

"Mr. Veliz told me the guy was going to do it," Mairena said. "Then we waited, and the sun was going down."

After it got dark, the man from the car wash walked nervously into the strip mall parking lot and got into the car. As they drove off, Veliz asked the man if he had assaulted Bernice Novack. The man explained that he'd been spotted by neighbors looking suspicious, so he had taken off.

The next afternoon, Cristobal Veliz met Mairena for another attempt at assaulting Bernice Novack. Soon after he arrived at Sanchez's house, Melvin Medrano pulled up in a Honda Accord with another man Mairena had never seen before.

After Veliz gassed up both cars, he and Mairena set off for Fort Lauderdale, followed by Medrano and his friend. During the trip, Veliz was in constant touch with Narcy, updating her on what was happening. That day, he made sixteen calls to his sister's secret cell phone.

At around 5:00 P.M., they arrived at NE Thirty-Seventh Drive and Veliz led Medrano and his friend past Bernice's house before both men parked the two cars a block away, by a bridge. Medrano and the other man then got out and walked back to the house, hiding behind some trash cans by the garage to wait for Bernice to come out.

Fifteen yards away, eighteen-year-old Drew Offerdahl was practicing piano in the living room of his family's home when he saw the two men sneaking through an alley toward Bernice Novack's garage. He called to his father, John Offerdahl, a former linebacker for the Miami Dolphins, and pointed them out.

"There were two guys who were suspicious standing next to Bernice's garage wall," the elder Offerdahl recalled.

When the Offerdahls came out and asked the men what they were doing, the two men ran away.

"We started chasing them," said John Offerdahl, "and the dogs were chasing after them, too. It was kind of curious. We're in a safe neighborhood, and people don't usually run away when they're asked what they're doing."

A few minutes later, Melvin Medrano and his friend returned to

Bernice's house, hurling her ornamental cast-iron garden frog through her front window before running away.

At home at the time of the attempted attack, Bernice Novack was startled by the sound of breaking glass. She dashed into her front room to find her heavy frog ornament lying inside on the carpet, with broken glass everywhere. She immediately called her son in a panic, asking what to do. Ben Jr. told her not to worry; that the incident was not worth reporting to the police. He assured her that everything would be all right, and reminded her to make sure the security alarm was on inside the house.

Nevertheless, the shaken eighty-six-year-old did call Fort Lauderdale Police, to report that her home had been vandalized.

Half an hour later, Fort Lauderdale Police patrol officer Scott Fry arrived in a police cruiser. Bernice gave a statement that she had heard a loud noise at about 7:00 P.M., before finding her front window broken and the cast-iron frog on the carpet inside.

Considering it a case of misdemeanor vandalism, the uniformed officer did not have the scene processed for evidence or take the frog into evidence.

Bernice was so upset by the incident that she asked Rebecca Greene, who lived directly opposite, to keep an eye out when she came home at night. She also arranged to have television surveillance cameras installed outside the house for extra protection.

"She was really, really nervous after that happened," said Estelle Fernandez.

After his second failed attempt to kill Bernice Novack, Cristobal Veliz left Miami with Laura Law, going back up north to regroup. He was angry and frustrated, and complained that he had already given Melvin Medrano $150 for the aborted job.

The plot was then put on hold, until Melvin Medrano could recruit someone else to help him. A couple of weeks later, a thirty-three-year-old illegal immigrant from Nicaragua named Alejandro Garcia started work at Medrano's car wash.

Garcia had first arrived in Florida in 2005 on a six-month work visa, staying on when it ran out. He was a street person and a crack addict with a long police record for theft, drugs, and petty crimes.

Five foot, ten inches tall and weighing around two hundred pounds, Garcia sported a large dragon tattoo on his right arm. He was blind in his right eye, after a machete cut it open in a childhood accident. Now he always wore sunglasses, as light troubled him, giving him dizzy spells and severe headaches.

Soon after they met, Medrano asked Garcia if he had ever beaten anyone up for money. When Garcia said no but that he was willing to do so, Medrano said he knew of a job to beat up an old lady.

"They were going to pay good money," Garcia later testified. "So I told him if [it's] an old lady, the job looks easy. I needed money, so I said okay."

Soon afterward, Medrano opened a new car wash, at a Vallero gas station a few blocks away, and hired Garcia to work there. Garcia would soon be meeting "Jefe" (the big boss), he told his new employee, who was bankrolling the old lady job.

The last week of March, Cristobal Veliz and Francisco Picado arrived at the car wash and met Garcia.

"Cristobal told me he wanted me to beat up an old lady," Garcia said. "The lady was his sister's mother-in-law."

Veliz explained that the old lady disliked his sister, Narcy, making her son, Ben, beat Narcy every day as part of the Jewish religion. He also told Garcia that Narcy had "big tits" that she didn't want, because her mother-in-law had given her a drink and she had woken up with them.

"He told me that [Ben] abused her sexually," Garcia would later testify, "and had sex up the ass without any tenderness, and made her give him blowjobs whenever he wanted. Horrible dirty things."

Veliz explained that he had sent others to try to assault the old lady, calling those other men "blood bunglers" because they had been too scared to do it.

Then he took Medrano and Garcia for lunch at a Subway restaurant near the car wash, to make the deal.

"Cristobal asked me how much I would charge," said Garcia. "I said, 'I don't know. I've never done this. Is a thousand okay?' He said, 'Okay, just do the job.'"

Veliz said that he and Medrano would follow the old lady's car and hit her from behind. When she got out of it, Garcia was to assault her.

"The plan was for me to give her a good beating," he explained, "and hit her in the teeth."

Before leaving, Veliz gave Garcia his cell phone number, which Garcia punched into his phone under the name "Jefe."

On Sunday, March 22, Temple Hayes and her partner, Barbara, stopped off in Fort Lauderdale, while on a cruise around Florida, to spend the day with Bernice. They drove over to the Coral Ridge Golf Course to collect Bernice and took her to Whole Foods, one of her favorite stores.

"And we sat there and talked for hours," said Hayes. "We were laughing with her about the great shape she was in. I said, 'Jeez, girl, you're my motivator, because you're almost in better shape than I am.'"

Then they went back to Bernice's house for a couple of hours, before they had to get back to the boat. At one point, Hayes asked how things were between her and Narcy.

"For some reason Bernice had softened around all that," Hayes said. "I think that she had let her guard down, and just said, 'This is the way it is, so I need to just be comfortable with it.' She was no longer talking about Narcy so negatively."

The following Saturday morning, March 28, Bernice Novack went to the Bank of America, in downtown Fort Lauderdale, to put a five-carat diamond ring in her safe-deposit box. On her way into the bank, she tripped over some broken sidewalk, landing facedown on the pavement.

The bank staff rushed out to help her, bringing her into the bank. They sat her down and treated the cuts to her head with rubbing alcohol. Bernice refused to let them call an ambulance, insisting she was fine. And after leaving the ring in her safe-deposit box, she drove herself home. Then she called Ben Jr., who was out of town, telling him she had fallen. He told her to go to the hospital immediately, but she said it was unnecessary.

"She was banged up pretty bad," said Rebecca Greene. "She had all kinds of cuts and bruises."

A few hours later, Ben Novack Jr. returned to Fort Lauderdale, driving straight over to his mother's house. He insisted on taking her to the Imperial Point Medical Center, where she was X-rayed, before being released.

Ben Jr. then decided to sue the Bank of America for negligence, because of the injuries caused to his mother by the broken sidewalk. The next day, Bernice asked Rebecca Greene to come over and photograph her injuries.

"She called me to take pictures of her face," said Rebecca, "and all because her son was going to sue them. He was one of those type people."

When Green arrived, Bernice gave her a digital camera to take the photographs.

"Bernice had this really thin skin," Greene recalled, "so if she cut herself or fell down, it would look just awful. That's the way she looked, because she had fallen and cut herself in several places, and skinned her face all up."

Apart from her injuries, Bernice appeared fine, and even opened a bottle of white wine to thank her neighbor.

On Monday morning, Bernice Novack drove to work as usual, but Ben and Narcy insisted on driving her home, saying she looked terrible.

"She tried to come back to work," said Charlie Seraydar. "That's the stamina that this lady had. Ben insisted that she go to another hospital for a second opinion."

Later that day, Ben Jr. e-mailed Seraydar the photographs of his mother's injuries, asking what needed to be done to file a negligence suit against the bank.

"She was all bandaged up," Seraydar said, "and had bruises on her legs, her arms, her elbows, and her face. I mean she looked like she'd had the shit kicked out of her."

Seraydar advised hiring private investigator Pat Franklin, who had worked on the home invasion incident seven years earlier, to photograph the sidewalk outside the Bank of America where Bernice had fallen.

After Bernice's fall, Narcy had been unusually sympathetic and helpful—for it would now be far easier to stage another accident for Bernice Novack, with her recent medical history of falls.

THIRTY-THREE

THE KILLING

At 1:00 P.M. on Friday April 3, Francisco Picado rented a red Chevy Scion from Rent Max in Miami, paying $118 in cash that he had been given by Cristobal Veliz. He then drove it to the car wash, where Melvin Medrano was waiting.

Two hours later, Medrano took the wheel of the Scion and collected Alejandro Garcia from the Blue Belle Trailer Park, where Garcia was renting a small room in the back of a trailer. He brought him back to the car wash, where Veliz was parked in his green Nissan Pathfinder.

After collecting a fourteen-inch monkey wrench, Medrano and Garcia followed Veliz to NE Thirty-Seventh Drive, Fort Lauderdale, and waited for Bernice Novack to come home. Several hours later, after she failed to appear, Veliz took his men out for dinner.

"Cristobal said that we were going to return," Garcia said.

On Saturday afternoon, they regrouped in the parking lot of a Checkers restaurant on East Sunrise Boulevard, Fort Lauderdale. Upon their arrival, Garcia stepped out of the Scion and walked over to the Pathfinder, where Veliz was receiving last-minute instructions from Narcy on his cell phone.

"He said, 'Mi Niña is giving me her route,'" Garcia later testified.

"His sister was giving him information, and he was writing down the make and license plate numbers of the old lady's car."

Veliz said the old lady would be at a strip mall near her house. So, after eating lunch, they drove there. When there was no sign of Bernice at the mall, he checked in with his sister, who suggested trying a nearby hair salon Bernice used. But there was no sign of her there, either.

Then Veliz ordered Medrano to follow him to Bernice's house, where there was a large black truck parked outside in front of her tan Infiniti.

Jefe told his men to wait for the old lady to come home and then attack her, before driving off and parking a few blocks away by a condo complex.

Melvin Medrano parked the red Scion at the end of the block and waited.

"I told Melvin I needed to buy a bottle of rum," said Garcia. "I was nervous because I had to attack the old lady. I can't do this if I don't drink something."

So they drove to a nearby liquor store, by the beach, and Medrano bought a large bottle of rum and a soda to mix with it, which Garcia began drinking.

Periodically, Medrano drove past Bernice Novack's house to see if the black truck was still there, as they were waiting until it had left before moving in. When Garcia finished the bottle of rum, he told Medrano to buy him another, so they drove back to the liquor store.

While there, Medrano decided to buy binoculars, for a better view of the old lady's house. So he drove to a drugstore and bought a pair for twenty dollars. Then, after discovering they were no good, he returned to exchange them for a better pair.

This time when they went back to Bernice Novack's house, they found that the black truck had now gone, leaving the coast clear for the attack.

That Saturday, Bernice Novack had stayed home all day, canceling her regular hairdressing appointment, as she was feeling unwell. She had spent the afternoon helping her longtime housekeeper Eduardo clean her home, which she enjoyed doing.

At around 5:30 P.M., Ben telephoned to check on his mother. Tomorrow was the thirty-fourth anniversary of Ben Sr.'s death, and Bernice told her son that she missed his father terribly.

Then she received a call from Estelle Fernandez.

"She had a very rough day," said Estelle. "She wasn't feeling well, but she was going to take it easy after Eduardo left."

The two friends made plans to meet the following day, and Bernice got off the phone saying she had to see Eduardo out.

"She said she'd call me back," said Estelle, "but she didn't."

After Eduardo drove off in his black truck, Bernice Novack locked all her doors, as she always did. She was feeling tired so she changed into her blue nightgown and poured herself a glass of chardonnay from the bottle she had opened the previous Sunday. Then she settled down on her sofa to watch television.

At around 8:00 P.M., Cathy Moffa was out walking her dog when she noticed a stocky Hispanic-looking man in sunglasses talking on his cell phone outside her neighbor Bernice Novack's house. Her dog started barking, and she became concerned. When she got home, she asked her husband to investigate. But by the time he went outside, the Hispanic man had disappeared.

At 9:22 P.M., Alejandro Garcia hid the large monkey wrench in his pants and grabbed the nearly empty second bottle of rum. He told Melvin Medrano to keep his cell phone on, so they could be in constant communication and Medrano would know when to come and collect him. Then he got out of the red Scion and walked down the street toward Bernice Novack's house.

When Garcia reached the house, he took out the monkey wrench and placed it between two large garbage cans with the bottle of rum.

Then he crouched down in the shrubbery, waiting for the old lady to come out and move her car, as Narcy had said was her custom.

"I was drinking all the time," said Garcia, "and talking to Melvin on the cell phone."

At 9:25 P.M., Garcia heard the double garage doors opening, and Bernice Novack came out in her blue nightgown.

"The lady's coming," Garcia whispered to Medrano on his cell. "I need to get out of here."

After turning on the speakerphone so his getaway driver could hear everything, Garcia put the cell phone in his pants. Then, as Bernice walked out of the garage and toward her car in the driveway, Garcia picked up the heavy monkey wrench.

He later recalled hearing a clicking noise as Bernice opened her car door remotely. Crouched down in the bushes, he watched her get into the car and start the engine. Then, as she drove past him, Garcia crept up behind the car, following it into the garage. Bernice Novack stopped the car inside and turned off the engine, taking the key out of the ignition.

Suddenly, as she opened the car door to climb out, her attacker lunged toward her, brandishing the monkey wrench.

"She looked at me and screamed," Garcia later testified. "Then I hit her. She fell down on the [passenger] seat. I leaned into the car and put my left hand on the steering wheel, and hit her again in the face. I don't remember how many times I hit her with the flat side of the wrench."

After Garcia had finished beating her, he carefully cleaned his fingerprints off the steering wheel with his shirt. Then he ripped Bernice's black piglet key ring out of her clenched hand, as Jefe wanted proof of the attack. Leaving the old lady slumped across the driver's seat in a pool of her own blood, he came out of the garage.

Melvin Medrano, who had heard everything on his cell phone, was standing in the driveway waiting.

"Let's get out of here," he said.

Garcia grabbed the monkey wrench and the rum bottle and jumped in the red Scion, parked outside with its engine running, and the two drove back to Miami.

. . .

The first savage blow from the wrench hit Bernice Novack squarely across the face, sending her glasses flying to the garage floor. It fractured her skull. The second blow broke her jaw, knocking out some of her teeth. Garcia had then delivered three more punishing blows to Bernice's head with the wrench.

After her attacker left, Bernice lay on the car's seat with her head bleeding, drifting in and out of consciousness. Terrified and in full shock, she somehow found the strength to get out of the car and stumble out of the garage. She opened the door to the house and entered by way of the laundry room, leaving a trail of blood as she did so.

Confused and trying to gather her thoughts, she staggered into her kitchen, through the living room, and into the bathroom, where she lost control of her bowels. She desperately tried to clean herself up, taking off her soiled underwear and trying to stop all the bleeding.

Suddenly, to her horror, she remembered that the door to the house from the garage was still open. Fearing her attacker was still out there and might return, and bleeding profusely, with her body shutting down, she staggered back out through the living room and kitchen and into the laundry room, where she locked the door.

Then she reached up to hit the panic button on the security control panel to summon help. But before she could do so, Bernice Novack collapsed facedown on the floor.

As they sped back to Miami, Alejandro Garcia called Jefe's cell phone at 9:38 P.M., informing him the attack had been successful. Veliz immediately called Narcy with the news. That day, the siblings were in constant communication, making fifteen calls to each other.

Back in Miami, Melvin Medrano parked the rented Scion outside Rent Max on NW Twenty-Eighth Street and waited for Cristobal Veliz to arrive. A few minutes later, Veliz's green Pathfinder drew up behind them, and Medrano went to collect their money for the job.

"Melvin came back and gave me six hundred dollars cash," said Garcia. "I asked him, 'What's this?' 'Well, he said, 'the man's not carrying more money; he'll give you more later.'"

Then, after going back to the trailer to wash Bernice Novack's blood off the monkey wrench, Garcia went off to a friend's house, spending the night smoking crack.

At 5:30 on Sunday morning, Rebecca Green went downstairs to get her newspaper. It was still dark outside, and she was surprised to see Bernice Novack's garage door open and the light on inside.

"She didn't get up early," Rebecca explained. "So I felt that was very unusual."

An hour later, when her husband, Bill, woke up, she told him something strange was going on, as Bernice's garage door was open.

"Well, don't call her," he said. "You'll scare her to death if you call this early."

So they waited another two hours before telephoning Bernice. As there was no answer, they decided to go over and see if she was all right. On the way over, they could see her tan Infiniti in the garage, with the lights still on.

Bill Green knocked on Bernice's front door. When there was no answer, he and Rebecca walked around to the back and peeked in through the sliding glass doors of Bernice's living room.

"Everything was like it had been left the night before," Rebecca recalled. "There were lights on, and the TV was going. Her glass of wine was sitting on the table. And I said, 'Something is wrong.'"

The Greens went back to their house and called Ben Novack Jr., telling him he ought to come over to his mother's house immediately and see if she was okay.

At 8:26 A.M., Ben Novack Jr. called Fort Lauderdale Police as he and Narcy raced to his mother's home. He asked them to check on his mother, saying her neighbors were concerned for her safety.

Ten minutes later, Ben and Narcy arrived at 2757 NE Thirty-Seventh Drive, where they were met by Bill Green.

While Narcy waited in the car, Ben Jr. unlocked the front door, and he and Bill Green entered.

"Ben and I walk in there," recalled Green, "and he yells, 'Hey, Mom! Hey, Mom!' He walks around into the kitchen and then we found her in a pool of blood, facedown. Her feet were toward the laundry room and her head was toward the kitchen.

"Ben used to be a policeman, so he went over and checked her pulse. And he said, 'Well, she's gone.'"

Then they looked around the room, which was covered in blood and feces.

"There's a little day toilet," Green said. "It looked like she had run in there, because there were blood spatters all the way around."

Then he and Ben went back outside, where Narcy was waiting in the car. Ben got in the car and told Narcy that his mother was dead, as several neighbors came over to see what was happening.

At 8:33 A.M., Ben put in another call to the police, reporting his mother dead.

"Ben was a little distraught and sat in the front of the car with his head in his lap," said Bill Green. "Narcy was there, and she didn't say anything."

At 8:39 A.M., two EMS officers from Fort Lauderdale Fire Department Rescue 54 officially pronounced Bernice Novack dead—thirty-four years to the day after her late husband's passing. Then patrol officers James Hayes and Kelli Phillips arrived and began securing the house with yellow crime scene tape.

They briefly interviewed Ben Novack Jr., who told them that his mother suffered from asthma.

"Novack did advise that his mother fell on a sidewalk a week prior," the officers later reported, "and had to go to Imperial Point Hospital. The hospital took X-rays and released Bernice Novack the same day."

At 8:55 A.M., Fort Lauderdale Police crime scene investigator Carol

Coval arrived to process the scene. By coincidence, she had also processed Ben Novack Jr.'s house after the 2002 home invasion.

The forensic investigator placed protective booties over her shoes before entering the house through the front door. She then did a cursory walk-through of the house.

"The house's flooring was large white tiles," she later wrote in her report. "Off the living room was a half bath and leading into and out of the bathroom was dried blood and fecal matter on the tile floor. The toilet was full of blood. Black panties were on the floor in front of the toilet."

She then followed the trail of blood through the living room, dining room, and into the kitchen. From there the blood trail went into the laundry room and out the door that led into the garage. It finished up in Bernice's car, which was covered in dried blood.

"Sitting below the open driver's car door on the concrete garage floor," wrote Coval, "were her eyeglasses."

Inside the car, Coval found blood on the front passenger and driver's seat areas, and on the center console.

"It appeared that blood had been smeared on the seat," Coval noted. "Blood was also found on the side of the driver's door."

Coval then examined Bernice Novack's body, which was lying face-down in the laundry room as if she had taken an ugly fall.

"She was cold to the touch," Coval reported. "She was in full rigor, it appears she broke her front teeth when she fell and she had a laceration to her left cheek. Her left middle finger was lacerated and broken."

Coval then removed several gold bracelets, necklaces, and an anklet from the body, placing them in a bowl in the laundry room. She also observed a full glass of white wine on the dining room table and "numerous prescription medications" in the bedroom.

At 9:25 A.M., Detectives Mark Shotwell and Brad Jenkins arrived at the house to investigate Bernice Novack's death.

"On entering the residence via the front door," Detective Shotwell wrote in his subsequent report, "I noted both drip and smear blood mixed with feces and a [pair] of soiled underwear in the bathroom off the living room."

Then, as Officer Coval carefully photographed the body and the death scene, Detective Shotwell went back outside.

"No signs of forced entry were noted," he wrote. "The front door was locked on Ben's arrival as were all remaining doors/windows with the exception of the garage."

He went back inside the house for a second look, finding nothing suspicious to make him think this was anything but a tragic accident.

"Nothing appeared disturbed or ransacked," he reported. "Novack's purse and jewelry were in open view. No footprints were found leading away from any of the blood trails or laundry room floor."

He also noted an almost full glass of white wine on the dining room table, and an empty 1.5 liter chardonnay bottle in the recycling bin.

Outside the house, he interviewed Ben Novack Jr., who said his mother had suffered a serious fall a week earlier and had been treated in a hospital emergency room.

"[Bernice] Novack had complained of dizziness and not felt well since," wrote Shotwell. "Ben Novack also stated that his mother did not drink white wine and questioned why the glass was on the table."

Novack also informed the detective that he was a retired police officer, and was concerned that the hospital where his mother was examined after her fall had missed something. He advised Shotwell to have the glass of wine tested.

Detective Shotwell also interviewed Bill and Rebecca Greene and several other neighbors.

The detective then went back inside the house to make a closer examination of the death scene. He concluded that Bernice Novack had been alone when she began bleeding and then collapsed, as all the doors leading out of the house were dead bolted and there were no footprints in her blood other than her own.

"The blood trail started inside or near her vehicle," he wrote in his report, "and then proceeded into the residence where she attempted to 'clean up' at the sink. Novack then moved to the bathroom as she lost control of her bowels, dripping blood and feces as she walked. Novack appears to have then reversed direction and moved back through the kitchen to the laundry room where she collapsed."

An hour earlier, Ben Novack Jr. had called Charlie Seraydar with the sad news, as Narcy comforted him in his car.

"He said he found his mother dead," Seraydar recalled, "so I ran over there and arrived before they [had] even removed the body."

Seraydar waited outside with Ben and Narcy while the police worked inside.

"[Narcy] was very close to Ben and very supportive," Seraydar said later. "She sat right next to him and held his hand."

Close to tears, Narcy told Seraydar how she and Bernice had planned to go shopping that very morning.

"I found that to be very odd," said Seraydar, "after all these years."

At around 10:30 A.M., the Broward County Medical Examiner's Office collected Bernice Novack's body, transporting it to the ME's office for autopsy. Bernice's prescription medications were also taken for analysis.

Fifteen minutes later, Detective Shotwell secured the house, giving Ben Novack Jr. his mother's jewelry and having him lock the door and set the alarm. Shotwell then placed evidence tape over the locks of the front door, the garage door, and the side door into the garage.

At 1:30 P.M., Dr. Khalil Wardak of the Broward County Medical Examiner's Office contacted Detective Shotwell, saying he wanted to view the residence to help him determine the cause of death.

Ben Novack Jr. then returned to unlock the front door and turn off the alarm.

Dr. Wardak arrived at 2:15 P.M. and spent about forty minutes inspecting the scene with Detective Shotwell and Officer Coval. He left at 2:55 P.M., and once again Ben Novack Jr. locked up the residence and reset the alarm.

At 9:30 that morning, Estelle Fernandez had called Bernice Novack, as they had plans to meet. There was no answer, so she'd left a message, saying she hoped Bernice felt better and assumed she was probably out early.

Several hours later, Fernandez received a phone call from Ben Novack Jr.

"He said, 'Bernice passed away,'" Fernandez recalled. "It was very cold . . . I was shocked."

He then put Narcy on the phone to explain what had happened.

"Narcy said there had been an accident," Estelle said. "That [Bernice] must have started bleeding from the nose. She then threw a tissue in the sink and ran to go to the bathroom and didn't make it and had a bowel movement over everything. That's what Narcy told me."

Narcy proceeded to explain in graphic detail how Bernice had tried to change her underwear and clean herself, but had then fallen down.

"She just couldn't deal with it and she passed away," Fernandez said. "That's exactly what Narcy told me."

THIRTY-FOUR

"THE MANNER OF DEATH IS DETERMINED TO BE: ACCIDENT"

A t 8:50 A.M. on Monday, April 6, crime scene investigator Carol Coval arrived at the Broward County Medical Examiner's Office at 5301 SW Thirty-First Avenue for Bernice Novack's autopsy. She walked in the morgue to find Bernice Novack's body on a metal gurney. Bernice was wearing her blue nightgown, covered in blood, and the sandals she had been found in. Coval photographed the body with 35 mm color film.

At 9:10 A.M., Broward County associate medical examiner Dr. Iouri G. Boiko began the autopsy by doing a rape kit. Detectives Mark Shotwell and Brad Jenkins were there as witnesses, as well as Investigator Coval.

Dr. Boiko opened up the body with the thoracoabdominal "Y" incision that stretched from the shoulders to the breastbone and extended down from the sternum to the pubic bone. Dr. Boiko then peeled back the skin and removed the chest plate. There were no injuries or buildup of fluid in any of the body cavities. He also found no evidence of blunt force or other injuries to the thoracoabdominal area. The cardiovascular system was in good condition for a woman Bernice's age, as was her respiratory system.

However, the medical examiner did find several serious blunt force injuries to the head. Bernice Novack had a left frontotemporal depressed fracture at the base of her skull, with internal bleeding. She had also suffered a traumatic brain injury, with bruising to her brain. Dr. Boiko found that her jaw was fractured in several places, and there were cuts and bruises all over her body. The third left finger, where she had once worn Ben Novack Sr.'s diamond wedding ring, was fractured.

He also observed crusted abrasions to her knees and her left leg, where she had fallen a week before her death. These were in the process of healing.

In his autopsy report, Dr. Boiko wrote that Bernice Novack had suffered from bronchial asthma, and noted her recent fall outside the Bank of America.

He listed the official cause of death as accidental, but did not clarify whether it had been caused by the earlier fall or this one.

"This 86-year-old white female, Bernice Novack," he wrote, "died as a result of blunt force injuries of head sustained in an unwitnessed fall at her home. The manner of death is determined to be: ACCIDENT."

Later, Dr. Khalil Wardak of the Broward County Medical Examiner's Office would claim he knew from the beginning that Bernice Novack had not died a natural death, but had been overruled by his superiors.

"When I examined the body," he later testified, "it did not speak of accidental death, because of the amount of injuries. From my training. I did not think it was a fall. I've never seen any injuries like this from someone falling. I expressed my concern."

A few hours earlier, Estelle Fernandez received a frantic phone call from Ben Novack Jr. complaining that his mother's treasured five-carat diamond ring was missing. "He said, 'You know my father gave my mother a ring,'" she said. "'Well I can't find it. Do you now where it is?'" Estelle said it must be around the house, as Bernice always wore it.

After hanging up, Novack called Charlie Seraydar, saying he suspected one of the crime scene officers of taking his mother's ring, and asked what to do. The ex-cop warned him not to accuse any officer of stealing the ring, otherwise he would get no cooperation into any ensuing investigation into his mother's death.

"He thought it had been taken off her body," Seraydar said. "I told him to wait until he could get into her bank safety deposit box, and make sure it was not there."

Nevertheless, Novack did call Fort Lauderdale Police, demanding they come back and search for the ring.

So, after leaving the Medical Examiner's Office, Detectives Mark Shotwell and Brad Jenkins returned to Bernice Novack's house. When they arrived, they were met by Ben and Narcy Novack and Charlie Seraydar. The detectives then made a complete video recording of the house, in case of any future legal action relating to the missing ring.

While in the garage, Detective Shotwell now concentrated on a sharp window frame over the driver's side door of Bernice's Infiniti. He theorized that Bernice may have been drinking before going out to the car, and then fell and hit her head on the window frame.

"The sharp corner appeared consistent in both size and height to have caused the puncture/skull fracture to the [left] side of Novack's head. This would also explain Novack's broken glasses found near the open driver's door."

Detective Jenkins then took blood swabs from the vehicle, laundry room, and bathroom. He also collected Bernice's broken glasses and the wineglass from the dining room table, placing them both in separate evidence bags.

At 3:00 P.M., 2757 NE Thirty-Seventh Drive was turned over to Ben Novack Jr., as the Fort Lauderdale Police Department's investigation was officially over.

After the police left, Charlie Seraydar walked through the death scene with Ben and Narcy Novack. The former detective saw nothing to make him think that Bernice Novack's death might have been the result of foul play.

"I didn't see anything out of place," Seraydar said. "This woman was a very independent lady, and she had [already] taken a very bad fall and injured herself."

Ben Jr. thought otherwise. He was convinced that his mother's death had been caused by something other than an accidental fall.

"Benji and I talked extensively," Seraydar said. "The bottom line was that there was blood everywhere. You could clearly see where she hit her head on the Formica table top, and it just looked like the lady had bled out."

Ben and Narcy then took Seraydar out for lunch at Alexander's Restaurant in downtown Fort Lauderdale. Over the meal, they talked about Bernice, as Narcy consoled her husband.

"We all had a very good talk," recalled Seraydar. "And there were questions that he brought up about the wineglasses on the table, saying she doesn't drink wine. I just said, 'Ben, your mother fell a week earlier.'"

Finally, Seraydar advised Ben to hire Pat Franklin to photograph the death scene, which he did. "He was very shook up and very suspicious," the private investigator recalled of Novack. "He didn't buy that her death was a fall. He goes, 'Something's wrong. My mom never drank white wine. There's no way she would leave a dirty glass either.'"

Novack also questioned why there was blood all over house if his mother had simply fallen. Somewhat wary of Ben Novack Jr. after working on his 2002 home invasion, Franklin advised waiting until police and autopsy reports became available.

"I said, 'Call me when the police have wrapped up their investigation, and when the ME's Office releases the body. I will go and get the autopsy report.'"

Novack replied that it would be difficult, as he was going out of town. When the investigator asked when he would be back, Ben said he didn't know, because he had business to attend to.

A few hours earlier, Narcy Novack had called her brother Cristobal complaining that Ben was furious as one of Bernice Novack's rings was missing. Soon afterward, Veliz confronted Alejandro Garcia at the car wash, demanding the ring back.

"Cristobal was kind of bossy," Garcia said. "He said, 'I'm looking for a gold graduation ring you took. I need that ring.'"

Garcia denied taking anything except Bernice's car key ring.

When Veliz asked how much money he wanted for the gold ring, Garcia became annoyed. "So I took out the old lady's key ring and he told me to throw it away," Garcia said. "So I threw it in a large garbage can in the gas station."

Veliz then congratulated Garcia on doing a good job with the old lady, and Garcia asked how she was.

"He said, 'She's fine,'" said Garcia. "'And don't worry as she's in hospital. Forget about her.'"

Then Garcia asked about the money still owed him. Veliz said he had already given Medrano $2,000 in addition to the $600 he already had. Realizing he'd been cheated, Garcia said he was going to beat up Medrano.

Veliz told him to calm down, saying he had a far bigger job in mind for him.

"He said, 'Don't worry, I have money for you,'" said Garcia. "This time I would be the boss and pay Melvin, so I could get even. He said I was going make some real money."

That night, Narcy Novack arranged for Bernice to be cremated as soon as possible, followed by a Friday memorial service. The cremation was carried out within twenty-four hours, at the Blasberg-Rubin-Zilbert Memorial Chapel on Seventy-First Street, Miami Beach, before any of Bernice's family or friends could be properly notified.

Maxine Fiel said that she was given no time to make arrangements to attend her sister's funeral. "She was cremated so fast," said Maxine. "Everything was done real quick. Details were kept from me about where it was taking place. Maybe they didn't want me there because I would have asked questions. Bernice was very upset about many things in that marriage."

. . .

Early Tuesday morning, Ben Jr. and Narcy went to the Bank of America to check the safe-deposit boxes he jointly owned with his late mother for her still-missing ring. He eventually found it in one of her boxes, and surmised that she had put it in there the day of her fall outside the bank.

Then Narcy helped him move all his mother's priceless jewelry and heirlooms into another of his safe-deposit boxes. Narcy paid special attention to the fabulous pieces of jewelry—many of which Bernice had worn at the Fontainebleau—for they would soon be hers.

THIRTY-FIVE

THE FUNERAL

On Thursday, April 9, *The Miami Herald* printed Bernice Novack's full-page obituary. Reporter Michael Vasquez conducted a rare interview with Ben Novack Jr., who revealed personal details that his mother had always kept hidden. She would have been even more horrified that the obituary, entitled "Fashion Model, Hotelier's Wife," said that she was a year older than she actually was.

"Bernice Novack, a foster child turned 1950s fashion model," it began, "and one half of the husband-and-wife team that brought the Fontainebleau to Miami Beach, died earlier this week from injuries sustained during a recent slip and fall. She was 87."

The article outlined her glamorous life with Ben Sr., entertaining famous celebrities and world leaders at the Fontainebleau.

"Bernice," it read, "after a bumpy childhood that included time in a foster home, worked as a fashion model for the likes of Salvador Dali and Coca-Cola. Her hair was a vibrant red—a color it would remain all her days."

Ben Jr. said his father had "flipped" for his mother, but there had been a problem as he was still married to Bella.

"She didn't want to date a married man," Ben Jr. explained, "and made it very clear to him. A year later or two years later he showed up with a divorce certificate and said, 'Now can we date?'"

Then Ben Jr. recalled his "glamor life," growing up in the penthouse of the Fontainebleau and meeting every president from Kennedy to Ford, as well as his friendship with Frank Sinatra and the "Rat Pack."

He said that after his parents divorced, they remained close until the end of his life.

"[They] never really parted ways," he said.

At 4:00 P.M. on Friday, April 10, a memorial service for Bernice Novack was held at Beth David Memorial Gardens in Hollywood, Florida. Rabbi Alan Litwak of the Temple Sinai in-North Miami Beach presided, although neither Ben Novack Jr. nor his mother were members of Litwak's congregation. All the rabbi knew about Bernice was what her son had told him in a brief telephone conversation the day before.

Wearing sunglasses and dressed in a fashionable black outfit, Narcy Novack greeted the mourners as they arrived at the synagogue. There to comfort her were her brother Cristobal, who had driven down from Philadelphia, and their sister Estilita, who was staying for a couple of days.

"Narcy was smiling," Estelle Fernandez recalled, "and seating everybody like she was at a convention. She was happy and pleasant, and you wouldn't have even thought she was at a funeral."

At first, Estelle hadn't even recognized Narcy, as she had her blond hair cut and dyed red for the occasion—like that of her late mother-in-law.

"She came over to me and shouted, 'Estelle! How are you?' Fernandez recalled. "And I looked at her and said, 'I'm fine, but I think you might have mixed me up with someone else. I don't think I know you.'

"And she said, 'It's me. It's Narcy.'"

When Estelle apologized for not recognizing her, Narcy said it was probably because of her new hairstyle.

"She went on and on about stupid stuff," said Fernandez. "No show of remorse. Nothing."

May Abad and her two teenage sons, Patrick and Marchelo, were also there, perfectly turned out. Ben Novack Jr.'s friend Jerry Calhoun had flown down in his private plane with his twin brother, Jack, and Prince Mongo to attend the service.

"Narcy came over to me," Mongo remembered, "and said, 'Bernice and I were getting along so good.' And I said, 'Oh, Narcy, I'm sorry and I hope things are going to be better.'"

Most of the mourners were elderly and had worked at the Fontainebleau while Bernice and Ben Sr. had presided over it. Bernice's longtime boyfriend George Rodriguez was late arriving, because he'd gotten lost. He was inconsolable throughout the service.

A marble urn containing Bernice's ashes had been placed at the front of the chapel. Next to it were photographs of her with Ben Jr., Narcy, and May with her sons.

"She would have never agreed to that," Fernandez said of the photos. "It was everything she hated."

When Estelle and her husband took their seats at the back of the hall, May Abad brought them to the front, to sit with the close family.

"I was shaking through the whole ceremony," Fernandez recalled. "I said, 'May, thank Narcy for sitting me up front. I really appreciate it.' And she said, 'She didn't do it. I did.' So they hated each other even then."

During the Orthodox service, Ben Novack Jr. delivered a eulogy to his mother from the pulpit. He began by saying that he had intended to prepare a speech the night before, but had not gotten round to it.

"To heck with it," he told the mourners. "I think I'll wing it."

"I was a little disappointed with Benji," said his old friend Pete Matthews. "I thought, 'Oh my God, to come up with something off the wall like that at your mother's funeral.'"

Ben Jr. then proceeded to announce his mother's age and that she had been a foster child, two of her most closely guarded secrets.

"It was everything Bernice didn't want anybody to know," said Estelle Fernandez. "I would have thought he'd be a little bit more caring."

Estelle was also appalled that throughout his eulogy, Ben constantly referred to his mother as "Bernice."

He also compared his mother's death to the tragic skiing accident that had killed film star Natasha Richardson just two weeks before. Initially, the actress had refused any medical attention, returning to her hotel room. But a few hours later she complained of headaches and was taken to the hospital. She died two days later.

"Bernice died the same way that that actress died," Ben Jr. told the mourners. "She fell outside the bank a week before, and this is the result."

Then he suddenly segued into his mother's often fraught relationship with Narcy.

"It was ridiculous," said Rebecca Green. "He hadn't prepared a thing and said he didn't know what to say. Then he stood up there and said, 'Well, Narcy and my mother didn't get on well, but in the last couple of years they have started getting along better.' And I'm thinking, 'What a thing to say.'"

After the service, Estelle asked Narcy what they planned to do with the ashes, as Bernice had often said she wanted her ashes mixed with those of her pet schnauzer before being scattered on the waters at the Fontainebleau. Narcy replied that they still had not decided, and were taking them home.

"Later she told me that she and Ben scattered them at the Fontainebleau," said Fernandez. "But I don't believe her."

After the service, everyone went to the Bonaventure Country Club in Fort Lauderdale for a catered reception. Narcy had organized everything, and had even asked Jerry and Jack Calhoun, who perform professionally as the Calhoun Twins, to play a lively set of country and western music.

"So these guys came in with cowboy clothes and everything," Bill Green remembered, "and start singing county and western songs and playing banjo. Then Narcy went up and started singing with them.

"That was strange, because Bernice didn't like country music. She was a very refined lady. I kept thinking, 'This is a funeral and not a nightclub.'"

. . .

In the days after Bernice Novack's death, her family and friends began to suspect that something was wrong. Guy Costaldo was so furious that his dear friend was being portrayed as "a fall-down drunk," that he called Fort Lauderdale Police Department to complain.

"She didn't fall in the afternoon with a couple under her belt," he said. "But they didn't want to have anything to do with me."

Maxine Fiel was also angry at newspaper stories focusing on the glass of wine found on Bernice's dining room table. "My sister was not a drinker," Fiel said. "She did like her wine to relax her, but under no means was she an alcoholic."

Ben Jr. even hired Pete Matthews's brother Joe, who specialized in homicide investigations, to review the case. After reading the Fort Lauderdale Police Department report and viewing photographs of the death scene, Joe Matthews agreed that Bernice Novack had died from more than a fall, and that Fort Lauderdale Police had carried out a shoddy investigation.

"It was an embarrassment," said Matthews, "and they did a terrible job in processing the scene. My biggest concern was that the crime scene was not done properly. I can't believe they could investigate any kind of death, and only take thirty to forty photos."

After reviewing all the reports and giving his opinion, Joe Matthews waited and waited to hear back from Ben Novack Jr.

"Maybe a month or two went by," said Matthews, "and I didn't hear anything. Pat [Franklin] and I would meet for a cigar together and fix all the problems of the world. One time I said to him, 'Whatever happened with Benji? Is he ever going to look into [his mother's death] or not?'"

In late April, Cristobal Veliz and Francisco Picado paid a short visit to Miami. While there, they drove to Fort Lauderdale in a rented car to meet Veliz's sister Narcy. When they arrived, Veliz directed his young friend to a particular street where a Cadillac Escalade was parked.

"It was his sister's car," Picado later testified. "We followed it to a diner and into a parking lot, and parked a few spots to the left."

Narcy Novack then got out of her car and went into the diner, closely followed by her brother, who told Picado to wait in the car.

"In approximately twenty minutes he came out with a bag with a newspaper inside," Picado said. "He opened it up and it had about three thousand to four thousand dollars, all in hundred-dollar bills. Then we went back to Miami."

In May, Ben Novack Jr. filed a wrongful death lawsuit against the Bank of America. It claimed that his mother's earlier fall on the bank's property had caused the internal injuries leading to the second fall that had killed her.

He hired a Miami Beach lawyer named Robert Switkes to handle the suit, sharing with Switkes his doubts over the official cause of his mother's death. After reading the Fort Lauderdale Police reports and autopsy report, Switkes agreed.

"This couldn't have been an accident," he said. "You just don't get up and fall. The injuries were totally inconsistent with somebody falling."

After Bernice Novack died, Narcy spent time at her house going through her things, and specifically sifting through her treasures from the Fontainebleau.

"Bernice had three bedrooms loaded with stuff," said Estelle Fernandez. "I don't know if it was valuable . . . and it might have been more sentimental than anything."

Narcy threw out Bernice's prized collection of books, explaining that she and Ben were not readers.

"I said, 'Why are you throwing out the books?'" Fernandez reported. "She says, 'We don't need them.'"

Then Narcy invited Estelle over to pick out anything she wanted to remind her of Bernice. Estelle told her that all she wanted was a photo-

The iconic Fontainebleau Hotel dominated Miami Beach in the 1950s and '60s. *(Courtesy of John Glatt)*

The Fontainebleau lobby and its legendary "staircase to nowhere." *(Courtesy of John Glatt)*

Ben Sr. and his sister Lillian at Ben Jr.'s first wedding. *(Courtesy of Jill Campion)*

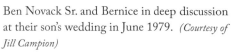

Ben Novack Jr. grew up at the Fontainebleau and was always close with Frank Sinatra. This photograph was taken backstage at a concert with his first wife, Jill. *(Courtesy of Jill Campion)*

Ben Novack Sr. and Bernice in deep discussion at their son's wedding in June 1979. *(Courtesy of Jill Campion)*

Bernice brought her longtime boyfriend George as her date to her son's first wedding. From left to right: Bernice, Ben Jr., Jill Campion, George Rodriguez. *(Courtesy of Jill Campion)*

Ben Jr. and Jill were deeply in love at their wedding. Unfortunately the marriage would be short-lived. *(Courtesy of Jill Campion)*

BOTTOM LEFT: Perry Como with Ben Jr. and Jill Campion at a gala dinner at the Fontainebleau. *(Courtesy of Jill Campion)*

BOTTOM RIGHT: Ben Jr. entertains President Ford at the Fontainebleau. *(Courtesy of Jill Campion)*

Ben Jr. was always especially close to Ann-Margret, whom he had known since he was a young child. From left to right: Ann-Margret, Ben Jr., Jill Campion, Roger Smith. *(Courtesy of Jill Campion)*

Stripper Big Fannie Annie took Narcy Novack under her wing and taught her the tricks of the trade when she joined the Follies International Club. Soon afterward, she would meet Ben Jr. *(Courtesy of Fannie Annie)*

LEFT: Ben Novack Sr.'s protégé Ahmed Boob had the run of the Fontainebleau in the 1970s. *(Courtesy of Jill Campion)*

RIGHT: After leaving the Fontainebleau, Bernice Novack moved to Fort Lauderdale and started a new life. *(Courtesy of Barbara Lunde)*

Ben Novack Sr. and his Fontainebleau manager Lenore Toby working at the hotel in the late 1970s. *(Courtesy of Lenore Toby)*

Soon after they married, Ben Jr. and Narcy moved into 2501 Del Mar Place in Fort Lauderdale. *(Courtesy of John Glatt)*

Narcy enlisted her older brother Cristobal Veliz to hire hit men to murder Bernice Novack and then her son, Ben Jr., after he cheated on her. *(Courtesy of United States Attorney's Office, Southern District of New York)*

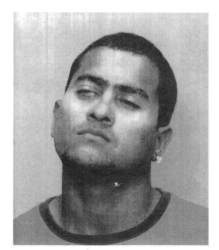

Ben Jr. at his home with some of his toys. *(Courtesy of United States Attorney's Office, Southern District of New York)*

Alejandro Garcia carried out the brutal murder of Bernice Novack, before killing Ben Jr. at the Rye Town Hilton. *(Courtesy of United States Attorney's Office, Southern District of New York)*

A week before she was murdered Bernice Novack took a fall outside a Fort Lauderdale bank. (*Courtesy of United States Attorney's Office, Southern District of New York*)

Former Hollywood police chief Jim Scarberry warned Ben Jr. in 2002 that Narcy would kill him if he didn't get out of the marriage. (*Courtesy of John Glatt*)

Joel Gonzalez attacked Ben Jr. in his Westchester hotel suite. (*Courtesy of United States Attorney's Office, Southern District of New York*)

GOVERNMENT
EXHIBIT
521
10 Cr. 602 (KMK) (ID)

Garcia used a monkey wrench like this one to batter eighty-six-year-old Bernice to death. (*Courtesy of United States Attorney's Office, Southern District of New York*)

Ben Novack Jr.'s Batmobile, which he got a few weeks before his murder. *(Courtesy of Charlie Seraydar)*

Maxine Fiel refused to believe that her sister Bernice had died an accidental death. *(Courtesy of John Glatt)*

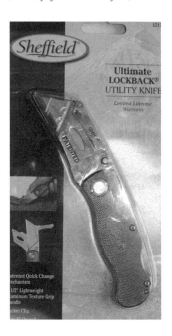

On Narcy Novack's orders, Alejandro Garcia gouged out her husband's eyes with a utility knife exactly like this one. *(Courtesy of United States Attorney's Office, Southern District of New York)*

The Woodlands Suite, where Ben Jr. was savagely murdered as his wife watched from the other room. *(Courtesy of United States Attorney's Office, Southern District of New York)*

LEFT: Dennis Ramirez was hired by his father-in-law Cristobal to drive the getaway car after Ben Jr.'s killing. *(Courtesy of United States Attorney's Office, Southern District of New York)*

RIGHT: Teenager Francisco Picado made a series of cross-country road trips with Cristobal Veliz, during the planning of both murders. *(Courtesy of United States Attorney's Office, Southern District of New York)*

Narcy and Cristobal's elder brother, Carlos, was implicated in a plot to maim May Abad, but has never been charged. *(Courtesy of United States Attorney's Office, Southern District of New York)*

Police found the mutilated body of Ben Novack Jr. lying bound and gagged on the floor of his suite at the Rye Town Hilton. (*Courtesy of United States Attorney's Office, Southern District of New York*)

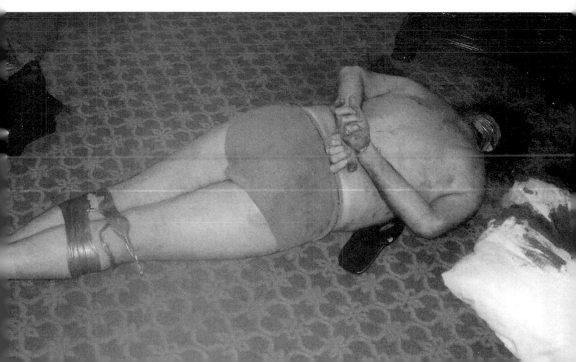

Garcia and Gonzalez were caught by a surveillance camera leaving the Rye Town Hilton after the murder. *(Courtesy of United States Attorney's Office, Southern District of New York)*

Narcy Novack looked daggers across a federal courtroom at her rival Rebecca Bliss, as prosecutor Andrew Dember questioned her. *(Courtesy of Candace Eaton)*

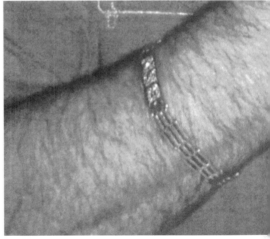

The notorious "BEN" bracelet, which prosecutors say Narcy gave Garcia after the murder, has never been found. *(Courtesy of United States Attorney's Office, Southern District of New York)*

Narcy Novack after her arrest in July 2010. *(Courtesy of United States Attorney's Office, Southern District of New York)*

graph of Bernice. Narcy said she had a very nice one on her nightstand, and promised to mail it to her.

"So I gave her my P.O. box address," said Fernandez, "but I never got anything."

One day, Bill and Rebecca Greene came over to find Narcy going through Bernice's freezer. "And Narcy says to us, 'Why don't you guys take this food?'" said Bill. "I said, 'No, I don't want it.' And she says, 'Well, there's nothing wrong with it. Bernice was very clean.' I thought that was a strange thing to say."

Ben Novack Jr. asked the Greenes to look after his mother's house, as they had a spare key and knew all the alarm codes. Over the next few weeks, Ben, who had now been appointed executor of his mother's estate, was a frequent visitor. As Bernice Novack's only child, he had inherited her estimated $2 million estate. The only other beneficiaries were her sister Maxine, who received $50,000 in cash, and her nieces Meredith and Lisa, who received $10,000 and $5,000, respectively.

According to Meredith Fiel, her aunt's amended will bequeathing most of her money to a Jewish charity still lay unsigned on a table.

THIRTY-SIX

THE BATMOBILE

Now that the first half of their plan had been successful, Narcy and her brother Cristobal moved into the second phase. After Bernice Novack's death had been ruled accidental, they now felt emboldened to move on and kill Ben Novack Jr.

Over the next several months, Cristobal Veliz crisscrossed the Northeast as he and Narcy plotted Ben's murder. They had decided to kill him in New York, believing it would give them a far better chance of getting away with it than in Florida.

Ben and Narcy Novack would next be in New York on July 9, for a Hispanic Amway convention they were organizing at the Rye Town Hilton, and it was decided that this was where they would strike.

Once again, the siblings planned to use Melvin Medrano and Alejandro Garcia for the hit, considering them a good team who had already proven themselves.

In May, Cristobal Veliz arrived at the car wash, telling Garcia to start preparing for the big job he had promised.

"Cristobal said the time . . . was getting close," said Garcia. "I asked him what it was to be. He said I had to beat up Señor Novack and cut off his balls. There was going to be an Amway convention in New York, and I was going to come in and do the attack. He said the object was that this man would be disabled, so he and his sister could take over the company."

Veliz then explained that Ben Novack had sex with little girls. He told Garcia that Novack also owned a factory that manufactured artificial limbs for children, and would trade these prostheses for sex.

"This made me hate him for what he was doing to the little children," said Garcia, who had a thirteen-year-old daughter back in Nicaragua.

On May 18, 2009, Melvin Medrano was arrested for driving without a license, and deported back to Nicaragua. Veliz then told Garcia to find a new partner, and offered him $15,000, as well as a good tip, for the Ben Novack job. Garcia said he knew a twenty-six-year-old Miami-born Cuban named Joel Gonzalez, who had just lost his job driving a lunch cart. He felt sure Gonzalez would come aboard. Soon afterward, Garcia approached Gonzalez about participating in the attack.

"I said we can tie him up, kick him, and get out of there," Garcia remembered. "He said, 'How much money?' I said three thousand, and he said, 'Fine, let's do it.'"

On May 5, Ben Novack Jr. had taken delivery of his eagerly awaited $128,000 Batmobile, blissfully unaware of the danger he was in. It was a fully working exact copy of the original Batmobile used in the 1966 *Batman* TV series, and had taken several years to build. It used castings from the original Batmobile molds, fitted onto a 1963 Lincoln frame.

With a rocket exhaust flamethrower, bat rockets, a bat ray projector, bat turbines, and an emergency bat turn lever, it was Ben Jr.'s dream car.

"He called me when he got it delivered," said Charlie Seraydar. "He wanted me to come over and see it. He was so excited. It was the culmination of many, many years of working to get it. It was his pride and joy."

The Batmobile was officially registered to Ben and Narcy Novack, with the personalized Florida plates BAT 1966. A delighted Ben Jr. happily posed for photographs in the driver's seat, wearing a white

T-shirt, denim cutoffs, and a baseball hat. Next, he told friends, he intended to buy a Batboat and a Batcopter.

He only ever got to drive his Batmobile once, to a gas station a couple of blocks away on Las Olas Boulevard, to fuel up. Then he parked it in his garage, where it would remain for months.

On Saturday, June 6, Ben and Narcy Novack attended the 2009 Florida Supercon, held at the Doubletree Hotel and Exhibition Center at Miami International Airport. Novack had previously given dealer Vincent Zarzuela a wish list of rare Batman comics and other collectibles he wanted.

When Zarzuela saw Novack on the convention floor, he thought the man appeared strangely subdued and preoccupied. "Something was off with him," Zarzuela recalled. "For lack of a better term, my Spidey sense was tingling."

So the New York dealer took Narcy to one side, asking her what was wrong with Ben. "And she whispered in my ear," Zarzuela said, "'His mother died recently.' And I said, 'Okay.'"

Then Narcy went off somewhere, leaving Ben behind at the booth to negotiate prices. As he and Zarzuela were looking through some comic books, a beautiful redhead, dressed up as the evil Batman villainess Poison Ivy, whose kisses are deadly poison, walked by the stall.

"She was very striking," said Zarzuela, "and we were both pretty blown away."

As the woman posed for photographs with fans, Zarzuela asked Ben if he wanted to be photographed with her.

"And he said, 'No, no, no. My wife's really jealous,'" the dealer recalled.

So Zarzuela took a photo of Poison Ivy on his digital camera, offering to send a copy to Ben.

"He said, 'Yeah, send it to me,'" said Zarzuela. "'You've got to tell me when you're sending it, because I want to make sure my wife doesn't see the picture.' And he actually seemed very serious about that, because she was apparently a very jealous woman."

. . .

One afternoon in mid-June, Alejandro Garcia introduced Cristobal Veliz to Joel Gonzalez at the car wash, where he was now working. Veliz immediately asked the overweight Gonzalez, who had a shaven head, if he had a driver's license and could follow a map. He said he could.

Then Veliz, who had just bought Garcia a pay-as-you-go cell phone for the upcoming attack, drove the two men to a nearby Nicaraguan restaurant for lunch. After they ate, Veliz dropped Gonzalez and Garcia off at their respective homes, telling them to shower and change clothes, as they were going somewhere.

After they had smartened up, Veliz told Gonzalez to drive his green Pathfinder to Fort Lauderdale. During the drive, Veliz, who was sitting in the backseat, pointed to a photograph of Ben Novack Jr. that had been attached to the dashboard. He told the man to pay special attention to it, because they were going to see him very soon.

"The objective [that day] was to get to know Señor Novack," Garcia explained, "and to find out who we were going to attack."

On the way to Fort Lauderdale, Veliz received a phone call from Narcy, giving the name and address of the restaurant where she and Ben would be. She told Veliz to look out for her husband's beige Cadillac Escalade SUV, in the parking lot.

Veliz in turn told his sister what Garcia and Gonzalez would be wearing, so she would be able to identify them.

"He told us that Señor Novack was going to be at the restaurant sitting with his sister," said Garcia. "When we came in she was going to do a signal so we could recognize [him]."

When they reached the diner in Fort Lauderdale, they soon found the Escalade in the parking lot. Veliz told the men to go into the restaurant.

The two men walked in and sat at the bar, ordering a glass of water. Looking over to their left, they easily recognized the bearded Ben Novack Jr., who was at a table with Narcy and another woman.

"I said to Joel, 'That looks like the man we're after,'" Garcia recalled.

"At that moment, [Narcy] started to stroke Señor Novack's hair, because that was the signal."

Because Veliz had told them to get as close to their target as possible, Garcia instructed Gonzalez to walk past Novack's table on their way to the bathroom. A couple of minutes later, they came out of the bathroom and went back to the bar, before leaving the diner.

Cristobal Veliz picked them up outside, and the three headed back to Miami. A few minutes later, Narcy called Veliz's cell phone. She complained that Gonzalez's bald head was "intimidating" and "scary," saying he would attract too much attention at the hotel.

Veliz told her not to be nervous, as Joel Gonzalez would be perfect for the job.

Soon afterward, Alejandro Garcia told Joel Gonzalez that Jefe now wanted him to play a bigger part in the attack.

"He wanted me to participate," said Gonzalez. "He would give me an extra five hundred dollars [in addition] to the three thousand I was promised."

Then Garcia gave him more details about the big job.

"Alex told me . . . we were going to attack Mr. Novack, because his wife wanted to take control of the business," said Gonzalez. "Novack was to be left disabled . . . and he showed me step by step how the assault would take place."

Then Gonzalez asked what would happen if he said no.

"He said it would be in my best interests," said Gonzalez. "That these were powerful people with money and they can make us disappear."

In late June, Ben and Narcy Novack went out to dinner with Ben's childhood friend Kelsey Grammer and his wife, Camille. They arranged to meet up in three weeks' time at Kelsey's rental in the Hamptons, when the Novacks came north for the Amway conference.

Kelsey Grammer would later tell investigators that Narcy was acting very strangely that evening, and that something was wrong.

On June 26, Ben Novack Jr. hired an attorney to file for divorce. Then, according to Joe Gandy, his attorney abruptly dropped the case after receiving threats.

Gandy said, "The lawyer called up Ben and said, 'I'm dropping the case . . . because I've been threatened.'"

In the final week of June, Cristobal Veliz was back in Miami finalizing arrangements for the imminent attack on Ben Novack Jr. With just over two weeks to go before the Amway convention in Rye Brook, New York, Veliz collected Alejandro Garcia and Joel Gonzalez at the car wash and took them to a nearby Nicaraguan restaurant for a briefing.

The Veliz siblings had now decided to buy a used vehicle for the attack, distancing themselves even further from it.

"Mr. Veliz asked us a lot about finding a car," Gonzalez recalled. "He said he needed a car for the trip to New York."

After inspecting several in Miami that were not up to scratch, Veliz told his hit men that they would be driving to Brooklyn, New York. He said he was buying an old Ford Thunderbird from his son-in-law, Denis Ramirez, and then towing it back to Miami for repairs.

On Wednesday July 1, the three men left Miami in Cristobal Veliz's Nissan Pathfinder, stopping off for the night in Jacksonville, Florida. Cristobal stayed with his daughter Karen Veliz, while putting up Garcia and Gonzalez at a Motel 6.

The next morning he met them in the parking lot, and a few minutes later Denis Ramirez arrived with Veliz's daughter Karen.

Ramirez then got into the back of the Pathfinder and, with Gonzalez doing the driving, the four men set off for New York, stopping only for food and bathroom breaks.

. . .

It was late afternoon when the green Pathfinder drew up outside 1499 Jefferson Avenue, where Francisco Picado was waiting. Ramirez then took his father-in-law to a fenced-in parking lot to the right of the brownstone, where his 1990 gray two-door Thunderbird with a broken windshield was parked. After starting the engine, Veliz agreed to pay Ramirez $800 later, saying he would have to get the car fixed in Miami.

Then, after buying everyone dinner at a Dominican restaurant in Brooklyn, Veliz drove Garcia and Gonzalez to the Crossbay Motor Inn at 137-27 Crossbay Boulevard in Ozone Park, Queens, where they would be spending the night. He handed Gonzalez $110 in cash to pay for the room, before leaving to stay with Laura Law.

At 9:08 P.M. Gonzalez officially registered, using his driver's license as identification. It was the first time in New York for both men, and they went out that night to a club, drinking and doing drugs. They also bought matching pairs of knockoff Valentino sunglasses from a bargain store.

At around 9:00 the next morning, Cristobal Veliz collected Alejandro Garcia from the hotel, leaving Joel Gonzalez in the room. The two men then drove to a PepBoys auto parts store in Metropolitan Avenue, Ridgewood, Queens, to buy towing lights and cables to haul the T-bird back to Miami.

Veliz told Garcia that there had been a change in plan, and instead of cutting off Ben Novack's testicles, Garcia would be slashing his eyes instead. Veliz told Garcia not to tell Gonzalez this, in case it scared him off.

After selecting magnetic tow lights and quick links for the towing operation, Veliz picked up a $9.99 Sheffield Lockback Utility Knife, asking Garcia if it would be suitable for blinding Ben Novack. Garcia said he thought it would.

"So he bought it," said Garcia, "and as he was paying, I took it out of the box and put it in my pocket."

They then drove back to the Crossbay Motor Inn and collected Gonzalez at 10:58 A.M. On the way to pick up the Thunderbird, Veliz stopped off at a True Value Hardware store, handing Garcia enough cash to buy a backpack for the tools they needed for the attack on Ben Novack.

Back at 1499 Jefferson Avenue, Veliz tried to hook up the towing lights and cables from the Pathfinder to the Thunderbird, but the plugs didn't fit. So he returned to the PepBoys to exchange them, before getting the lights working.

It was early afternoon when Veliz, Garcia, and Gonzalez set out in the Pathfinder on the 1,350-mile journey to Miami, towing the Thunderbird behind them.

On the July Fourth weekend, while her brother was finalizing preparations to kill her husband, Narcy helped Ben Jr. run a Hispanic Amway family convention in Fort Lauderdale. It was being held at the Broward Convention Center, where Mark Gatley was now general manager. He had not seen Ben since the late 1990s, and it was his first meeting with Narcy, who struck him as highly competent.

"She held herself up professionally and dressed well," Gatley said, "as a loving wife and business partner."

At Friday's preconvention meeting, Ben Novack Jr. attacked the Broward Convention Center for incompetence. This set the tone for the rest of the convention.

"All of us were a little embarrassed," said Gatley, "and he picked up on that. He did a number on the G.M. of the hotel there, saying the restaurant was less than average, and needed to be fixed. And he picked on our convention and visitors' bureau a little bit, for things that [we] should or shouldn't be."

After the meeting, Gatley and Narcy struck up a conversation. Gatley remembered: "And she said to me, 'You know, Ben has so many enemies. He has so many people that don't like him.'" She then asked if Gatley had observed her husband's behavior at the meeting, and Gatley agreed that it had been bad. "And she said, 'Yeah, but I'm here,'" said

Gatley. "'I have to protect him. I'm the one that has to look out for Ben. Somebody has to.' I said, 'Great.'"

The next morning, at registration, Ben Novack Jr. was in a better mood and was even chatty. As Narcy helped sign in the convention guests, the Convention Concepts Unlimited employees Matt Briggs and May Abad, and three freelancers, worked behind the scenes.

Ben Novack Jr. sat to one side of the registration desk with Gatley tinkering on his laptop computer. Suddenly, he became introspective, and began discussing his father and his childhood at the Fontainebleau.

"Ben and I were having these conversations about his father's hotel," said Gatley. "And he was Googling the Fontainebleau on his computer while I was sitting [there]. He told me that he and Steve Wynn of Las Vegas were very good friends. He said Steve Wynn grew up in his dad's hotel, and learned the hotel business there. And that one of his first hotels was a tribute to the Fontainebleau."

Novack also spoke about his upcoming plans to relocate to Seattle, Washington, and start taking things easier.

"Ben told me [he and Narcy] were buying properties there," said Gatley. "He said, 'We've already been up there and looked at places. I know I can dock my boat there.'"

Then Narcy came over, telling Ben to apologize to everyone he'd upset at yesterday's meeting, and suggesting they take those people out to lunch. She said she always had to look out for Ben, as he caused trouble.

"Ben just shrugged it off," said Gatley. "He didn't pay any attention."

On Sunday morning, after the conference ended, Ben Novack Jr. met with Mark Gatley to settle his bills. As usual he quibbled, complaining that things at the conference center had not been up to snuff, but then reluctantly paid with his black American Express Card.

As they said good-bye, Gatley said he was looking forward to hosting Novack's upcoming five-thousand-person Amway convention in September, as had been agreed. Then the convention planner dropped a bomb, saying that this was not a done deal by any means.

Novack explained that he had a long-standing beef with the Broward County Sheriff's Department for not allowing him to park outside one of the terminals at Fort Lauderdale Airport.

"Those were things that he would not just let go," said Gatley. "He was getting all red-faced about it."

Novack explained he had already e-mailed the sheriff, county administrator, and other local notables, inviting them to a meeting on Wednesday. They had not replied, so he now wanted Gatley to use his influence to make them attend. Becoming angry, he threatened to pull the upcoming convention, which the city badly needed financially, if they dared snub him.

Gatley promised to do his best to make the Wednesday meeting happen. Then, as they were leaving, Narcy called him over.

"Ben has so many enemies," she whispered in his ear.

Late that night, Ben Novack Jr. called Mark Gatley at home, checking on his progress.

"He called me several times," said Gatley. "'Is that meeting going to happen? What do you think?' I said, 'I'm pretty sure it will, Ben. They know about your September convention here, and everybody wants to make sure that happens.'"

A few hours earlier, Cristobal Veliz and his two hit men towed the broken Thunderbird into Miami. As Jefe had nowhere to stay, Garcia offered to have him and Gonzalez sleep in the small room he rented in a trailer, which belonged to an elderly lady named Gladys Cuenca.

"They came over and asked if they could stay for a few days," Cuenca later testified. "I said yes."

On Monday morning, Cristobal Veliz towed the Thunderbird to a mechanic in Miami, leaving it to be repaired. On his return to the trailer, he asked Garcia to persuade Gladys Cuenca to register the car in her name with the Florida department of Highway Safety, so it could never be traced back to him.

"I said Cristobal was going to give it to me as a gift and both of us could use it," Garcia explained. "I never told Gladys what we really needed it for, and she agreed because she didn't have a car."

Later that day, Veliz drove his two hired hands to a Kmart to buy equipment for the Ben Novack Jr. job.

"We were looking for something to beat the man," Garcia later testified, "and we found some handheld dumbbells."

In the sports department, Garcia picked out for himself a pair of blue dumbbells weighing about five pounds, and a pink pair weighing eight pounds for Gonzalez.

"We were also looking for [duct] tape to tie up Señor Novack," said Garcia. "That was Cristobal's idea. It was two inches thick with fibers in it and pretty strong."

Veliz also purchased two pairs of baseball gloves, so as not to leave fingerprints behind at the attack, and a showerhead and some bathtub mats, as a thank-you present for Gladys Cuenca.

Jefe paid for everything with his credit card.

On Wednesday afternoon, July 8, Ben Novack Jr. got his meeting with the Broward County sheriff and local government officials. It began with the angry convention planner standing up and railing against the Sheriff's Office for incompetence.

"He did his usual thing," said Mark Gatley, who also attended the meeting. "It didn't really have much to do with our meeting."

Novack castigated the sheriff for the incident several years earlier when police had ordered him not to park outside a terminal, as it breached security.

"It was a stormy meeting," said Gatley. "He just wanted to review how incompetent the Sheriff's Office was."

Novack also complained that security was far too strict, with too many police checkpoints at the airport and the convention center.

"He is a very aggressive person," said Nikki Grossman, the president of the Greater Fort Lauderdale Convention and Visitors Bureau, who was also at the meeting. "He wanted to make everyone aware of his issues."

Finally, at the end of his long tirade, Novack issued an ultimatum. He threatened to pull the plug on the lucrative September convention if he did not get a letter promising to remedy the situation by the time he returned from New York.

After the meeting, Ben and Narcy Novack took their yacht *White Lightning* out on the water for the first time since it had broken down a year earlier. Since then, it had been in a boatyard having a $2 million refitting.

They had invited Prince Mongo to accompany them on the yacht's maiden voyage, but he was too busy campaigning to become the mayor of Memphis.

"He said, 'Come on. Fly down and ride on the boat with me,'" said Mongo. "I couldn't just pick up and ride on the boat."

Trouble soon struck as they sailed down the Intercoastal Waterway, when a water hose came loose.

"So they had to turn around," said Mongo, "and limp back to the dock and back to the boatyard."

Late that night, Ben Novack Jr. called Mark Gatley at home, asking for his thoughts on the meeting.

"We chatted for about half an hour," recalled Gatley. "He went on about, 'Do you think they paid attention? Are they going to take care of this? You know if they don't, I'm not coming back.'"

Gatley assured him that the Broward County Sheriff's Office would take care of things for his September convention, and do a good job.

"He would go off on these rants that were unrelated," said Gatley. "I got the sense that he was really looking for someone to talk to, as much as anything else."

Novack suddenly became emotional, complaining that nobody really listened to him or cared about his business.

"He was just rambling on," explained Gatley. "I mean some of the stuff was so left field. I got off the phone that night thinking, 'This is just a lonely person who wants to talk to somebody.'"

. . .

A few hours earlier, Cristobal Veliz had collected the Ford Thunderbird from the mechanic and driven it back to the Blue Belle Trailer Park. He then instructed Garcia and Gonzalez to pack their best clothes for "the big date," as he was now calling the attack on Ben Novack Jr.

"That's when Mr. Garcia said we are going to do something shady," Gonzalez would later testify. "That we were going to commit a crime. Mr. Veliz told me that I knew as much as I needed to know."

Veliz then ordered Gonzalez to drive Garcia back to New York in the Thunderbird, while he went separately in his Pathfinder.

But the two hit men were barely out of the greater Miami area when the Thunderbird overheated and they had to pull into a gas station.

"Mr. Veliz appeared five minutes later," said Gonzalez. "He opened the hood of the car and tried to figure it out, and bought cooling fluid to try and cool it down."

When the Thunderbird refused to start, a furious Veliz reattached the towing lines to his Pathfinder to haul the car back to New York.

He then called Denis Ramirez from the road, complaining that his car had broken down again. Ramirez insisted on being paid the agreed-upon $800 anyway, "but he said he was only paying me $300, because the car was no good."

Early Thursday morning, Cristobal Veliz pulled off the I-95 in Jessop, Maryland, and stopped off at a drive-through Bank of America ATM to withdraw $200. Wearing a baggy T-shirt and a baseball cap, he was photographed at 6:18 A.M. by a CCTV camera making the withdrawal.

Three minutes later, his green Nissan Pathfinder was captured by the surveillance camera leaving the bank towing the gray Thunderbird back to New York.

THIRTY-SEVEN

"PREPARING FOR THE BIG DATE!"

A t around noon on Thursday, July 9, Ben and Narcy Novack flew into JFK Airport from Fort Lauderdale, to prepare for that weekend's Amway convention at the Rye Town Hilton. Before leaving, a jubilant Ben Novack Jr. had e-mailed Charlie Seraydar the news that the Miami Beach Police Department had finally agreed to put a plaque with his name on it on the wall of police headquarters, recognizing his thirty-one years of volunteer service.

"We had been trying to do that for him for a long time," said Seraydar, "and so that was a very ego-boosting thing for him."

He also called Kelsey Grammar to arrange dinner at his Hamptons spread. But the actor couldn't make it, as he was in Los Angeles shooting a movie.

When a limousine from the Rye Town Hilton was not there waiting outside the terminal, Novack went ballistic. He called up the hotel's associate director of events, Angelica Furano, and yelled at her, before hanging up and hailing a cab for himself and Narcy.

At 2:00 P.M., Ben and Narcy Novack walked into the lobby of the Hilton at 699 Westchester Avenue in Rye Brook, New York, where they were welcomed by Furano. Ben did not mention the limo problem.

Furano, who would be on call 24/7 during the Hispanic convention, escorted Narcy to the Woodlands Suite, on the fourth floor, where they would be staying.

A few minutes later, Ben Novack Jr. walked into the suite with the hotel's general manager, Alon Ben-Gurion, whose grandfather David Ben-Gurion had been Israel's first prime minister. The luxury suite consisted of a large parlor doubling as an office, a bedroom, and two bathroom/toilets (one of which was broken).

Two hours later, after unpacking and settling in, Ben Novack Jr. went to the John Halstead Room on the second floor for a preconvention meeting. The three-hour meeting was also attended by Convention Concepts Unlimited employees May Abad and Matthew Briggs, and by Furano, duty manager Jeremy Morris, the hotel chef, and the food and beverage manager. Narcy Novack did not attend the meeting, remaining in the Woodlands Suite to make calls.

The president of Convention Concepts Unlimited began by castigating Furano again for having failed to have the limousine waiting for him at the airport. Then he outlined in detail exactly what he expected the Hilton staff to do during the convention. He said that his stepdaughter, May Abad, would be handling the event, and that hotel staff should liaise with her.

Back in the Woodlands Suite, Narcy Novack was busy finalizing arrangements for the attack on her husband, now just three days away. While Ben was busy at the briefing, Narcy was talking to Cristobal, who had now reached Philadelphia.

While Ben was away, Narcy called her brother four times, with one call lasting forty-five minutes.

"They are discussing what is going to happen on July twelfth," assistant U.S. attorney Andrew Dember would later explain. "They are mapping it all out. Narcy knows her husband is in a long meeting with staff. She doesn't have to worry."

In Philadelphia, Veliz took the Thunderbird to a mechanic, who told him it was beyond repair. So after removing the license plates and title papers, Veliz left the car in the mechanic's yard and drove on to New York in the Pathfinder with Garcia and Gonzalez.

When they arrived, Veliz drove straight to his son-in-law Denis Ramirez's house at 1499 Jefferson Avenue, Brooklyn. Outside on the sidewalk, Veliz ordered his son-in-law to get him a car for "the big date" on Sunday morning, and told him that Ramirez would now be driving. He handed Ramirez fifty dollars to buy a cell phone for the job.

"We were going to beat somebody up and rob [them]," Ramirez would later testify. "He said he would pay me a thousand dollars and told me not to drink anything on Sunday night."

After Cristobal Veliz left to drop Garcia and Gonzalez off at the Crossbay Motor Inn, where they would be staying, Ramirez called an ex-girlfriend who drove a taxi, who agreed to lend him her Lincoln Town Car for the weekend.

At 8:00 A.M. on Friday, Ben Novack Jr. held a briefing for his staff in the parlor of his Woodlands Suite. Late the previous night, Narcy Novack's niece Leslie Goyzueta, Maria Gallegos, and Gallegos's sister Theresa Rivas, had all flown in for the convention, which they would be working on a freelance basis.

While Narcy stayed in the adjoining bedroom, Ben Novack issued last-minute instructions to his team. Then he sent them off to the Westchester Ballroom to begin setting up the two registration areas, as the Amway Hispanic attendees would soon be arriving.

Thirty miles away, in Ozone Park, Queens, Cristobal Veliz was collecting Alejandro Garcia and Joel Gonzalez to scout out the Rye Town Hilton. He arrived at 2:00 P.M. in his Nissan Pathfinder and drove them straight to the hotel, parking just outside.

On the way there, he had instructed them to familiarize themselves with the hotel and visit the Woodlands Suite, on the fourth floor. They were also to pay special attention to getting in and out of the hotel, avoiding hotel surveillance cameras at all costs.

After getting out of the Pathfinder, the two men casually strolled into the parking lot. Garcia, who was wearing his new Valentino sunglasses with his white T-shirt and jeans, and carrying a backpack, coolly asked an attendant where the Amway function was being held.

At 2:50 P.M. the two hit men were photographed by a hotel surveillance camera walking through the front lobby of the hotel. Ironically, Ben Novack Jr. also happened to walk straight past them on his way to Angelica Furano's office, near the front desk.

"I saw the gentleman in the diner at Fort Lauderdale," Gonzalez recalled.

Then Garcia led his partner up several flights of stairs to the guest rooms on the fourth floor, turning left and walking toward Rooms 453 and 454, comprising the Woodlands Suite.

"We found it," Garcia said. "I said to Joel, 'This is where the money is going to be.'"

Garcia then decided to leave through an exit just across the hallway, thinking it would be a faster way out.

At 2:58 P.M. Garcia and Gonzalez were photographed in the lobby leaving the hotel, and then again walking out into the hotel parking lot to the Pathfinder.

"Cristobal asked us if we had gotten to know the area and found [Novack's suite]," said Garcia. "I said yes, everything was fine, and we knew the path we were going to take."

From the Pathfinder, Veliz telephoned Narcy inside the hotel, telling her everything was going according to plan.

By the time the hit men arrived back in Brooklyn it was late afternoon. Cristobal Veliz stopped off at a RadioShack on Knickerbocker Avenue, buying a $140 TomTom GPS device. Then he took Alejandro Garcia next door to the Turbo men's store to buy him some smarter clothing, so he wouldn't stand out on Sunday morning at the Amway convention.

"He asked me to look for a shirt, shoes, and pants," Garcia recalled, "so I would look more presentable for the attack."

After picking out a black dress shirt, loafers, and a pair of pants,

Veliz paid the ninety-five-dollar bill with his Bank of America credit card.

He then dropped both men off at the Crossbay Motor Inn for the night; he would be staying at Laura Law's house in Bay Ridge, Brooklyn.

Back at the Rye Town Hilton, the Convention Concepts Unlimited staff was struggling to cope with the unexpectedly large crowds that had started arriving for the Amway convention. That weekend set records, with more than 1,900 Hispanic Amway distributors attending, more than twice as many as the 450-room Hilton could accommodate.

At 5:00 P.M., two hours before the convention's first scheduled event, there was a growing line of angry attendees snaking out into the parking lot. Over the next few hours, the Hilton staff scrambled to find alternative accommodation nearby, for the overflow, while Ben Novack Jr. seethed with anger.

Nevertheless, the first event of the convention started on time and went off without a hitch.

At 11:00 P.M., as things were winding down, Ben Novack Jr. was sitting at a conference table alone with the hotel's associate event director Angelica Furano when he began discussing his plans for the future.

"He said he was very proud of May [Abad] and all the hard work she had done," Furano would later testify. "And he was looking forward to retiring . . . and letting May do more of the day-to-day work, while he stayed in the background."

On Saturday, July 11, Ben Novack Jr. and his Convention Concepts Unlimited staff worked a sixteen-hour day.

"We started early at 7:00 A.M., said freelancer Maria Gallegos. "We registered additional people and continued to collect money."

About mid-morning, Ben and Narcy Novack came down and joined their orange-uniformed employees at the registration desk, issuing name tags and taking money from attendees for the various events.

That night there were two separate banquets, at 6:00 P.M. and 8:00 P.M., with little downtime at the two registration desks.

After the banquets ended, the Convention Concepts Unlimited staff retired to their respective rooms with blue pouches containing a total of $110,000 in cash that they had collected at the registration that day.

"That was standard procedure," Leslie Goyzueta explained. "We would collect all the money and put it in pouches given to us by Mr. Novack. At the end of the day I would count the money and put the pouch in my room safe."

Ben and Narcy Novack remained downstairs, requesting that the Tulip Tree Restaurant stay open so they could order dinner. Not wanting to upset her "difficult" client, Angelica Furano arranged for this to happen.

Just before midnight, Narcy Novack offered to help out Angelica Furano at breakfast the next morning, something she had never done before.

Then, at 12:07 A.M., Ben and Narcy used one of their key cards to enter the Woodlands Suite. As Narcy went to sleep in the bedroom, Ben settled down at his computer. As usual, he worked through the night on convention business, as well as searching eBay for Batman comics and memorabilia.

Late Saturday night, Cristobal Veliz called Francisco Picado, asking if he could drive some people to Miami the next morning. Picado agreed, as he knew his mentor always paid well.

Thirty-Eight

"FINISH HIM OFF!"

At 3:00 A.M. on Sunday, while Ben Novack Jr. was still at work in his suite, Cristobal Veliz pulled up in front of 1499 Jefferson Avenue in his Nissan Pathfinder. He called Denis Ramirez, saying he was waiting outside. After hastily dressing, Ramirez came downstairs and got into the borrowed black Lincoln Town Car and followed his father-in-law's Pathfinder to a gas station to fill up.

They then proceeded to the Crossbay Motor Inn, where Alejandro Garcia and Joel Garcia had packed and were ready to go, wearing their "professional-looking attire."

At 4:06 A.M. Gonzalez checked out of the motel and walked out with Garcia to the Pathfinder, putting their bags in the trunk. Garcia, wearing his fake Valentino sunglasses, kept his backpack, which contained all the weapons for the attack.

Then they got into the Lincoln Town Car, which Ramirez drove, following Veliz in his Pathfinder to the Rye Town Hilton.

Driving in convoy, the vehicles took the Belt Parkway, crossed over the Whitestone Bridge, and took the Hutchinson River Parkway to Rye Brook in Westchester County, New York.

It was still dark when they arrived at the Rye Town Hilton at 5:10 A.M. There was a light on in the Woodlands Suite, where Ben Novack Jr. was still working at his computer.

"We showed Denis [Ramirez] the area inside the parking lot where he was going to wait for us," Garcia later testified. "Then Cristobal said we needed to wait for a cell phone call from his sister, to tell us when we could attack the man."

Ramirez then drove the Town Car behind the green Pathfinder off the hotel grounds and to a gas station in Port Chester, just five minutes away. Veliz parked the Pathfinder on the road, while Ramirez stopped the Town Car by a Dumpster on the gas station forecourt.

Then the conspirators all waited nervously for Narcy Novack's call.

While Ramirez went inside the gas station to buy cigarettes, Garcia and Gonzalez got into the Pathfinder for final instructions. The previous day, Garcia said he would need a bottle of rum for the job, and Veliz had promised to bring one along.

"[Cristobal] said, 'I have a present for you,'" said Garcia, "and he gave me a bottle of rum. I said I'm going out to buy a bottle of soda and start drinking. I was nervous."

After buying the soda, Garcia got back into the Town Car with Ramirez and started drinking the rum cocktail. As the rum began taking effect, Ramirez started teasing Garcia about having beaten up an old lady in Fort Lauderdale.

"I said the lady had died," said Ramirez. "He got upset and said that Cristobal had to pay him more money because the old lady [had] died. Cristobal [had] told him she hadn't."

By the time Joel Gonzalez returned to the Town Car after smoking a cigarette, Garcia had worked himself into a frenzy.

"Mr. Garcia was very angry," Gonzalez recalled, "and wanted to know if it was true [about the old lady dying]. He said, 'Don't mess with me! Don't play with me!' Denis [Ramirez] was laughing and joking and not telling him if the old lady had died or not."

. . .

At around 6:30 A.M., it was just getting light when Ben Novack Jr. turned off his computer, stripped down to his boxer shorts, and got into bed for a couple of hours' sleep.

Investigators believe that Narcy waited until Novack fell asleep before sneaking out of bed and into the adjoining room, where she quietly called her brother's cell phone at 6:39 A.M., setting in motion their murderous plan.

After her call, Cristobal Veliz summoned Garcia to the Pathfinder, announcing, "She's ready. Let's go."

Garcia walked back to the Lincoln Town Car, took a long drink of rum, and told Ramirez to drive back to the Rye Town Hilton.

At 6:45 A.M. Denis Ramirez drove the Lincoln Town Car onto the grounds of the Rye Town Hilton and parked on a service road. Garcia told him to keep the engine running, so they could make a quick getaway. Then he and Gonzalez emptied out their pockets so nothing incriminating could fall out, before getting out of the Town Car and walking toward the hotel.

Inside the hotel, associate events director Angelica Furano had just arrived at the ballroom to help with breakfast. She was alarmed to discover a crowd of Amway attendees already lining up by the registration desks, with no Convention Unlimited staff to take care of them.

At 6:54 A.M. she called Ben Novack Jr.'s cell phone, asking him to send someone to the registration desk immediately.

"He answered the phone," recalled Furano. "He told me to call Nando [from Amway] and have him go to the registration. He sounded fine . . . normal."

After hanging up, Ben Novack Jr. went back to sleep.

. . .

The two killers entered through a side door, went up two flights of stairs, to the fourth floor, and turned left, as they had done two days earlier.

It was around 7:00 A.M. when they approached the Woodlands Suite. Narcy Novack was waiting in the doorway, gesturing to them to hurry up. She was dressed in a smart brown business suit, but had not done her dyed red hair or her makeup.

She ushered them in through the double doors and closed them. Then she put her index finger to her lips and made a shushing sound, pointing toward the bedroom. Inside, they saw Ben Novack Jr. fast asleep in bed, wearing only gray Hanes boxer shorts and black socks.

Then Narcy led the two men to a kitchen area, where Garcia placed his backpack on the counter and took out the dumbbells, duct tape, and gloves.

Both men removed their dress shirts and shoes, and while they were changing, Narcy told Garcia to remove his sunglasses. He ignored her, as the light hurt his eyes.

Finally, they put on the sports gloves and picked up the dumbbells, gripping them hard.

As they tiptoed past Narcy and into the dark bedroom, Garcia whispered that on the count of three they would attack.

Then they took their positions on either side of the double bed, where Ben Novack Jr. was asleep. Garcia quietly counted to three.

"We grabbed the dumbbells and started to hit him hard," Garcia later testified. "On the head, the chest, the ribs, and the abdomen."

Ben Novack woke up and started screaming, as he desperately tried to defend himself, furiously lashing out at Garcia. In the struggle, he broke an arm off his attacker's Valentino sunglasses, and his own gold Rolex watch came off, both falling onto the bed.

As Novack frantically fought back, Gonzalez got scared and walked out of the bedroom, leaving Garcia alone with Ben Novack.

"Narcy was angry," Gonzalez said. "She ordered me to get back there and help [Garcia]."

When Gonzalez returned to the bedroom, Narcy handed him a pillow and told him to use it to muffle Ben's screams, as he was making too much noise.

On the bed, Ben Novack was grappling with Garcia, who was still beating him with a dumbbell. Gonzalez put his knee onto the mattress, leveraging all his weight to smother Novack with the pillow.

"Mr. Novack swerved to the left and hit [Garcia] in the neck with his fist," Gonzalez recalled. "I dropped the pillow and left them wrestling with each other and walked out of the room."

Narcy was furious to see Gonzalez leave again, and screamed at him to go straight back and help his friend.

When he came back he found Ben Novack on the carpet, with Garcia standing over him and still pounding him hard with the dumbbell. As Novack was no longer moving and was just moaning in agony, Gonzalez said it was enough. Garcia stopped, and apologized for losing control.

Then, while he held Ben Novack down, Garcia told Gonzalez to duct-tape Novack's hands behind his back and his legs together.

"I taped his legs, and there was no resistance," Gonzalez recalled. "He was breathing very hard. There was a lot of blood coming out of his mouth."

Then, for the third time, Gonzalez went back to the kitchen, where Narcy was pacing nervously.

Alone in the bedroom, Garcia stood over Ben Novack, who was hogtied on the carpet, and took out the utility knife.

Then, grabbing a large clump of Ben Novack's long, thick hair, Garcia lifted up his head and thrust the sharp blade into Novack's left eye and turned it sharply. Ben Novack moaned in anguish. Then Garcia took out the knife and plunged it into Novack's right eye and twisted it.

When Garcia came back into the parlor, Narcy asked him if he had cut Ben's eyes. After confirming that he had, she asked if he was certain Ben would never see again. Garcia said he did not think so, but offered to cut the eyes some more. Narcy said that would not be necessary.

At this point, Gonzalez walked into the bedroom and saw what Garcia had done to Ben Novack's eyes. He came back into the parlor looking shaken.

"Did you do that?" he asked.

"Yes," Garcia replied.

Inside the bedroom, Ben Novack Jr. was still alive, making weak groaning noises.

"Finish him off," Narcy reportedly ordered.

So Garcia returned to the bedroom and wrapped duct tape around Ben Novack's head and mouth so tightly that he choked on his own vomit and died.

At the wet bar at the far end of the parlor, Narcy handed the two killers towels. She then turned on the faucet so they could wash off her husband's blood. While they were cleaning up, she went into the bedroom and took off Ben's wrist his treasured gold bracelet, which had "BEN" spelled out in diamonds. She handed the bloody bracelet to Garcia, who put it in a plastic bag and then into his backpack.

After the attackers put back on their dress shirts and shoes, Garcia returned to the bedroom to retrieve his sunglasses, which had come off during the attack. They were on the floor by Ben Novack's dead body, now lying facedown in a growing pool of blood. But Garcia forgot to take the smashed temple piece, leaving it on the bed alongside Ben's blood-soaked Rolex.

The original plan had been for them to tie up Narcy, leaving her in the suite with Ben to make it look like a robbery. But Narcy had changed her mind, suddenly announcing that they would all leave the suite together.

Less than ten minutes after they'd first entered the Woodlands Suite, the two killers left with Narcy Novack. After she closed the double doors, they all turned right into the hallway.

Garcia and Gonzalez took a left exit into a stairwell, and Narcy Novack continued down the hallway.

At the bottom of the stairs, the killers came out, made a wrong turn, and got lost. They walked around the entire hotel to the swimming pool, searching for the way out.

They wound up in the main lobby, where they spotted Narcy Novack wheeling a small suitcase. Then, as they walked out at 7:11 A.M., both men were photographed by the hotel's video surveillance camera

One minute later, they were photographed again, walking out into the parking lot and toward Denis Ramirez, who was waiting in the Lincoln Town Car to whisk them away.

At 7:14 A.M., as they made their getaway, Ramirez called Cristobal Veliz, informing him the mission had been accomplished. Veliz in turn called Narcy, telling her that Garcia and Gonzalez were safely out of the hotel and would soon be on their way home to Miami.

THIRTY-NINE

THE GRIEVING WIDOW

At 7:09 A.M., Narcy Novack appeared in the corridor between the ballroom and the kitchen pulling her large roller bag, and was caught by a hotel surveillance video camera. Prosecutors believe that during the last couple of days, she had scoped out the hotel, carefully noting where the CCTV cameras were placed.

Although there were already long lines of people outside the ballroom, snaking up to the fourth-floor guest rooms for breakfast, Narcy calmly planted herself directly in front of another surveillance camera in the corridor. For the next eighteen minutes, she stood with her distinctive suitcase, calmly making calls on her cell phone. She appeared completely unaware of all the frenzied Amway breakfast activity around her.

At 7:19 A.M., Narcy called May Abad, who was still in her room, and spent two minutes and thirty-nine-seconds on the phone. Then, at 7:31 A.M., she called Ben's cell phone for a forty-two-second call, as part of her elaborate alibi. At 7:33 A.M., she called her daughter again, a forty-eight-second call. Then she wheeled her case out of the corridor and disappeared out of camera shot.

A few seconds later, she arrived at the Amway registration desk, where Angelica Furano was standing by the entrance of the Port Chester Suite.

"I apologized for calling Mr. Novack so early," Furano recalled, "and I was sorry if I woke him up. [Narcy] said he had been up all night working and had just gone to sleep."

Furano told her that because of the huge crowd, the hotel had run out of china plates and mugs, and was resorting to plastic ones. Narcy said she would tell Ben, who would be furious.

She then wheeled her case over to the registration desk, where the Convention Concepts Unlimited staff had started to arrive.

"She was coming to the table . . . like she was in a rush," recalled Leslie Goyzueta. "She looked . . . a little bit flustered. I was really surprised to see her there, because typically, on a Sunday morning, Narcy and Mr. Novack wouldn't come downstairs."

When May Abad came over to hug her, Narcy pulled away.

"May said, 'You look like shit,'" said Goyzueta. "[Narcy] said Mr. Novack had rushed her out of the room to take care of the breakfast. She wasn't wearing makeup. She always wore makeup."

After spending five minutes at the registration desk, Narcy announced that she had to "go and wipe my ass," and wheeled her heavy suitcase toward an exit stairwell on the right.

"There was a young Hispanic man there," said Goyzueta, "and he tried to help her down with the suitcase. She just said no and went downstairs."

Detectives believe that Narcy, who could easily have taken an elevator to the Woodlands Suite instead of carrying the heavy case up the stairs, had other intentions. They think she now dumped the secret 954-816-2089 cell phone, with all her incriminating calls to her brother Cristobal Veliz. They also suspect that Veliz may have been at the hotel to collect the phone personally from Narcy.

At around 7:40 A.M., a seventy-four-year-old Amway guest named Rigoberto Wilson was on his way to breakfast when he got lost. Suddenly he saw Narcy Novack wheeling her suitcase along a fourth-floor corridor wearing her brown jacket and slacks. He immediately recognized her from the previous night's banquet, where he had been told she was running the convention.

Wilson then followed Narcy, thinking she was probably on her way to the breakfast. She stopped at an exit door and turned around to see Wilson a few feet behind her.

"She saw me and I saw her," he later testified. "She was frightened."

Narcy opened the exit door and went through it, and Wilson walked past. He went downstairs through another exit, and got even more lost, searching for the dining room.

A few minutes later, Narcy Novack came back to the fourth floor. She went to the Woodlands Suite, letting herself into the bedroom at 7:45 A.M. with her key card. She went inside, walking past her husband's bloody remains and into the parlor, where she took off her brown jacket and left her suitcase.

Then she came back out and left the door ajar, sitting down in the corridor to decide on her next move.

Suddenly Rigoberto Wilson reappeared, still searching for the dining room.

"She was leaning against the wall in the hallway," he recalled. "She looked toward me and started screaming, 'Help me! My husband!'"

Wilson asked what was wrong, and she ignored him and started pounding on the nearby guest room doors.

Then Wilson noticed one of the doors to the Woodlands Suite was open, so he went in to investigate, surmising that that's where she had come from.

"I saw blood on the bed," he later remembered. "The man was tied up, with his feet and arms tied behind his back. He had duct tape over his mouth. He was facing down with his head turned to the left and there was blood around his neck."

Wilson then took out his cell phone and began taking photographs of Ben Novack's smashed-up body, as he could still hear Narcy screaming in the corridor. He took a close-up of Ben's head, another of his whole body, and a third of some of his jewelry.

Then he came back out to find a crowd had gathered in the corridor around Narcy Novack, who was still screaming hysterically. Wilson remembered she had been wearing a brown jacket and had had a suitcase when he'd first seen her, which she no longer had with her. So he went back into the suite to look for them.

"I said to myself, 'That's the lady who was rolling a suitcase. She must have gone out to give it to someone,'" he explained. "Then I went back into the room with the dead body to look for the suitcase."

Unable to find it, he came out again, where Narcy was still screaming, "My husband! My husband!"

"I went into the room for the third time," said Wilson. "Then the lady came in and looked at the dead body. She opened her legs, as if she wanted to get on top of him, and started pulling on his shoulders, screaming, 'Why! Why!'"

He watched in astonishment as Narcy began beating her husband's lifeless body on the shoulder blades with her clenched fists.

"Then she got on top of him, as if she was riding a horse," said Wilson. "She sat down on his buttocks and grabbed his arms but she couldn't lift him."

Finally, Wilson asked Narcy in Spanish if she wanted to tell him something. When she ignored him and carried on screaming, he left.

At 7:50 A.M., Rye Town Hilton Hotel security officer Mark Rivera received a call, reporting a heart attack in the Woodlands Suite. He ran to the fourth floor, where he saw a crowd outside.

"The door was ajar and I went in," said Rivera. "The first thing I saw was Mrs. Novack down on her knees [and] over the body. There was no one else in the room. She was screaming, 'Why me! Why is this happening?'"

Then he saw Ben Novack facedown in a pool of blood.

"My first reaction was to calm down Mrs. Novack," Rivera explained.

"I was trying to remove her from the body so nothing would be tampered with."

The tall, muscular security officer then picked up Narcy, carrying her over to a chair behind her husband's body.

"She kept trying to get back to Mr. Novack," he said. "I kept her right there."

While Rivera was restraining Narcy, the hotel's security chief, Louis Monti, arrived, closely followed by acting manager Jeremy Morris.

"I walked in and Mark [Rivera] was physically holding her back," Morris later testified. "They were both on their knees and he had his arms wrapped around her. She was crying and saying, 'Why!' She was hysterical, yelling and screaming."

When Monti saw Ben Novack's battered body facedown on the carpet, he felt ill.

"Mr. Novack was duct-taped on the floor in his underwear," Morris remembered. "There was blood all over the bed."

After ensuring that the police were on their way, Monti left the suite to secure the scene, and made sure no one else came in.

At 7:56 A.M. Kerri Conrad and Alex Miller from Rye Brook Emergency Services arrived at the hotel, responding to a 911 call reporting a heart attack. They parked their EMS truck by the lobby and went straight to the Hilton security station. They were directed up to Room 453, where Rye Brook police officers Neil Moore and Mark Rampolla had arrived three minutes earlier.

"It was incredibly crowded," Conrad recalled, "and there were people all over the place. I went into the [bed]room and saw he was facedown on the floor with his arms behind him. There was blood on the sheets."

Conrad then put her hand on Ben Novack's bloody neck, under his thick gold necklace, noting the congealed blood in his matted hair and in his eyes, and checked his pulse.

"I didn't feel anything," she said. "He was flatlined. I hooked him up to a heart monitor and checked the body temperature. He was maybe room temperature. He was blue. Cyanotic. It was obvious he was dead."

After Officer Neil Moore tilted the body over so Conrad could look at the face, she officially pronounced Ben Novack Jr. dead at 7:59 A.M.

Then she went into the adjoining parlor, where Narcy Novack was sitting on a couch.

"I offered my condolences," Conrad said. "She grabbed my wrist and said, 'Are you sure he's dead?' I said, 'I'm sure.' She had no emotions. She did not seem upset."

It was at that point that May Abad called duty manager Jeremy Morris's cell phone, asking what was going on. Without elaborating further, he invited her up to the Woodlands Suite. A couple of minutes later May Abad rushed into the parlor and asked her mother what was happening.

"He's dead! He's dead!" Narcy screamed at her daughter.

"May seemed stunned," said Rivera. "She wasn't crying. There was blood everywhere. What was weird was the daughter asked the mother, 'Where's the money?' Mrs. Novack couldn't answer because she was so upset and crying."

At 8:05 A.M., May Abad called Matthew Briggs in his room, informing him that Ben Novack was dead. He immediately rushed up to the fourth floor and saw Jeremy Morris in the hallway, who confirmed the news.

"I ran into the parlor area," Briggs recalled. "May was distraught, crying and screaming. She was on the couch . . . going back and forth hugging [Narcy]."

Narcy told him to go and get the money collected at the convention immediately and put it in the hotel safe-deposit box.

Then a wheelchair arrived to move Narcy Novack to Room 481, diagonally across the hallway, to get her away from her husband's body.

"She couldn't walk," Rivera said. "She was very upset, so I wheeled her in the wheelchair to another room."

Outside in the hallway, May Abad told her mother to pull herself together.

"May told her to shut up and stop it," said Morris, "or it was going to make her throw up. She seemed to be upset at her mother's behavior."

. . .

Downstairs at the Amway registration desk, things had quieted down after breakfast, as the guests went off for the first event of the day. The three remaining Convention Concepts Unlimited staffers were unaware of the drama taking place upstairs.

"The girls and I were going to take turns for breakfast," said Leslie Goyzueta. "Maria and I left to go to the hotel restaurant."

They were just about to start eating when Matt Briggs burst into the restaurant, demanding their convention cash immediately.

"Matt seemed flustered, alarmed, and scared," Maria Gallegos recalled. "I had never seen him like that before."

When she asked him to tell them what was wrong, Briggs looked at them with tears in his eyes, saying, "Ben's dead."

"We were in shock," Maria said. "We started to cry."

After handing over the blue pouches full of money, they returned to the registration desk and tried to compose themselves.

After picking up the killers, Denis Ramirez sped off toward Brooklyn to meet up with Cristobal Veliz. He took I-287 toward the Tappan Zee Bridge and got on the New York Thruway going south toward the Triborough Bridge.

Soon after they got in the Lincoln Town Car, Alejandro Garcia said that Ben Novack had broken his Valentinos, and he showed Joel Gonzalez the sunglasses, now missing an arm. He asked Gonzalez to sell him his identical pair, but he refused.

Gonzalez then asked Garcia why "he had to do that" during the attack. When Ramirez asked what Garcia had done, Garcia replied that he had taken out Ben Novack's eyes.

"I remember Mr. Garcia looking at the reaction in my face," said Gonzalez. He said, 'Don't think about what happened. The worst part is over.'"

Then Cristobal Veliz called, telling Ramirez to take the Tuckahoe Road exit and meet him at a gas station in Yonkers. Soon after they arrived there, the green Pathfinder suddenly appeared and parked in front of them.

Garcia got out to speak to Jefe, taking the backpack containing the bloody dumbbells and the utility knife. He threw it into a Dumpster at the back of the gas station.

He then returned to the Town Car and told Ramirez to follow the Pathfinder to Brooklyn. Cristobal Veliz then led Ramirez south along local roads and over the Triborough Bridge into Brooklyn, finally stopping at the Apex Bus garage, where Veliz occasionally worked.

Then the two attackers got into the Pathfinder, took off all their clothes, and changed into clean ones.

"I had the undershirt I had worn when I attacked Señor Novack," said Garcia. "I needed to take it off because it stank. It had a bad smell."

Garcia then tried to clean all the blood off himself.

"He was wiping down his feet," Gonzalez recalled. "He had a lot of blood on his toes, socks, and shoes."

After learning that Garcia and Gonzalez were safely out of the Rye Town Hilton, Cristobal Veliz had telephoned Francisco Picado and woken him up. He told him to get dressed and meet him at the Dunkin' Donuts at the intersection of Knickerbocker and Myrtle avenues, Brooklyn, saying he would pay him $500 to drive his hit men back to Miami.

At around 8:30 A.M., Veliz parked outside the Dunkin' Donuts, while Ramirez stopped next door in a Burger King parking lot. The two killers got out of the Lincoln Town Car and went over to the Pathfinder. Garcia sat in the front passenger seat, while Gonzalez got in the back.

Veliz then paid them off in $100 bills, handing Garcia $7,000 and Gonzalez $3,000. He told them to count the money to make sure it was correct, which they did.

"After Cristobal paid me, I told him I was very nervous," said Garcia. "I said I need to get out of here. I need to go to Miami. He told me don't worry, Frank is coming, and he'll take you."

. . .

Just before 9:00 A.M., Francisco Picado appeared at the Dunkin' Donuts on foot and went straight over to the green Pathfinder. He asked Veliz for money for gas and tolls to Miami. Veliz replied that Garcia would take care of expenses.

Then, as Picado climbed into the driver's seat of the Pathfinder, Veliz told him to drive carefully to Miami and have a safe trip.

Several minutes later, Picado was driving along Bedford Avenue when Garcia announced he had to get rid of something.

"Alex asked me to look for a garbage Dumpster," Picado said, "to throw a bag he had out. I saw a firehouse with a Dumpster, and he threw out the bag. Later he told me it was some clothes he had been wearing [in the attack].

"Then I started driving to Miami. I got to 95 and just went straight down."

FORTY

"ONLY A MONSTER CAN DO THIS EVIL THING"

R ye Brook police chief Gregory Austin was in Maine on a family vacation when he received a call about Ben Novack Jr.'s murder. He immediately headed back to Westchester County to take charge of the investigation.

There are few major crimes in the affluent village of Rye Brook, twenty miles north of New York City. The last murder the twenty-eight-member police department had to investigate was in 2003, and it remains unsolved.

It was obvious that Ben Novack Jr.'s brutal murder would require far larger resources than the Rye Brook Police Department had available, so several other Westchester County law enforcement agencies were called in.

At 9:50 A.M. Detective Roger Piccirilli of the Westchester County Division of Public Safety arrived at the Rye Town Hilton to process the crime scene. He was then briefed by Detective Sergeant Terence Wilson of the Rye Brook Police, who had already been appointed lead detective for the investigation.

"We conducted a walk through two hallways and a staircase," recalled Detective Piccirilli. "Rye Brook police had noted some stains on the carpet. They decided [it was linked] with what had happened in Room 453."

The crime scene specialist then donned a Tyvex suit and went into the Woodlands Suite to supervise the photographing and documenting of the murder scene.

"My initial observations were that there were no signs of a struggle," said Piccirilli. "At the far end of the room by the window was a white male lying on the floor with his hands and legs bound by duct tape. There was duct tape covering his mouth.

"In the whole bedroom there was nothing knocked over and nothing to indicate any sort of struggle. All the activity was on the bed. On the left side was a very large amount of blood."

Stepping into the parlor, the detective observed a table with Ben Novack's business papers on it and a laptop computer. Nearby was a blue pouch with about $15,000 in cash inside, alongside a television remote wrapped in a plastic bag.

Detective Piccirilli noted how there were no cabinet drawers pulled open or items on the floor, the obvious signs of a robbery.

He then went over to the wet bar at the far side of the parlor, observing red staining on the sink.

"Again I noted no signs of a struggle," said Piccirilli. "It appeared [the blood was confined] to two areas of the wet bar and where the victim lay on the floor."

The crime scene specialist also noted there were no signs of any forced entry into the suite, and none of the windows were damaged. He then led his team outside, where they photographed and swabbed possible blood stains on the two hallways and stairway by the Woodlands Suite. To protect the crime scene, all fourth-floor guests would now be accompanied to and from their rooms by police.

Later that morning, Piccirilli returned to the Woodlands Suite to retrieve evidence. On the bed, he found Ben Novack's blood-soaked gold Rolex watch, which had come off his wrist during the attack. Next to it was the temple piece of a pair of sunglasses.

At 12:45 P.M., Rye Brook Police detective John Arnold interviewed Narcy Novack. She told the detective that Ben had seemed unusually nervous over the last few days. He had picked at his fingers until they bled and was not sleeping.

The previous night, he had stayed up working, finally going to bed at 6:30 A.M. Half an hour later, Narcy had left him asleep in the bedroom, going to the other end of the hotel to supervise breakfast for the Amway guests.

"She told me that her husband had asked her to cuddle a little bit in the morning," Detective Arnold later wrote in his report. "A little after 0700 hrs [sic] she ran out to go to the breakfast."

Narcy explained that there had been such a big crowd for the breakfast that the hotel had run out of china and had resorted to using plastic plates. Knowing her husband would strongly disapprove of this, she had called his cell phone to inform him. When there was no answer, she had returned to their room to tell him.

"She entered the room through the suite doors," Detective Arnold wrote. "She was going to use the bathroom in the parlor area, because the toilet was 'plugged up' in the bedroom. She did use the bathroom . . . when she entered the parlor area she called out to her husband and said, 'Novack, you're not going to like this,' but he did not answer."

Narcy said she had then walked into the bedroom and "tripped over" Ben's body. After looking down and seeing him lying on the floor "in need of medical attention," she had started screaming and called the front desk. Then she'd rushed out of the suite, banging on nearby doors for help.

Detective Arnold then asked if Ben had any enemies. Narcy said he had, including some at the Miami Beach Police Department. She explained that after retiring from the Reserves, Ben had wanted his photograph displayed on the ceremonial wall of honor, alongside those of the other retired officers. After his request was denied, there had been "a big battle," ending with Ben asking the mayor to intervene.

"Narcy stated that she did hear her husband on the phone," wrote Detective Arnold, "mentioning something about spilling the beans if they do not put him on the wall."

At 4:15 P.M. Rye Brook Police detective Steven Goralick arrived at the room, with instructions to make Narcy as comfortable as possible.

By this time Narcy was talking about suicide, saying she wanted to swallow some pills and end it all. Goralick then arranged for a rabbi to come and counsel her, after she told him she was Jewish.

At 5:24 P.M. the acting chief medical examiner for Westchester County, Dr. Kunjlata Ashar and her assistant arrived at the Woodlands Suite to view Ben Novack Jr.'s body. They rolled him over on his back, and his horrific injuries were photographed. Then his hands and feet were bagged, to preserve any evidence. Still bound in duct tape, he was put in a body bag on a gurney and taken to the Medical Examiner's Office for an autopsy.

At 7:30 P.M. senior investigator Edward Murphy of the Westchester County District Attorney's Office, arrived at Room 481 to interview Narcy Novack. He had just spent an hour interviewing May Abad, and had many questions for her mother.

"I introduced myself and extended my sympathy," said the former New York City homicide cop. "I told her how the investigation was going to proceed. We were going to be starting from scratch, and I needed to know everything about Ben Novack: his personal life and anyone that he owed money to. She was very agreeable and said she'd do anything to help investigators find out who killed her husband."

For the next two hours, Murphy, who was later joined by Detective Alison Carpentier, interviewed Narcy, looking for any leads.

Once again she told the detectives that Ben had enemies, saying he had recently been "hanging out" and "doing business with weird people."

She said her husband often attended comic book trade shows, and had recently agreed to pay $43,000 for a Batman comic book. Then, about three weeks ago, he had gotten into a dispute with a comic book dealer who'd shown up at their residence. According to Narcy, Ben and the dealer, whom she did not know, began to negotiate prices for a comic book. She had heard shouting, and the dealer saying, "Now, you are going to Jew me down!"

Then Ben had had her retrieve a "bag" of cash, which he gave to the dealer, who then left.

During the interview, Lieutenant Christopher Calabrese of the Westchester County Police Department brought in the gold Rolex watch and temple piece from a pair of sunglasses, which had been found on the blood-soaked bed.

"I placed the watch in front of Mrs. Novack," Lieutenant Calabrese later reported. "She looked intently at the watch and stated, 'the watch belonged (past tense) to her husband, he always wore it . . . yes he was wearing it last night.'"

He then showed Narcy the broken temple piece from a pair of knockoff Valentino sunglasses. She said it came from a pair of her sunglasses that had broken on the flight over. When the detective asked how it had gotten on the bed, Narcy replied that Ben had been trying to mend them.

"He liked to fix things," she told the detective, "so he might have just decided to fix them in bed."

When Calabrese asked where the rest of the sunglasses were, Narcy looked "perplexed." After a pause, she said that she had lost them on the plane. He followed up by inquiring how Ben could possibly have been trying to fix them without the rest of the sunglasses, and Narcy had no answer. When he repeated the question, she replied, "I don't know."

At around 11:00 P.M. Narcy Novack and her daughter, May, were taken downstairs to Room 262 to spend the night. Detective Sergeant Terence Wilson offered to post a uniformed officer outside their door in case the killer was still out there, but Narcy said it would not be necessary.

Just before midnight, a police officer accompanied May Abad and Matthew Briggs to the hotel safe-deposit box to pay off the Convention Concepts Unlimited staff. May Abad then took the box into a small room, where she removed cash for the three freelancers and Briggs. She also took out $2,200 for Briggs to run a scheduled event for a church organization in the Bahamas the following week, which would go ahead as planned.

. . .

Early Monday morning, as the killers arrived back in Miami, Rye Brook Police chief Gregory Austin issued a media release appealing for any information about Ben Novack Jr.'s murder. Chief Austin said his detectives were now investigating the homicide with the help of the Westchester County District's Attorney's Office and the Department of Public Safety.

"Based on the information available at this point," read the release, "this incident appears to be centered on Mr. Novack. Investigation is on going."

The chief also announced a special tips line, promising that any information provided would remain confidential.

Around 9:50 A.M., Dr. Kunjlata Ashar performed an autopsy on Ben Novack Jr.'s body at the Westchester County Medical Examiner's Office in Dana Road, Valhalla. She was assisted by two other medical examiners. Detective Sergeant Terence Wilson of the Rye Brook Police was there as an observer.

Dr. Ashar began by cutting the duct tape that still bound Ben Novack's hands and legs and logging it into evidence for forensic investigation. She then took off the heavy gold chains around his neck, a diamond-studded gold ring, and a gold pinkie ring.

Dr. Ashar began by taking a cursory look at the numerous injuries to Ben Novack's head.

"His head had every kind of blunt force injury as well as sharp injuries," she later testified. "The back of the head had three lacerations to the left side."

One of the injuries on the top of the head was star-shaped, clearly bearing the imprint of the side of a dumbbell. Later, when his head was shaved, the doctor found a tiny blue piece of material from the weapon embedded in the wound.

"I looked at all the fractures," she said. "There were fractures on the front of the skull as well as the back. One was a depressed skull fracture."

The medical examiner also noted the horrific injuries to both eyes.

"His left eye had an incised wound that went inside the eyeball and it had collapsed," she said. "The eyeball is usually filled with fluid, and when cut, the fluid comes out and [the eyeball] shrivels up. The right eye had mixed sharp and blunt injuries and an incised wound. There were three other additional incised wounds on the eyelid."

She then opened up Ben Novack's body using the traditional Y-shaped thoracoabdominal incision and inspected his internal organs and ribs.

"He had multiple fractures on the right side as well as the left," said the pathologist.

She also found twenty fractures to his ribs, which were so badly smashed they resembled chicken bones.

In total, Dr. Ashar counted a total of thirty-four blunt force injuries and twelve sharp-force injuries to Ben Novack's battered body. He had actually died choking on his own vomit, after Garcia wound the duct tape tightly around his mouth and throat.

In her autopsy report, Dr. Ashar listed the cause of death as "Blunt and sharp injuries of body with fractures of skull and ribs, contusions of brain and lungs; hemorrhages; aspiration of gastric contents; found bound and gagged. Homicide."

Back at the Rye Brook Hilton, Westchester County District Attorney's Office investigators Michael LaRotonda and Art Muhammad had learned that $105,515 in cash from the Amway convention was in the hotel front desk safe. Under the present circumstances, the hotel management was "uneasy" having such a large sum of money there, and wanted it removed as soon as possible.

Narcy Novack offered to take the cash back to Fort Lauderdale, but the detectives suggested she deposit it in a local bank instead, for security purposes. At 10:30 A.M. they drove her to a nearby Wachovia Bank, where she had a joint account with Ben, and the cash was counted and deposited.

At the bank, Investigator LaRotonda observed a teller handing Narcy Novack a pile of money, which she put in her bag. Later, back at the hotel, the investigator saw Narcy's bag on a table and looked inside and saw $5,000 in cash.

"It was open," he later testified. "I observed currency on its side in thousand-dollar straps. There were five of them."

Later that morning, senior investigator Edward Murphy asked Narcy Novack to come to the Westchester County Police Department headquarters in Valhalla to give a full written statement before returning to Florida.

"[She] agreed," said Murphy, "indicating that she wanted to be as helpful as possible to the law enforcement officials investigating her husband's death."

But first, Narcy said she had to take care of some personal errands, including getting a new charger for her cell phone. Detectives Murphy and Carpentier then drove Narcy and May Abad in an unmarked police car to a nearby Verizon store to buy one.

At 11:30 A.M. Chief Austin held a press conference at Rye Brook Village Hall. The tiny hall was packed with local and national TV news crews and reporters.

Standing at a lectern, the youthful police chief said the attack did not appear to be random. There were no reports of screams from the room, he told reporters, and no valuables were missing.

"We feel the person who did this was not a stranger who anonymously, randomly picked him up," said Chief Austin, "but had some sort of connection which we haven't determined yet. We have no suspects at the moment."

The chief said there were "visible signs" that Novack had been beaten to death but refused to elaborate on the weapon used. He said an autopsy was now taking place and he needed to see the results before releasing any further details.

Answering reporters' questions, Chief Austin said Ben Novack Jr.

and his wife had checked into the Hilton on Thursday night, to work together on the conference. He refused to name the victim's wife, warning that security at the hotel had been heightened, and no reporters were being allowed inside.

He said detectives were now busy reviewing hotel surveillance video for any leads and interviewing Amway delegates and anyone who had been staying on the fourth floor on Saturday night.

"We're hoping people at the hotel may have seen something or heard things," said the chief. "We're trying to put the pieces together."

A few hours later, Chief Austin gave a telephone interview to *The Miami Herald*, providing one further detail about the murder.

"He was bludgeoned with some sort of blunt instrument," Austin said. "We have no suspects at this time."

On their way to Westchester County Police headquarters, Investigator Murphy told Narcy that he did not expect her to identify Ben's body, as it was in such bad condition. But Narcy said she wanted to see her husband one last time.

"She insisted on seeing her husband at the morgue," Murphy later wrote in his report, "and making the identification."

Murphy and Detective Alison Carpentier then drove Narcy and May Abad to the medical examiner's office, arriving at 3:50 P.M. The two women were led into the morgue, where Ben's butchered body was laid out on a gurney, a blanket strategically placed across his face, where his eyes had been gouged out.

Unprepared for such horrific injuries to her stepfather, May was physically sick, and had to be taken away. Her mother just coldly stared at her husband's body without a hint of emotion.

"Narcy stood at the window with me for fifteen minutes," said Murphy. "She was very calm. She didn't say much."

After Narcy officially identified the body, she and May were driven to the Westchester County Police headquarters in Hawthorne, New York, to be formally interviewed.

. . .

Just after 5:00 P.M. Charlie Seraydar called Ben Novack Jr.'s cell phone. When there was no answer, he called May Abad.

"Narcy and May were at the police station," Seraydar recalled, "and then May handed her phone to Narcy, who started saying that she had come back to the room and found Ben dead."

Narcy then got off the phone, saying the police wanted to interview her, and May would explain everything.

"So May gets on the phone with me," said Seraydar, "and we talk for about fifteen to twenty minutes. Then she says, 'I've got to go. The cops want to talk to me.'"

When detectives questioned May Abad, she told a different story from her mother. She claimed that Narcy had not come down for breakfast until around 7:20 A.M., and then had left at around 7:40 A.M. to go back to the suite.

After making her statement, May texted Charlie Seraydar, asking if her mom and Ben had been fighting.

"And I just sent her a text message back," said Seraydar, "and I said, 'Call me.' And that alerted me that the cops already knew that there was something going on."

As investigators Ed Murphy and Alison Carpentier prepared to interview Narcy Novack, they had several reasons to suspect she had been involved in her husband's murder. The electronic door lock codes for the Woodlands Suite had now been examined and it had been determined that no key cards had been used to enter the room between the time Narcy and Ben entered the suite the previous evening at midnight and when Narcy returned from breakfast at 7:45 A.M. to discover Ben dead.

Detectives were also skeptical of Narcy's implausible claim that the arm of the fake Valentino's sunglasses had come from a pair she had broken. How could Ben have tried to fix them, they asked, if the remaining parts were missing?

Also, after learning from Narcy about Ben's fondness for being tied up, investigators wondered if this had played any part in his murder. It seemed more than just coincidence that his body had been found bound in duct tape, in the exact same bondage position that he so enjoyed for sex.

Additionally, a few hours earlier they had received a tip-off from Florida that Ben Novack Jr. had been the victim of a 2002 home invasion, and that Narcy was behind it.

At 6:01 P.M. on Monday, Investigator Edward Murphy and Detective Alison Carpentier turned on a video recorder in a small interview room at Westchester County Police headquarters. Then Narcy Novack was brought in, without being told that the interview was being recorded.

Over the next eight hours, a team of five detectives would take turns questioning her about her husband's murder. Narcy had not eaten since Sunday morning, and over the course of the interview, she refused repeated offers of a slice of pizza, water, or even a visit to the restroom.

The two investigators began by asking what Narcy and Ben's movements had been since arriving in New York on Thursday night for the Amway conference.

Narcy said the Amway conference had posed "a lot of problems," after 1,900 people turned up instead of the 1,200 expected. The detectives sympathized as Narcy explained that it had been double the amount of work for everyone.

Narcy seemed chatty, describing herself as her husband's "eyes and ears" and his "foody partner."

"When Ben says, 'Come,' I run like a maniac," she told the investigators.

Slowly they steered the questions around to 6:30 on Sunday morning, when Narcy claimed that Ben had finally come to bed and woken her up.

"He just snuggle a little," she said, "and he was playing with my hair."

As soon as he fell asleep, she had gotten up and taken a shower. Then the phone rang and Ben had answered it and had a brief conversation with Angelica Furano. He had then ordered Narcy to leave so she wouldn't be late for breakfast.

"And he start barking at me," she told the detectives. "He was rushing me [and] he realized that I was leaving without giving him a kiss, and we don't do that. He said, 'Come on, give me a besito.' So I went back. I kiss him and I left."

Narcy had then wheeled her suitcase, containing her computer and makeup, along the corridor to the banquet hall, where a large crowd had gathered for breakfast.

"The line is humungous," she said.

A few minutes later, after her daughter, May, and Matt Briggs had come down, the caterers ran out of china and silverware.

"When I find out it was plastics and disposables," Narcy said, "I knew right away that I had to get hold of Ben. Ben doesn't like surprises."

She had tried to call his cell phone but there had been no answer, so she had gone back to their suite to tell him.

"And I said, 'Novack,' you're not going to like this," Narcy told investigators. "And I usually called him 'Novack' when we . . . have a problem. He didn't answer, so I thought he was asleep."

After using the bathroom in the parlor, she went into the bedroom.

"And that is when all hell broke loose," she said. "I walked in . . . and I trip on something . . . and I realize that he was on the floor. It did not look like Ben. Ben won't be on the floor. Something was not right. When I saw him I started screaming. And I don't know if I got on the phone. I was screaming on the phone . . . and then I run outside the hallway, through the bedroom door. I was screaming and knocking on every door."

She said a couple had then come to her assistance and followed her back to the suite.

"I was holding Ben and rubbing his leg," Narcy said.

"Holding him where?" Detective Carpentier asked. "Show me?"

"From his underwear and his butt," she replied. "I was just rubbing his leg and holding his butt and trying to move him. Somebody grabbed me. They were trying to get me away. I was hysterical."

When Investigator Murphy asked if she had seen Ben's face, Narcy was evasive.

"He's very hairy," she said, "so I knew that was him and he was not moving."

Murphy asked if she had tried to help him and turn him over, as he was facedown on the carpet.

"I have a problem with blood," Narcy replied. "If I have a little cut or something. I cannot see blood. If they take blood out of my arm I faint."

"Did you faint?" Carpentier asked.

"No," she said. "I'm afraid of blood. I don't know if I passed out at that time. I blacked out. Something happened to me."

After a hotel security guard had sat her on a couch, she said, she tried to grab his gun and commit suicide.

"I just wanted to kill myself," she explained. "They were telling me he was gone. I said I want to be gone too and I want it to be quick. So I just grabbed his gun and I guess he was quicker than me."

Detective Carpentier said she felt bad that May had been physically sick after seeing her stepfather's body in the morgue. "Nobody should have to see that," Carpentier said.

"I wanted to see him," Narcy stated. "I didn't go there to see the injuries. I wanted to see him and I was happy I went to see him."

"I wish we could have done more," Carpentier said. "His condition is bad and they had to try to put the blanket in a way that wouldn't . . . really upset you."

"Only a monster can do this evil thing," Narcy replied.

A few minutes later, observing how Narcy had already revealed how Ben liked "kinky sex" and being tied up, Investigator Murphy asked if his murder could be connected to this.

"Shhh, she doesn't know," Narcy said, referring to Detective Carpentier.

Murphy then informed her that Rye Brook Police had received a call from Florida about Ben being attacked during a 2002 home invasion.

"Was he ever a victim of a home invasion?" Murphy asked.

"He was not! He was not!" Narcy said indignantly. "And that's why we went back together, because he lied. He was not!"

Narcy then explained that her husband "likes a lot of weird things" involving "dirt" that she didn't want to dig up.

"He likes rough stuff," she told them. "He made up the home invasion. He thought that he would convince me to have sex."

She claimed that in 2002 she had merely handcuffed Ben to a chair before taking her own jewelry and watches from a safe and leaving.

"He say[s] that I had the house robbed. No," she snapped. "I took my stuff. I have the right to leave the house. I'm not his prisoner. I'm not his sex slave. I was fed up. I find some weird stuff. I freaked out."

She then accused Ben of being a pedophile, saying she had found his collection of pornographic pictures of children, which he feared she would use against him.

"He wants me to come back and [not to] expose that," she explained. "And he would do anything not to have that out, because he knew they would put him in jail."

Narcy said Ben had dropped the criminal complaint and they'd reconciled after she returned the pictures, which he'd had stored in a warehouse. As a precaution, Narcy said she had kept a few of the pedophile pictures back, and Ben had been suspicious.

She also claimed her husband courted young female amputees, taking them out on dates and promising to buy them prosthetic limbs.

"He likes somebody to be . . . helpless," she said. "I guess that they cannot run away from whatever he does to them, because they don't have the legs."

Narcy said when she discovered his fetish for amputees, it had freaked her out.

"I was in love with him," she explained. "And when you love somebody and they explain to you that it's a screw loose, you've got to hope it's gonna get better."

She also claimed to have seen his love letters from amputees dating back to his youth at the Fontainebleau.

"He would promise them," she said, "okay, you come to the hotel [and] I'm going to wine and dine you. I want [us] to get to know each other and when you're comfortable . . . we will start dating. But his only purpose was to have sex with them."

After the 2002 incident, Narcy told the detectives she had shown Bernice Novack her son's amputee photographs, some dating back to when he lived with her.

"I said, 'Bernice, I loved your son, but he's sick, and since I'm leaving him I think I owe it to you . . . he needs help.'"

According to Narcy, her mother-in-law had refused to believe her until she saw the pictures, along with envelopes addressed to Ben at her address. Then she had commended Narcy for having the "courage and honesty" to tell her that Ben was so sick, and for staying with him.

Changing the subject, Investigator Murphy asked if anyone had pressured Narcy to let them into the suite to rob Ben.

"I'm so confused," Narcy replied. "What are you telling me?"

Murphy told her that a young boy had seen two men go into the Woodlands Suite, and a lady coming out shortly afterward.

"That woman has to be you," he told her.

"Beats me," Narcy replied, throwing up her hands.

Again Murphy asked if she had been threatened, but Narcy insisted she would have called the police if she had been.

"Suppose they tell you," Murphy pressed, "if you don't let us come in and take the money, then we're going to kill him."

"No," Narcy replied.

"I'm not saying that you knew something was going to happen," said Murphy. "I think that's why you black out when you went back into the room, because you didn't expect to see that."

"Wait a minute," Narcy said. "You're telling me that I saw the people that went into the room?"

"I'm saying that you opened the door for them," Murphy said.

"No I did not," she snapped.

"You had to open it," Detective Alison Carpentier said.

"There would have been a reason for it," Murphy added.

"Nobody's threatening me," Narcy replied. "Nobody's threatening."

"Narcy," Murphy said, "every one of these crimes always gets solved, okay."

"I hope it does," she replied.

"And when the people get caught they always try to point fingers," Murphy continued. "I just want you to tell me now if . . . somebody threatened you, and they told you that they wanted to go in because they wanted to make some money, all right. And they weren't going to harm your husband . . . did that happen?"

"Okay," Narcy snapped. "Do you think I'm a suspect . . ."

"I don't think you're a suspect," Murphy replied calmly.

The detectives then asked about Ben Novack Jr.'s wrists and legs being bound with duct tape prior to his murder, which closely resembled his favored sexual position. Confronting Narcy with the obvious similarities, they asked if a sex game with a stranger could have led to his killing.

Narcy said what they did in bed was "very private" and "embarrassing." She explained that Ben could get an erection only by taking Cialis or Viagra forty-five minutes before sex.

"He takes it every day," she told them. "I'm pouring my heart out to you."

"But we need to know everything," Detective Carpentier said. "We're not trying to make you embarrassed."

"Yeah, but you've got to understand this is my husband that we're talking about, and I don't want you to look at him as a pervert."

"I'm not looking at him as a pervert," Murphy said. "We're not taking any of this personally. Everybody has their own lives."

"But I should not be saying this," Narcy continued. "This is betrayal."

Then Carpentier asked if Ben had taken Viagra or Cialis Sunday morning.

"No," Nancy replied.

"Would you be surprised if we find it in his system?" Carpentier asked.

"He told me on Saturday to come up because he was going to take it," Narcy said, "and I told him that I was busy."

"And what about Sunday?" Carpentier asked.

"I don't know," Narcy said. "I don't count the pills."

Carpentier then asked about their unconventional sex life.

"He played rough," Narcy said. "We [both] played rough. It's a thing that we did."

Narcy said that they had always used Ben's Miami Beach Police Department handcuffs for bondage purposes, until he had retired from the Reserves. Now they made do with belts from hotel robes.

Detective Carpentier then asked if she wanted Murphy to leave so she would be more comfortable talking to another woman about such intimate details. Narcy said yes, so Murphy left them alone.

Carpentier asked if Ben liked to be in control during sex.

"Yes," Narcy replied. "He ties [my knees] or he does it between my boobs. I have implants. And he likes to show me different things to do. Sometimes he likes the vibrator. But not inside him."

She said that Ben had recently wanted to experiment with erotic asphyxiation, after seeing a program about it on television. But she'd refused, as it was too dangerous.

"He's been asking me . . . to do the passing-out thing," she said. "He said it must be fun. We left that alone because . . . somebody might die."

Detective Carpentier then asked how Ben liked to be tied up.

"He will ask somebody to tie him up to the armpit," Narcy replied, "because [of] his hair there."

Ben also loved to be blindfolded, and Narcy said they have a special chair with restraints in their bedroom at home.

"He has special blinders," she explained. "They have little balls. I don't mean to be sick, but when we do it, it's fine. I don't want you to think bad of me."

"Listen, I'm in a marriage, too," Carpentier said, trying to relate to her. "I appreciate that this is difficult for you. I'm not judging you at all."

Narcy said Ben loved being tied up and helpless, and became very excited after taking Viagra. She said Ben also tied her up and left her alone for hours while he went into another room to work on his computer.

Then the detective asked how long before foreplay would Ben take

Cialis or Viagra. Narcy said anywhere between forty-five minutes and an hour and a half.

Carpentier then questioned whether Ben might have invited someone else into the room for bondage sex.

"Ben was not doing anything," Narcy snapped. "He's married."

"Narcy, don't you think it's odd," Carpentier reasoned, "that he dies in a position that he finds sexually arousing? So that's why we're asking you about the sex part of it."

"But he doesn't like anybody hitting him," she said.

"But isn't it odd," the detective repeated, "that he dies in the same manner as he gets pleasure in life? It's a little ironic?"

Then Detective Carpentier asked Narcy if she had any involvement in her husband's death.

"No," Narcy replied resolutely.

"Narcy, would you take a lie detector test on that?" the detective asked.

"I will," she replied. "I will take a hundred lie detectors. I do whatever you want me to do."

Investigator Murphy then came back in the room and offered Narcy a glass of water, which she refused. Carpentier stepped out, and the seasoned investigator Murphy remained. He now concentrated on Narcy's exact movements before leaving the suite to go to breakfast. As he tried to pin her down, Narcy became increasingly dramatic.

"I want to die," she declared. "So if by any chance you think I'm a suspect or something, let's kind of clear the path. I'm very fragile. I'm afraid my husband is not around to protect me. I don't know who to trust. Let's be a little bit compassionate."

She then accused the two detectives of playing "good cop/bad cop" with her.

"We're wasting time. I'm hurting" she told Murphy. "All I want to do is kill myself and forget about the whole thing. Nothing is bringing my husband back."

Over the next four hours, one by one, the detectives took turns trying to break Narcy, without any success. The marathon interview went into many areas.

Narcy discussed Ben's affairs, their marital problems, his relationship with his mother, and his obsession with Batman, which she'd never understood. She even talked about Ben's childhood at the Fontainebleau hotel, which she referred to as "Dirt Castle."

"He was like a child in a lot of ways," she told detectives, "because he was naïve. He was born with a silver spoon in his mouth. He didn't have friends to play with because he was raised in a hotel. He was born in a hotel."

She said that Ben had had a miserable childhood at the Fontainebleau, having to deal with his father's business and growing up around entertainers. "A lot of misbehaving and all kinds of stuff," she said. "He was exposed to a lot of things, and the parents did not see anything wrong with that because that was their lifestyle."

Narcy claimed that mental illness ran on the maternal side of Ben's family, and he had received psychological counseling for his amputee fetish. "He has a disease," she told the detectives. "His grandmother was committed, his mother was on medication and always to the psychologists. When my husband was little he started [going to] a psychologist, medication and the whole thing. He stuttered."

Calling Bernice Novack "this old biddy," she said their relationship had been difficult at the beginning, but they had eventually become very close.

"But that was the Jewish mother," Narcy explained. "I did not take it personal. My mother-in-law will give her life for me . . . I used to tell my husband."

As the interview progressed, Narcy became increasing agitated, frequently putting her head down on the table whenever a prying question upset her.

When Detective Art Mohammed, who had now replaced Detective Carpentier, accused her of having a selective memory, Narcy lashed out.

"I don't need you or anybody else to yell at me or to put pressure on me," she told him. "I cannot take it. Just give me an electric chair and put me out of my misery. I cannot take this anymore."

At the end of the interview, Narcy suggested her husband might have committed suicide.

"I wish he did kill himself," Investigator Murphy replied gravely. "I really do. At least there'd be a reason behind it. Unfortunately he was severely beaten to death. There's a lot of rage there. I promise you we'll get to the bottom of this one. We always do."

At 2:00 A.M. on Tuesday, Detectives Roger Piccirilli and Dwayne Tabacchi arrived at the Rye Town Hilton to search Narcy Novack's wheeled suitcase, which was in May Abad's room. When the investigators opened it, they found a series of hand-scribbled notes relating to Rebecca Bliss. These included cell phone numbers and addresses of Bliss's mother and her old boyfriends, showing just how deeply Narcy had investigated her rival.

Among the Post-it notes was the address of the Marina Bay apartment Ben Novack had set Bliss up in, and the names and contact numbers of the manager and other Marina Bay staff.

Narcy had also investigated Bliss's former career as a porn star. There were e-mail addresses and cell phone numbers for Bliss's alter egos, Mona Love and Meela Love. Even more disturbing, Narcy had listed Bliss's mother's home address in Grand Rapids, Michigan, along with that of the ex-boyfriend who had shot Bliss.

The detectives carefully logged the two dozen notes into evidence, and seized two more computers and a bag of papers for analysis. Later, back at police headquarters, hardened detectives would be shocked at some of the esoteric pornographic images they discovered on Ben Novack's laptop.

While Narcy Novack's luggage was being searched, Murphy and Carpentier were driving Narcy, accompanied by May, to a New York State Police facility for a polygraph examination. After signing a voluntary consent form, Narcy was questioned about her husband and his violent death. She failed the test several times, with her answers showing indications of deception.

As Narcy was being confronted with the negative results, May burst into the polygraph room screaming. She then tried to attack her mother, and had to be physically restrained by detectives.

May later claimed that her mother had failed the polygraph exam five times. She had been cooperative at the start, but became incensed when the examiner kept asking whether she'd killed Ben. At one point, she declared that the police should not attack her while she was grieving her dead husband.

"She kept saying, 'This is ridiculous, I'm supposed to be mourning my husband,'" said May, "and she kept getting angry."

Finally, Investigator Murphy drove Narcy back to the Rye Town Hilton, dropping her off at 9:00 A.M. on Tuesday.

A few hours later, while Narcy was flying back to Fort Lauderdale, the Rye Brook Police asked the Florida Department of Law Enforcement to place her under surveillance.

FORTY-ONE

"MY MAMA KILLED MY DADDY!"

On Tuesday morning, *The Miami Herald* ran a front-page story about Ben Novack Jr.'s murder, labeling it "a targeted hit." With the banner headline "Resort Creator's Son Slain in N.Y.," the story caused an immediate sensation.

"Ben Novack Jr. grew up in the penthouse of Miami Beach's most fashionable hotel," the article read, "watching his parents hobnob with U.S. presidents and Hollywood royalty. This week, 55 years after his father opened the legendary Fontainebleau Hotel, Novack was found bludgeoned to death in a much more modest venue—the Hilton Rye Town in Rye Brook."

The Fort Lauderdale *Sun-Sentinel* also ran a front-page story, headlined "Lauderdale Businessman Slain in New York Hotel."

"News of his death stunned South Florida's business community," read the story, "where Novack was known as the son of the couple who founded the Fontainebleau in 1954."

The story reported Rye Brook Police chief Gregory Austin's press conference the previous day, adding that the name of Novack's wife had still not been released to reporters.

Now retired, Fort Lauderdale detective Steve Palazzo, who had investigated the bizarre 2002 Novack home invasion, was eating break-fast when he read the story.

"I picked up the phone immediately and called [the police in] New York," said Palazzo, "and said, 'Was Narcy Novack in New York at the time of the murder?' Because to me it was evident she was involved in the murder."

He told the Rye Brook detectives to immediately get a copy of his 2002 police report and read it.

"I said, 'Look, here's what you need to know,'" Palazzo recalled. "'If Narcy Novack was [there] she is probably responsible for his death. And you need to send somebody straight to the house and secure it, because it's got millions of dollars worth of property and that's what it's all about.'"

He also offered his help, explaining how Ben Jr. had shown him all the hidden safes and hiding places in his house. "I told them that I'd been in the house, and Ben shared some secrets with me back then," Palazzo said, "but I never heard from them."

Jim Scarberry, who had not spoken to Ben Novack Jr. since the home invasion, was at his son's wedding in Las Vegas when he received a call from a *Miami Herald* reporter friend of his.

"She called my cell phone," said the now-retired Hollywood police chief, "and said, 'Did you hear about Benji?' And I said, 'No, what happened?' She said he was murdered in New York, and I immediately said, 'Well, where's Narcy? I know she has something to do with it.'"

Later that day, a Rye Brook detective called private investigator Pat Franklin in Fort Lauderdale for background information on Ben and Narcy Novack.

"The first thing they told me," said Franklin, was "'Well, Ben Novack's been murdered. What do you think?' I said, 'You'd better check the wife.'"

The former cop also immediately suspected that somehow Bernice's and her son's deaths were connected. "It was highly coincidental that first Bernice goes and then Ben," he said. "That's remarkable—within three months of each other."

. . .

That afternoon, Special Agent Terrence J. Mullen of the Florida Department of Law Enforcement (FDLE) began preparing a search warrant for the Novack house, looking for evidence. And Sergeant Terence Wilson of the Rye Brook Police Department's Detective Bureau, who was now leading the murder investigation, contacted Charlie Seraydar for assistance.

"The search warrant was predicated on my testimony," Seraydar explained. "They needed the information on the house for the warrants, and I gave them that. I happened to know where all the safes were because we picked out the locations when [Ben] bought the house."

As soon as she landed in Fort Lauderdale, Narcy Novack hired twenty-four-hour security guards for 2501 Del Mar Place, from the Louken Security Company.

On Wednesday morning she headed to Wachovia Bank at 350 East Las Olas Boulevard, a five-minute drive from her home. When she asked for the $100,000 in cash she had deposited two days earlier in New York, the teller manager, Katherine Di Fiore, said the bank didn't have that much cash. She suggested Narcy take half in cash and the rest in cashier's checks.

Narcy reluctantly agreed, and at 2:22 P.M. was given $50,000 from hers and Ben's joint account, in twenty-five straps of $2,000 bundles made up of $20 bills. The manager also gave Narcy a bank check for $50,000, but on her way out Narcy changed her mind. She now wanted two $25,000 checks instead.

After leaving, Narcy went to another Wachovia Bank branch nearby, where she rented a large safe-deposit box, although she already had two smaller ones there.

At around 5:30 P.M. on Wednesday, Fort Lauderdale Police were called to 2501 Del Mar Place to investigate a domestic disturbance. Narcy

Novack and her niece Karla Veliz, who had just flown in from New York, had tried to evict May Abad from the guesthouse, and things had gotten violent. During the altercation, May and her cousin, who had never met before, got into a slapping match in Ben Novack's office.

"I saw May in Ben's office," Veliz later testified, "and she was just leafing through the folders and files. She was combing through everything. She kept repeating, 'My father has something for me.' She was going through the folders looking for something."

Karla then ordered May out of the office, and as she was leaving, her mother appeared brandishing a crowbar. Then Narcy came after May, swinging the heavy weapon at her daughter's head. As May raised an arm to protect herself, she was hit. The violent confrontation between mother and daughter was captured by a video surveillance camera.

After receiving a distress call from May, Charlie Seraydar arrived in the middle of the fight, and separated Narcy and May.

"They're kicking the shit out of each other in the driveway," Seraydar said. "I separated them and then I called the Fort Lauderdale Police."

When the police arrived, May Abad ran out of the Novack compound screaming, "My mamma killed my daddy! My mamma killed my daddy!" Then she started knocking on nearby doors, accusing Narcy of murdering her stepfather.

Prince Mongo received a call from a friend, who told him about what was happening. "She said May is going crazy," said Mongo. "She's banging on my door and screaming that her mamma killed her daddy. I said, 'My God, who is her daddy?' Because she did not like Ben at all, and all of a sudden she called him 'daddy.'"

Meanwhile, Seraydar went inside to calm Narcy down.

"I went in and talked to her," he said. "She wouldn't let the cops in, and I was just shaking my head, thinking, 'You guys just got done doing an affidavit for a search warrant, and she's in the house before you serve it. Get her out of here!' They couldn't do it. Very inept."

Seraydar helped May Abad pack up her stuff and then drove her to a friend's house. That night, she filed a complaint against her mother with Fort Lauderdale Police for aggravated battery. Detectives later investigated May's claims, but no further action was taken.

. . .

The next morning, Narcy Novack flew back to New York to take care of business. She gave one of the $25,000 certified checks to her brother Carlos's common-law wife, Melanie Klein, and the other to New York attorney Howard Tanner, for unspecified legal services. Later she would be accused in federal court of money laundering.

"Narcy Novack is running back and forth between New York and Fort Lauderdale," said assistant U.S. attorney Andrew Dember, "moving money like crazy. She empties Ben's accounts and takes $14,700 from their joint account and gives it to Melanie Klein to write more checks. She's really busy moving money after her husband's death."

Her brother Cristobal Veliz had also been busy moving money around. The day after Ben Novack's murder, he withdrew $6,500 from his Bank of America account, and the following day he took another $500.

Later he would testify that he had given the money to his brother, Carlos, for Narcy, who needed it.

That day, Cristobal had received a call from Alejandro Garcia, who asked him what to do with Novack's distinctive "BEN" bracelet, which Narcy had handed to Garcia after the attack.

"He said, 'Throw it away, it's my gift to you,'" Garcia later testified. "So I decided to keep it."

On Thursday morning, July 16, Rye Brook Police lead detective Terence Wilson arrived in Fort Lauderdale to investigate Ben and Narcy Novack, speaking to as many people who knew them as he could. It would be the first of almost a dozen trips to Florida he would make over the next two years.

Later that morning, Broward County Circuit Court judge Matthew I. Destry signed an affidavit for a search warrant to enter 2501 Del Mar Place looking for any evidence leading to Ben Novack Jr.'s murderer. The seven-page warrant, prepared by the Florida Department of Law Enforcement, revealed that in June 2002, Ben Novack Jr. had been the victim of a home invasion, which he had accused Narcy of organizing.

"The Fort Lauderdale police report indicates that Ben H. Novack Jr.," the warrant read, "claimed his wife Narcy orchestrated the robbery with unknown males and disabled the alarm system. [We have] determined that this 2002 home invasion has not resulted in any arrest or criminal prosecution."

The warrant also revealed that Narcy had been given a polygraph test that "showed indications of deception when questioned to her knowledge of this homicide."

Special Agent Mullen wrote that he wanted to seize records and documentation of the Novacks' "business activity, travel and financial transactions" and video surveillance inside and outside the premises. He was also looking for silver-gray duct tape and any other relevant evidence to the murder.

"Your affiant has learned that pursuant to this investigation," wrote agent Mullen, "a long time family friend Charlie Seraydar was interviewed and stated that he has known Ben H. Novack for approximately 35 years and has been inside the premises at 2501 Del Mar Place . . . and has observed approximately four to five safes in the residence which are believed to contain US currency, personal effects and business records of the decedent Ben H. Novack, Jr."

Later that day, *The Miami Herald* dug up Ben Novack Jr.'s 2002 divorce petition, in which he accused Narcy of trying to kill him for his fortune.

Reporter Julie Brown interviewed Novack's divorce lawyer, Don Spadaro, and three other sources.

Spadaro provided *The Miami Herald* with Ben's 2002 divorce petition, which contained Narcy's damaging quote that the only reason he was still alive was because she had intervened to stop him from being killed.

"If I can't have you, no one will," Narcy was quoted as saying. "The men that helped me . . . will come back and finish the job."

Jim Scarberry told Brown of Ben's claim that Narcy had "fessed up" to the robbery. His and Ben's long friendship had ended, Scarberry said, after Ben refused to press charges and called off the divorce action.

"I chewed him out," Scarberry was quoted as saying. "I said, 'You are absolutely nuts, Benji.'"

The Fort Lauderdale Police Department refused to release the damning 2002 police report to the *Herald*, saying it was now part of an ongoing murder investigation.

When questioned if the prior incident made Narcy Novack a suspect in her husband's killing, Rye Brook Police chief Greg Austin said absolutely not, as he did not want to impede his detectives' current investigation.

"Everything she has told us has checked out," he told the *Herald*. "Just because of the home invasion doesn't mean she's a suspect. [It] may open up something that will change that, and we agree it is an important part of the case."

That afternoon, Agent Mullen served the warrant on Narcy Novack, and he and his officers searched the Del Mar Place compound from top to bottom. They seized video equipment from the master bedroom, plus eight 8 mm videocassettes and a Beta videotape. They then went into Ben's cluttered upstairs office and removed a Dell computer, miscellaneous paperwork, a phone book, and a day planner. In the garage, they discovered five rolls of duct tape.

Agent Mullen and his men then searched the building next door, which housed the offices of Convention Concepts Unlimited. From there they removed five computers, one laptop computer, and an external hard drive.

Everything seized from the property was then flown to the Westchester County District Attorney's Office for forensic examination.

The next morning, Narcy Novack hired prominent New York criminal attorney Howard E. Tanner to represent her. His first action was to request a second independent autopsy on Ben Novack Jr.'s body, still on ice at the Westchester County Medical Examiner's Office.

Now feeling threatened, Narcy had her eldest brother, Carlos Veliz, move into 2501 Del Mar Place as her bodyguard. He would remain there for the next year.

"He was basically protecting her," said Charlie Seraydar, "and she very rarely left the house."

Seraydar was one of the few people Narcy allowed into the house, and they remained on friendly terms. On several occasions, he asked her what had happened in the Hilton Rye Town hotel suite. And Narcy always stuck to the same story she had told detectives.

"And I said, 'Narcy, now you can understand why people think you're involved,'" said Seraydar. "'It sounds stupid. It sounds not plausible.'"

On Thursday, July 16, *The Miami Herald* asked the Broward County Medical Examiner for a copy of Bernice Novack's autopsy report. But the office refused, saying that the autopsy report—which is usually a public record—had now been "put on hold."

The following day, a spokeswoman for Broward County medical examiner Joshua Perper claimed that the Fort Lauderdale Police Department had asked that the autopsy report not be released. "They are going to be reviewing whether to reopen the investigation or not," the spokeswoman explained.

However, when a *Herald* reporter called the police department for confirmation, she was told there were no plans to take another look at Bernice Novack's death.

"This is a closed case," said Fort Lauderdale Police Department spokesman Frank Sousa, "and at this time there are no plans to review it."

Late Friday afternoon, thirteen hundred miles away in Westchester County, Chief Greg Austin appealed for any information on a pair of Valentino sunglasses that had been found, asking anyone who saw someone wearing them on Sunday morning to come forward.

FORTY-TWO

THE LETTER

Soon after Ben Novack Jr.'s murder, Meredith Fiel phoned Narcy to offer her condolences on her cousin's death.

"So I started talking to Narcy," Meredith recalled. "I said, 'Well, what happened?' and then, oh my God, she befriended me." Narcy complained of police harassment, accusing the press of ruining her and Ben Jr.'s good names. "She talked to me for hours about how they're accusing her," Meredith said, "and they're besmirching her name."

Then Narcy invited Meredith to Florida, offering to give her some of her late aunt Bernice's things to remember her by.

When Meredith said she was scared of flying, Narcy said her brother Carlos could drive her down to Fort Lauderdale, as he was coming to take care of her. "She was talking about him being her bodyguard," Meredith said. "And that she was afraid."

Over the next year, the two women talked on the phone regularly, as Meredith tried to gather enough evidence against Narcy to reopen the investigation into her aunt's death.

"I was suspicious of Narcy," Meredith said, "The police never even [interviewed] me about her. So I was trying to get information from her all on my own."

Several times, Meredith asked Narcy about the morning of her cousin's murder. Narcy told her a different version of events from the one she'd told investigators—and Meredith found her very persuasive.

Narcy said that Ben was still up working that Sunday morning when she finally went to bed at around 5:00. Two hours later she got up and went down for breakfast. The hotel manager told her they had run out of silverware because of the bigger-than-expected turnout, and they would have to use plastic knives and forks. Narcy said she knew how Ben despised plastic cutlery.

"Her story was that she called him to say they had to go to plastic," Fiel said, "and when he didn't pick up the phone, she got a little angry. She thought that he must have gone to bed and went up to tell him about the plastic and found him [dead]. So when she told me that story, I believed it."

Narcy also reached out to Bernice's best friend, Estelle Fernandez, telling her a similar story with slight variations.

"Narcy called me," Fernandez said, "and kept me on the phone for two hours, feeling me out. I knew what she was doing, but I wouldn't let on."

Narcy said she and Ben were asleep in bed when he had woken her up, telling her to go and do the convention breakfast. "So she went downstairs," Fernandez said, "and there was a problem with the silverware, because they'd overbooked. So she called him and he said, 'Okay, I'll be down in a little bit.'

"When he didn't come down, she called again, and he didn't answer. So she left May in charge and went back upstairs, and that's when she found him. That's what she told me."

At the end of the conversation, Estelle asked Narcy what she planned to do, as Narcy was now rich and no longer had to work. Narcy replied that she had no intention of winding up the business, and was already booking new conventions.

On Tuesday, July 21, the Miami Springs Police Department received an anonymous letter containing details only the police knew about Ben

Novack Jr.'s murder and his mother's death. Dated July 21, the five-page letter, handwritten in Spanish, accused Narcy and her brother Cristobal of masterminding a murderous plot to gain control of the Novack family fortune. It also warned that Narcy's daughter, May Abad, would be the next victim.

"I am a person who had heard rumors," it began, "but true without a doubt. I write out of respect for God and the precious life of human beings. [These murders] were undoubtedly committed by the wife of Mr. Novack and her brother.

"Together they killed . . . his mother Mrs. Bernice Novack in the most ruthless way [with] an overdose of medication to make her mad or extremely nervous. That night they went to her house. The daughter-in-law had keys to the house and had taken the cellular phone. They beat her up so bad that she could not call her son Ben. The killers assassinated the defenseless [old woman] that they had pursued for months. For weeks they had scared her through the windows and doors."

The letter writer knew that Bernice Novack had fallen a week before her death, and had been treated in hospital.

"That's what made the murderers' crime so perfect," the anonymous correspondent wrote, adding that the killer had laughed at Fort Lauderdale Police for failing to realize Bernice Novack had been murdered.

The letter warned that Narcy and her brother would stop at nothing to get their hands on the Novack millions.

"This woman is related to other crimes," the letter stated. "She is also highly dangerous, ruthless and ambitious for Mr. Ben Novack's money. This woman should not be at liberty at home. Her daughter is innocent and could be the next victim. Protect her."

After receiving the letter, the Miami Springs Police sent it to Rye Brook Police, who took it very seriously. They processed it for DNA and fingerprints, but were unable to identify the writer.

"We believe that it's probably [written by] a religious person," Detective Sergeant Terence Wilson said. "Maybe an older person, possibly a Spanish female who is very close to the family and knows a lot of the players in the family."

Almost three years later it would be revealed that the letter was

THE PRINCE OF PARADISE · 313

written by Narcy's elder sister Letitia Turano, a very religious woman who strongly disapproved of what her siblings had done.

The same day the letter arrived, Broward County medical examiner Joshua Perper met with Fort Lauderdale Police to take another look at Bernice Novack's autopsy results, after receiving numerous calls from Maxine Fiel and other relatives.

After reviewing the autopsy results, Perper confirmed that Bernice had died from an accidental fall, and that there had been no foul play. He also refuted any suggestions that there was a connection between her death and her son's subsequent murder.

Bernice's eighty-three-year-old sister, Maxine, was livid when a reporter asked for her reaction. "They both died suddenly and really violently," she told the Westchester *Journal News*. "Both died from blunt force. At this point I'm very concerned my sister was murdered."

Maxine vowed to do everything she could to get her sister's case reopened and to get justice for her. "I went on a mission," she said. "I said, 'My poor sister was murdered,' and I kept calling the Fort Lauderdale Police and the Medical Examiner's Office, refusing to take no for an answer."

Soon after the meeting between the medical examiner and the Fort Lauderdale Police, somebody leaked the Fort Lauderdale Police's 2002 report of the alleged Novack home invasion to *The Miami Herald*. With its lascivious details of bondage sex games, amputee pornography, and death threats, the story made headlines all over the world, taking things to a new level.

"Details of Novack Home Invasion Describe Sex Games," screamed the next morning's *Miami Herald* front-page headline. The accompanying article went on to provide sensational details about the wealthy couple's unusual sex life.

"The turbulent marriage of Ben Novack Jr. and his wife Narcy," began reporter Julie Brown's story, "is detailed in a 2002 Fort Lauderdale police report that describes a home invasion planned by his wife and thugs with mob ties, robbery and death threats, surprise breast implants and peculiar sex games."

The *Herald* said that it had sent Narcy a certified letter seeking her comment on the 2002 report, which Rye Brook detectives were now examining, but had received no response.

The Associated Press also ran a wire story, which was picked up by hundreds of newspapers coast to coast. "The wife of a man who was killed last week in a suburban hotel," the story read, "told police in 2002 that he often hit her and once broke her nose. [She said they] had a very violent past together.

"The 18-page report included references to the Novacks' use of portable urinals, to nude photos of women with artificial limbs, to a roomful of Batman collectibles and to a claim from Narcisa Novack's mother-in-law that Narcisa tried to poison her."

A few hours later, Narcy Novack appeared in public for the first time since her husband's death with her new criminal attorney, Howard Tanner. She told reporters that the accusations against her were "getting wilder by the minute."

Tanner said his client was "distraught" over her husband's murder and should not be considered a suspect. She had nothing to gain from Ben's death and was cooperating with investigators, he added.

"Any allegation that she was involved," said the veteran defense attorney, "is absolutely ridiculous."

In the last week of July, Maxine Fiel received a telephone call from a woman claiming to be the writer of the anonymous letter, warning her to be careful, as she was in danger.

"I spoke with her on the phone," Maxine recalled. "She was an old lady and very religious, and had this very heavy [accent]. I think she was a member of Narcy's family."

The woman, who wouldn't give her name, told Maxine that Narcy had planned everything.

"She told me that I should be very careful," said Maxine, who never reported the call to police, "and she wants me to know that my sister had been stalked before her death."

After the call, Maxine vowed to have her sister's death reexamined, and began calling all the various law enforcement agencies involved in the Novack case.

"I wouldn't stop," she said. "I just kept calling everybody and clawing like a dog with a bone."

At the end of July, Rebecca Bliss was evicted from her luxury apartment at the Falls at Marina Bay, as she could no longer afford the rent.

"Ben was no longer there," she said, "and my lease was up."

Down and out, she lived in a women's shelter for a couple of months, before moving into the garage of the same ex-boyfriend who had once shot her and ended her career as a tattoo artist.

Forty-Three

FAMILY FEUD

On August 1, three weeks after Ben Novack Jr.'s murder, his body was still on ice at the Westchester County Medical Examiner's Office. Judaism dictates that a body should be buried within twenty-four hours of death, and Ben Novack Jr.'s had been ready for release to a funeral home since his autopsy.

"Nobody has claimed it," said Westchester County deputy medical examiner Kunjlata Ashar. "It's up to the family members . . . we are done with whatever we had to do."

Maxine Fiel said she was shocked that her nephew had still not been buried. "Here is the Prince of the Fontainebleau," she told *The Miami Herald*, "and he is being treated no better than a homeless person."

Maxine said that Kelsey Grammer had even offered to pay for his friend's burial, but Narcy refused permission.

"Kelsey offered to pay," said Fiel. "When I heard I wanted to call him and thank him, but [Narcy] was stalling and let him lay out there."

Howard Tanner explained that his client was attempting to resolve "certain issues," so a proper memorial could be held.

"She's been through an unbelievable trauma, the murder of her husband," he told a reporter. "This [delay] has caused unspeakable grief, and she wants to resolve the matter."

. . .

After Ben Novack Jr.'s killing, there was some confusion over whether his widow would inherit his estimated $10 million estate.

In his June 2006 will, Ben had left everything to Narcy, including all his yachts, cars, Batman collection, and the proceeds from his late parents' respective estates. He also bequeathed her all his business interests, although Convention Concepts Unlimited was not mentioned by name. There were also likely millions of dollars more squirreled away in offshore accounts.

In the event that Narcy were to die first, he had bequeathed $100,000 to her daughter, May Abad, and $250,000 each to her grandsons, Marchelo and Patrick Gaffney. He had also provided for his mother, if she survived him, giving her $30,000 a year for the rest of her life.

Fort Lauderdale probate attorney Carl Schuster, now handling both Bernice and Ben Novack Jr.'s estates, said probate courts usually appointed a personal representative whom the decedent had named in his will. But in this case it was complicated, as Bernice Novack had appointed her late son as hers.

"Because of the circumstances of [Ben Jr.'s] death," Schuster told the *Journal News*, "it's muddied up the waters, for sure."

Then on July 29, Narcy Novack officially asked Broward County Circuit Court to appoint her as her late husband's executrix. She also asked for permission to have Ben's body cremated. But the court refused, as his will requested that he be buried, with Narcy's remains, next to his father in the Novack-Spier family mausoleum in Mount Lebanon Cemetery in Queens, New York.

On Wednesday, August 5, 2009, Cristobal Veliz had Francisco Picado drive him to Miami in his black Murano to retrieve Ben Novack's bracelet. With the ongoing police investigation, he and Narcy did not want the bracelet being found and linking them to Ben Novack's murder.

"He wanted the bracelet back," said Garcia. "I said, 'You gave it to me as a gift.'"

When Veliz offered Garcia something else in exchange, Garcia replied he wanted the rest of the money still owed him for the Ben Novack job.

"So he agreed and he came to Miami to give me my money," said Garcia. "He said to meet up at the gas station where Melvin used to have the car wash."

At the appointed time, Garcia sat down with Jefe and Picado at a Subway restaurant near the car wash for the exchange. During lunch, Veliz told Garcia to go to the restroom, where Picado would hand him the money.

"I went into the bathroom with Frank," Garcia recalled, "and waited until some people left. Frank handed me $3,000 [in $100 bills], which I put in my pocket. I counted it later."

They all then went back to the Murano, where Garcia gave Picado back the bracelet.

Suddenly Garcia demanded another $10,000, saying that as Ben Novack had died, he was owed more. Then he warned Jefe that if anything were to happen to him, he had written a letter to Crime Stoppers detailing Veliz's part in the two murders, and it would be mailed out.

"I was nervous," Garcia later testified. "I said if anything happens to me, then someone will send that letter. He said everything is cool and he's going to give me more money."

The next day, Veliz and Picado were back in Brooklyn, going straight to Laura Law's house in Bay Ridge.

"He took out Ben's bracelet," Picado said, "and put it in a yellow envelope with bubble wrap inside. Then he went to take it to someone in the house."

Then, after filling up the Murano's gas tank and getting an oil change, Veliz had Picado drive him back to Miami.

On Friday, August 7, May Abad filed a legal objection to her mother being appointed executrix of Ben Novack Jr.'s estate. Abad had now hired a Fort Lauderdale attorney named Stephen McDonald to represent her in the estate dispute.

"Considering Narcy's . . . still a potential person of interest . . . in the murder," explained probate attorney Carl Schuster, representing Ben Jr.'s estate, "It just seems inappropriate for her to be the one appointed under these circumstances."

While her daughter was filing papers to prevent her gaining control of her late husband's estate, Narcy Novack was visiting the North Federal Highway branch of the Bank of America. Although she had no right to do so, she had persuaded a bank employee to allow her to access Ben Jr.'s and Bernice's safe-deposit boxes, using a key she had brought with her.

Then she removed valuable items of jewelry and other family heirlooms, including the diamond necklace Frank Sinatra had given Bernice.

Five days later, Rye Brook Police launched a special Web site, seeking information from the public to try to crack the case. The new site, www.bennovackjr.com, asked for tips and any new details about the murder. It also sought information about anybody near the hotel who had been wearing imitation Valentino sunglasses. There was also a photo of the victim's treasured gold bracelet, with "BEN" set in diamonds, and text stating that it may have been taken from the hotel room.

Rye Brook Police chief Greg Austin told *The Miami Herald* that it was by far the biggest case in his tiny village's history. He had now assigned three detectives and a uniformed officer to work on it full time. Additionally, said Chief Austin, Westchester County Police and investigators from the district attorney's office were assisting his team.

Austin refused to discuss any details, except to say that the Web site had already generated a few tips, which were now being pursued.

"This is a complicated case," he explained.

In the weeks after her husband's death, Narcy Novack attempted to dispose of Ben's property. She emptied all three safes in the house and tried to sell off the boats and several antique cars.

On Friday, August 14, May Abad's attorney persuaded a circuit court judge to freeze her stepfather's assets. Narcy Novack was also removed as the executrix of her husband's will, while the murder investigation was going on.

The Broward County Probate Court then appointed attorney Douglas Hoffman, of the Fort Lauderdale firm of Rudolf and Hoffman, as curator of Ben Novack Jr.'s estate. Hoffman's first order of business was to arrange for Ben Novack's burial in the family mausoleum, according to his wishes.

"It was horrible," Hoffman recalled. "He'd already been left in the morgue for like thirty days before I was appointed. All this time Narcy's not cooperating with people. She's refusing to pay for [his burial,] and other members of the family are accusing her of killing him. It was very emotionally charged and a media circus."

Hoffman was also empowered to "collect and preserve" all the decedent's assets and deliver them to the legally appointed personal representative for his estate.

"After Ben passed away a caveat was filed by May Abad that she was going to contest her mother being appointed as personal representative," Hoffman explained. "And the court, knowing there was going to be a fight, appointed a curator, someone to handle the administration while the fighting went on. The inventory for the estate is complex, voluminous, extensive. [Ben] was quite a collector."

Within hours of Hoffman's appointment, Narcy Novack and some helpers emptied out four of the six warehouses containing her late husband's multimillion-dollar Batman collection. She lied to the warehouse manager, saying that Ben was fine and had given his permission for the items to be removed. Then she broke the locks on the warehouses and looted them, driving numerous boxes of collectibles away in a truck.

"Mr. Novack has six warehouses filled up to the rafters with Batman memorabilia," Hoffman's partner, Gary Rudolf, later testified in probate court. "He was supposedly the second largest Batman collector in the world. Narcy Novack went out to the storage facilities [and] emptied four of them."

. . .

The previous day, Thursday, August 13, four New York homicide investigators had driven to Philadelphia to interview Narcy's brother Cristobal Veliz, now living in an apartment at 1219 Race Street, in the heart of Chinatown. When they arrived at the seedy four-story brick apartment building, they rang his apartment 21's entrance buzzer, but there was no answer. The detectives eventually tracked down Veliz's landlady at a nearby Chinese restaurant, who arranged to have her daughter let them into Velez's apartment.

When they returned to the building in the afternoon, an investigator recognized Veliz's old red Porsche parked outside. They were taken upstairs by the landlady's daughter, who knocked on the door of the apartment. When there was no answer, she used a key to let herself in and called out, "Veliz!"

Cristobal Veliz immediately came out from a back bedroom. After showing him his police identification, Senior Investigator Edward Murphy explained that they were investigating his brother-in-law Ben Novack's death. Veliz invited them inside, and Murphy went in with Detective Sergeant Terence Wilson, while Detectives Alison Carpentier and Michael LaRotonda waited in the hallway.

Sitting at the kitchen table, Murphy asked Veliz if there were problems in Narcy's marriage, and if Ben had been cheating. Veliz said there had been marital problems a few years earlier, resulting in Ben breaking his sister's nose. At the time, he had told Narcy not to divorce Ben and to work things out.

"Within the past year Narcy had told Cristobal about Ben having a girlfriend," Murphy wrote in his official report, "and Cristobal told her to be patient, that it was normal for men to look outside of their marriage."

Veliz said that when he'd stayed with them recently in Fort Lauderdale they had seemed very much in love. He denied knowing anything about the 2002 home invasion.

Murphy then asked Veliz when he had last spoken to Narcy. Two or three days ago, Veliz replied, adding that whenever they spoke after

Ben's death, she would be crying. When the investigator asked when he had last been in Florida, Veliz said in April, for Bernice Novack's funeral, which was the last time he had seen Narcy and Ben.

Murphy then asked if Narcy had ever discussed Ben's girlfriend Rebecca Bliss. He said yes, and he had told his sister that Ben had made a mistake.

Then the detectives asked Veliz to accompany them to the Philadelphia Police headquarters, a few blocks away, to give a written statement. He agreed to do so, and went into the bedroom to get ready.

During the interview, the two detectives had noticed a Western Union money transfer receipt lying on top a pile of other papers on the kitchen table, where they were sitting. Murphy had immediately recognized one of the names on it, Francisco Picado, as Denis Ramirez's cousin, and an address in Brooklyn he'd visited a week earlier as part of the investigation.

When Veliz left to get changed, Murphy copied down the details in his notebook.

Sender, Francisco Picado   Receiver, Alejandro Garcia
347-398-3329   Miami, Fla
1499 Jefferson Ave   8/12, $533
Brooklyn, NY 11237   tarjeta 9075011
Nombre Mi Terro   Chucho

A couple of minutes later, Veliz walked back into the kitchen and saw Investigator Murphy staring at the Western Union receipt. He did not say a word.

At 5:40 P.M., Investigator Murphy and Detective Alison Carpentier carried on interviewing Cristobal Veliz in a Detective Squad interview room at police headquarters. Veliz gave a one-page written statement before saying he was more comfortable speaking English than writing it and continued orally.

He said he had first learned of Ben Novack Jr.'s death when his brother, Carlos, called him the next day. Narcy had telephoned later. He said she had never discussed the manner in which Ben had been killed.

Questioned why he had not come to Florida to be with his sister, Veliz replied that he was a bus driver and couldn't just take off work.

He said that Narcy's house phone had been broken, so he had been calling his brother Carlos's cell phone to speak to her, as he was staying with her. Investigator Murphy then asked why he didn't just call Narcy's cell phone, and Veliz said, "It's okay. I called Carlos's phone."

Veliz also claimed not to have seen any media coverage of his brother-in-law's death, and asked how Ben had been killed. The two detectives replied that he had been a victim of an assault that had resulted in death, without going into further detail.

When Murphy then asked Veliz if he had any idea who might have killed Ben Novack, Veliz replied, "May Abad." He said that Narcy had complained to him that May drank too much and that her two teenage sons took drugs.

Veliz was then asked where he was on the morning of Ben Novack's death. He replied that he had finished his bus driving shift in Philadelphia at 11:00 P.M. on Saturday and had then driven to his girlfriend Laura Law's apartment in Bay Ridge, Brooklyn, to spend the night. On Sunday he had slept in, before taking Laura for dim sum. He had spent Sunday night with her before leaving to return to Philadelphia at 8:30 A.M. Monday, to start an 11:00 A.M. shift.

At the end of the interview, after Veliz allowed a police doctor to take a sample of his DNA, the detectives asked Veliz to suggest a good Chinese restaurant for dinner, before they returned to New York. He then took them to the Rising Tide, on Race Street, and even offered to pay for their meals, which they declined.

After the meal and before leaving Philadelphia, the investigators arranged to collect surveillance video from a Western Union office in Chinatown that would provide the smoking gun to break the case wide open.

Early the next morning, Cristobal Veliz drew up outside 1499 Jefferson Avenue, Brooklyn, in his red Porsche.

"He called me at six o'clock in the morning," Francisco Picado later testified, "and said the detectives had been to his house the night before and we had to drive to Fort Lauderdale . . . to see his sister. I didn't want to drive him again but I ended up going."

During the seventeen-hour drive down I-95, Veliz spoke about the attacks on Ben and Bernice Novack, asking the teenager to point the finger at May Abad if police ever questioned him.

"He told me that he had paid Alex and Joel to assault Ben," Picado later testified. "My cousin Denis Ramirez had picked them up and driven them to the [Rye Town Hilton] and back. He said that if investigators ever came to me to try and blame it on him, I should tell them it was May Abad who told me to do it."

Veliz also claimed that after Gonzalez and Garcia had left the Woodlands Suite, May had come in and cut her stepfather's throat.

When they reached Jacksonville, they stopped off at Cristobal's daughter Karen's house. He then told Picado to drive back to New York, as his son, Christopher, would drive him to Fort Lauderdale.

FORTY-FOUR

STILL ON ICE

On Sunday, August 16, *The Miami Herald* carried a front-page story headlined, "Wealth, Privilege, and Murder." The story, which had a three-column photograph of a smiling Ben Jr. and Narcy Novack sipping champagne, superimposed on top of the Fontainebleau, contained new details about the murder and the bitter battle for Novack's estate.

"The violent death of Ben Novack Jr., son of the Fontainebleau founder," read the story, "has unleashed a vicious family feud and spilled a torrent of tawdry secrets."

Breaking her silence, May Abad told reporter Julie Brown that she was so close to her late stepfather, she even called him "Dad."

"He was everything to me," she was quoted as saying. "I never went to my mother for anything. He was the one who always helped me out."

May also revealed that her stepfather had set his mistress up in an apartment, paying all her bills. According to Abad, the relationship had become so serious that Ben was planning to meet her family.

"My mother was very jealous," said Abad, who denied knowing anything about his affairs until recently. "He had a girlfriend on the side, close to 40."

She also discussed the morning of Ben Novack's death, describing walking into the Woodlands Suite suite to find her mother throwing herself on the floor, screaming, "He's dead. He's dead."

And she revealed how her mother had failed a lie detector test at Rye Brook Police Station the next day. "She flunked it five times," May said. She couldn't understand how she failed the "simple test," since police merely asked: "Did you kill Ben Novack? Do you know who killed your husband? Where were you when it happened?"

In the article, May accused her mother of deliberately delaying Ben Novack's burial while she was considering cremation.

Narcy Novack refused to be interviewed for the piece, leaving her attorney to respond to her daughter's damaging allegations.

"I can only say that I'm troubled by what May's agenda could possibly be," said Howard Tanner. "If she had credible evidence, then I'm sure that evidence is being investigated by police."

The following day, *The Miami Herald* published details of Ben Novack Jr.'s last will and testament, revealing that he had left his entire fortune to Narcy. It also noted that if his widow were involved in his murder, most of his estate would go to May Abad's two sons, with May receiving $150,000.

"Novack's body continues to decompose in a Westchester County morgue," read the story, "as the family battles over where he should be laid to rest."

At 2:11 P.M. on Monday, August 17, Cristobal Veliz left a voice-mail message on Investigator Ed Murphy's cell phone, saying that he had something important to tell him. A few minutes later, Veliz called again, and Murphy answered.

During the conversation, Veliz gave certain details about Ben Novack Jr.'s murder. He also asked for a fax number, saying he wanted to send Murphy something. Murphy gave him the number, and at 2:36 P.M., Veliz sent a letter in Spanish addressed to "Ed Murrly."

The translation read:

I appreciate how professional you acted with me. You asked me a lot of things and I answered what I knew and that is my truth but I have found out other things and if I stay quiet it won't [sic] he good. Francisco told me that he did a favor for the daughter of my sister Narcisa. I refer to May Azalea Abad. Of which has me disturbed. It's really ugly what she's doing to her mother. The reason May wants everything and wants to run the business that belongs to my sister. Where does she get the money to pay for lawyers and she already moved. I went looking for her to ask her about her bad attitude and I didn't find her. I believe they are laughing at me.

She has stolen valuable stuff from my sister. Her and her two kids they drink and have drug problems that you already know. As for the drugs people commit crazy acts.

If this helps you with something use it. Please use discretion with my name. [May] has a lot of money at this time and is capable of doing something stupid against me. If she doesn't love her mother me less.

Cristobal Veliz

Over the next two weeks, Cristobal Veliz telephoned Investigator Murphy five more times, each time providing additional information about Ben Novack's murder, implicating his niece.

Now that May Abad was becoming a real threat to Narcy's inheriting Ben Novack Jr.'s estate, the siblings decided to have her arrested. In mid-August, Alejandro Garcia had been caught robbing a Home Depot store in Fort Myers, Florida, and was briefly incarcerated before posting bail. Soon afterward, Cristobal Veliz summoned Garcia to the Donde Martica Colombian restaurant in Boca Raton for a meeting.

Over lunch, Jefe offered to pay Garcia $6,000 to plant some weapons and drugs inside May Abad's black Toyota Tacoma truck.

"Someone was then going to tip off the police," said Garcia, "so she would be arrested. He asked me to find a driver for the job."

Garcia called his friend Yader Tinako, whom he had recently met in jail, who agreed to drive. Several days later, Garcia introduced Tinako to Veliz, who said he needed a place to stay for a couple of days. Tinako agreed, and Veliz paid him $300 to stay with him and his girlfriend.

The next afternoon, Garcia and Tinako spent a few hours driving around Fort Lauderdale looking for May's truck, but were unable to find it. Then Veliz told Garcia that his brother, Carlos, would give him the weapons to place inside May's truck. He said Carlos would meet him outside a gas station in Boca Raton the next day. He then gave him $100 to buy marijuana to plant with the firearms.

At the appointed time, Garcia and Tinako arrived at the gas station. A few minutes later, a white Mercedes pulled up next to them and a middle-aged Hispanic man got out.

"I asked him if he was Cristobal's brother, Carlos," Garcia recalled. "He said, 'Yes. I'm going to give you a canvas bag.'"

Garcia put the bag into the trunk, then Tinako drove him to his girlfriend China's apartment in Miami, where Garcia was now living. When they arrived, Garcia took the canvas bag into his bedroom and opened it on the bed.

Inside were seven different types of firearms, including a Magnum revolver, a 357 Magnum revolver, a pocket-size semiautomatic, and a larger semiautomatic.

"Each weapon had its own ammunition inside a plastic bag attached to it," Garcia said.

That night, Alejandro Garcia went out and, instead of buying marijuana, as instructed, spent the $100 Cristobal had given him on women, crack, and heroin. Later he told Veliz that police had raided his girlfriend's apartment and seized the marijuana.

"Cristobal asked what happened with the weapons," Garcia said. "I said they were hidden. He told me not to worry. He was going to give me money to buy more marijuana to leave in the truck."

On August 21 the new curator of Ben Novack Jr.'s estate, Douglas Hoffman, wrote a letter to Narcy Novack's probate attorney, Henry Zippay Jr., asking that Zippay's client turn over all estate assets immediately. The letter also demanded that Narcy return $105,000 belong-ing to Novack Enterprises, which she had taken after her husband's murder.

"These were the specific proceeds of the New York convention," Hoffman wrote, "and was the result of cash assets belonging to the cor-poration being placed into the individual account and control of your client. This transaction was well documented by the New York Police. Both the cash kept by your client and the cash placed into her individ-ual account needs to be returned to the auspices of the corporate entity forthwith."

The letter also demanded titles to every single asset belonging to Ben Novack or his company, including "all vehicles, boats, watercrafts, etc."

Four days later, Hoffman submitted his first report on the state of the Ben Novack Jr. estate to the Broward County Probate Court. He stated that he had now located Ben's second cousins, who owned the Novack-Spier family mausoleum in Mount Lebanon Cemetery in Queens, New York. There were four plots available in the mausoleum, but the owners were asking $93,000 for just one of them.

Hoffman had then contacted the cemetery, who told him that there were several plots available just outside the mausoleum for $7,500, in-cluding perpetual care.

"After further negotiations," Hoffman reported, "the owner of the Novack-Spier Family Mausoleum agreed to the sum of $17,500.00 to be paid to the family owners thereof so as to carry out the decedent's burial wishes."

The curator added that only one plot was now needed, as Narcy no longer wanted to be buried next to Ben, as he had requested. Hoffman asked the court to authorize the purchase of the one cemetery plot and the necessary funeral expenses.

The following day, August 26, Narcy Novack returned to the Bank of America and cleaned out Ben Jr. and Bernice Novack's three large ten-by-ten safe-deposit boxes. Although she was not authorized to access these boxes, she'd brought along keys. She handed bank employee

Colleen Gratz her Florida driver's license, before signing the card, and Gratz brought her up to the second floor and provided a master key so Narcy could access the boxes.

After leaving Narcy alone in a private room with the three boxes, Gratz called her superior, Andrea Fernandez, saying she needed to see her urgently.

"So I went up upstairs," said Fernandez, "and she showed me the records and said 'Look at this.'"

To Fernandez's horror, she saw that only Bernice and Ben Novack Jr. were authorized to access these safe-deposit boxes.

"Narcy Novack wasn't in there," Fernandez later testified. "So, I said, 'Where is the customer?'"

At that point, Narcy Novack came out of the private room wearing a bulging black backpack and clutching a full shopping bag. Fernandez asked her who Bernice was, and without missing a beat, Narcy replied that Bernice Novack was her now-deceased mother-in-law.

"So I look in the folder," Fernandez said, "and I found a photocopy of the death certificate from Bernice."

She then asked who Ben was, and where he was right now.

"He's my husband," Narcy replied. "Oh, he's in the house."

Fernandez explained that they now needed to update the safe-deposit records, as they were now out of date. "So I said to her, 'I need you to upgrade them. When do you think you can bring Ben into the store?'"

Narcy replied she had to run some errands first, but she would bring her husband in that afternoon, for the necessary paperwork. Fernandez said she would appreciate that, so Ben could approve her being substituted in the safe-deposit box records for Bernice.

After Narcy left with the backpack and the shopping bag, Fernandez asked her assistant, Keisha Hall, to place a sign in the Novack deposit boxes that they were not to be accessed until the records had been updated.

Unlike her boss, Hall had read the stories about Ben Novack Jr.'s murder and wanted no part of it. "Oh, no, I'm not touching it," Hall told Fernandez. "He's dead. It was all over the news."

Fernandez then went online and Googled "Ben Novack Jr." and learned all about his savage death and its lurid aftermath.

"[I read] that he was killed in New York," she later testified. "He was found in a hotel [and] Narcy was getting investigated for his murder. And that's when I freak. I said, 'Lock it up! Nobody accesses those boxes until you hear from me.'"

Then she alerted her boss, the bank's legal department, and the personnel department.

At 10:45 A.M. on Thursday, August 27, a probate hearing was held at the Broward County Courthouse to determine how to proceed with the difficult Ben Novack Jr. estate. Although Narcy Novack did not attend, she was represented by her criminal defense attorneys Howard Tanner and Robert Trachman, and her probate lawyer, Henry Zippay Jr. May Abad was represented by her team of lawyers, Stephen McDonald and William Crawford. The Ben Novack Jr. estate was represented by its recently appointed curator, Douglas Hoffman, and his law partner, Gary Rudolf.

The high-profile case was now attracting a lot of national media attention, and in the press gallery were a news crew from NBC News, a producer from *Dateline NBC*, and a *Sun-Sentinel* reporter and photographer.

"Don't put that camera on me," Judge Dale Ross snapped at the start of the eighty-five-minute hearing. "Don't you dare do that."

Gary Rudolf began by telling the judge that the most pressing matter was to get Ben Novack Jr. a proper burial, as his body was still in the morgue forty-six days after his murder.

"That [is] the first priority," said Rudolf, "and we have taken that very seriously. We have tried to follow the dictates of Mr. Novack."

Rudolf explained that Narcy had previously informed them that she no longer wanted to follow her late husband's burial instructions and be buried by his side.

"However, this morning," Rudolf told Judge Ross, "I was told by counsel for Narcy, just prior to entering the courtroom, that she has changed her mind regarding that issue and wants to now have us adhere to the terms of the will and . . . buy side-to-side plots."

Rudolf said the Novack-Spier family was refusing to sell two plots in the mausoleum, as these were being reserved for three other family members. However, there was a community mausoleum next to the Novack/Spier one, where they could purchase a tandem plot, where Ben Jr., and eventually Narcy, could be buried one on top of the other.

He estimated that it would cost approximately $25,000 for the upper and lower plots and burial expenses, including $500 for the services of a rabbi.

"It is Miss Novack's position," Zippay told the judge, "that the terms and the provision of the will be followed."

Then Rudolph said that Narcy, as next of kin, would have to sign off on the burial arrangements. There was also the question of whether there would be a graveside service.

"I have spoken with Mrs. Novack," said her criminal attorney Howard Tanner, "and she wants a private service."

The estate curator, Douglas Hoffman, agreed to make arrangements for the funeral, which Narcy Novack had already indicated she would not be attending.

Then he told the judge that there were problems administering Bernice Novack's estate, as she had appointed her late son as her personal representative.

"The Estate of Bernice Novack will flow into the Estate of Ben Novack," said Hoffman. "In the interest of economy it has been discussed . . . that I be placed in the position of successor personal representative to finish . . . administration of Bernice's Estate."

McDonald said Maxine Fiel had also expressed an interest in doing so. "She is the only surviving blood relative of Ben Novack Jr.," he said. "I will be candid with the court . . . she has expressed an interest in becoming representative of both estates."

Judge Ross said it would be more economical to have a personal representative in Florida, and Fiel lived in New York, so he appointed Hoffman to be interim personal representative for both estates.

Gary Rudolf then moved on to the assets of the Ben Novack Jr. estate, describing them as "complex and unique." To give the judge some idea of the difficulties, he handed him a pile of photographs showing the inside clutter of the Novack house, with Batman and other collectibles stacked to the ceiling.

"As you can see there is a tremendous amount of Batman and other memorabilia in the home," said Rudolf. "There are also other substantial assets in what's called the museum room, where . . . there are numerous Batman items. Cluttered is fairly accurate."

"My gosh," said the judge in amazement, looking at the photographs.

"[We] have the original Batmobile which Mr. Novack had made from the original mold from the movie," said Rudolf.

He also showed the court photographs of the yacht *White Lightning* and a party barge, which he described as "more or less homemade."

Rudolf told the judge that he had concerns about protecting the estate assets.

"There were at least three safes in the home," he said. "All three safes have been emptied and we have no knowledge concerning the whereabouts or the contents of those safes. We have asked and been told that nobody knows."

Yesterday, he told the judge, when he had visited the six warehouses housing Ben Novack Jr.'s enormous Batman collection, he learned that Narcy had already emptied out four of them.

"There are a smattering of some little items that might have some value," he said, "but all the other items have been taken by Narcy Novack. The present whereabouts are unknown. The problem . . . at this point in time is to try and collect and then safeguard all these assets."

Then Narcy's attorney Henry Zippay stood up and pointed out that the curator had failed to identify what property his client had co-owned with her late husband.

Judge Ross said that could be done later, but in the meantime he wanted to stop anything further being removed from the house or the warehouses.

"I appreciate that, Judge," said Zippay, "Just the selective application that everything belongs to the deceased, and for twenty-some years of marriage that she has nothing, is an assumption that should not be portrayed."

Rudolf said it was vital to safeguard the remaining assets immediately.

"These items could easily disappear," he told the judge. "We have not even located the comic book collection yet that we understand is quite valuable."

The judge was then told that Narcy Novack still resided at 2501 Del Mar Place, which she was fully entitled to do. However, she had informed the curator that she could not afford to maintain the house. Since her husband's murder, she hadn't kept up the monthly payments on the $750,000 mortgage, or paid the electric bill. She had asked for a monetary advance, but this was complicated by the fact that this wasn't a probate issue.

"I'm concerned about . . . the house being foreclosed on," said Hoffman.

The judge deferred making a decision until a later date.

Gary Rudolf then moved on to the future of Convention Concepts Unlimited, which still owed debts for the Rye Brook convention and three others.

"There are people that are due monies," said Rudolf. "There is a $770,000 American Express bill for outstanding business as well."

"I didn't know you could get a limit that high," said Judge Ross.

"He's got a black card," Rudolf explained.

The lawyer told the judge that Convention Concepts Unlimited had basically been "a one man operation," with his employees Narcy, May Abad, and Matthew Briggs.

"Prior to her death, Bernice Novack was also an employee," he added. "Other employees were hired as needed for those events. For the most part, Mr. Novack handled his own finances."

He said that the curator had come to the conclusion that although it was still a "very lucrative" company, Novack Enterprises should be liquidated, as the other employees refused to work with Narcy.

"Matthew Briggs, who was involved in the financial end," Rudolf explained, "will not work for the company if Narcy Novack is involved.

We're told May Abad will not work for the company if Narcy Novack is involved. If the court directs us to employ Narcy Novack, we feel that we are going to be unable to manage the company because of the lack of those other two key employees at this time."

Henry Zippay pointed out that his client had worked for twenty years with her late husband in the business. "[She was] operating the business," he said. "Not part time, not anything. She was an intricate part of his business, and it's her desire that the business continue. And, fine, if these other people don't want to work in the business, don't let them work in the business. She could run the business just as easily."

Judge Ross said he was inclined to give Narcy the opportunity to "run with the ball" and see if she could make a go of it. "Why not let her take the darn thing," he said.

Rudolf replied that there were other reasons why the employees refused to work with Narcy. "Both of them are deathly afraid to work in this business right now," he told the judge without elaborating.

"It's her business," the judge said. "It's going to be her business . . . until something else happens. That something could happen, but you know until that does happen and if these folks are going to actually quit, well, I guess that's their choice."

Then Rudolf suggested that, as estate curator, his partner, Douglas Hoffman, take over running Novack Enterprises himself. "Mr. Hoffman then makes the decision as to who he is going to employ," he said, "and [we will] sit down and interview Narcy and find out if she has the capability."

The judge said he did not want to harm the business, especially if Narcy were to end up with it eventually. "I want to preserve the business," he said, "if it's preservable."

May Abad's lawyer Stephen McDonald told the judge that others involved in the upcoming conventions also had problems with Narcy. "They won't work with her," he said. "Flat out won't work with her. At the end of that convention in New York, Mrs. Novack took some $95,000 and deposited [it] into an account in her own name. That was business money. Now, that concerns me."

Rudolf said he had written to Narcy's probate attorneys demanding the return of those funds to the business.

Finally, the judge agreed that Doug Hoffman be elected to the board of directors for Novack Enterprises, and decide whether to wind the business up or not.

"And if these folks want to object," the judge said, "you're going to have to come in here fast and object to that. Okay."

Outside the court, Howard Tanner gave an impromptu press conference to reporters. "She had nothing to do with her husband's death," he said. "Narcy feels horrible about these baseless, uncorroborated allegations. She will be exonerated."

At 2:00 P.M. on Monday, August 31, Cristobal Veliz telephoned senior investigator Edward Murphy in New York, saying he had discovered who had killed Ben Novack Jr. He said he had overheard Francisco Picado arranging to give money to the killer, Alejandro Garcia, at a Miami gas station at 7:30 the very next morning.

"He said he was at his sister Narcy's house in Fort Lauderdale," Murphy said of Veliz. "And it would be good if we went down to Florida to see them at the gas station."

The investigator asked for details about Garcia, and where he could be found.

"[Cristobal] told me he was a tall, dark Hispanic," Murphy said. "He stated he did not know how to get in touch with him."

As soon as he got off the phone, Murphy rounded up Detectives Terence Wilson, Alison Carpentier, and Mike LaRotunda, and they all flew down to Miami that night.

At 6:45 on Tuesday morning, the detectives set up surveillance units at various vantage points around the gas station, on the corner of Forty-Second Street and Twenty-Seventh Avenue in downtown Miami. The New York investigators had called in the Florida Department of Law Enforcement to assist them.

Shortly after 8:00 A.M., Alejandro Garcia appeared on a bicycle wearing a T-shirt and sunglasses and carrying a dark backpack. As the investigators in unmarked police cars moved in, Garcia, who had come to collect another $100 for marijuana to plant in May Abad's truck, pedaled into an alleyway behind the gas station and disappeared.

The alley was too narrow for the police cars, so they backtracked to see if Garcia would emerge from the other side, but he never did.

"We searched a four- to five-block area," said Detective LaRotunda, "and gave a description of the subject to four or five other police cars. It was apparent that he had been riding around looking for somebody."

After giving up on finding Garcia, Investigator Murphy drove to 2501 Del Mar Place in Fort Lauderdale looking for Cristobal Veliz. A security guard at the front door said neither Narcy nor her brother were home.

The previous day, Maxine Fiel had asked the Broward County Probate Court to appoint her the executrix of her nephew's estate. May Abad's attorneys had now persuaded Fiel to work with them, to prevent Narcy Novack from inheriting her husband's estate, under the Florida "Killer Statute."

"The surviving spouse is a person of interest," their petition noted, "in an ongoing investigation of the murder of the Decedent in the State of New York and elsewhere. Under Florida's so-called 'Killer' statute, NARCY NOVACK may be determined to have 'killed' the decedent."

Under the Killer Statute, someone who murders or causes the murder of the decedent cannot benefit from that crime in any way. The estate is then administered as if the killer had died first.

"Accordingly," the petition read, "the surviving spouse, NARCY NOVACK, may not ultimately inherit under the decedent's last will and testament even if she is never adjudicated guilty of murder in any degree in any court of law."

The petition also observed that if Ben Jr.'s widow were disqualified under the Killer Statute, the estate would then pass to her grandsons, Patrick and Marchelo Gaffney.

"May Abad is the natural guardian of these children," the petition read, "and, on behalf of the minor children, she has waived any preference and consented to the appointment of Maxine L. Fiel as personal representative. It is in the best interest that the minor children of May Abad be represented by a family member who will appropriately protect their interest in this estate and properly administer this estate."

FORTY-FIVE

"HE GOT BURIED WITH HIS FATHER"

At 1:00 P.M. on Wednesday, September 2, 2009, Ben Novack Jr. was finally laid to rest in Mount Lebanon Cemetery in Queens, New York—fifty-two days after his murder and on Narcy Novack's fifty-fourth birthday.

Despite asserting earlier that she would not attend, Narcy came to the private service wearing a black suit with a small matching fedora and silver cat's-eye sunglasses, but deliberately avoided many of the mourners. Maxine Fiel was there with her husband, David. May Abad and her sons, Patrick and Marchelo Gaffney, also came. Also in attendance were several fully armed law enforcement officers.

The previous weekend, estate curator Douglas Hoffman had purchased two plots in the Novack-Spier family mausoleum, after tracking down Ben's distant cousins in Iowa and England.

"I believe he's buried where he wanted to be buried," said Hoffman.

At the private ceremony conducted by Rabbi Samuel Waidenbaum of the Rego Park Jewish Center, Maxine Fiel movingly recited a poem from Walt Whitman's *Leaves of Grass*.

"I feel at peace today," Maxine later told a reporter. "He got buried with his father. It should have been done immediately. She let him lay there for fifty-two days, and he would have gone to Potters' Field. I understand Kelsey Grammer paid for the funeral."

During the service, Narcy Novack played the role of grieving widow, pointedly ignoring the rest of the family and standing by herself at the service.

"She turned her back on me," David Fiel said. "I saw she tried to shed some tears, but I think she's a big actress."

After the funeral, Rye Brook Police chief Gregory Austin said his officers were still rigorously investigating Ben Novack Jr.'s murder.

"The case is still active," he said, "and continues to move forward."

The next day, attorney Gary Rudolf wrote to Narcy Novack's attorney Henry Zippay demanding that his client return all the Batman memorabilia she had taken.

"Your client emptied four large storage units," the letter read. "These warehouses contained a substantial number of Batman memorabilia . . . and your client must have transferred them to new or other storage locations. Please provide the Curator with a list of all items removed by your client . . . within one week from the date of this letter."

The following day, Rudolf fired off another letter, this time seeking information about what Narcy Novack had done with the missing $105,000 from the Rye Brook Amway convention.

"You have yet to respond to any of our letters requesting information regarding the assets which your client has taken," wrote Rudolf. "Specifically we asked for the information and return of approximately $105,000 of cash assets from the New York convention which she has deposited in her own name (or taken as cash) and you have yet to give us any information regarding the whereabouts of the four warehouses of memorabilia taken by her."

A few hours later, Broward County Circuit Court judge Dale Ross ordered Narcy Novack not to remove any further items from her late husband's estate. "[You] are hereby enjoined from transferring, selling, assigning or otherwise disposing of such assets," the order stated. He also ordered Curator Hoffman to begin assessing the Ben Novack Jr.

estate and to hire independent appraisers to go into 2501 Del Mar Place and the various warehouses and draw up a complete list of assets.

"The sheer volume of it is overwhelming," Hoffman said. "It's more than just the Batman stuff; it's furniture, cars, collectibles . . . we have a lot of appraisers working on it."

On September 10, May Abad publicly accused her mother of murdering Ben Novack Jr. In a probate court petition, Abad's attorney William Crawford argued that Narcy Novack should not be appointed the personal representative for her late husband's estate, because she had murdered him.

"Narcy Novack unlawfully and intentionally killed or participated in the procuring of the death of the Decedent, Ben H. Novack, Jr.," Abad's petition read. "Accordingly, Petitioner Narcy Novack is not entitled to any of the benefits of the last will and testament of Decedent under the Florida Probate Code."

When contacted by ABC News for comment, May Abad, who now stood to inherit millions with her two sons if Narcy were disqualified, said she was no longer giving interviews. "I spoke to one and that was it," she explained.

In the ABC story, Westchester County communications director Donna Greene said both mother and daughter had laid claim to Ben Novack Jr.'s body before internment.

"[Novack was kept] on ice, literally and figuratively," she said.

Around mid-September, Cristobal Veliz decided to lie low awhile until things had quieted down. As he disappeared from view, his brother, Carlos, started becoming more visible.

Carlos Veliz contacted Alejandro Garcia to arrange another meeting, saying he wanted to get to know him better. They met at the Donde Martica Colombian restaurant on Sandleford Boulevard, Boca Raton. Over a meal, Carlos Veliz said he was looking for Cristobal, whom he had not heard from for some time. Garcia said he had not spoken to

Cristobal either, and he wasn't answering phone calls or returning messages.

Carlos then asked Garcia what his favorite color was, and Garcia replied it was blue.

"I'm going to call you 'Azul,'" Carlos replied, referring to the word *blue* in Spanish. He wrote down Garcia's cell phone number on the back of the restaurant's business card.

Then he asked Garcia to do another job, and showed him a photograph of May Abad, whom Garcia didn't recognize.

"He gave me the picture," said Garcia, "and said, 'I want you to beat up the woman and leave her a cripple.'"

According to Garcia, Carlos explained it was because she was interfering in his sister Narcy's inheritance, and had kidnapped Cristobal.

Garcia agreed to do the job, taking an initial payment of $3,000 with a promise of getting the rest of the money owed him for the Ben Novack job.

Over this period, Meredith Fiel remained in close touch with Narcy Novack, still trying to get incriminating evidence against her. But with her mother, Maxine's, alliance with May Abad, Meredith walked a tightrope. During their weekly conversations, Narcy often attacked May Abad, claiming she was not her real daughter.

"Narcy hated May," said Fiel. "She wanted to do DNA testing, because she thought that May wasn't her daughter, and there had been a mix-up at the hospital."

One time, an excited Narcy called Meredith saying that she had now found Orthodox Judaism. "Narcy was seeing a rabbi," said Meredith. "She talked about making potato latkes and how everyone in the family had loved her [Jewish food]. The whole thing was just sick. I mean she did voodoo stuff, too."

Later it would be discovered that Narcy had now embarked on a passionate affair with a Fort Lauderdale rabbi.

Charlie Seraydar, who had also heard that Narcy was romantically involved with a rabbi, was still a frequent visitor to the house, where

Carlos Veliz had been living for months. On one occasion, Seraydar brought along his young son to see the Batmobile, which was still parked in the garage.

"I went over to the house and I spent time with [Narcy]," said Seraydar. "I saw Carlos [there] a lot," said Seraydar. "[Narcy] said that he came from New York and had been away from his family for several months, and he needed to get back."

On Friday, September 25, Broward County probate judge Dale Ross held a twenty-five-minute emergency hearing, after Douglas Hoffman filed a motion to depose Narcy Novack under oath. The curator had now discovered that after emptying the four warehouses, Narcy had moved the Batman collection into her house, where it was piled up to the ceiling in boxes. He now wanted to question her on the stand about her husband's collection and all his other assets.

"This is a very complicated estate," Narcy's attorney Henry Trachman told the judge. "Mr. Novack, putting it diplomatically, was very eccentric. He saved everything. This home is just a maze of physical things, documents, items, memorabilia, collectibles."

Trachman said that after the murder, homicide detectives had searched the house from top to bottom.

"Narcy Novack's residence has been tossed by the police," he said. "It was absolutely reprehensible what the police did to that place. They left that place a mess."

He said he understood the court's concern that his client might be selling off assets, but there was no evidence to support this.

"Dissipating assets is one of those things after the fact," the judge countered. "You don't know it's being done until after it's been done, and after it's been done, it doesn't matter anymore."

Trachman told the judge that the Novacks' had had "a lengthy marriage," with Ben doing the payroll while Narcy ran the business. "There's a tone of the way this is being handled," he told Judge Ross, "obviously because of the undercurrent of the fact that she's a person of interest. All the things in her home were her's and her husband's. To say, 'Well, this was Ben Novack's, but Mrs. Novack, you had no entitlement to it.' It's disingenuous. This was a household. Money that came in from the business is what ran this household."

The judge said that until Narcy Novack was officially charged with a criminal offense, the court would presume everything belonged to her. "There's a potential here," he explained, "that somebody's going to go to prison for many, many years. Now, if she's charged, and even I know in the criminal division you're innocent until proven guilty."

Representing the Ben Novack estate, Curator Gary Rudolf accused Narcy Novack of "ducking answering questions" about it.

"We know she's taken assets," he told the judge. "We know she's hidden assets. There's not even a question about that. The question is where are they and why are we being denied access to them? That's why we need to take her deposition."

Rudolf then complained that Narcy and her brother Carlos Veliz were obstructing the curator's court-ordered task to protect and appraise the estate.

"Mrs. Novack impedes," he said. "She has her brother Carlos Veliz there impeding us. She doesn't let us take documents. She says, 'I want to keep these.' This is not a free exchange of information and access. I'm sorry."

Visibly frustrated, Judge Ross asked the attorney what more he could possibly do to protect the estate. "We already entered an order that no-body has access to the home or warehouse," he said. "Is there anything else I can do to kind of use the criminal analogy—can I put an ankle bracelet on somebody?"

On September 25, Narcy Novack officially laid claim to her late hus-band's $1 million life insurance policy. On the claimant's form, she asked for the money to be paid in one lump sum, writing that nothing would be due for his funeral.

At 9:45 A.M. on Monday, October 5, property appraisers Diane Marvin and Robert Hittel arrived at 2501 Del Mar Place for three days of work.

They had been hired by the estate curator to prepare a room-by-room inventory of both the house and the adjoining office building.

The two appraisers were met at the door by Narcy and her brother Carlos, who were hostile from the outset.

"I was instructed by Narcy to address them as Mrs. Novack and Mr. Veliz," Marvin later reported, "because she did not want to be on a first-name basis."

Diane Marvin explained the appraisal process to Narcy and her brother. "[I] proceeded to share our game plan with her," said Marvin. "Narcy became uncooperative and insisted we begin with the Coca-Cola collectibles and comic books."

The appraisers explained that they had arranged for a comic book expert to visit on Wednesday, to prepare an inventory. They also said they must be very "methodical," due to the large number of unorganized items and boxes piled up throughout the residence.

"At this point it became apparent that Narcy was not going to cooperate," said Marvin, "as she wanted to be in control of the appraisal process. She became very argumentative and made unnecessary, inappropriate comments and challenged me to appraise her 'panties.'"

Diane Marvin then called the curator's office, saying they were having problems with Narcy. They were then told to move next door to the Convention Concepts Unlimited offices "to defuse the situation."

Soon after they began working there, the cleaning lady arrived. Then Narcy and Carlos started berating them in front of her. "Carlos stated that I was 'doing the lawyer's dirty work,' and that I was really conducting an 'investigation,'" said Marvin. "I assured him that I was only doing my job as an appraiser and was treating this assignment as I would any other assignment. Meanwhile, Narcy continued to be vocal about her opinions, made derogatory remarks, and used foul language. Carlos made a number of derogatory remarks about [Ben Novack Jr.]"

When the appraisers attempted to examine her gym equipment, Narcy refused even to allow them to touch it, saying she was "germophobic."

For the rest of the morning, as Narcy and her brother looked on, the two appraisers inventoried everything in the Novack Enterprises offices, with the exception of the Batman collection.

At around 12:30 P.M. they told Narcy they needed to return to the main house and start working there, but she refused to allow this. "Narcy insisted we leave them for an hour," said Marvin, "so that she could 'have a break' from us, and would not permit us to continue working."

When they returned an hour later, Narcy's behavior became even stranger and paranoid. "Narcy was agitated," Marvin explained, "and shouted she didn't know me and demanded to make a copy of my driver's license. She complained that she had been robbed and did not trust us. She spoke in a raised voice and shouted that I was 'trying to screw' her.

"She challenged me in a sarcastic manner to appraise the food in her pantry. She spoke in a taunting way and tried to engage me in an argument. She and Carlos stated they would not cooperate with us or do anything to help facilitate the appraisal."

Then Narcy told Marvin that she was so angry she was going to "explode." She also threatened to have her "fired."

"At that point I told her we would leave," said Marvin, "and come back when it would be more convenient for her."

The appraiser then called the curator's office to ask for help. Soon afterward, Narcy's criminal lawyer Robert Trachman arrived.

The two appraisers remained outside the house while Trachman went in to reason with Narcy. Narcy insisted that she did want Diane Marvin inside the house again that day, although she agreed that Robert Hittel could resume work tomorrow with someone else.

Two days later, Diane Marvin wrote up a report, saying that Narcy and Carlos's "difficult" behavior would delay the appraisal by at least three weeks, when the Batman collection could be appraised by an expert.

"In summary," Marvin wrote, "I found Narcy Novack to be uncooperative, controlling, hostile, combative and verbally abusive. Carlos was also controlling, protective of Narcy and made threatening remarks."

Marvin also requested that an outside observer be present when she and Hittel returned to complete cataloguing the Batman collection.

"The appraisers need protection from being accused of stealing," she wrote, "and someone should be there to act as a buffer."

. . .

The following week, curator Douglas Hoffman filed a motion in Broward County Probate Court complaining that Narcy Novack and her brother Carlos were making his job impossible. Using Diane Marvin's report as Exhibit A, he asked Judge Dale Ross to order Narcy to cooperate.

"Narcy Novack has been an obstructionist with the appraiser carrying out her duties," the motion stated. "Furthermore, Narcy's brother, Carlos Veliz, has been intimidating, threatening and uncooperative."

Hoffman said a New York expert in Batman memorabilia was flying to Fort Lauderdale at the end of October to carry out the appraisal, but he feared Narcy would try to stop it.

"The Curator believes," Hoffman wrote, "that there will be a likelihood of irrevocable injury to the Estate if he cannot fully and timely carry out his duties. [And] that items may continue to be secreted or otherwise lost to the Estate, and that Narcy Novack will continue to be uncooperative in allowing the Curator to efficiently carry out his duties to locate, appraise and safeguard the assets of the Estate."

The motion also asked Judge Ross to order Narcy to allow Diane Marvin and her staff to continue their appraisal, appointing a "neutral third party" to ensure the appraisers' safety. It asked the judge to ban Carlos Veliz from the house while the appraisal was taking place.

In the wake of the motion, Narcy Novack's attorney Howard Tanner was interviewed by *The Miami Herald*. Once again, he stated that his client was totally innocent and had been wrongfully accused of killing Ben Novack Jr. by her daughter. Tanner pointed out that May Abad and her two young sons had a motive for lying, as they would inherit everything if Narcy Novack were convicted of murder.

He also maintained that as her husband's sole beneficiary, Narcy now owned his entire Batman collection. "She was married to him for nineteen years," Tanner said. "It was purchased during their marriage."

He explained that Narcy had no money, as she was unable to access their marital assets. A month earlier she had requested a family allowance from the probate court, which had still not been ruled on.

"She's a victim," Tanner explained. "Not only of losing her husband to a crime—now she's a victim of a system that is punishing her for no reason at all."

Rye Brook homicide detectives were now busy interviewing everybody who had ever come into contact with Ben and Narcy Novack. Lead detective Terence Wilson had already met many of Ben and Narcy Novack's friends and business contacts, looking for any leads.

The New York detectives also believed that Bernice Novack's death had been no accident, and started sending their colleagues in the Fort Lauderdale Police Department leads on things to follow up. But these were met with an icy reception.

In mid-October, the Fort Lauderdale Police announced it was satisfied that Bernice Novack had died from a series of falls, and that absolutely no foul play was involved.

"So far every lead [Rye Brook Police] have given us has been looked at," said spokesman Sergeant Frank Sousa, "but they all led to dead ends."

A few weeks later, the FBI quietly moved in, taking over the investigation into Bernice Novack's death.

FORTY-SIX

NARCY SPEAKS

On Tuesday, October 20, Judge Dale Ross ordered Narcy Novack to allow the appraisers three days of access to 2501 Del Mar Place, to complete their job. She must also make everything available to the appraisers, and reveal where any missing items were. Carlos Veliz was ordered to vacate the premises during the appraisal.

Hours after the ruling, Narcy Novack appeared in Broward County Circuit Court for her long-awaited deposition. After Narcy was sworn in, May Abad's attorney William Crawford stood up to begin his often confrontational questioning.

"Have you ever been known by any other names other than Narcy Novack?" he asked.

"There's a list of them," Narcy replied in her thick accent. "Narcy Saveles, Narcy Saveles Novack."

"And how about Narcisa Sero Felez Backham?"

"Yes," she agreed.

After Narcy told the court that she had a college-level education in Ecuador, Crawford asked about her employment history after coming to America.

"I'm going to object to that," interrupted her criminal attorney Howard Tanner.

Crawford then amended his question, asking about her work history after her marriage to Ben Novack Jr.

"In meeting, planning industry," Narcy replied. "Event producing."

Her daughter's attorney then asked how many children she had.

"That's an interesting question," replied Narcy. "One."

"One. Okay. The name of the child?" Crawford asked.

"Do I want to say that name?" she asked her other lawyer, Trachman, who told her to answer.

"May Abad," she replied.

"And by whom did you have your child May Abad?" Crawford asked.

"My first marriage, Angel Abad," she replied.

Then Crawford asked straight out if she had murdered her husband on July 12, 2009?

"No," Narcy replied resolutely.

"Did you conspire with another person to kill him on July 12, 2009?

"Certainly not," Narcy said.

"Did you plan to murder him on July 12, 2009?

"No."

"Did you direct someone to kill your husband on July 12, 2009?"

"No."

"Do you know who killed your husband on July 12, 2009?"

"No."

Then Crawford asked how many key cards been issued to her and her husband when they had checked into the Rye Town Hilton.

"I'm going to advise my client to invoke the Fifth Amendment," Tanner said.

"Describe the appearance of your husband when you found him on July 12, 2009, after breakfast?"

Again, Tanner told his client to invoke the Fifth Amendment to that question, as well as a further one as to whether she knew Ben Jr. had been having an affair prior to his death.

Then Crawford moved to the 2002 home invasion, asking Narcy if she had conspired to kidnap her husband.

"No," she replied defiantly.

"Okay," Crawford continued. "On or about June 10, 2002, did you extort any money or property from your husband?"

"No."

"Did you admit to participating in a scheme whereby your husband was bound and gagged on or about June 10, 2002?"

"That's exaggerated," Narcy replied.

"Did you admit to that on June 10, 2002?" Crawford pressed.

"I don't recall," Narcy said evasively.

"Did you participate in tying up and gagging your husband on June 10, 2002?"

"At this point we're going to invoke the Fifth Amendment," Tanner interjected.

"Did you ever say to any Fort Lauderdale Police Department detectives, on or about June 10, 2002," Crawford asked, "'If I can't have Ben, No one else can'?"

"No."

"Did you ever extort money or property from your husband Ben Novack, in exchange for your silence with respect to certain sexual practices in your marriage?" Crawford asked.

Once again, Tanner invoked Narcy's Fifth Amendment rights, and then again for a question about why Ben had declined to file charges against her in 2002. He also refused to let her answer whether Ben had given her a pay rise after the 2002 incident.

"Do you practice voodoo?" Crawford asked. "Do you have black candles at your house?"

Tanner again stepped in, invoking Narcy's Fifth Amendment rights.

Crawford then asked the name of her husband's life insurance company, which she had applied to for a payout after his death.

"I don't remember," she answered.

"Is that the policy with a million dollars in it?" Crawford probed.

"Yeah," she replied.

Then after half an hour on the stand, Bill Crawford had no further questions, and Narcy Novack stepped down from the witness box.

. . .

The next day, Narcy Novack's civil attorney, Henry Zippay Jr., filed a motion asking the Broward County Probate Court to decide whether May Abad's opposition to her mother's appointment as the estate's personal representative had any merit. The motion also asked Judge Dale Ross to rule on whether the Florida "Killer Statute" was sufficient grounds for denying Narcy the right to oversee her husband's estate.

"Narcy Novack hereby requests," the motion read, "this honorable court to specifically set a time for the trial/final hearing of the two objections as filed by May Abad relating to the allegations that Narcy Novack 'unlawfully and intentionally killed or participated in the procuring of the death of the Decedent, Ben H. Novack, Jr.' And further, upon failure to advance and/or prove said evidence, that the court appoint Narcy Novack as Personal Representative . . . and award her the requested family allowance."

Three days later, May Abad's attorney William Crawford responded, again asking Judge Ross to appoint Maxine Fiel as the estate's personal representative. His motion repeated the allegation that Narcy Novack had murdered her husband, and therefore should be disqualified from running Ben's estate under the so-called "Killer Statute."

Later, Maxine would explain that she had reluctantly agreed to become involved in the probate case to protect her family's estate from Narcy Novack. "[Stephen McDonald] called me up and asked me to be the [personal] representative," she explained. "I was not too happy about doing it, but he said this way you can protect your sister's [and Ben's] money, because as his wife, she would inherit everything."

On November 9, May Abad's attorneys filed a new motion, citing the 1991 prenuptial agreement as sufficient grounds for Narcy's not being appointed personal representative.

"Prior to the parties' marriage," the motion stated, "Narcy Novack waived and relinquished all statutory rights as surviving spouse . . . in the selection and appointment of an executor, administrator or other personal representative of the decedent's estate."

The motion also alleged that Narcy Novack had "surreptitiously" deposited money belonging to Novack Enterprises into her personal bank account, contravening the Florida Probate Code. She had also refused to return the money to the court-ordered estate curator.

"Narcy Novack is further incapable of complying with . . . Florida law," the motion read, "by reason of her deliberate surreptitious removal of Batman memorabilia and collectables [sic] and hiding and concealing [them] from the duly appointed Curator."

Two weeks later, attorney William Crawford filed yet another motion into probate court, this time concerning Narcy's role in the June 2002 home invasion. It accused her of conspiring with others to "kidnap and batter" Ben Novack Jr., and of stealing $350,000 in cash and jewelry.

"Narcy Novack stated . . . to another," the motion read, "that she did what she did . . . to decedent Ben H. Novack, Jr. to get what she needed to get."

The motion observed that Ben Jr. had been bound with duct tape in 2002, just as he had been when he was murdered seven years later. It alleged that Narcy had "extorted" her husband to pay her $6,500 a month, so she would not "reveal photographs . . . involving nude bodies with amputated arms and legs." It also accused her of an ongoing campaign of extorting money and property from Ben Jr. "in exchange for her remaining silent about the intimate facts and circumstances concerning their private marital relationship, including their sexual relationship."

Soon afterward, Narcy Novack's attorney Howard Tanner hit back, hiring a private investigator named Robert Crispin to go through May Abad's trash looking for incriminating evidence. The retired Coconut Creek Police Department detective was put on retainer for an ongoing program of "trash pulls." His first one was on November 8, and over the next six months he would conduct at least half a dozen, taking various bills and final notices that Narcy Novack hoped to use against her daughter at a later time.

FORTY-SEVEN

THE BIG BREAK

On Wednesday, November 18, investigators were finally ready to move in and arrest Alejandro Garcia for Ben Novack Jr.'s murder. Over the last few weeks they had been busy gathering evidence against him. He and Joel Gonzalez had now been clearly identified on surveillance video at the Rye Town Hilton at the time of the murder. Detectives had also interviewed Gladys Cuenca, who told them that Garcia had introduced her to Cristobal Veliz, who had then spent three days in her trailer with the two suspected killers.

The investigators' endgame was to arrest Narcy Novack and her brother Cristobal for Ben's and Bernice's murders, but they would start with Garcia and Gonzalez and try to get them to cooperate.

That morning, investigators Ed Murphy and Mike LaRotunda arrived at the car wash on Twentieth Street and Seventeenth Avenue, Miami, where Garcia worked. They brought him down to Miami Police headquarters on an outstanding bench warrant.

At the station, Garcia was brought into an interview room and seated at a table with the two detectives and a female Spanish-language interpreter.

At 12:20 P.M. the detectives turned on a video recorder and asked

Garcia about his background and how he had come to America. Wearing sunglasses, a gray T-shirt, and a heavy silver chain, Garcia appeared relaxed, saying he was "confused" as to why he was there.

Over the next half hour, he answered Murphy's general questions about his life in Miami, admitting to being in the country illegally.

Then Murphy casually said he wanted to play Garcia an audiotape, but would first have to read him his Miranda rights.

"We need to know if you recognize the voices on that tape," Murphy said. "Am I clear?"

"I don't know, I'm confused," Garcia replied. "I need an attorney, because I don't know what I'm being accused of. I can't sign this."

Finally, he agreed to sign the Miranda rights form, and Murphy played him cassette tapes of his three telephone conversations with Cristobal Veliz in which Veliz implicated Garcia in Ben Novack Jr.'s murder.

"I just remembered that Alejandro Garcia committed a crime," Veliz is heard saying on one tape.

After playing the tapes, Murphy showed Garcia photographs of people connected to the case, including Joel Gonzalez. He also displayed surveillance pictures of Garcia and Gonzalez at the Rye Town Hilton on the morning of Ben Novack's death.

Garcia was evasive, initially denying that he had ever been to New York. Eventually, after seeing the irrefutable evidence of him at the Rye Town Hilton with Gonzalez, he admitted going to New York to do some painting and laboring for Carlos Veliz.

"We cleaned, we painted, we removed trash," Garcia said. "We cleaned the house. My conscience is clear that I haven't done anything. I didn't do anything to anybody. I didn't harm anybody."

Murphy told Garcia he was sympathetic and knew he had only played a small part in the murder. He said he was far more interested in the people behind it.

"We're trying to help you, Alejandro," Murphy said. "Obviously there are other people who are blaming you."

Finally, Murphy and LaRotunda left the interview room after more than an hour of questioning, and Detective Alison Carpentier came in.

"Alejandro, I'm Alison," she told him through the interpreter. "I'll let you know what's going to happen from here. You're gonna be booked on charges of murder."

On December 18, Douglas Hoffman submitted his second curator's report, asking for Judge Dale Ross's permission to liquidate Novack Enterprises and file bankruptcy.

"The corporation is insolvent," he wrote, " and could not be maintained as an ongoing concern."

He noted that the company's assets were approximately $350,000, and the outstanding debts on Ben Novack Jr.'s black American Express card were $769,763.81. Additionally, there were claims for unpaid bills for the Batmobile totaling $18,650.00, as well as $50,000 for work on Ben's yacht, *White Lightning*.

Convention Concept Unlimited staff Joe Gandy, Matthew Briggs, and May Abad were also asking for nearly $30,000 in unpaid wages, while Charlie Seraydar was owed $3,000.

"It was my position that the company had no value without Ben Novack," curator Doug Hoffman later explained. "And ultimately that's what the court decided."

On Saturday, January 23, 2010, the top-rated TV show *America's Most Wanted* featured the Ben Novack Jr. case and appealed for anyone with information to come forward. Producers invited Narcy Novack to be interviewed, but she refused.

Several days earlier, Rye Brook Police had released the anonymous letter to the media, in a new attempt to break the case open. It would be another year before they discovered it had been written by one of Narcy's sisters.

Police chief Gregory Austin said that he had been initially skeptical of the letter, but during the ongoing investigation, it had proved uncannily accurate.

"What we found interesting in the letter," said Chief Austin, "is that there were names in it at the time we were not aware of. As we did our own investigation, we found that information to be true."

Lead detective Terence Wilson, who was interviewed for the *America's Most Wanted* segment, called the anonymous letter a key piece of evidence. "We processed the letter for fingerprints, DNA," he said, "to try and find out who the person was that wrote the letter. Unfortunately we were not able to do so."

Narcy's criminal attorney Howard Tanner told *The Miami Herald* that the anonymous letter should never have been made public while the investigation was still ongoing.

"It is astonishing to me," he said, "that the chief of Rye Brook police would give it to the press."

On Monday, February 2, Broward County probate judge Charles M. Greene suddenly handed Narcy Novack control of her husband's multimillion-dollar estate. In a dramatic ruling on the first day of the probate trial, the judge dismissed May Abad and Maxine Fiel's lawsuits that she be disqualified under the "Killer Statute."

Abad's attorneys, Stephen McDonald and Bill Crawford, had asked the judge to dismiss their petition without prejudice, so they would still be able to challenge Ben Novack Jr.'s will. Their case had fallen apart after attempts to subpoena a Rye Brook homicide detective to come to Florida and testify were shot down in case this compromised the ongoing criminal investigation.

After the ruling, Howard Tanner told reporters that May Abad's attack on her mother was based on "rumor and innuendo," and called it a "miscarriage of justice."

"If it can happen to her, it can happen to anyone," he said.

Under the ruling, Narcy could now dispose of all her husband's assets, and inherit her late mother-in-law Bernice's estate.

The following day, Narcy Novack's three attorneys submitted bills to the estate for their services. Her criminal lawyers Howard Tanner and

Robert Trachman billed legal fees of $883,000 and $650,000, respectively. Her probate attorney, Henry Zippay Jr., wanted $36,190 for his work on the case.

On Thursday, Judge Greene abruptly reversed his decision, seizing the estate back from Narcy. His about-face came after he learned that a federal grand jury was about to convene in New York to investigate a broad criminal conspiracy involving Narcy Novack.

The judge had also based his new ruling on Narcy Novack's request to use $1.6 million from her husband's estate to pay off her legal team. He questioned whether her criminal legal team's work benefited the estate or just defended Narcy from possible criminal charges.

Judge Greene then appointed Doug Hoffman as the new personal representative for both the Ben Novack Jr. and Bernice Novack estates. He ordered that the estates' liquid assets be placed in a court depository so they could not be accessed without court permission.

After the hearing, Tanner said that his client would fully cooperate in any investigation, as she had done from the start. "Authorities have nothing but unsubstantiated rumors," he told reporters.

Cristobal Veliz was becoming increasingly worried that Alejandro Garcia might cut a deal with the government. He still did not know of Garcia's arrest, and started calling Joel Gonzalez, asking where his friend was.

"I lost count of how many calls there were," said Gonzalez. "I didn't tell him [about Garcia's arrest] because Mr. Garcia had told me not to tell him a thing."

Finally, Veliz surmised that Garcia had returned to Nicaragua, and he decided to have him killed there so he couldn't give up him or Narcy to the police.

In early 2010, Veliz contacted Juan Carlos Castillia, saying he needed to talk to his lover, Melvin Medrano, who had been deported to Nicaragua after the Bernice Novack job.

"Cristobal was worried and wanted to know about Alex [Garcia],"

Castillia later testified. "He was worried Alex would talk to the cops. He wanted to . . . have him killed."

On February 19, Castillo arranged a three way telephone call between Veliz and Medrano, who agreed to make Alejandro Garcia disappear.

At the beginning of March, the FBI seized assets belonging to the Ben Novack Jr. estate, under federal forfeiture regulations, in connection with allegations of financial fraud. When Narcy attempted to take title of Ben's Batmobile and several other antique cars, a federal judge signed sealed warrants preventing her.

The Miami Herald reported that the sealed warrants meant that the FBI Violent Crimes Task Force now believed it had sufficient evidence to persuade a judge that Narcy Novack had been involved in illegal activity for financial gain. The forfeiture was ordered under a seldom-used maritime and admiralty law. Among the items seized were the Batmobile, a 1957 Ford Thunderbird, a 1970 Jaguar, a 1962 two-door Ford coupe, and a thirty-five-foot barge.

In early April, on the first anniversary of her sister Bernice's death, eighty-four-year-old Maxine Fiel flew to Fort Lauderdale to try to get the case reopened. She was accompanied by her husband, David, who was seriously ill, with only a few weeks to live.

"I refused to believe Bernice died naturally," Maxine said. "So we went to Florida and started investigating."

When the Fiels arrived, they were met by Estelle Fernandez, who took them to Bernice Novack's house and introduced them to Bernice's friends and neighbors.

"They told me that Bernice said there were men in front of her house," Maxine said. "She was being stalked, which is what it says in the anonymous letter."

During their visit, May Abad was particularly attentive, as she needed Maxine's help to challenge Ben Novack Jr.'s will. A few weeks earlier she had given birth to her third son, whom she had named Ben, in honor of her late stepfather.

"May knows how to charm you," Maxine said later. "She's a good talker and can be very open. She'll tell you about her mother at the drop of a hat. They don't get on. She thinks her mother did it."

Maxine was surprised at how May continually referred to Ben Novack Jr. as "Dad." "She never called him 'Dad' before," Maxine said. "Bernice would scream if she could hear it. He was never that."

While in Florida, Maxine gave an interview to *The Miami Herald* criticizing the way Fort Lauderdale Police had handled her sister's death.

In a front-page story headlined "Two Bodies, Few Answers in Novack Family Mystery," Maxine questioned why Fort Lauderdale Police had failed to take the anonymous letter seriously. "The letter lays it all out. She was murdered," Fiel said. "They tried to say she was confused, but she was not."

Maxine labeled as rubbish the Fort Lauderdale detectives' theory that Bernice had fallen and then tried to drive to hospital before changing her mind. "My sister would never have gone out in a nightgown," Fiel said. "It seemed to me that she was being chased, not that she was falling around the house. There was blood smeared everywhere, and her injuries were horrific."

Fort Lauderdale Police spokesman Frank Sousa repeated that there was absolutely no new evidence to warrant the case being reopened. "That letter doesn't prove anything," he told *The Miami Herald*. "At this point, there is nothing to indicate anything different from our [initial] finding."

Broward County medical examiner Joshua Perper agreed, reiterating that Bernice Novack had died from a series of falls.

Soon after Alejandro Garcia began cooperating with the government, investigators realized that May Abad was in great danger. At the beginning of June, Westchester County Police flew her to New York, warning her that her life was in danger. Then they sent her straight back, promising to relocate her and her two sons to a safe house. Unfortunately, they explained, this could take months, due to all the paperwork involved.

"They told me I was in danger," said Abad, who was now waitressing at a Chili's restaurant at the Fort Lauderdale Airport, but "they didn't do anything about it except to tell me to protect myself."

Over the next several weeks, Abad called Fort Lauderdale Police numerous times reporting strange men hanging around outside Chili's. On one occasion, she told them, someone followed one of her sons home from school.

Finally, Westchester County Police detective Alison Carpentier, who had become close friends with May Abad during the investigation, became so concerned for her safety that she loaned her $5,000 out of her own pocket to get an apartment in Naples, Florida.

"If Alison didn't help me," Abad said, "who knows what would have happened."

Forty-Eight

THE ARRESTS

A t 6:00 a.m. on Thursday, July 8—just days before the one-year anniversary of Ben Novack Jr.'s murder—the FBI descended on 2501 Del Mar Place. Narcy Novack was still asleep when agents burst into the house and arrested her. Simultaneously, in Brooklyn, New York, Cristobal Veliz and his son-in-law, Denis Ramirez, were also taken into custody. An FBI arrest warrant was then issued for twenty-five-year-old Joel Gonzalez, who was considered armed and dangerous.

As there is no federal murder statute, they were all charged with conspiracy to commit interstate domestic violence and stalking. Federal prosecutors said further charges were likely. The 1994 federal domestic violence law—which was passed after the murder of Nicole Brown Simpson—meant that they all faced life in prison if convicted.

In the unsealed federal indictment, prosecutors accused fifty-three-year-old Narcisa Veliz Novack of plotting her husband's murder, as she feared he was about to walk out of the marriage, leaving her penniless. The indictment alleged that on the morning of July 12, 2009, Narcy opened the Rye Town Hilton suite door to Gonzalez and Garcia, who beat and slashed her husband to death. She even handed them a pillow to hold over her husband's face while he was being assaulted. Finally, she gave Garcia her husband's favorite diamond bracelet on the way out.

Later that morning, a handcuffed Narcy Novack, wearing a black top and patterned skirt, was led into federal court in Florida, where she was arraigned in front of U.S. magistrate Barry Selzer. She was then extradited to Westchester County, New York.

During her brief court appearance she said nothing, beyond acknowledging that she understood the charges against her. A bond hearing was set for the following Wednesday, and her lawyer Robert Trachman said she would not be appealing the extradition.

As Narcy appeared in federal court, the FBI and the Westchester County District Attorney's Office held a joint press conference, announcing that they had solved the Ben Novack Jr. murder case.

"The plot that led to the brutal death of Ben Novack was a family affair," U.S. attorney Preet Bharara declared. "Today, just four days short of the one-year anniversary of the heinous killing . . . we announce the indictment of four individuals allegedly responsible for his death."

Questioned about Narcy's motive, Bharara replied that prosecutors were filing a civil complaint seeking the forfeiture of the estate, in addition to Ben Novack Jr.'s $1 million life insurance policy, to prevent Narcy from benefiting.

Then a reporter asked what, if any, significance the arrests would have on the case of Bernice Novack's death.

"We are taking a look at that, as you would expect we would," Bharara replied, "and we may have more to say about that later."

Westchester County D.A. Janet DiFiore then spoke, describing the plot to kill Ben Novack Jr. as "diabolical."

"What transpired on the morning of July 12, 2009, in Ben Novack's hotel room, was nothing short of a calculated plot," she said, "[Narcy Novack] was intent on eliminating her husband and taking his family fortune for her own."

Then George Venizelos, who was in the charge of the New York FBI office, spoke about his bureau's key role in the complicated interstate investigation.

"The killing of Ben Novack was not a spur-of-the-moment crime of passion," he told reporters. "It was the endgame of considerable planning. Likewise the case was solved by a great deal of dogged police work by a well-coordinated team."

The final speaker was Rye Brook Police chief Gregory Austin, who thanked the other law enforcement agencies for their help in breaking the case.

"The stalking and violent attack of Ben Novack Jr. that led to his death," said Chief Austin, "was an act of violence never before seen in Rye Brook, and I'm proud that these defendants will be held accountable for this crime."

Late in the afternoon of July 8, Cristobal Veliz and Denis Ramirez were arraigned in federal court in White Plains, New York. During their appearance, assistant U.S. attorney Elliott Jacobson revealed that Bernice Novack had been murdered by hit men hired by Cristobal Veliz.

"That was the assault that resulted in her death," Jacobson told the court. He also disclosed that Veliz had tried to frame and assault May Abad, as she threatened Narcy Novack's inheriting Ben Novack Jr.'s estate.

Maxine Fiel told the *Journal News* that although she was glad about the arrests, the investigation should now widen to include her sister's murder. "They need to connect the dots," she said, "between my sister's murder in April 2009 and her son's murder a few short months later. Fort Lauderdale closed that investigation very quickly . . . that investigation needs to be reopened now."

Reacting to her mother's arrest, May Abad expressed surprise that prosecutors were alleging that Narcy was actually in the hotel room during the murder and had participated in it. "I never thought she was actually there," Abad told *The Miami Herald*. "I thought she went back to try and stop it. Maybe it's me just trying to see the good in her. This is my mother. No matter what the investigators said, I was trying to see the last little bit of good in her—but maybe there isn't."

. . .

On Friday morning, Fort Lauderdale Police finally agreed to reopen the investigation into Bernice Novack's death. Police spokeswoman Kathy Collins told the *Sun-Sentinel* that detectives had no further comment.

However, Broward County medical examiner Joshua Perper told the *Sentinel* that he had already been contacted by Fort Lauderdale detectives about the case. "My understanding is police are continuing their investigation," he told the newspaper.

At 2:00 P.M. that same day, Joel Gonzalez walked into the Miami Police headquarters and surrendered. He was immediately booked and taken into custody. The FBI said he would be arraigned on Monday.

The following Wednesday morning, July 14, Narcy Novack was back in federal court, at a bail hearing. Looking unkempt in blue prison scrubs, with straggly, dyed red hair, Narcy remained silent throughout the bail proceedings, sitting passively in handcuffs. Several of her relatives and friends were in the public gallery.

Arguing against bail, U.S. attorney Elliott Jacobson revealed new gruesome details of Ben Novack Jr.'s horrific killing, and the part Narcy had allegedly played in her mother-in-law's death.

The prosecutor said that during the investigation into Ben Novack's death, he had asked the Westchester County medical examiner to take a look at the death scene photos and other evidence in Ben's mother's death. The medical examiner had done so and immediately declared it a homicide.

Jacobson told federal magistrate Robin Rosenbaum that Narcy and her brother Cristobal Veliz had hired two men to assault Bernice Novack three months before her son's murder. Then, using information provided by Narcy Novack, the men had savagely beaten Bernice to death with a monkey wrench.

"Narcy Novack was complicit in the homicide of Bernice Novack," Jacobson declared. "She died after she was struck several times."

He also disclosed that Alejandro Garcia—whose identity was being kept secret—had already pleaded guilty to domestic violence charges, and was now fully cooperating with law enforcement. Jacobson said Garcia's testimony implicated Narcy Novack in both murders. Joel Gonzalez was also helping police, said Jacobson, and had fully backed up Garcia's version of the murders.

The prosecutor told the court that Ben Novack Jr. had been beaten to death with dumbbells, and Narcy had ordered one of his killers to gouge out Novack's eyes with a utility knife. "In Spanish, she urged them to cut out his eyes and finish him off," Jacobson said.

Both killers were then captured on Rye Town Hilton CCTV video leaving the Novack suite after the murder.

Jacobson also accused Narcy of trying to mislead investigators by claiming that an arm of Garcia's fake Valentino sunglasses had belonged to her.

Howard Tanner protested his client's innocence, in both deaths. He told the magistrate that Narcy had fully cooperated with police since her husband's murder, and pointed out that she had been interrogated without a lawyer present.

"They want to strengthen their case by implicating her in a so-called homicide," he said, "that has no basis in fact."

Federal magistrate Robin Rosenbaum found more than enough evidence to hold Narcy Novack in custody. She was confused by Narcy's response "It's in good hands" when asked where her passport was.

"I don't know what that means," the magistrate said, "and it is a concern."

The next day, Thursday, July 15, medical examiner Joshua Perper, reversed his previous findings that Bernice Novack had died an accidental death. After an early morning call from Fort Lauderdale Police, he amended the manner of death on her death certificate to read "homicide." Later he explained that the new evidence was "very solid" and there was no question "it is a homicide."

Perper also defended his earlier decision to rule it an accidental death, saying that he had taken into account Bernice's recent history of falls. He maintained that there had been nothing to suggest that a weapon had been used in the blunt force trauma injuries she had suffered.

"In view of the history of falls and no indication that anyone was assaulting her," he explained, "accidental death was the likely determination."

The medical examiner said that when he had learned from Fort Lauderdale Police of Alejandro Garcia's eyewitness testimony, it had completely matched the crime scene. "The evidence they have is very firm," he told the *Sun-Sentinel*, "because it is consistent with our findings."

The Fort Lauderdale Police Department also defended its work on the case. "There is no physical evidence that would have got us a conviction as a homicide," said spokesman Frank Sousa. "We received information due to Ben Novack's investigation, but we had to hold off on our case until their case was done."

When Maxine Fiel learned that she had finally won her courageous fight to have her sister's death declared a homicide, it was a bittersweet victory. In May, David, her beloved husband of more than fifty years had died, and she was now in the process of moving to upstate New York to be nearer her daughter Meredith.

"My poor, poor sister," she said on hearing how Bernice had died. "She must have been so scared. She was such a fighter."

FORTY-NINE

VALHALLA

At the end of July, Narcy Novack was brought back to New York and taken to the women's unit of the Westchester County Jail in Woods Road, Valhalla, where she would remain until her eventual trial. It was a long way from the luxurious lifestyle she had grown accustomed to.

On Monday, August 9, 2010, Narcy appeared in federal court in White Plains, pleading not guilty to charges related to her husband's murder. Handcuffed and wearing gray prison garb, she looked tired and drawn.

After Narcy made her plea, Howard Tanner asked federal magistrate Paul Davison to grant bail, saying his client would agree to be electronically monitored.

Prosecutor Elliott Jacobson argued against bail, calling Narcy a flight risk and a danger to the community. He also revealed new damning evidence against her.

"We have learned of efforts to kill another witness," said the federal prosecutor without elaborating. He described Ben Novack Jr.'s killing as "extraordinarily grisly," adding that the "Veliz Family" had also plotted to frame and assault May Abad.

Tanner countered that it was "unfair" for the government to make such serious allegations without backing them up. "The government will simply throw out allegations that are not based on any fact," he told the magistrate. "Anyone can say anything they want about plots, but there is going to come a time, and it will come at the trial, where they're going to have to be put to their proof."

Tanner also denied that Narcy Novack was a flight risk. "My client allegedly committed these crimes a year ago," he said. "She had a passport the whole time and could have left the jurisdiction, but she didn't."

Magistrate Davison refused Novack bail, saying his decision had nothing to do with the government's new allegations, but was based solely on the indictment.

In late August, Narcy Novack requested a public defender, claiming she could no longer afford to pay her attorney Howard Tanner. In a letter to U.S. District Court judge Kenneth Karas, now assigned to the Narcy Novack case, Tanner said his client was broke, as she was unable to access her husband's estate. It would later be revealed that Narcy had already paid Tanner the "vast bulk" of the $105,000 Rye Brook convention money she had taken after her husband's death.

In a financial affidavit, Narcy claimed to have received no income in the previous twelve months, and to having just $1,500 in her bank account. She listed her assets as her marital home, worth $7.8 million, plus automobiles, collectibles, and other personal assets worth $500,000, along with $800,000 worth of jewelry. She also wrote that she owed $53,000 on credit cards, with monthly payments of $1,200, plus $480,000 in back payments on the $9,000-a-month mortgage for 2501 Del Mar Place.

"The above assets are unavailable to me," she wrote at the bottom. "All assets have been frozen or seized by the government."

In an accompanying letter, Tanner requested that Judge Karas allow him to continue to represent his client, and offered to work for the basic public defender's salary. "Her inability to pay is due to the fact that all estate assets have been frozen," Tanner wrote, "as a result of civil forfeiture actions initiated by the government and/or probate proceedings pending in Broward County, Florida. Accordingly, all funds have been rendered unavailable to her and she cannot borrow against these assets."

He told Judge Karas that a new counsel would be "unduly prejudicial" to Narcy Novack, and that he knew the case intimately, having represented Narcy in both criminal and probate matters since her husband's death.

After reading the letter, Judge Karas agreed to allow Tanner to remain, as long as he was compensated only as a court-appointed public defender.

Even from jail, Narcy Novack and Cristobal Veliz were still trying to frame May Abad for Ben and Bernice Novack's murders. Joel Gonzalez, who had now cut a deal with the government, saw Veliz almost every day at Valhalla jail. One Sunday morning, when they were attending church together, Veliz made him an offer.

"He offered me money," Gonzalez later testified. "He said once I went over to him, he would pay $150,000 into an account. Then, after Mrs. Novack [was free,] he would put another $150,000 in an account."

Veliz, who had no idea Gonzalez was cooperating with prosecutors, said if the government asked who had orchestrated the assaults, he should say May Abad had hired him and Garcia to do them.

Gonzalez refused to commit himself, stringing Veliz along for a while.

"He kept asking me, 'Are we going to do it?'" Gonzalez said. "He kept telling me to give an account number to put the money into. I kept saying, 'I'll talk to you the next time I see you.' I never gave him a direct answer."

Eventually, Cristobal Veliz resorted to threats.

On October 10, Gonzalez was in his cell when another inmate handed him a handwritten note from Veliz. It contained Bible verses from Deuteronomy and Luke, which Gonzalez perceived as a direct threat.

"One witness is not enough to convict anyone of any crime or offense they may have committed," read the passage from Deuteronomy 19:15.

"A matter must be established by the testimony of two or three witnesses."

Gonzalez interpreted this to mean that if Alejandro Garcia was cooperating with the government and he, Gonzalez, was not, it would be enough to destroy the case against Narcy Novack.

At 10:00 A.M. on Thursday, December 16, Narcy Novack, dressed in a gray prison outfit and chained around the waist, was back in federal court for a routine status conference. Also in the courtroom were her brother Cristobal Veliz, his son-in-law Denis Ramirez, and Joel Gonzalez.

On the way from the Westchester County Correctional Center, Gonzalez had been placed in a holding pen with Narcy. "She asked me if it was hard to set her free," said Gonzalez, "and to do her this favor. I was the only one that could help her. The only one that could give her freedom. She was reiterating what Mr. Veliz had said."

Later, at the hearing, Howard Tanner asked Judge Karas for a sixty-day adjournment, in order to review discovery turned over by prosecutors. Then, as the attorneys discussed possible dates for the next status hearing in late February, Narcy Novack became visibly agitated.

When Tanner told the judge that he would be out of town for the week of February 20, Narcy exploded, startling the courtroom. "While you're away," she snapped at her lawyer, "I'm going to be locked up here in Valhalla."

Judge Karas then set the next status hearing for February 10, and Narcy and the other defendants were led out of the court by bailiffs.

After the hearing, Tanner told reporters that his client was understandably frustrated by having to remain behind bars until her trial. "Nobody's happy being in jail," he explained. "Jail is a new experience for her."

On Thursday, February 10, 2011, Joel Gonzalez was conspicuous in his absence at the next status hearing. This time Narcy Novack appeared more composed, chatting to Howard Tanner throughout the brief hearing. Sitting behind another table were Cristobal Veliz with his lawyer, Stephen Lewis, and Denis Ramirez with attorney Ismael Gonzalez.

Joel Gonzalez's absence went unmentioned by both Judge Karas and prosecutor Elliott Jacobson.

During the hearing, Jacobson told the judge that he would soon decide if the government would file additional charges against Narcy Novack and the other suspects in connection with Bernice Novack's murder. He said a grand jury was now considering new federal charges, and might issue a superseding indictment in the next few weeks.

After the hearing there was much speculation that Joel Gonzalez had already pleaded guilty, strengthening the government's case even more.

"Whatever it is, if he's admitted anything," Howard Tanner told reporters, "I don't believe that he will hurt my client, because my client continues to assert her innocence."

One week later, Denis Ramirez threw in his cards and pleaded guilty, too. He admitted to driving Garcia and Gonzalez to the Rye Town Hilton for what he believed was to be an assault and robbery.

In federal court, Cristobal Veliz's thirty-six-year-old son-in-law and the father of his grandchildren pleaded guilty to conspiracy and domestic violence charges. He denied knowing that Ben Novack Jr. was the target for murder, and claimed he thought he was driving the two men to the hotel to commit a violent robbery. During the hearing, prosecutors named their star witness and Ben and Bernice Novack's confessed killer, Alejandro Garcia, for the first time.

Federal prosecutor Jacobson also revealed further new details about Ben Novack Jr.'s murder. It had been Narcy Novack, he said, who had made the crucial call to the killers at 6:39 A.M. from the Hilton Hotel, instructing them to proceed. Then, about half an hour later, she had let them into the hotel suite to commit the murder.

Two weeks later, the *Journal News* reported an unidentified law enforcement source claiming that Garcia had told investigators that Narcy's oldest brother, Carlos Veliz, had offered him money to murder Ben

Novack Jr. Carlos, who had not been charged, denied having anything to do with Ben's murder.

"They are dealing with people who have a rap sheet up to the ceiling," Carlos told the *Journal News*. "One thing I know, my name will not dance in that (jail). I've got nothing to do with it."

FIFTY

FRUSTRATION

On Tuesday, April 5—the second anniversary of Bernice Novack's death—federal prosecutors finally charged Narcy Novack with orchestrating the murder. In an eleven-count superseding indictment filed in White Plains federal court, Novack and her brother Cristobal Veliz were charged with racketeering in the April 2009 death and with attempting to have Alejandro Garcia killed so he couldn't testify against them. Narcy Novack was further charged with laundering $95,000 out of the $105,000 she took the day after Ben Novack Jr.'s murder.

"This indictment alleges racketeering acts that run the gamut from murder to robbery to obstruction of justice," said U.S. attorney Preet Bharara. "A bloody and corrupt chain of events for which the defendants will now have to answer to a jury."

Prior to the media learning of the new charges, Maxine Fiel had received a courtesy call from the Westchester County prosecutor.

"I knew she had been killed," an elated Fiel told *Journal News* reporter Jonathan Bandler with regard to her sister's death, "and felt it was me against the world. But now it's an indictment. I hate to think of my sister and the fright she felt that day. [Narcy's] an evil woman and I hope she never sees the light of day again."

. . .

Three days later, Narcy Novack and Cristobal Veliz were arraigned on the new charges at White Plains federal court. They both pleaded not guilty.

At the hearing, federal prosecutor Elliott Jacobson dramatically upped the stakes, revealing that the government was now considering charging the siblings with murder in the aid of racketeering, which can carry the death penalty.

Narcy sat next to Cristobal, the two flanked by their respective attorneys. She wore an orange prison jumpsuit; her lank brown hair was streaked with gray. Carlos Veliz's wife, Melanie Klein, also attended, sitting quietly in the back row of the public gallery.

As Prosecutor Jacobson told Judge Kenneth Karas that the government was now considering a capital case, Narcy suddenly became animated. She began wagging her finger at Howard Tanner as the prosecutor explained that if the death penalty were brought into play, the Capital Crimes Unit would come in to review the case, which could delay the trial for months.

"This process is glacial," Judge Karas noted.

At 4:59 that afternoon, Prosecutor Jacobson sent an e-mail to Howard Tanner and Stephen Lewis, giving their clients one final opportunity to plead guilty before he went ahead with the new capital charges.

"It is our intention," Jacobson wrote, "to proceed with several violent crime in aid of racketeering counts (including a murder in aid of racketeering count) in a superseding indictment. These counts were approved by the Department of Justice this afternoon.

"We will hold off returning the superseder until 9:00 A.M. on Monday, April 25, 2011. Please contact me if you wish to resolve this matter by plea."

The morning of the deadline, Cristobal Veliz wrote a letter to Judge Kenneth Karas informing him that he had now fired his attorney, Stephen Lewis. He accused Lewis of trying to railroad him into pleading guilty and testifying against his sister, and telling him that his case was already lost. Veliz's letter also made a series of unsubstantiated allegations against Ben Novack Jr., May Abad, and Denis Ramirez's cousin Francisco Picado.

Veliz claimed that his niece had told him that Ben Novack had raped her in 1991, when she was growing up. In 2009, Veliz claimed, May had told him she'd caught her stepfather receiving oral sex from one of her sons. He said he had confronted Ben Novack with May's accusation, but he had denied it.

"[Her] anger . . . caused her to send people to kill Ben," Veliz wrote. "She's claiming the money that belongs to her mother as a personal reward for the traumatic rape that she went through and also what Ben did to her son."

Veliz also claimed that Ben Novack had made "strange videos" about "handicapped females in wheelchairs" having sex.

"My only fault in this matter," Veliz told Judge Karas, "is that I should have been honest with my sister and told her what had happened."

At the next status hearing, held on Friday, May 6, Prosecutor Elliott Jacobson told Judge Karas that the Department of Justice needed a further six weeks to decide whether to seek the death penalty. If it became a capital case, the defense would have to bring in new attorneys, experienced in death penalty cases, to join the defense teams—a process that could take months.

With attorney Stephen Lewis also announcing that he would no longer be representing Cristobal Veliz, things would be delayed even further, as a new lawyer would have to be brought up to speed on the case.

After the hearing, Judge Karas met with Veliz and Lewis in his chambers to discuss Veliz's letter. It was decided by "mutual agreement" that Veliz would get a new attorney.

A few months earlier, Bernice Novack's home had been put on the market, with an asking price of $875,000. And in May, her treasured possessions, including many from the Fontainebleau, were sold off.

The grand piano that Frank Sinatra had supposedly given her fetched $6,897.97, and the prized bronze and marble statues that had once adorned the hotel went for a total of almost $19,000. The remaining jewelry that hadn't been taken by Narcy sold for nearly $15,000, and her dresses and other clothing, $5,350.

The sale made a total of $182,983.37, less the appraisers' 20 percent commission, giving her estate $146,386.70.

"They cleared everything out of the house," said Rebecca Greene. "It was so sad to see these total strangers going into that house and taking Bernice's things. She was such a private person, and to have total strangers go in there and box it all up and take it away in U-Hauls was just devastating."

On May 19, Cristobal Veliz took his case to Supreme Court judges John Roberts and Stephen G. Breyer. In a letter written on his behalf by Laura Law, he appealed for justice.

"I am a wrongly accused man," he stated. "I have not been involved in any way in the crime that I am arrested and jailed for. The legal system has been treating me badly."

He accused his former attorney Stephen Lewis of teaming up against him with prosecutor Elliott Jacobson, and the FBI and the Westchester County District Attorney of conducting a "lousy" investigation without "a single clue or evidence."

He copied the letter to the *New York Post*, the New York *Daily News*, *El Diario*, and the *Journal News*, but not one story appeared.

On Thursday, June 23, Narcy Novack was back in White Plains federal court with Cristobal Veliz. Throughout the status hearing, at which prosecutors announced that the Justice Department had still not made up its mind about the death penalty, Narcy appeared visibly upset and agitated. Wearing a cream prison outfit, her brown hair tied back with a blue ribbon, she repeatedly shook her head in annoyance.

"I've instructed her that there's no basis for a bail application," Tanner explained to the judge. "She's frustrated."

"I understand," Judge Karas replied.

At the end of the hearing, as Narcy was being led out of court by a bailiff, she banged the government's table in anger and glared at the prosecutor.

A few minutes later, outside the courthouse on Quarropas Street, Laura Law handed out to the reporters assembled there a protest letter from Cristobal Veliz.

Each week, Laura Law, who worked as a nurse at a Brooklyn hospital, caught a bus to Westchester County Jail in Valhalla, New York. In the morning she would visit Cristobal Veliz, and then walk over to the women's jail to see Narcy Novack in the afternoon.

Narcy had now been locked up for a year, having little to do with the other inmates. She spent her days working on her case in her cell, remaining in daily touch with her brother Cristobal by mail. She kept a strictly kosher diet inside the jail.

"She doesn't share a cell," said Laura Law. "She don't want to talk to nobody over there. She's just living alone because she doesn't like the other people."

Law said that Narcy had started writing a book about her once-glamorous life with Ben Novack Jr., giving her version of his murder.

"She writes it down like a story book," said Law. "She likes to show it to me. She says it's a very good story and that it might be a movie one day."

FIFTY-ONE

"A SICK,

VICIOUS CYCLE"

On July 16, 2011, *The Miami Herald* carried a recap of the case, headlined "The Novack Murders: A Tale of Greed, Sex, Betrayal and Shocking Brutality." In the story, reporter Julie Brown interviewed defense attorney Howard Tanner, who insisted that Narcy Novack was totally innocent and that prosecutors had no evidence against her.

"The puzzling thing," said Tanner, "is that prosecutors are making deals with people who are admittedly involved in the murder of Ben Novack, and they are going after Narcy, who had nothing to do with the murder . . . They are making deals with a variety of devils."

Two weeks later, at a status hearing, Prosecutor Elliott Jacobson told Judge Kenneth Karas that the government would not be seeking the death penalty, but would be asking for a mandatory life sentence instead. Narcy Novack had no visible reaction to the news.

Jacobson said that he was still pressing ahead with a new superseding indictment, including murder in aid of racketeering, which would be ready in a couple of weeks.

"Naturally my client is frustrated by the whole process," Tanner told the judge, who replied that he "appreciated" that.

The judge officially appointed defense attorney Larry Sheehan to represent Cristobal Veliz.

Toward the end of the morning's hearing, Jacobson complained to the judge about defense attorney Tanner's recent interview with *The Miami Herald*, taking exception to his saying that prosecutors were making a deal with "a variety of devils."

Judge Karas issued a gag order on attorneys giving any further interviews to the press, saying he was concerned that it might prejudice the jury pool for the upcoming trial.

On Tuesday, September 20, the long-awaited second superseding indictments were filed against Narcy Novack and her brother Cristobal. The six new felony counts included one of murder in aid of racketeering, alleging that the two were part of an interstate plot to enrich themselves. It carried a mandatory life sentence without parole if they were found guilty.

Two weeks later, Judge Kenneth Karas set an April 16, 2012, date for the murder trial to begin. After Narcy was formally arraigned on the new charges, pleading not guilty, Howard Tanner announced he was considering asking the court for separate trials, as there was a "good basis" to do so.

At the hearing, Veliz's arraignment was postponed after he told the judge he had not yet discussed his plea with his new lawyer, Larry Sheehan. Then, against Sheehan's advice, Veliz held up a copy of the letter he had written to Judge Karas and waved it around.

"They did this, not me," he declared angrily. "I'm not guilty."

Two weeks later, Veliz was arraigned on the new charges; he pleaded not guilty to all of them. He also asked Judge Karas for permission to leave Westchester County Jail for a few hours so he could marry his fiancée, Laura Law (already described as his wife in his letters), at a nearby town hall.

"You want to marry Laura Law?" the judge asked.

"Yes, please," Veliz replied. "Please give me the opportunity."

Judge Karas said he would check with federal marshals, and told the defendant to "hang in there."

. . .

On November 15, Ben Novack Jr.'s collection of Batman comics and other collectibles was auctioned off in Beverly Hills, California. In a three-day auction, his rare comic book collection fetched a total of $268,000, including a record $101,575 for a restored 1939 *Detective Comics* No. 27, which marked the very first appearance of Batman.

In mid-February 2012, Maxine Fiel hired top genealogist Harvey E. Morse to investigate the Novack family tree and prevent her nephew's fortune from going to May Abad and her two sons. Fiel's attorney, Mark Hanson, then petitioned Broward County Probate Court, asking it to decide exactly who the rightful heirs to Ben Novack Jr.'s millions were. He said the Novack family's purpose was to "cut off [Narcy's] bloodline," so neither she nor any of her descendants could profit.

"The law as a matter of public policy," attorney Hanson said, "does not want the murderess to benefit in any way under the will."

Hanson, who is based in Daytona, Florida, already claimed to have located three of Ben Novack Jr.'s cousins, who could lay claim to his now estimated $10 million estate.

Fiel said the last person Bernice would have wanted to inherit her money and valuable jewels was her daughter-in-law. "Not one of my children or I have ever discussed the money," she said. "I want justice. I want that woman [Narcy] put away forever and never [to] see the light of day."

Asked by a local Miami TV station for her comment, May Abad lashed out at her stepfather's family. "They have no dignity whatsoever," she said. "All they're after is the money. Where have they been all these years?"

On Friday, February 28, at a pretrial hearing, it was revealed that Narcy Novack had been receiving regular visits at the Westchester County Jail from criminal attorney Gary Greenwald, whom she had put on a retainer. Her longtime attorney Howard Tanner had found out only a day earlier, after Greenwald asked Judge Karas to allow Narcy to use her assets to pay his, Greenwald's, fees.

Tanner was also unaware that two months earlier Narcy had transferred the ownership of a 1995 Mercedes to Greenwald, who had registered it in the name of a consulting firm he ran. In January Narcy had also transferred $18,797.05 from an insurance policy to the lawyer.

The portly attorney, based in Chester, New York, arrived in court with a female assistant carrying a bag of jewelry valued at $200,000, which Greenwald claimed belonged to Narcy Novack.

In August 2010, Narcy had signed an affidavit claiming to be penniless. Since then, Tanner had been representing her at a fraction of his normal fee as a public defender.

"I've received a letter giving some indication that Mr. Greenwald now represents Miss Novack," Judge Karas said. "With the trial date fast approaching, I find it perplexing."

Then Greenwald asked the judge for a special hearing to determine if Narcy Novack could use assets currently tied up in Florida probate court to pay his fees. He explained how the $200,000 worth of jewelry he had brought to court had recently come to light through a family member.

"The taxpayers have been paying for Miss Novack," Karas told Greenwald angrily, "and the taxpayers should be reimbursed for Mr. Tanner's hard work. You have a retainer. Now all of a sudden there's jewelry to pay for it."

Then Tanner told the judge that his client wanted to address the court, although he'd warned her not to.

"I'm going to echo that advice," said the judge. "What Mr. Greenwald has said in this court could hurt your cause in ways you don't even think."

Ignoring him, Narcy got to her feet and declared, "I'm tired of this. I'm fighting corruption. I've been framed."

"We're not here to try your case," the judge told her.

"Please let me use my wedding band to defend myself," she said. "Because the Florida court has used my assets to pay my accuser's lawyers' bills. I can't use my own [money.]"

"You told me in a sworn statement that you had nothing to pay an attorney," Karas told her sternly. "Now you're telling me you want to use [jewelry]

"After I find out later that I have this," she snapped. "Please let me use my assets, so I can use Mr. Greenwald to defend myself. I need more than what I have."

"I can answer that in one word," the judge told her sternly. "No."

Judge Karas then denied Greenwald's request for a hearing, saying Narcy Novack already had a court-appointed attorney. "She just wants to have her proverbial cake and eat it," said the judge. "She has no right to multiple counsel. I will leave it to the government as to what it wants to do with the jewels. The application is denied."

Judge Karas then called a short recess, leaving Narcy and her brother Cristobal alone in the courtroom except for two marshals and a couple of reporters.

"Bastards!" Narcy hissed at her brother, sitting behind her. Then she turned around to the press bench, grinned, and said, "Happy Halloween."

When the court reconvened, Judge Karas told Veliz he was denying his request to marry Laura Law, as it posed too many security problems.

"He's just going to have to wait," said the judge.

Two days later the government named Ben Novack's secret mistress in a sensational motion. It asked Judge Karas to allow the jury to hear about the Novacks' 2002 home invasion, claiming it established "a sick, vicious cycle" leading to the two murders.

It also revealed that, before his death, Ben had been supporting one-time exotic dancer and tattoo artist Rebecca Bliss in an apartment in Fort Lauderdale. After discovering the affair in the summer of 2008, the motion claimed, a furious Narcy telephoned the landlord and ordered him to terminate the lease, as her husband was dead and there would be no further payments.

Then she had then gone to the FBI and accused Ben of arranging sham marriages, with Bliss being one of the unlawful brides. A month later, Narcy notified Mexican customs officials that her husband had smuggled $10,000 in currency into Mexico.

The motion contended that after the FBI failed to act, Narcy and her brother Cristobal began hatching the plan to murder Bernice and Ben Novack.

Ten days later, an all-day pretrial hearing was held to rule on a defense motion that Narcy Novack's seven-hour videotaped police interview should be inadmissible. Senior investigator Edward Murphy testified that Narcy Novack had fully cooperated with law enforcement after her husband's murder.

He admitted, however, under Howard Tanner's questioning, that she had not been informed that the interview was being videotaped.

"We chose not to tell her," he said. "She was not a suspect."

After a lunch recess, Narcy Novack dramatically took the stand. Wearing a Westchester County Correctional Center standard orange jumpsuit, her graying brown hair in a ponytail, she was sworn into the witness box.

She told her attorney Howard Tanner that she had been suicidal in the hours after Ben's murder. "There was a uniformed police officer with a gun on his belt," she said. "I tried to grab the gun. My husband was gone and there was nothing I could do for him."

Narcy claimed that all her statements after her husband's murder were coerced, as she had been told that her questioning was a normal procedure she had to follow. She also maintained that initially she had refused to take a lie detector test, but had been intimidated into it by detectives.

"They asked me to sign [the polygraph test forms]," she told Judge Karas. "I said, 'No, I'm tired.' Then they locked me in the polygraph room and left me for twenty minutes. They came back with May Abad and said she had taken hers and passed and was free to go. [I took it] because I just wanted to be clean and recover the body and do what I wanted to do."

Narcy said that after failing the polygraph test, the detectives' attitude to her changed drastically. "The detective came over and he was screaming at me and calling me names," she claimed. "I said, 'Let me sleep for a couple of hours . . . either arrest me now or let me call a lawyer. Then May Abad entered the polygraph room and she was going to hit me. One of the [detectives] grabbed her, saying, 'Leave her, we're going to get her ass.'"

In cross-examination, Elliott Jacobson asked Novack if all the statements she had made to investigators were involuntary.

"I did not care to answer to anyone," she snapped. "I wanted to be left alone."

At the end of the daylong hearing, Cristobal Veliz took the stand and claimed that Detective Murphy and Detective Sergeant Terence Wilson had entered and searched his apartment without his permission. During his testimony, Narcy's brother baffled the courtroom by insisting that the "Ed Murphy" who had questioned him was not the same "Ed Murphy" who had testified earlier.

"I have never seen him before in my life," Veliz told the judge in a thick accent.

Under his attorney Larry Sheehan's questioning, Veliz said four investigators had entered his Philadelphia apartment and woken him up. He said he thought he was under attack and had gotten a knife to defend himself. Veliz also claimed that there had been no papers whatsoever on his kitchen table and a detective had opened his briefcase while he was changing in the bedroom, and had found the Western Union wire transfer.

Veliz also claimed that a detective had later asked him if he suffered from hemorrhoids, after seeing a box of Preparation H, which had also been inside the briefcase.

"Could you see the Preparation H without opening up the briefcase?" Sheehan asked.

"Impossible," Veliz replied.

"Was there anything on that table when they went into the apartment?" the lawyer asked.

"No," Veliz said.

Before dismissing Veliz from the stand, a confused Judge Karas asked him if Detective Edward Murphy had come to his apartment.

"Not this one," Veliz relied resolutely. "He looked different."

. . .

On March 12 the government's case took a major hit when it was revealed that Detective Alison Carpentier, who had since retired, had given May Abad $5,000 to enter a safe house. Prosecutor Elliott Jacobson had written a letter to the court flagging certain issues that might arise during trial. One of them was the question of Detective Carpentier's loan, which was never paid back.

"Following Ben Novack's murder," Jacobson wrote, "Abad was increasingly isolated from her family. [She] felt threatened by them."

The letter also asked Judge Karas to stop the defense from showing the jury the photographs of female nude amputees found on Ben Novack's laptop computer. "Neither those pictures, nor evidence about them," Jacobson wrote, "should be admitted in evidence. Ben Novack is not on trial and whether he had such a fetish is not an appropriate issue for the jury to consider."

Four days later, Howard Tanner wrote to Judge Karas demanding that prosecutors be ordered to produce complete details about Detective Carpentier's loan to May Abad, and all the phone records and e-mails between the two women dating from Ben Novack's murder onward.

"Detective Carpentier's payment to Ms. Abad raises substantial issues," Tanner wrote, "of the integrity of the law enforcement investigation, which is crucial to the defense of this case. Apparently, Detective Carpentier was the subject of an investigation and was subsequently either fired or forced to resign . . . a fact not revealed by the Government."

On Friday, March 23, Judge Kenneth Karas ruled that Narcy Novack's videotaped police interviews could be played for the jury only if she took the stand. After watching the seven-hour interview and reading the complete transcript, Judge Karas said he found Narcy's behavior more "melodramatic" than "suicidal." He noted that she hadn't been arrested, restrained, or searched during the police questioning, and had repeatedly said that she knew she was free to leave but wanted to do everything to help the investigation.

"Mrs. Novack is not a wallflower," the judge said. "She has a very strong personality and . . . a will of her own. She appears to be chatty in discussing some remarkably intimate details."

The judge found that Narcy's statements, although given voluntarily, would be admissible at trial only if she testified. Judge Karas also found that the police had acted properly in entering Cristobal Veliz's apartment and that none of his rights had not been violated. He said he found it "incredible" that Veliz had claimed that he had never seen Investigator Murphy before.

"It just doesn't make sense," Judge Karas said, and ruled that any information "gleaned" from the visit to Veliz's apartment would be admissible at trial.

On Wednesday, April 11—five days before the start of her trial—Narcy Novack telephoned the *Journal News* offices and gave an exclusive jailhouse interview.

"You guys have demonized me," she told reporter Jonathan Bandler. "Well, now I don't have answers at the courtroom, well, guess what? I'm going to make this very public. They want this to be a federal case, well, let's have a federal case."

Narcy then claimed that she was lucky to be alive, and had been almost murdered with her husband. "At the last moment my plan changed," she explained. "For the grace of God I left the room."

In her rambling interview, the accused murderess questioned whether the government could even prove Ben was dead. "One of my questions is," she asked, "is my husband alive? And they don't have the answer."

Narcy also claimed her mother-in-law, Bernice Novack, had not been murdered. "I don't believe she was killed," she railed. "Not on my orders and not on anybody's orders. That did not happen."

Then she attacked the prosecutors for being corrupt and setting her up. "They can lock me in Valhalla," she declared, "but you know the truth will come out, because I'm going to expose these rat bastards. And believe me they're going to regret this."

. . .

On Monday, April 16, the day before jury selection, the defense scored a major victory when Judge Karas ruled that the contentious 2002 home invasion incident would be inadmissible at trial. But the jury would be allowed to hear Narcy Novack's statements to Fort Lauderdale Police describing her marriage as a "sick, vicious cycle" and saying she had left Ben as many as sixty times. The jury also could not be told that Narcy Novack had repeatedly failed a polygraph test, as it would be unfairly prejudicial.

During this final pretrial hearing, Narcy insisted on addressing the court several times, despite warnings from the judge and her attorney not to do so. Now she wanted the judge to postpone the trial so she could be better prepared for it.

"Enough already," she told Judge Karas. "I'm fed up. Put on hold everything . . . so I can have a proper defense. Let's wait for two or three months until I'm comfortable. I'm not ready to fight for my life, [and] you're just rushing me."

Judge Karas denied her request, expressing surprise that she now wanted to delay the trial after having made "abundantly clear" her frustration at the slow pace of the proceedings.

Then prosecutor Elliott Jacobson read out portions of Narcy Novack's recent interview with the *Journal News*, accusing her of criminally threatening federal prosecutors.

"The federal government has eyes and ears," he warned Narcy. "We're not talking about some small police department in Podunk. If there's any attempt to intimidate us there will be hell to pay."

After lunch, Tanner told the judge that, as a protest, his client was now insisting on wearing bright orange Westchester County Correctional Center scrubs at trial, although her brother Cristobal would wear civilian clothes.

"Her position is her clothing has been seized and is not available," Tanner explained. "She has no idea what type of clothes [will] be given to her."

Once again, against Tanner's advice, Narcy insisted on addressing the court.

"Why sugarcoat?" she asked. "They have turned my life inside out, upside down. [I'm] an innocent widow and I want people to know. The world needs to be educated. I'm not going to be made a puppet and have them dress me from Kmart."

After reading of her mother's intention to wear standard jail uniform at trial, May Abad offered through her attorney to personally select clothes from Narcy's wardrobe, and send them to her mother.

FIFTY-TWO

THE TRIAL

On Tuesday, April 17, fifty prospective jurors filed into Judge Karas's fifth-floor courtroom to see if they could be fair and impartial in the wake of the enormous publicity the case had generated. After being questioned one by one by the judge and attorneys from both sides, most claimed to be unaware of any details of the case.

On Wednesday morning, more potential jurors were examined, and by 11:45, the no-nonsense judge had selected eight men and four women jurors, along with six alternates.

After the jurors were dismissed until opening statements the following Monday, Judge Karas ordered Narcy Novack to stop the "name-calling."

The unrepentant defendant apologized for calling the prosecutors "rat bastards," explaining her remarks had been directed solely at the Rye Brook Police Department.

"They did me wrong," she explained, "and I will always be mad at them. There's no sugarcoating it. Mr. Jacobson is dealing with tainted information."

As Judge Karas warned her to remain quiet during the trial, Narcy began to try to explain herself.

"You will not interrupt me, ever!" the judge told her angrily. "It's not my job to be your lawyer . . . I don't think it's helpful for you to make these statements, but that's for you to figure out."

At 9:30 A.M. on Monday, April 23, as Narcy Novack and Cristobal Veliz were brought into the U.S. District Courthouse for the first day of their trial, a nor'easter was raging outside. As promised, Narcy wore standard-issue orange jail scrubs, with her graying hair tied in a pony-tail. Her brother Cristobal had a crumpled off-white shirt with a vest underneath, which he would wear for the next month. Although he spoke good English, Veliz requested a Spanish-language interpreter for the duration of the trial.

At 10:00 A.M. the twelve jurors and six alternates entered courtroom 521, taking their seats in the jury box. Then special assistant U.S. at-torney Perry Perrone stood up to deliver the government's opening statements.

"Cut his eyes! Break her teeth!" he began. "Words from a script to a grade-B horror movie? Nope. You will hear that on July twelfth, 2009. For Ben Novack and his mother, Bernice, these actions would become a gruesome reality."

The tall, youthful prosecutor told the jury that "these horrible acts" had been carefully orchestrated by Narcy Novack and her older brother, and the motive was "jealousy, retribution and greed."

Perrone explained how Ben Novack Jr. was having an affair with an "exotic dancer" called Rebecca Bliss, and Narcy feared he would divorce her, cutting her off from his multimillion-dollar fortune.

After failing to buy off Bliss, Narcy had gone to the FBI and accused her husband of arranging sham marriages, and named Bliss as one of the brides. When the FBI failed to act, she enlisted her brother Cristobal to hire "savages" to assault first Bernice Novack and then her son.

"They're not nice guys," the bespectacled prosecutor acknowledged. "Their actions are horrible. But Narcy Novack and Cristobal Veliz chose them for that reason. They made them witnesses in this case."

Winding up his ninety-five-minute opening argument, Perrone told the jury it was "a very complex case," but they would find "overwhelming proof" that the two defendants were guilty beyond a reasonable doubt.

Then Cristobal Veliz's attorney, Larry Sheehan, told the jury that the killers, Alejandro Garcia and Joel Gonzalez, would say anything to save their skins. "The government makes deals with the devil," said Sheehan. "What kind of man hits someone with barbells and then cuts his eyes out?"

He said that in federal court, the only way out of prison is in a pine box. "They will say anything to get out," he said. "It's a get-out-of-jail-free card."

Sheehan then accused May Abad of not only hiring the two killers, but also of kidnapping and torturing his client before threatening to kill his grandchildren. He told jurors that "wild horses" could not stop Cristobal Veliz taking the stand in his defense.

In his opening statement, Howard Tanner accused the Rye Brook Police Department of being "inexperienced" and of immediately focusing on Narcy Novack like "a laser beam." "From the moment Ben Novack's body was discovered by his wife," said Tanner, "the fingers started pointing at my client. Whispers in the ears of detectives by May Abad. It soon turned into a tainted investigation."

Tanner accused Detective Alison Carpentier of compromising the whole murder investigation by giving money to a person of interest. "She gave May five thousand dollars in cash," Tanner told the jury, "and deposited it in her bank account. Even after she was taken off the case, Alison Carpentier gave her [another] gift months later. May Abad never paid her back."

He acknowledged that Ben and Narcy Novack had an unconventional marriage, as jurors listened in rapt attention. "We're going to get to the amputee sex," he told them. "We're going to get to the deviant sex. This is not about whether this was a normal marriage. But the fact remains it worked for them."

Tanner said the only evidence against his client came from "two lying monsters," and that everything that had happened inside the Woodlands Suite at the Rye Town Hilton was uncorroborated.

"Narcy Novack was not in the hotel room," he declared. "She had absolutely nothing to do with Ben or Bernice Novack's deaths."

After a brief recess, the government called its first witness, now-retired Fort Lauderdale Police Department detective Steve Palazzo. Although the jury could hear nothing about the 2002 home invasion, Palazzo was able to describe how Narcy Novack had brought her husband's photo collection of naked female amputees into police headquarters.

"Did she show you any of them?" prosecutor Elliott Jacobson asked.

"Yes," replied Palazzo. "She told me she wanted to bring to my attention photos that would show the unusual sexual desires of her husband. There were real old photos and magazines. Some of the women were undressed and missing limbs. She said they were into bondage and he was into fantasies about having sex with amputees."

Palazzo said Narcy had described hers and Ben's marriage as "a sick, vicious cycle," saying she had walked out on him on many occasions.

Then Howard Tanner asked if some of the photographs had been Polaroids, intimating that they had been taken by Ben Novack himself.

"They may have been," he replied.

That night, *The Miami Herald*'s Julie Brown asked May Abad her feelings about the prosecution strategy of accusing her of masterminding the killings.

"The whole thing is a joke," she said. "They are making a circus out of this. To me, they are going to say whatever they can to save their own asses."

On the second day of the trial, Ben Novack Jr.'s estate lawyer, Carl Schuster, testified that Narcy Novack would have inherited far more if her husband died than in a divorce. The Fort Lauderdale attorney said that under the Novacks' 1991 prenuptial agreement, Narcy would have received only $65,000 plus moving expenses in a divorce. But under his June 2006 will, she stood to gain millions.

"Financially," said Schuster, "she would have been better off if he was dead."

Later that morning, federal marshals led Rebecca Bliss into court to testify about her affair with Ben Novack Jr. The heavily tattooed former prostitute and pornstar, who was in custody in Michigan for DUI and nonpayment of child support, had been granted immunity by the government to testify.

Looking pale and haggard with her messy brown hair tied back and curls falling into her face, Bliss seemed nervous and uncomfortable. As Bliss took the stand to be sworn in, Narcy Novack glared at her across the courtroom from the defense table.

Under assistant U.S. attorney Andrew Dember's direct questioning, Bliss described how in early 2008, Ben Novack Jr. had answered her online "escort ad." After an exchange of e-mails and phone calls, they'd met for a two-hour sex session and he had paid her $600.

"The first date was just sexual relations," she told the jury, "but we got a lot closer."

In early June, she said, Novack persuaded her to give up prostitution and move from Miami to Fort Lauderdale, promising to support her and find her a place to live. He installed her in a luxury hotel spa for two weeks while she looked for an apartment.

He then signed a lease on a luxury condo in the Marina Bay Club, a short drive away from his home, telling her to furnish it at his expense.

"He asked me not to work anymore," she told the jury, "not to continue to escort. He paid for all my food and utilities."

Bliss testified that although her sugar daddy paid for everything and was very generous, she rarely saw him. During her year there, they had sex "maybe twice."

She told the jury they were in love, and that Ben Novack had promised to leave Narcy for her and get a divorce.

"As his girlfriend," Bliss told jurors, "I was being very patient."

Then, in January 2009, Bliss received a barrage of furious calls from Narcy Novack. "She asked, did I know he was married," Bliss testified. "I said, yes, I did. She told me there were a lot of other girls and I wasn't the only one."

She said Narcy then offered her $10,000 to break off the relationship and never talk to her husband again. Bliss refused.

At this point, Judge Karas overruled Howard Tanner's objection, allowing Bliss to testify that Narcy Novack had told her, "If she couldn't have him, no other woman was going to have him."

In an often-hostile cross-examination, Tanner ridiculed the idea of love between Bliss and Ben Novack.

"You put yourself out there as a prostitute?" Tanner asked.

"Yes," Bliss replied, unfazed.

"You charge three hundred dollars an hour to have sex, is that your stated price?" he continued.

"Yes, you have to set the price the same as the other girls in Florida. But I have limits on what I will do."

Then, referring to the $10,000 she claimed Narcy had offered her to stop seeing Ben, Tanner questioned whether it had been enough money. "How much would it have taken?" he demanded to know. "Everybody has their price."

"I told her there wasn't one," Bliss replied. At the defense table, Narcy Novack stuck a finger in her mouth, as if she were about to throw up.

On Wednesday morning, two burly marshals led Alejandro Garcia to the witness stand. He was wearing thick black wraparound sunglasses and an Orange County, New York, jail jumpsuit.

For the next five days, through two Spanish-language interpreters, the government's star witness would describe, without a hint of emotion, coldly killing Bernice Novack and then her son, Ben.

Under assistant U.S. district attorney Elliott Jacobson's questioning, Garcia told the jury that in March 2009 he'd been recruited by Melvin Medrano to assault an old woman. Soon afterward, he said, Medrano had introduced him to Cristobal Veliz, at the Miami car wash where Garcia worked. Jefe, as he knew him, was organizing the job for his sister Narcy Novack, and would pay him $1,000.

After several failed attempts and after drinking two bottles of rum, Garcia had sneaked up behind Bernice Novack's car and attacked her with a monkey wrench in her garage.

"She looked at me and she screamed," he testified. "And right away I hit her."

Over the next several days, he described Cristobal Veliz's preparations for the next attack, on Ben Novack, for which Garcia would be paid $10,000. As Medrano had been deported back to Nicaragua, Veliz had recruited Joel Gonzalez for the attack.

Garcia told the jurors that the original plan had been to castrate Ben Novack, but that had changed to cutting out his eyes. He said Veliz told him the reason was so that Narcy could continue running Convention Concepts Unlimited, using her disabled husband's business expertise to help her.

On Friday morning—the fifth day of the trial—jurors heard the gruesome details of the July 12, 2009, attack on Ben Novack. Garcia described how a cell phone call from Narcy Novack had been the signal to go to the Rye Town Hilton, and how she had let them into the suite.

"I went to one side," Garcia testified. "Joel went to the other side without making noise. And we started to beat up the man. We grabbed the dumbbells and started to hit him on the chest, the ribs, and the abdomen."

"Did you strike him anywhere else?" prosecutor Jacobson asked.

"Yes," replied Garcia. "I hit him in the face. In the head. But that was not the plan."

"Why did you do it?" Jacobson asked.

"Because he wouldn't quiet down," Garcia said matter-of-factly.

Garcia testified that Narcy had then handed Gonzalez a pillow to muffle her husband's screams.

After Gonzalez had duct-taped Novack's hands and feet, he walked out of the bedroom.

"Then I took the utility knife," Garcia said, "and I cut out the man's eyes."

"Who told you to do that?" Jacobson asked.

"Cristobal did," Garcia replied. "The plan was to cut his eyes."

As Ben Novack was still "groaning and complaining" on the floor, Garcia said he decided to gag him. He wrapped the heavy gray duct tape around the back of his head and mouth so tightly that Ben Novack finally choked on his own vomit and died.

Then Narcy Novack had asked Garcia if he had cut her husband's eyes.

"I said yes," Garcia testified. "She said, 'Are you sure, he won't be able to see?' I said, 'If you want I can keep cutting more,' and she said, 'It's fine.'"

He then described how Narcy had gone back into the bedroom as he and Gonzalez were washing up in the wet bar area.

"She gave me a thick gold bracelet with some initials in diamonds," he said. "I put it in the pocket of my pants."

Garcia said the plan had been to tie up Narcy and make it look like a robbery, but she suddenly changed her mind.

"When I went looking for her with the duct tape," said Garcia. "She wasn't there anymore.

On Friday afternoon, Garcia testified that a few months later, Cristobal Veliz had offered him $6,000 to plant some guns and drugs in May Abad's truck. He eventually collected seven firearms from Veliz's elder brother, Carlos, at a garage.

Then, a few weeks later, at another meeting, Carlos had handed him a photograph of Narcy's daughter, May Abad, offering him $3,000 to beat her up and leave her a cripple. But before Garcia could go through with it, he was arrested on November 18, 2009, for Ben Novack's murder.

On Sunday night, Carlos Veliz—who has never been charged with anything—gave an interview to the *Journal News* denying any involvement in the case.

"I sleep every night with my head very quiet," he said. "I don't have to be worried. I'm not involved whatsoever."

On Monday, April 30, Alejandro Garcia was back on the stand for the start of the second week of the trial. Prosecutor Jacobson asked him about the deal he had made with the government to testify against the two defendants.

"What do you understand of the agreement?" Jacobson asked.

"That whatever I say," he replied, "cannot be used against me."

Jacobson told the jury that on April 7, 2010, Garcia had pleaded guilty to interstate domestic violence and to his role in the murders of Ben and Bernice Novack. Under the agreement, Judge Karas would take into account his part in killing Bernice Novack at sentencing.

"Other than pleading guilty," Jacobson asked, "what are your obligations?"

"To tell the truth," he replied.

Then Cristobal Veliz's attorney, Larry Sheehan, stood up to begin his cross-examination.

"Was it you and Joel Gonzalez's intention to kill Ben Novack?" Sheehan asked.

"No," replied Garcia.

"Despite hitting him twenty to thirty times with barbells?"

"I didn't say that."

"How many times have you hit him?"

"I don't know."

"Have you ever seen a picture of what Ben Novack looked like after you hit him?" Cristobal Veliz's attorney asked.

"No."

The attorney then showed the jury a series of gruesome color photographs of Ben Novack's trussed-up body, including one particularly gory close-up of his slashed eyes. Several members of the jury looked away in horror. Narcy Novack put her head in her hands.

"That's how Ben Novack looked," Sheehan stated.

"I don't know. I don't remember," Garcia replied.

"He was bleeding," Sheehan continued. "You had cut his eyes. Both eyes."

"I don't know," Garcia said. "I can't tell you. First I saw like water. I imagine it is fluid in the eye."

"And then blood?"

"That's right."

"A lot of blood?"

"That's right."

On Tuesday, Narcy Novack's attorney Howard Tanner cross-examined Garcia, who had now been on the stand five days.

The attorney noted that Garcia had still not been charged with Bernice Novack's murder in Florida, where he still faced the death penalty.

"As a condition of the [government] agreement," Tanner asked, "you are not required to plead guilty to killing Bernice Novack?"

"Not yet," Garcia replied.

"There's a specific understanding that the State of Florida can't punish you if you were to plead guilty to Bernice Novack's death?"

"Well, I'm not to be punished again."

"As part of the cooperating agreement," Tanner continued, "the State of Florida is prohibited in seeking the death penalty?"

"That's right," Garcia agreed.

Under Tanner's questioning, Garcia admitted meeting prosecutor Elliott Jacobson numerous times to discuss the questions he would be asked at trial, the last time as recently as two Friday's ago.

"You told them the answers you were going to give at this trial?" the defender asked.

"Yes."

"Is it fair to say that as you sit here today, you would do anything to avoid a life sentence? Is that fair to say, sir?"

"I don't know what you mean by 'anything,'" Garcia replied angrily.

"You would certainly lie, as you have in the past, to avoid a life sentence. Isn't that correct?"

"I did that in the past, but then I told the truth. I already swore to tell the truth, and up to this moment I have."

Just before the lunch break on Wednesday, Alejandro Garcia was dismissed from the stand after five and a half days of testimony.

The eighth government witness was Miami hair salon owner Gladys Cuenca, who had rented a small space in her trailer to Garcia. She said he had allowed Cristobal Veliz and Joel Gonzalez to sleep on his floor for several days at the beginning of July 2009.

The elderly woman testified that Veliz hardly spoke to her while he stayed in her trailer, but installed a new showerhead and made other bathroom improvements while there. She also testified how Veliz had her register in her name two of the vehicles used in the Ben Novack killing, and that she had briefly assumed ownership of his Nissan Pathfinder before Veliz took it back.

On Thursday, May 3—the ninth day of the trial—Joel Gonzalez took the stand. Over the next two days, Gonzalez, now twenty-nine, would give his account of the brutal killing of Ben Novack Jr. in fluent English, attempting to minimize his role in it.

Describing the attack at the Rye Town Hilton, Gonzalez testified that Narcy Novack let them into the fourth-floor suite. When Ben Novack woke up and fought back at the beginning of the attack, Gonzalez said he became "startled" and "backed off." Narcy Novack had then ordered him back into the bedroom, handing him a pillow to muffle her husband's screams.

"Mr. Garcia was still hitting him with the dumbbells," Gonzalez said. "I placed a pillow over Mr. Novack's face."

As the attack continued, Gonzalez said, he'd stepped back into the parlor twice more, and each time, Narcy had ordered him back to help Garcia. Finally, she had instructed him to go tell Garcia to cut her husband's eyes.

"Had anyone ever told you that was part of the assault plan?" Dember asked.

"No," Gonzalez replied.

After leaving the hotel, Gonzalez testified, Garcia had told him to forget what had happened in the suite.

"I was feeling pretty bad," Gonzalez said. "I was feeling pretty disgusted with myself."

After being arrested in July 2010, Gonzalez said that Cristobal Veliz had offered him $150,000 to implicate May Abad in her stepfather's death. The offer had come while they were both incarcerated in Westchester County Jail. He was promised another $150,000 when Narcy Novack was freed.

"Mr. Veliz advised me to place the blame on someone else," Gonzalez said.

After refusing to commit himself, as he had secretly cut a deal with the government, he encountered Narcy Novack on the way to a federal court hearing.

"She asked is it hard to set her free," Gonzalez testified, "and do her this favor. That I was the only one who could set her free."

In his cross, Larry Sheehan pointed out that although he might have felt disgusted that Garcia had cut out Ben Novack's eyes, Gonzalez had still taken the money.

"In Miami," said Sheehan, "did Mr. Garcia go out every day doing crack?"

"Yes," Gonzalez said, "Mr. Garcia was spending a lot of money on crack and prostitutes. He was bringing prostitutes back to the apartment where we lived."

In his cross-examination, Howard Tanner asked why he had left the bedroom during the attack on Ben Novack.

"I felt bad. I felt guilty. I had a lot of emotions," Gonzalez replied. "I didn't want to be around what was going on."

"Yet you went back into the room," Tanner countered, "because you were told to by a fifty-three-year-old lady?"

"Correct."

"Did she threaten you?"

"No."

"You continued to take part in the assault?"

"Yes."

"You know that Mrs. Novack," Tanner said, "had absolutely nothing to do with the plot to assault and kill Ben Novack?"

"No," Gonzalez said.

On Monday, May 7—the eleventh day of the trial—the jury heard from some of the peripheral members of the conspiracy. Cristobal Veliz's son-in-law, Denis Ramirez, testified how he drove the two killers to the Rye Town Hilton on July 12, 2009, in a borrowed Lincoln Town Car. The thirty-seven-year-old Nicaraguan-born truck driver testified that he had sold Veliz his 1994 Ford Thunderbird for the Ben Novack job, but it had broken down. Then he had arranged to borrow a former girl-friend's Town Car as a replacement.

He testified that his father-in-law had offered him $1,000 to do the driving, but he had only received $100.

Then Ramirez's cousin Francisco Picado, now twenty-two, testified how he had driven the killers back to Miami after Ben Novack's murder. Under assistant U.S. attorney Andrew Dember's direct questioning, Picado claimed he had found out about the assault only during the drive to Miami, when Garcia showed him Ben Novack's bracelet and told him about the brutal beating.

"He said [he had] just come from beating [Ben Novack] up," Picado told the jurors. "Joel tied him up with duct tape and held him down while [Garcia] had cut out his eyes."

Picado, who had cut a deal with the government in return for immunity, also recounted his role in Bernice Novack's murder. He admitted knowing about the plan to assault the old lady, and to renting the red Scion to be used in the attack.

"[Cristobal] said his sister was basically paying him to pay someone to assault her mother-in-law," Picado testified.

On Tuesday morning, when Larry Sheehan questioned Picado about his testimony regarding never meeting May Abad, Narcy Novack suddenly slumped forward and broke down in tears.

Howard Tanner then asked for a brief recess so his client could compose herself. After the jury was excused, Narcy suddenly turned toward Picado, yelling, "I'm innocent, and you're helping him!"

Then she turned to prosecutors, shouting, "When are you going to arrest that guy? This is not right."

A female marshal led a still-weeping Narcy out of the courtroom and into a holding pen, where she threw a tantrum and started screaming.

Fifteen minutes later, when Narcy was brought back into the courtroom, Elliott Jacobson complained to Judge Karas about her behavior. "She maybe upset," said the prosecutor, "but I get to do my job free of intimidation."

"Why don't you arrest the witness!" Narcy yelled back at him.

Once again, Howard Tanner apologized on behalf of his client, saying he was sure his client had nothing personal against Jacobson. "She was just venting and it wasn't a threat," he told Judge Karas. "I'll tell her to vent to me right now."

Then Narcy stood up and apologized to the judge. "This is your courtroom," she told him. "I'm sorry, Your Honor. I just feel I'm treated unfairly. I've taken a lot. I'll try my best."

Judge Karas sternly told her that he would not tolerate any further outbursts.

"These are serious allegations," he said. "I understand you and Mr. Veliz are feeling a lot of pressure, but nothing will be directed at the government for doing their job. You and I will just have to agree to disagree about whether you're being treated fairly. You may not like the evidence that's come in. You may not like what the witnesses have said. But what you are not here to do is disrupt this trial."

That night, Narcy Novack telephoned Channel 12 reporter Tara Rosenblum from Westchester County Jail, claiming the trial was "unfair" and she was being persecuted.

"I was sobbing and poking holes at my skin," she told Rosenblum, "bracing myself so I wouldn't go up there and grab [Garcia] and say, 'Why? Why? Why?' I have never met [Garcia]. I have never seen [Garcia]. I can swear to you on a stack of 17 bibles."

During the thirty-five-minute interview, she also dismissed Rebecca Bliss's claim that Ben had ever loved her. "Whatever she says," said Narcy, "doesn't prove anything, because I know him longer than she did."

At the end of the interview, Narcy appeared to question her brother Cristobal's innocence, saying she would be "devastated" if he had been involved. "I know my brother and he's not a criminal," she said. "I think someone used him."

Next morning, Larry Sheehan called for a mistrial, saying the interview had jeopardized his client Cristobal Veliz's right to a fair trial. Judge Kenneth Karas denied this request, saying there was no reason to believe any of the jurors had seen it. But he said he was concerned that Narcy Novack was "inflicting legal wounds" on her brother.

He then issued a gag order, banning Narcy from speaking to the media for the duration of the trial.

"This is not a permanent ban," Karas explained. "After the verdict she can comment all she wants."

At the start of the fourth week of the trial, prosecutors called a procession of witnesses who had been at the Rye Town Hilton the morning of Ben Novack's murder. Rigoberto Wilson testified about Narcy Novack's strange behavior outside the Woodlands Suite, before following her inside to discover Ben Novack's bloody body trussed up in duct tape.

He testified that rather than call 911, he started taking photographs with his cell phone. This seemed to take prosecutor Andrew Dember off guard.

"Why did you take pictures?" Dember asked.

"I like taking pictures," Wilson replied.

He then described how Narcy had straddled Ben Novack's face-down body, shaking his shoulders and repeatedly screaming, "Why!"

Prosecutors then called paramedic Kerri Conrad, who had pronounced Ben Novack dead. In damaging testimony to the defense, she testified that Narcy Novack was emotionless about her husband's death.

The government's next witness was Angelica Furano, who had been the Rye Town Hilton's events manager in July 2009. Under prosecutor Andrew Dember's direct, she told of a conversation that she had had with Ben Novack late Friday night at the Amway convention.

"Did Mr. Novack tell you about his future plans for the company," Dember asked.

"Yes," Furano replied. "He said he was very proud of May and all the hard work she had done."

She testified that Novack said he would soon be retiring from his company's day-to-day operations, and his stepdaughter would be taking over.

In his cross, Howard Tanner noted that Furano had told investigators about this conversation only four days after the trial had started.

Then, in further damaging testimony for the defense, Hilton security officer Louis Monti testified that the killers had not used key cards to enter the Woodlands Suite, which proved that somebody must have let them in. He had checked the two locks for the suite, and they had not been used between Saturday midnight and 7:45 Sunday morning, when Narcy Novack had returned from breakfast.

On Tuesday, May 15—the sixteenth day of the trial—the government began calling investigators and CSI forensic experts to tell the jury about the murder investigation.

Criminal investigator Richard Corvinus of the Westchester County District Attorney's Office testified that Alejandro Garcia's cell phone listed contact numbers for Narcy Novack, Cristobal Veliz (under the name "Jefe"), and Carlos Veliz.

Joselyn Chernjawski of the Westchester County Forensic Laboratory testified about the voluminous DNA testing done in the Woodlands Suite, and on evidence recovered from it. Not surprisingly, the only blood that had yielded DNA profiles came from Ben Novack.

To bolster Narcy Novack's claim that the broken arm of the Valentino sunglasses belonged to her, Tanner questioned the absence of Alejandro's Garcia's DNA on the arm. Chernjawski explained that all the blood on it had made it impossible to swab a DNA sample.

In redirect, Perry Perrone observed that there was also no forensic evidence that Narcy Novack had ever touched the glasses.

"Correct," the forensic investigator replied.

Just before afternoon recess on May 16—the seventeenth day of the trial—prosecutor Elliott Jacobson handed each juror a series of FBI Situational Information Reports, under a stipulation agreement with the defense. For the next fifteen minutes the jurors read the three FBI reports, which contained a list of unsubstantiated accusations against Ben Novack Jr., presumably coming from his widow.

Most explosive was an October 1, 2009, "Criminal Activity Alert" for the Miami Division claiming a possible affair between Ben Novack and May Abad.

"Ben Novack may have had a romantic/abusive relationship with his stepdaughter May LNU," the FBI report read. "Narcy Novack reportedly found explicit love letters from May LNU to Ben Novack. Narcy allegedly gave a package containing the letters to her lawyer."

Another listed Ben Novack Jr.'s alleged criminal activities, claiming his employee Joe Gandy supplied him with "baseball-sized quantities of cocaine."

It also mentioned his partnership in Jerry Calhoun's Entertainment Coaches of America company, noting that Calhoun's spread in Leesburg, Florida, was equipped with a runway for Calhoun's $5 million private jet.

"Calhoun and Novack utilized this aircraft for trips to Mexico," the report stated, without elaborating further.

The report also stated that Narcy Novack had observed her husband viewing "online child pornography," and he was physically abusive toward her.

"He offered to pay her $500,000 if [she] agreed to a divorce," the report read. "She refused the divorce because she [had] helped build their very lucrative business."

The report also mentioned Narcy's "two trusted associates," Bob Walton and Robert Hodges, aka Prince Mongo. It observed that after Ben Novack's death, Narcy spent two hours on the phone with Walton.

The next day, these allegations would make front-page headlines all over America. But the jury would be left wondering about their significance, as no further mention of them was made at trial.

At the beginning of the fifth week of the trial, the jury was shown gruesome photographs of the horrendous injuries sustained by Bernice Novack and her son, Ben.

On Tuesday, May 22, Dr. Khalil Wardak of the Broward County Medical Examiner's Office testified that he had visited the death scene at Bernice Novack's home in April 2009, and had immediately suspected foul play.

He told the jury that the eighty-six-year-old woman had injuries all over her body, including a 3.5-centimeter left frontal skull fracture. The bone of the skull had been pushed against her brain, an injury that would have required a tremendous amount of force and was inconsistent with a fall.

Dr. Wardak testified that he had told the Broward County Medical Examiner he had made a mistake in his finding of accidental death.

"Did you express your concern," Howard Tanner asked in his cross.

"Yes, I did," Dr. Wardak replied.

The following day, the acting Westchester County Medical Examiner, Dr. Kunjlata Ashar, took the stand, detailing Ben Novack's appalling injuries and his torturous death.

Under prosecutor Perry Perrone's direct examination, Dr. Ashar illustrated Novack's injuries for the jury, using color photographs from the murder scene. Several members of the jury turned away, as the uncensored photographs were displayed on monitors in front of them. The medical examiner testified that Ben Novack had still been alive when his eyes were gouged out.

During the autopsy, she had found his last meal still in his bronchial pipe, and explained that his multiple rib fractures had made him vomit. She said the duct tape over his mouth had made him choke to death.

"Is it unusual for a man to ejaculate when he's dying?" Perrone asked.

"Not at all," the medical examiner replied.

Dr. Ashar said in May 2010, at the request of federal prosecutors, that she had reviewed Bernice Novack's autopsy and police reports.

"It didn't take me one day to determine this wasn't an accident," she said. "I came to the conclusion almost immediately."

As the trial entered it's sixth week and the government started wrapping up its case, there had been much speculation that May Abad would take the stand against her mother and uncle. Ultimately, prosecutors were confident that they had a sufficiently strong case without putting her through such an ordeal.

. . .

On Thursday May 24, the government called its forty-ninth witness, senior investigator Edward Murphy of the Westchester County District Attorney's Office. Under Andrew Dember's direct, the retired New York City homicide detective told jurors that he had first sat down to interview Narcy Novack on the evening of Sunday, July 12, 2009, about twelve hours after her husband's killing.

During the interview, Murphy said that Lieutenant Christopher Calabrese of the Westchester County Police Department had entered the hotel room with a Rolex watch and the broken arm from a pair of sunglasses.

"He showed [the arm] to her," Murphy testified, "and asked if she recognized it. She said, 'Yes, they're from my glasses. They're Valentinos.'"

When Calabrese asked how the piece had gotten on the bed, Narcy replied that her husband had been trying to fix them.

"She said she had broken them on the plane over from Florida," Murphy said. "Ben bugged her to let him fix them."

When, Lieutenant Calabrese asked where the rest of the glasses were, Narcy said she must have left it on the plane. When he asked how Ben could have fixed them, then, Narcy did not reply.

"He asked her again," Murphy said, "and she said she didn't know."

Later that day, jurors were shown an August 12, 2009, Philadelphia Western Union video showing Cristobal Veliz wiring $500 to Alejandro Garcia, with Francisco Picado's forged signature on the form.

Murphy said that the next day, Veliz had been wearing the same T-shirt and baseball cap as in the video, when he (Murphy) and three detectives had arrived at his Philadelphia apartment to interview Veliz.

Murphy told the jury that while Veliz was out of the room changing he spotted a receipt for a money transfer on a table, showing the $500 payment to Garcia. He had quickly copied down the details, recognizing Francisco Picado's 1499 Jefferson Avenue address in Brooklyn.

"If it was significant," Murphy said, "I didn't want him to know I'd seen it."

In his cross-examination, Howard Tanner asked about Murphy's interview with Narcy on the evening of her husband's murder.

"Is it fair to say she appeared visibly distraught?" Tanner asked.

"You'll have to explain that," the investigator replied. "What do you mean?"

"She was crying," Tanner said.

"Not when I was with her," Murphy said. "When I first saw her I expressed my sympathy for her loss. She was calm. She was in control. She said she would do anything to find out who killed her husband."

At the end of the day, before Judge Karas recessed for the long Memorial Day weekend, Howard Tanner expressed concern about his client's mental condition. "I want to put on record that she has been visibly disturbed all day," he said. "She has been crying throughout the day and I have not been able to communicate with her. It may be she's just having a bad day."

Then Tanner asked the judge for time to prepare Narcy to take the stand in her own defense, in the event she decided to do so. "If she's going to testify," he told the judge, "I'm going to have to have her ready, because Mr. Jacobson will have a lot of questions."

On Tuesday, May 29, the jury returned from the four-day Memorial Day recess, as the trial entered its sixth week. The government now wrapped up its marathon case by presenting an elaborate four-hour-long PowerPoint presentation. Prepared by the government's fiftieth and final witness, Dean DeLitta, a Cisco Systems cell phone expert, it would irrefutably link the two defendants and the killers to one another during both murders.

The jury watched as DeLitta tracked Cristobal Veliz and the two killers in real time, driving to the Rye Town Hilton on July 9, 2009, for a reconnaissance mission. Then he showed the jury how they had returned to the hotel two days later for Ben Novack's murder.

The government's coup de grace was the 6:39 A.M. call from Narcy Novack's secret phone to her brother Cristobal, launching the attack. The presentation graphically illustrated her call from the hotel bouncing off a cell tower less than a half mile away to Veliz's phone at a Port Chester gas station just five minutes away from the Hilton. The records showed it was the only call her secret 954-816-2089 cell phone would make that morning.

The presentation also tracked Alejandro Garcia's and Melvin Medrano's cell phones on April 4, 2009, the night Bernice Novack was murdered. It showed numerous calls between them and Cristobal Veliz that night.

The voluminous cell phone records corroborated much of the two killers and their accomplices' testimony. Under defense cross-examination, DeLitta conceded, however, that there was no way of knowing what was said during the phone calls or even who was making them.

On Wednesday at 11:50 A.M. DeLitta was excused, and the government rested its case against Narcy Novack and Cristobal Veliz after almost twenty-five days and fifty witnesses.

FIFTY-THREE

THE DEFENSE

After the lunch recess, Cristobal Veliz took the stand in his own defense. With newly cropped receding hair and wearing a new shirt, his first change of clothing since the start of the trial, Veliz would spend the next four days testifying through two Spanish-language interpreters.

Veliz told his attorney, Larry Sheehan, that May Abad had reached out to him as a teenager after an incident with Ben Novack Jr. "She asked me for help," he testified, "so I went down [to Florida] to help her."

Judge Karas refused to allow Veliz to tell the jury what he claimed his niece had said, except that it had led to a conversation between him and Ben Novack.

"As a result of what May had told you," Sheehan asked, "did you see a change in Ben and May's relationship?"

"It changed a lot," Veliz replied, "because she seemed to take control over him."

"How?" Sheehan asked.

"She would ask him for gifts," he said. "Everything she wanted she would get."

In early July 2009 he had encountered May at a barbecue at Keyling Sanchez's house in Miami, and they had had a conversation.

"We can't say anything about the conversation," Sheehan said, "but would it be fair to say she was speaking loudly?"

"She was almost out of control," Veliz said. "She was very upset."

"Did she indicate something she was going to do to Ben Novack?"

"Yes."

"Did she say she was going to cut off Ben Novack's testicles?"

"Yes."

"As a result of the conversation, did you speak to Ben Novack?"

"Yes."

A few days later, Veliz testified, just before Ben Novack's murder, he had met Alejandro Garcia for the first time. He had been pumping gas at a Miami gas station a couple of blocks from Sanchez's house when May pulled up in her Honda. Inside the car was Alejandro Garcia, whom Veliz claimed never to have met before, and another Hispanic man who he later discovered was Joel Gonzalez.

Veliz claimed his niece asked him to drive "her friends" to New York, where they were working for Ben Novack at a convention. He had refused, saying he had to drive a girlfriend somewhere.

Veliz also testified that his niece had seemed very happy at the gas station. "She said Ben Novack had just given her fifty thousand dollars," he told the jury, "and had told her that in his will he had left a hundred and fifty thousand for each of her children and herself."

Sheehan's next question, regarding where Veliz was in the early morning of July 7, 2009, appeared to throw the defendant off balance.

"We skipped a lot," Veliz replied uncomfortably. "I was on my way to New York from Miami."

He testified that he next saw May Abad at 10:30 P.M. on Friday, July 10, two days before Ben Novack's murder. She had unexpectedly turned up outside the Apex Bus stop on Allen Street, New York, as he came off his driving shift.

"She was in a car with three people," he said.

"Recognize any of them?" his attorney asked.

"Yes. Alejandro Garcia."

"Did May ask you for anything?"

"Yes," he replied. "She asked me to get her a taxi."

Veliz said his niece wanted Garcia and Gonzalez to be taken to a convention at a hotel in Westchester. She asked him to call his son-in-law Denis Ramirez, knowing he worked part time as a taxi driver. Veliz said he had then called Ramirez, who arrived soon afterward.

"I told him my niece wanted to speak to him," Veliz said, "and they made the deal."

Then, according to Cristobal Veliz, the two men had gotten into the car with Ramirez and driven off.

The defendant also offered elaborate explanations to counter all the government's cell phone evidence, and the two trips to New York the killers claimed Veliz had made with them. Veliz explained he always kept his cell phone in his Nissan Pathfinder, which was often used by Francisco Picado.

"I had many complications," he told the jury, "because a lot of women would call me, and I didn't want my wife to find out."

He claimed Laura Law, who was a nurse, had become "very sick" from radiation from the X-ray machines she used. She suffered acute allergies and asthma, leaving her too weak for sex.

"I chose to love her instead of making love to her," he explained. "If I wanted to do something as a man, I would do it outside."

"So that's why the phone was in the car?" Sheehan asked.

"I had a lot of women," Veliz replied, as several jurors laughed.

His attorney then asked about his trip to Florida in early July 2009 with Picado. Veliz explained that he had become intimate with a very high-class lady from Hong Kong during a ten-day Canadian bus tour. When it was over, as she still had a week's vacation left and wanted to see Miami, he had offered to take her sightseeing there.

He was so embarrassed at the state of his old Pathfinder that he had borrowed Picado's brand-new Nissan Murano for the trip, letting Picado use his vehicle while he was away.

"The woman was very refined," Veliz told the jury. "And Frank's SUV was new and nicer than my old Nissan."

. . .

On Monday, June 4, Cristobal Veliz was back on the witness stand, as the trial went into its seventh week. That morning, Larry Sheehan read him a long list of accusations that had been leveled at him by government witnesses. And over the next two and a half hours, the defendant replied "No" more than two hundred times, denying any involvement whatsoever in the murders of Ben Novack Jr. and his mother, Bernice.

He categorically denied everything the two confessed killers had testified about him, insisting that he had never recruited them or paid them, let alone accompanied them to the Rye Town Hilton for Ben Novack's murder. He claimed that his Pathfinder had been stolen, along with his credit cards, which had been used to frame him for the murders.

"I had nothing to do with this," he maintained. "I never touched my brother-in-law."

That afternoon, Veliz testified that May Abad had had him kidnapped on September 3, 2009. He said he was on his way for a Chinese meal when he was attacked in a Philadelphia underpass and knocked unconscious. He had then woken up in a basement blindfolded and tied up. Over the next eighteen days he had been kept prisoner, he said, eating only his four jailors' leftovers.

"[I was] treated like an animal," he told the jury.

He claimed that May Abad had eventually come to the basement, at which point he begged her not to kill him or hurt his grandchildren. She had then ordered his release, after he agreed to have Narcy give her money from Ben Novack's estate.

Veliz had wanted to testify that May Abad had also confessed to murdering Ben Novack, telling him, "Ben got what he deserved," but Judge Karas had ruled it hearsay and disallowed it.

"It's a way for Mr. Veliz," said the judge, "to try and contort the rules of evidence to pin this on someone else."

Late Monday afternoon, assistant U.S. attorney Andrew Dember began his cross-examination of Cristobal Veliz, picking apart his testimony piece by piece. For almost four hours on Tuesday, Dember confronted Veliz with his bank statements and bank withdrawals, pointing out glaring inconsistences in his sworn testimony about his movements up and down the East Coast during the first seven months of 2009.

Facing the prosecutor's questions, Veliz was often evasive, and lost his temper several times after Judge Karas cut him off for hearsay.

Although he acknowledged giving Alejandro Garcia his phone number in August 2009, when he claimed to have first spoken to him, he could not explain why the confessed killer's cell phone contact list had his number logged under the name "Jefe," which means "the Boss" in Spanish.

"It's because you were Alejandro Garcia's boss, weren't you?" Dember demanded to know.

"That's what they wrote," Veliz replied.

"My question to you was," said Dember raising his voice, "Were you Alejandro Garcia's boss?"

"No," came Veliz's defiant reply.

On Wednesday morning, Andrew Dember played the jury a surveillance video. It was recorded at 6:18 A.M. on July 9, 2009, at a Bank of America drive-through ATM in Jessup, Maryland, and showed Cristobal Veliz withdrawing $200. Prosecutors say he withdrew the cash during his second trip to New York with Garcia and Gonzalez, while towing the broken Thunderbird back north for repairs.

When Dember asked Veliz to account for his movements that day, Veliz insisted that he had been driving an Apex bus to an amusement park in Virginia, parking it a hundred meters away from the ATM to withdraw money. He vehemently denied Garcia's and Gonzalez's claim that he was driving them to New York to assault Ben Novack Jr.

After Veliz agreed that it was him in the video, Dember played the rest of it. Following the cash withdrawal, the video shows Veliz walking out of the camera's view. Then, two minutes later, a green Pathfinder can plainly be seen in the distance towing a Thunderbird out of the parking lot.

"Mr. Veliz," Dember said sternly. "Do you see a green Pathfinder on the video?"

"That's not my car," he replied testily.

"That's not your green Pathfinder towing your Thunderbird out of the parking lot?"

"No."

Later, it would be revealed that prosecutor Perry Perrone had discovered this smoking gun only at 3:00 that morning, after reviewing the ATM video in preparation for the day's questioning. He had then alerted the other prosecutors, and they had worked through the night to duplicate a series of still photographs to show the jury that morning.

For the rest of the day, Cristobal Veliz seemed a beaten man, trying to ward off further blows to his credibility. During one particularly heated exchange, Dember accused the defendant of fabricating the "refined lady from Hong Kong," whom Veliz had finally named as "Chin Chu Lancha," to place him in Miami instead of in New York with Garcia and Gonzalez. The prosecutor noted how Veliz had used the exact same name for another lady he had claimed to have gone shopping with on August 13, when investigators had first come to his apartment.

When confronted with this, Veliz tried to laugh it off as a joke. Then Dember pointed out that Chin Chu Lancha was actually a derogatory adaptation of the well-known Spanish expression *sin su lancha*, meaning "straight off the boat."

"It's used to make fun of how Chinese people speak," Dember explained to the jury. "It's the phony name you keep for women."

"You're humiliating me," Veliz replied.

"Mr. Veliz," Dember thundered. "You make up these names for people because they don't exist."

"You're humiliating me," Veliz repeated, gripping his hands together. "Don't humiliate me anymore."

"You say it for a joke," Dember accused. "You say it for a laugh, as you giggle in the witness stand."

All through the trial, there had been great anticipation that Detective Alison Carpentier would be called as a witness. In opening statements, both defense attorneys had told the jury that the whole murder investigation had been tainted by one of the lead detectives' having given $5,000 to May Abad.

As a succession of investigators took the stand, the two defense attorneys had never missed a chance to refer slyly to Carpentier's gift, reminding the jury of its implications.

Ultimately, the defense backed off calling Detective Carpentier to the stand, after Judge Karas warned that her testimony could open the door for prosecutors to ask her about Narcy Novack's having repeatedly failed a lie detector test.

On Thursday morning, Cristobal Veliz stepped down from the stand, as his attorney, Larry Sheehan, had no further redirect questions for him. Then, after playing the jury a seventy-three-minute video of Alejandro Garcia's original interrogation—to demonstrate to the jury how he looked when he was lying—Sheehan rested his case.

Then Howard Tanner called his first defense witness, Narcy Novack's former probate lawyer, Henry Zippay Jr. Describing himself as "100 percent disabled," the attorney testified by video link from his Fort Lauderdale office. Tanner sought to discredit the government's contention that, in a divorce from Ben Novack Jr., his client would have gotten only $65,000 based on their prenuptial agreement. Zippay testified that under a postnuptial agreement, which had never gone into effect, Narcy would have received far more.

In his cross-examination, Elliott Jacobson got Zippay to admit that even if the postnuptial agreement had been valid, as the defense claimed it had been, Narcy would have received twice as much with Ben dead than in a divorce.

"Were you paid for your service?" Jacobson asked Zippay.

"I received an initial retainer," Zippay replied, "but Mrs. Novack never paid me any more money. I received ten percent of what I was owed."

The next defense witness was retired police detective Robert Crispin, whom Tanner had hired to try to discredit May Abad. The private investigator testified that he was paid $5,000 to conduct six "trash pulls" between November 2009 and February 2010. He said he had waited for

May Abad to put her trash out in front of her home before rifling through it.

Crispin testified that he found several shut-off warnings from the electric company and late-payment notices for Abad's Toyota. Then, on June 28, 2010, he found a two-page handwritten list of May's future aspirations. Written on notepaper adorned with butterflies and lady-bugs, May's long-term goals included: having fifteen to twenty properties within five years; moving into a five-bedroom house on the water with a pool and a small boat; and spending more time with her three sons. She also wanted to buy a "hole in the wall bar," as well as make $1 million by the age of forty and retiring.

"Would you agree," Tanner asked, "the note reflects the wishes of someone who wants to become very rich?"

Prosecutor Jacobson objected, but Judge Karas allowed him to answer.

"Yes," Crispin replied.

The private investigator also testified that he had visited 2501 Del Mar Place looking for any sunglasses with missing temple pieces. He had found about six pairs in that condition and placed them on a small glass table to be photographed. None of them had been Valentinos.

In his cross, Jacobson asked Crispin if he had been given specific instructions to look for a pair of Valentino sunglasses with a missing temple piece.

"I may have," Crispin replied.

"And you didn't find any Valentino sunglasses?" the prosecutor asked.

"No," he replied.

Jacobson noted that Narcy Novack had lived at the house until she was arrested in July 2010 and could easily have broken off the temple pieces.

"You have no idea if the sunglasses were accidentally broken or intentionally broken," Jacobson asked.

"I do not," Crispin replied.

Crispin conceded that he also did not know where or when Abad's "Long Term Goals" note had been written, agreeing that there had been no attempt made to destroy it.

"These notes," Jacobson asked. "What kind of trash were they found with?"

"Food and garbage," the investigator said.

"'Trash pulls' isn't that a fancy way of saying you're going through somebody's trash?"

"Yes," Crispin said.

"You have no way of knowing if the aspirations, hopes, and dream for her to have her life changed, [were written after seeing] a seminar at a convention?"

"Yes," Crispin acknowledged.

The next defense witness was Jeremy Morris, the Rye Town Hilton manager on duty the weekend of Ben Novack's murder. He testified that Narcy was visibly distraught over her husband's death.

"There was a lot of screaming and crying," Morris told the jury.

"Would you describe her as emotionless?" Tanner asked.

"Definitely not emotionless," Morris replied.

During his questioning, Morris suggested that May Abad had appeared more upset with her mother's behavior than her stepfather's murder.

"May told her to shut up and stop it," Morris testified, "or it was going to make her throw up."

On Friday morning—the thirtieth day of the trial—Howard Tanner announced that Narcy Novack would not be taking the stand in her own defense. This followed a report in *The Miami Herald* that Narcy was so furious that Detective Alison Carpentier would not be called as a defense witness that she had threatened her lawyer after court recessed on Thursday.

"My client has instructed me to put on the record that she does not wish to testify," Tanner said. "I met with my client . . . on numerous occasions to discuss this issue. She has stated to me that she has said what she is going to say. She continues to assert her innocence."

Then Judge Kenneth Karas asked the defendant to verify that it was her signature on a document Tanner had just given him stating her intention not to testify. Narcy Novack refused to answer the judge directly, going through her attorney instead.

"She has just whispered, 'Yes, I do,'" Tanner said.

"Is the decision [not to testify] made by you of your own free will?" the judge asked.

"Yes," her attorney relayed to the court.

"This is for the record," Judge Karas said. "Mrs. Novack has elected not to communicate with me directly and through Mr. Tanner."

For the rest of the trial, Narcy Novack would not utter a single word, staring straight ahead defiantly. It was as if she no longer recognized the federal court.

That afternoon, Howard Tanner called Carlos Veliz's daughter Karla to the stand. Narcy Novack's niece testified that she flew down to Fort Lauderdale a couple of days after Ben Novack's murder to stay with her aunt.

"She's a human being," Karla said. "I wanted to be there emotionally for her."

Previously, Judge Karas had ruled that the jury could not hear about Fort Lauderdale Police being called to 2501 Del Mar Place, or about May Abad's allegation that her mother had attacked her with a crowbar. But Karla would be allowed to describe what had led up to the confrontation.

"Comes a time you had an interaction with May Abad?" Tanner asked.

"Yes," Karla Veliz replied, explaining that it was first time she had ever met her cousin.

"When you went into the guesthouse, what happened?"

"I saw [May] in Ben's office," Karla said, "and she was just leafing through the folders and files. She kept repeating, 'My father, my father—he has something for me.'"

In his cross-examination, Elliott Jacobson asked Karla if she was Carlos Veliz's daughter and if Melanie Klein was like a stepmother.

"She's my father's partner," Karla said.

"Are you aware that there's been evidence that your father gave a bag of guns to Alejandro Garcia," the prosecutor asked, "to plant in May Abad's trunk?"

"No," she replied.

"Are you aware that your father attempted to have Garcia maim May Abad?"

"No."

"Are you aware your father has been implicated in racketeering?"

"No."

In redirect, Tanner asked Karla what May Abad's demeanor was while rifling through Ben Novack's papers.

"She was extremely nervous," Karla replied. "She wanted to get in and out. She was going through each and every folder feverishly."

On Friday afternoon the defense rested its case after calling just eight witnesses. The government then began its rebuttal case, and after the jury was dismissed for the weekend, Howard Tanner called for a mistrial.

"I don't believe the government has submitted evidence of a sufficient nature to convict my client," he declared.

"I deny the motion," Judge Karas ruled. "I find there is more than sufficient evidence to convict on these charges."

FIFTY-FOUR

"IF EVER THERE WAS A PLOT HATCHED IN HELL"

On Tuesday, June 12—the thirty-second day of the trial—as assistant U.S. attorney Andrew Dember was about to deliver the government's closing arguments, Cristobal Veliz insisted on addressing the court, against his attorney's advice.

Speaking in fluent English, Veliz now claimed to have known everything about the plot and said that the government knew only 25 percent of it.

"If I know who the killers are," Veliz told Judge Karas, "I can give a full explanation of what happened. Then you can judge me."

"Mr. Veliz," the judge said. "The evidence is over. Let the jury decide. Have a seat. Your testimony is done."

Then prosecutor Dember walked over to the lectern in front of the jury to begin his closing argument.

"You've sat and listened over the last seven weeks to an extraordinary amount of testimony and information in this case," he began. "You've seen two different orchestrations that led to the deaths of Ben and Bernice Novack. They hired hit men and bought people to carry out their enterprise—to punish Ben Novack for his marital indiscretion and take over his business and assets."

Dember then began methodically laying out the evidence, likening it to large and small pieces in a jigsaw puzzle.

"Garcia and Gonzalez were the hit men," he told the jury. "They didn't come into these homicides, these acts, by accident. They were brought into this by these defendants—"

"By May Abad!" Cristobal Veliz suddenly yelled from the defense table.

Judge Karas immediately dismissed the jury, and started reading from a U.S. Supreme Court decision that the right of a defendant to be present in court is not absolute. He then castigated Veliz for his behavior throughout the trial, by banging on his desk and often shouting to get his points over.

"You are not allowed to intervene," he told Veliz. "I expect you and everyone in this courtroom to act with sufficient respect for the system of justice. You are not allowed outbursts. If you can't abide by these simple instructions, you will be placed in a pen. Do you understand?"

"Yes, I stay quiet," the defendant replied.

Judge Karas then brought the jury back, and Dember continued.

"Garcia and Gonzalez were hired by Mrs. Novack and Mr. Veliz—these people over there," he declared, pointing at the defense tables. "So much of the defense case is that it wasn't them that hired the killers. It's May Abad. It's May Abad. This is frankly incredible."

The prosecutor told the jury that Garcia and Gonzalez were just hired hit men with absolutely no loyalty to May Abad. "There is no relationship between [them] and May Abad," he said. "They don't even know who she is."

Sifting through all the evidence against the two defendants in both killings, Dember said the phone call that Narcy Novack made to her brother Cristobal's "dirty phone" at 6:39 A.M. on July 12, 2009, was especially damning.

"It's go time," Dember said, "and Mr. Veliz tells Garcia it's time. [The killers] didn't rely on luck. They didn't knock down the door. They didn't drill [the lock]. They didn't use a key card. Narcy Novack ushers them into the room and they inflict a vicious, brutal attack on Ben Novack."

Once again Dember led the jury through all the cell phone and credit card records, placing Cristobal Veliz at key locations at the same time as the killers. He ridiculed Veliz's claims that May Abad had set him up, and that Francisco Picado had used his Pathfinder, cell phone, and credit cards at critical times.

Dember then accused Veliz of distancing himself, in a calculated manner, from everyone doing his dirty work. "It's all a question of Cristobal Veliz trying to outsmart everyone," the prosecutor said.

On Wednesday morning, Andrew Dember systematically picked apart Narcy Novack's alibi for the morning of her husband's death, saying she had made a lot of mistakes.

"[There were] real doozies," he told the jury. "The first one was that they had a plan to tie up Narcy and her husband, so it looked like a robbery." He said she had put "the kibosh" on that without thinking out the consequences.

"Narcy Novack did not have an endgame," he said. "She didn't have an exit strategy about what happens next."

Dember told the jury, Narcy could not just get into a car and drive off, or be found in the suite "unharmed and untied," either. Therefore, she needed an alibi.

Although she showed up at the Amway breakfast to make it look like she was helping out, all she did was park herself in front of a hotel security camera. "She makes an appearance so she can be seen," the prosecutor said, "so people can say, 'Oh, I saw Narcy Novack.'"

Her big flaw was that she was visible only after the killers had left the hotel.

"It's all after the fact," Dember said. "It doesn't help her."

At the end of his six-hour summation, Dember told the jury that there was not "a scintilla of evidence" that May Abad had had anything to do with either of the murders.

"The evidence is overwhelming against Narcy Novack and Cristobal Veliz," he said. "There is only one logical and natural conclusion to be drawn from the evidence in this case. We will ask you to reach a verdict that speaks the truth—a verdict that beyond a reasonable doubt Narcy Novack and Cristobal Veliz are guilty."

Judge Karas then called a recess, and as the U.S. marshals were taking the defendants out of court, Cristobal Veliz suddenly shouted, "I want to change my plea!"

When the court reconvened an hour later, at 1:30 P.M., Larry Sheehan clarified that his client wanted to change his plea only as it related to May Abad. Once again Sheehan told Judge Karas that, against his advice, Veliz wished to address the court.

"I want to plead guilty," Veliz told the judge, "and I want to speak on my behalf. I want to tell the real truth [in English]."

He then attacked his attorney for not asking him enough questions, and working with the prosecution against him.

Judge Karas refused to allow him to change his plea, or to testify again.

"You had a chance to answer the larger questions," Karas told him. "To the extent you don't think your testimony went the way you want, it's over."

"It's not over!" the defendant defiantly replied.

"It's over," the judge reiterated. "The evidence is all in. Your testimony is over. If you can't sit quietly there's a place for you in the pen."

At 1:45 P.M., after the jury had filed back into the courtroom, Larry Sheehan walked over to the jury box to begin his closing argument.

"It's been a long trial," he told the jury. "I've got the summation jitters. I've got to tell you it's been a long road, and you have no idea how happy I am to be here."

For the next forty minutes, Sheehan methodically recited dozens of inconsistencies between Alejandro Garcia's and Joel Gonzalez's testimony. He attacked them as "sociopaths" who would lie "at the drop of a hat."

"They're people without conscience," he told the jury. "They're people without souls. They can't get their stories straight, folks, because they're lying. Were they testifying or testi-lying."

Sheehan's summation went into Thursday morning, as he suggested that May Abad had masterminded the killings. He told the jury that it would take only a single doubt to find his client not guilty.

"Reasonable doubt begins with Garcia and ends with Gonzalez," he declared. "My job is now over and yours begins. It's time to reach a good verdict. Please take your time and discuss it and you'll come back with a just verdict of not guilty."

Then Howard Tanner stepped up to the lectern for his closing argument.

"The government's case is as flimsy as a house of cards built on a shaky foundation, based on suspicions, assumptions, hearsay, and speculation," he told the jury.

He said the government was trying to get into his client's head and guess at the motive. "They're missing facts, firsthand witnesses," he said. "Not people who say what they heard that Narcy Novack said."

Tanner said the real reason prosecutors had made a deal with two sociopathic killers was because they didn't have anything else. Calling Garcia and Gonzalez "monsters," he said they had lied to prosecutors, hoping to get out of prison one day.

He also questioned whether Narcy Novack had even made that crucial 6:39 A.M. cell phone call that set the attack in motion, saying "a phone is not a person."

He claimed Narcy had never brought her so-called secret phone to New York, although someone else obviously had, he added, intimating that it was Narcy's daughter, May.

"If someone wanted to make it look like Narcy Novack made that call," Tanner said, "it would be very easy to use that phone to do so."

Although he was suggesting that May Abad was behind everything, he acknowledged that he couldn't be certain. The reason, he explained, was that investigators had never bothered to search May's hotel room, or properly question her about where she was when Ben Novack was killed.

"I don't have to prove May Abad is guilty," he told the jury. "I don't have to solve this crime. They have to prove Narcy Novack is guilty."

At 1:38 P.M. on Thursday, it was prosecutor Elliott Jacobson's turn to have the final word, before the jury went out to deliberate. Wearing his trademark red bow tie and an immaculately pressed checked suit, the wiry prosecutor told the jury that the only way the killers had had access to Ben Novack was through his wife. He said no one else in the entire world would have known the exact time to send in the killers to carry out "these horrific and savage crimes."

"If ever there was a plot hatched in hell, it was this one," the prosecutor said.

He then compared Cristobal Veliz to a child telling fairy tales on the stand under oath.

"It was perjury so palpable," he said, "that many of you were laughing. You knew what he said up there doesn't [comport] with reason and logic. Why did he pitch that nonsense? Because Cristobal Veliz has been buried under a mountain of investigative evidence, and will say just about anything not to go to jail for the rest of his life, for the brutal slaying of two human beings."

At the end of his summation, Jacobson told the jury that Narcy Novack was ultimately responsible for these "brutal and particularly sadistic" murders.

"They didn't just want to kill these people," the prosecutor said. "Somebody wanted to make them suffer. Somebody was out for revenge. Someone wanted to make sure that Bernice Novack would never speak again. Someone wanted to make sure Ben Novack would never look at another woman again. That someone was, and is, Narcy Novack."

FIFTY-FIVE

THE VERDICT

At 11:00 A.M. on Monday, June 18—the thirty-sixth day of the trial—the eight men and four women of the jury entered their deliberation room to try to reach a verdict. Over the nine-week trial there had been nearly sixty witnesses, more than three hundred exhibits, and four hundred pages of testimony to examine.

Ninety minutes into deliberation, the jurors sent a note to Judge Karas requesting the testimony of Gladys Cuenca and Francisco Picado. Then, at 6:00 P.M., the jury left, ending its first day of deliberation.

Deliberation resumed at 9:45 on Tuesday morning, and an hour later the jury asked Judge Karas for the legal definition of "robbery." This was significant, because to find the defendants guilty of Ben Novack's felony murder, the government had to prove that the two killers had taken his diamond bracelet, making the crime a robbery. The bracelet had never been recovered.

While the jury continued to deliberate throughout the day, Larry Sheehan and Howard Tanner remained outside the courtroom chatting with journalists and trying to keep a positive spin on things.

Late Tuesday afternoon, jurors asked the judge to clarify some of the charges as far as they related to racketeering conspiracy. After consulting all the attorneys, the judge called the jury back into the courtroom and did so.

At 5:30 P.M., jurors sent in a note saying they wanted to leave for the day, and they were excused.

On Wednesday morning, temperatures hit 93 degrees in White Plains as jurors began their third day of deliberations.

Then, at 11:45 A.M., lead court security officer Tom Delehanty walked into Judge Karas's courtroom holding a white envelope. The judge, who was now presiding over another trial for illegal gun possession, opened it and announced, "We have a verdict."

It had taken the jury sixteen hours to reach it.

Over the next hour, there was great expectation as word of the verdict spread. As the gun case continued, Court 521 began filling up with some of the major players in the Novack/Veliz case. Westchester County district attorney Janet Di Fiore took a front-row seat in the public gallery, alongside Rye Brook Police chief Greg Austin and Detective Sergeant Terence Wilson, who came with former detective Alison Carpentier.

At 12:20 P.M., after the gun trial recessed for lunch, the prosecutors and defense attorneys for the Novack/Veliz trial retook their places for the verdict.

A U.S. marshal brought in Cristobal Veliz, but there was no sign of his sister. A few seconds later, Howard Tanner walked in from the holding pen, shaking his head.

"Your Honor," he said. "My client has informed me that she doesn't want to be present for the verdict. I recommended that she be there, but she nevertheless wants to decline that right. She can hear everything from outside."

After confirming Narcy Novack's right not to be present at her own verdict, Judge Karas requested that she be brought in to confirm that she in fact didn't want to attend it. She was led into the court, looking defiant and refusing to acknowledge the judge.

"Is she going to talk through you?" Judge Karas asked her attorney.

"Yes," Tanner replied.

"Is it your intention," the judge asked, "that you not be in the courtroom when the jury give its verdict?"

"She whispered in my ear, 'Yes,'" her attorney replied.

"Miss Novack," Jude Karas said. "If you want to leave, you can leave now."

A few minutes later, the jury filed into the courtroom to deliver its verdict. The jurors were given no explanation for Narcy Novack's absence from the defense table.

Then the clerk of the court read out the charges one by one, and the jury forewoman, Aro Edwers, responded to each charge in a loud, clear voice.

The jurors found both defendants guilty of all the charges except one, violent crime in aid of racketeering. This meant that they were not guilty of the felony murder of Ben Novack, as the government had failed to prove that Novack's gold bracelet had been taken and that a robbery had been committed.

Narcy Novack, who could hear the verdict from a holding pen, was convicted of twelve of the thirteen counts against her. Her brother Cristobal Veliz was convicted of fourteen of the fifteen counts against him. He showed no visible reaction.

The verdict meant that the siblings now faced spending the rest of their lives in federal prison.

Then the judge dismissed the jury and set sentencing for November 1, at 10:00 A.M.

Outside the courthouse, Detective Sergeant Terence Wilson of the Rye Brook Police Department, who had devoted three years of his life to bringing Narcy Novack and Cristobal Veliz to justice, said he was delighted with the jury's decision.

"We are very happy," he said. "Bernice can now rest in peace."

Maxine Fiel also applauded the verdict, saying she hoped Narcy

Novack died in prison, for what she did to her sister. "That is such good news, I'm crying," said Fiel. "The woman's a sociopath. I hope she never sees the light of day again."

Westchester County D.A. Janet DiFiore, who'd turned the case over to federal prosecutors at the end of 2009, refused to comment on the verdict as she left the courtroom. A few hours later she issued a statement: "These defendants, modern day 'public enemies,' planned, orchestrated, enlisted accomplices and assisted in the brutal killing of Ben Novack Jr. here in Westchester and his mother Bernice Novack in Florida."

U.S. attorney Preet Bharara also issued a press statement, saying justice had been served. "Narcy Novack and her brother, Cristobal Veliz, will now have to answer for the blood of Ben Novack and his elderly mother."

Hours after the verdict, the fight began for Ben Novack Jr.'s millions. If Narcy Novack is barred from her share of his estate by Florida's Killer Statute, May Abad's sons, Patrick and Marchelo Gaffney, will inherit it, with their mother receiving $150,000.

Within days of the verdict, a lawyer representing Ben Novack's adopted half-brother, Ronald Novack, filed a suit contesting the will. Maxine Fiel and her two daughters are also expected to challenge it, and Ben Novack's cousin Andrea Danenza Wynn, who is married to Las Vegas casino mogul Steve Wynn.

But there could be complications, as the jury did not technically convict Narcy of murdering Ben, so she may still try to argue that she is exempt from the Killer Statute and claim her husband's estate.

EPILOGUE

At 11:00 A.M. on Monday, December 17, Narcy Novack and Cristobal Veliz were brought into Judge Kenneth Karas's courtroom for sentencing. Dressed in a dark blue prison uniform, her long graying hair severely tied back in a ponytail by two rubber bands, Narcy stared straight ahead defiantly. Her sixty-year-old brother Cristobal, wearing beige scrubs and looking drawn and haggard, sat down at the defense table with his new attorney, Michael Keesee. After his guilty verdict he had fired Larry Sheehan.

Five jurors were back in the jury box for the sentencing, and producers for *48 Hours* and *Dateline* were in the public gallery.

A week earlier Harold Tanner had appealed to Judge Karas to send his fifty-six-year-old client to prison for just twenty-seven years, instead of the life sentence the government was demanding. In his sentencing recommendation Tanner wrote that this would still be a "virtual death sentence" and sufficient punishment.

But federal prosecutors disagreed, saying the siblings should never be freed.

"They are evil; they are dangerous; they are remorseless; and they are relentless," read the government's recommendation. "They bear responsibility for the untold suffering and horrific deaths of two innocent human beings, one of them an eighty-six-year-old woman."

Tanner began by telling Judge Karas that Narcy Novack did not wish to attend her sentencing. After questioning Novack to ascertain that she was doing so voluntarily, Judge Karas dismissed her from the courtroom and she was led out to a holding area where she could hear the proceedings.

Her attorney then asked the judge not to sentence Narcy to life, saying there was only circumstantial evidence against her in Bernice Novack's killing. However, Judge Karas disagreed, saying there had been "plenty of evidence" against her.

Veliz's new attorney, Keesee, was also pleading for leniency on his client's behalf, claiming he was less culpable than his sister for the murders.

"Cristobal Veliz is not the evil monster the government claims," read his sentencing recommendation. "He did not deliver the blows that caused Mr. Novack's death."

Lead prosecutor Elliott Jacobson then addressed the court, branding the siblings "pathological liars" and "extraordinarily dangerous psychopaths," going on to add: "The only sentence that would ensure the safety of the law-abiding community is a sentence that assures these defendants will spend the rest of their lives in jail," he declared.

Before being sentenced, Cristobal Veliz exercised his right to address the court, still protesting his innocence.

"I was tricked," he told Judge Karas through a Spanish interpreter. "I was deceived. The real criminal, the one who arranged this whole thing, was May Abad. They have no evidence against me."

Karas then turned his attention to the siblings' sentencing. He began by saying he could find no mitigating factors for Narcy Novack's crimes.

"There's really nothing to explain what she did," he said. "She lived a life of privilege. If she had a marriage she wasn't happy with . . . she could have gotten a divorce."

He then sentenced Narcy Novack and Cristobal Veliz to spend the rest of their natural lives in prison for orchestrating the "vile" killings of

Ben Jr. and Bernice Novack. He described the two murders as "gruesome," saying they sent "a shiver" down his spine.

"At the end of the day it was because of Ms. Novack's greed and her selfishness," said the judge, "and what she thought was her ability to manipulate people, there are two innocent people—her husband and her mother-in-law—who are dead."

Judge Karas said Narcy's refusal to remain in court for her sentencing only proved she was a coward.

"Her final act of cowardice was walking out of this courtroom today," he said.

Judge Karas said Narcy had believed she could "outsmart" everybody, and her motive for killing her husband and mother-in-law was "old-fashioned greed."

"She even tried to manipulate this whole trial through the press," he said. "At the end of the day she's a coward."

The judge also fined her $250,000 as well as ordering both defendants to pay $105,515 to Novack Enterprises, the amount stolen at the Amway convention after Ben Novack's murder.

Judge Karas then addressed Cristobal Veliz, saying he had never witnessed a worse case of perjury in his entire career, describing it as "an affront to the criminal justice system.

"It's shameful," he told Veliz. "I've never seen anything like it. After he said his name, I'm not sure he said a truthful thing."

Westchester County District Attorney Janet DiFiore later applauded the life sentences.

"Today Narcy Novack and Cristobal Veliz are finally being held accountable for their gruesome and brutal conduct," she stated. "It was pure greed that drove their evil scheme to steal millions of dollars from the Novack family by murdering Ben Novack Jr. [and] his elderly mother. This dangerous brother-sister team will now be where they belong—behind bars for the rest of their natural lives."

After the sentencing Harold Tanner said Narcy Novack would be appealing the verdict on several unspecified grounds.